KINGDOM
QUARTERBACK

KINGDOM
QUARTERBACK

Patrick Mahomes, the Kansas City Chiefs,
and How a Once Swingin' Cow Town Chased
the Ultimate Comeback

MARK DENT and
RUSTIN DODD

DUTTON

DUTTON

An imprint of Penguin Random House LLC
penguinrandomhouse.com

Map on page 13 by David Lindroth
Photograph on page 67 courtesy of the State Historical Society of Missouri
Photograph on page 125 courtesy of AP/Charlie Riedel
Photograph on page 229 courtesy of the authors

Library of Congress Cataloging-in-Publication Data
has been applied for.

ISBN 9780593472033 (hardcover)
ISBN 9780593472040 (ebook)

Printed in the United States of America
1st Printing

Book design by Tiffany Estreicher

In those days the distances were all very different, the dirt blew off the hills that have now been cut down, and Kansas City was very like Constantinople. You may not believe this. No one believes this; but it is true.

—Ernest Hemingway, "God Rest You Merry, Gentlemen," 1933

When I was growing up, Black folks lived on the other side of the tracks. Now they live on the other side of the freeway.

—Mildred Dudley, Kansas City community meeting,
The Call, 1976

Football began as a runner's game. But it prospered and grew with the discovery of flight. Only one man commands the flight of the football. He is the quarterback.

—John Facenda, *NFL's Best Ever Quarterbacks*,
NFL Films, 1979

To Frank and Mary Dodd and Paul and Debbie Dent

CONTENTS

Contents

KINGDOM
QUARTERBACK

PROLOGUE:
THE KANSAS CITY SPIRIT

On the morning of October 25, 1919, Kansas City held a parade. Which is to say, it threw a massive party. It started downtown, near the corner of Ninth Street and Grand Boulevard, where, at precisely 11 A.M., seven thousand marchers split into divisions and, carrying flags, poured into the heart of the city—less than a mile from the chalky river landing where Kansas City was born. The Liberty Memorial parade, which launched a fund-raising drive for a new war monument, was one of the largest spectacles in the town's history: Veterans from the American Legion numbered in the thousands. Schoolkids donned autumn sweaters and lined storefronts along the route. The cadet band from Lincoln High School—the city's first for Black children—played patriotic tunes in the crisp morning air. The city, everyone said, was on the cusp of greatness—a future with no limits.

A century later, the reason for this optimism might sound strange: The people of Kansas City simply thought that constructing a giant new memorial would change the destiny of the place. In the months after the Treaty of Versailles, civic leaders determined they needed a monument to honor the 441 local men who had died in World War I. Towns across America were doing the same, of course, but Kansas City, sensing an opportunity, took it to another level. Its citizens wouldn't just erect any memorial. No, they decided they'd privately raise $2.5 million (close to $45 million in today's dollars) to build one of the finest pieces of public art in the world, a magnificent structure to rival anything in Rome or Athens, a centerpiece for a civic project that would turn Kansas City—a growing little hub in the heart of America—into one of the leading metropolises in the country. "Kansas Citians are awake to the opportunity to do something big for a cause that will draw the admiration of the nation," one business leader said. "It will make this city bigger, broader and grander."

Again, if this seems grandiose, if it sounds odd that a city known mostly for its stockyards would think that a monument could change everything, it's fair to say you don't know the people of Kansas City. (Don't worry. You will.)

Back in the first part of the twentieth century, it still seemed possible for an American city to move up in the world, to become the next New York or Chicago. In 1919, Kansas City was not yet seventy years old. What had once been a tiny trading post on the frontier had bloomed into a wide-open, freewheelin' river town, a rollicking den of gambling and booze, a second-tier financial center for the cattle and wheat industries, and a place where the locals came to carry a fascinating contradiction: For the most part, everyone was *very midwestern*—nice and polite with a lingering self-doubt. When a writer visited almost a decade later, he noted "all the frailties of the Kansas City psychology," including "a wholly unnecessary inferiority complex." But just under the surface, where you couldn't always see it, there was an unceasing confidence in the city's potential. The inhabitants of the place came to call this ethos the "Kansas City Spirit," the idea that something small would become something grand if only the people believed. Civic leaders dreamed of a beautiful "city of a million," turning the phrase into a marketing slogan. They built winding boulevards and sprawling parks. They watched the population boom. On that fall Saturday morning in 1919 when the Liberty Memorial parade took over downtown, *The Kansas City Star* newspaper called the project the most important in the city's history, "the beginnings of one of these dream cities built in imperishable stone."

Civic boosters pictured a memorial scraping the sky on a hill above downtown, across the street from the city's palatial Union Station, surrounded by art museums and opera houses and auditoriums, a project to rival the "White City" at the World's Columbian Exposition in Chicago in 1893. If any fiscally conservative citizen voiced their objection to the ambitious cost, *The Star* had a quick retort: "Kansas City isn't a hundred thousand dollar town." If that wasn't enough, the project's backers had another advocate, a Kansas City man named Horace Ray Palmer, a lieutenant who had served in the 164th Field Artillery Brigade. Before the war, Palmer had been an assistant city editor at *The Kansas City Star*. He was bookish, with thinning hair and glasses, a few months away from turning forty. In the annals of Kansas City, he's barely a footnote, a forgotten newspaperman who grew up in St. Louis, spent fifteen years chasing stories around Kansas City, went to war in Europe, and then moved on to a career in advertising, ultimately ending up in New York.

On the day before the Liberty Memorial parade, Palmer wrote a piece for his former newspaper, imploring his fellow citizens to raise the $2.5 million, tapping into the Kansas City Spirit and a collective fear that never seemed to go away.

"Kansas City is right now at the turn of the road," Palmer wrote. "Shall it become a great city, a city of beauty, a city definitely committed to artistic development, to culture and the finer things of life?

"Or shall it develop as a great, ugly town?"

ONE hundred years later, on a frosty winter morning, there was another parade in Kansas City, this one larger and louder and with an almost unlimited supply of cheap beer. It was February 5, 2020, three days after the Kansas City Chiefs won their first Super Bowl in fifty years, coming from behind in a 31–20 victory over the San Francisco 49ers. To celebrate, the city was throwing one of the biggest parties in its 169-year history. The celebration had already raged for roughly sixty hours, bleeding into the workweek, draining office productivity, canceling school, and postponing surgeries at a local hospital. On the morning of the parade, close to half a million people were expected to flood into downtown. Everyone was still buzzing about "Wasp," the play that had jump-started the Chiefs' improbable comeback.

The route started on Grand Boulevard—same as the Liberty Memorial parade's—and ended in front of Union Station, creating a two-mile line through the heart of the city. The forecast called for snow flurries and frigid temps. But when Quinton Lucas arrived downtown around 4:30 A.M., the streets were already filling up with football fans, jubilant and dressed in red. To Lucas, Kansas City's thirty-five-year-old mayor, it looked like a movie.

At 11:30 A.M., a cavalcade of seventeen double-decker buses began rolling down Grand Boulevard, past restaurants and bars and office towers. Around noon, the parade pulled past the glass exterior of the Sprint Center, the twelve-year-old sports arena that was built to spur a downtown revival, and for a moment, one of the buses stopped. As the crowd began to chant—"MVP! MVP!"—a man behind a security barrier clutched a can of Miller Lite in his right hand and yelled up toward a group of football players and executives who were standing on the bus's second deck. The fan cocked his arm and flung the full can into the air, a brewski Hail Mary that sailed close to forty feet before beginning its descent, winding up in the outstretched right arm of Patrick Mahomes, the team's star twenty-four-year-old quarterback, who happened to be wearing ski goggles and leaning perilously close to the edge.

It's probably hyperbolic to say that the throw and snag were more impressive than anything that happened three days earlier, in Super Bowl LIV, but if you were standing on Grand in that moment, surrounded by a mass of humanity and joy, you'd be forgiven for thinking that. It was a stunning feat of coordination and focus, of timing and showmanship. *Holy shit.* It was incredibly clutch.

Then, as the fans on Grand erupted into more cheers, Mahomes popped open the beer and started to chug.

ON the evening of November 5, 1919, Jesse Clyde Nichols walked to the front of the Pompeian Room at the Hotel Baltimore and began to speak to a crowd of campaign workers. It had been eleven days since the Liberty Memorial parade, and the hotel had been transformed into a fund-raising headquarters, hosting daily luncheons for organizers and pep rallies for workers. Nichols, the vice chairman of the project, wanted to deliver a quick message: "I love this city," he said.

Kansas City, as everyone expected, had rallied to the cause. Big-money donors forked over thousands. Schoolchildren smashed piggy banks. On the eighth day of the campaign, pledges had surpassed $1.9 million, and *The Kansas City Star* blasted out a simple headline, hoping to keep the pressure on: "Come On!"

When city leaders first decided to build a war memorial, they formed a committee to guide the project. The chairman was a local millionaire and philanthropist, Robert A. Long, an unassuming co-founder of the Long-Bell Lumber Company. The real engine behind the scenes, however, was Nichols, a young real estate developer who'd grown up across the state line in Kansas, then built a small fortune by designing neighborhoods for Kansas City's elite. In time, Nichols would become one of the most influential real estate men in American history, partially responsible for every suburban cul-de-sac and shopping center, a popularizer of restrictive covenants that changed the landscape of cities. On this evening inside the Hotel Baltimore, though, he was still nine months shy of his fortieth birthday, sporting oval-rimmed glasses on his roundish balding head.

Nichols had spent the last week pushing volunteers to canvass the city, to hustle from house to house to house and convince the city's citizens that they had more to give. "If we can't make the money this week," Nichols told the volunteers, "every man and woman of your workers must stay with the ship until we do."

The campaign, however, was working. Kansas City didn't want to fail, and the donations were coming from everywhere. A week into the campaign, police busted an illegal gambling game on Fifth Street, in the city's North End, a hive of organized crime. When the establishment's operator and customers appeared before Judge John Kennedy, the fines added up to $115, which was turned over to the Liberty Memorial campaign. "If you know anybody you can have arrested," Long told volunteers the next day, "be sure he is taken before Judge Kennedy."

This was the Kansas City Spirit in action, a bubbling up of pride and hope, a fear of failure that had caused more than eighty-three thousand citizens of all races and classes to give money for a war memorial, and it was still present on the night of November 5, as volunteers crammed inside a hotel ballroom. If everything went as planned, they could surpass the $2.5 million that night. Soon after dinner, Long announced they had done it, to rapturous applause lasting for two and a half minutes.

In the middle of it all was J.C. Nichols. He had stood before the crowd in a coat and tie, overwhelmed by emotion, his voice struggling to rise above the din, declaring his love for Kansas City.

"It is a wonderful thing to live in a town with people such as these," he said. "In no city will one find such people as you who will do so much for your city and believe so much in your city's future."

Of course, what the volunteers in the room did not know was that Nichols, the man who was molding Kansas City, who was shaping the very idea of what it meant to live in American cities and suburbs, who, according to Long, was a tireless and selfless advocate for his hometown, was already in the process of splitting the city apart.

THE Super Bowl parade continued down Grand, passing a bar named the Cigar Box, where a lounge singer named Al Latta sings Sinatra on Friday nights, and passing the old brick headquarters of *The Kansas City Star*, completed in 1911 in Italian Renaissance architecture, where a young Ernest Hemingway took a reporting job and learned to write. It passed hipster coffee shops and retro jazz clubs and the twelve-story Western Auto Building, with its iconic glowing sign atop the roof, and finally it passed Twenty-First Street and turned right onto Pershing Road, pulling up to the side of Union Station, where the Chiefs players were ushered onto a temporary stage and Patrick Mahomes cradled the Super Bowl trophy in his arms.

Mahomes, an easygoing Texan who immediately embraced the city, was, at that moment, the greatest football player on planet earth: the most brilliant talent at the most valuable position in sports, the youngest quarterback to win Super Bowl MVP, the owner of a magical right arm that seemed touched by some unseen football deity. Since being drafted in the first round in 2017, he had done the following:

1. Spent one season as a backup/understudy to veteran starter Alex Smith.

2. Won the NFL's MVP Award while throwing fifty touchdowns.

3. Overcome a gruesome knee injury and led the Chiefs to their first Super Bowl championship in a half century, an angelic run that included epic comebacks in all three playoff games.

4. Expanded the very notion of what a quarterback could be.

In other words: There was nobody like Patrick Mahomes. The son of a Black father and a white mother, he was a transcendent star in a league that had once pushed young Black quarterbacks to other positions. He was capable of defying physics with his passes, unleashing a barrage of sidearm, no-look, and (occasional) left-handed throws, pushing the sport into the future, like an NFL version of Steph Curry. ("I love that style," Curry said. "The same kind of way that I play.")

He was still just twenty-four, in the embryonic stages of cultural stardom, theoretically in the first years of his physical prime, and he belonged to Kansas City, a football-obsessed town that had refused to draft a quarterback in the first round and subsisted for a generation on retread QBs—game managers and backup quarterbacks from the coasts.

The Chiefs, as a franchise and a brand, had been in Kansas City since 1963, when the franchise's founder, Lamar Hunt, uprooted the Dallas Texans and found an eager city in the heartland. It was, in most ways, love at first sight. The Chiefs had represented the American Football League in two of the first four Super Bowls, winning a championship in the 1969 season. The city adopted the players as their own. But in the decades that followed, the fate of the team had come to mirror that of the city itself: heartbreaking losses, widespread stagnation, a once proud institution that could not repay the adoration of its true believers.

As Mahomes stood onstage, he took a microphone and began to speak. From the front of the stage, he could look out toward the horizon and see a giant sea of red, which was really a few hundred thousand Chiefs fans, all gathered on a grassy hill above downtown. Behind him was Union Station, with its grand Beaux Arts architecture, and behind that was the city's skyline, and *behind that*, somewhere, was the Missouri River, where a port had once been formed on a small landing below the bluffs. If Mahomes looked up, however, he would have seen one thing: the Liberty Memorial, a 217-foot tower nestled between two halls.

The memorial had taken seven years to finish. A New York architect, Harold Van Buren Magonigle, was hired. Plans were adopted. When the monument was dedicated in 1926, President Calvin Coolidge spoke to a crowd of 150,000 and praised the city's spirit.

The project's leaders thought the Liberty Memorial would help catapult Kansas City to national prominence, but that's not what happened. Not quite, anyway. The city continued to boom throughout the 1920s and '30s, but it wasn't because of the Liberty Memorial. "Looked more like a silo to me," said Will Rogers, the actor and humorist.

The novelist Sinclair Lewis wasn't a fan. Neither was Amelita Galli-Curci, the famous opera singer, who said it looked like a saltshaker. The years passed. The crowds dissipated. The city continued to grow. But mostly, it pushed along like always, a cow town in the middle of the country. After a while, even people in Kansas City started complaining about the Liberty Memorial. They said it looked like a smokestack.

It closed to the public in 1994. Years of freezing and thawing—and more freezing and more thawing—had caused the concrete to crack and steel to corrode. According to an engineering firm that conducted a study, the deterioration extended to 80 or 90 percent of the structure's sub-deck. It was as if the whole Liberty Memorial was rotting from the inside.

IF it is not clear already, this book is two stories: It is the story of Kansas City and the story of Patrick Mahomes, its quarterback. If you are a reasonable person, you may believe there are limits to what a superstar quarterback can mean to a city. Peyton Manning, after all, did not cause Fortune 500 companies to flock to Indianapolis, and while Aaron Rodgers may have been extraordinary on the field, Green Bay is still Green Bay. That's true from a literal perspective, of course, but cities are more than a ranking of GDP or population. They are living, breathing organisms—a source of cultural and metaphysical energy, a place to work and live and find a community, an idea that becomes an identity.

The authors of this book grew up in Kansas City. More specifically, we come from its manicured suburbs, which were first dreamed up by J.C. Nichols. We grew up during the late 1980s and '90s, during a particularly fallow period for the city. Its downtown was essentially dead. Its football team was known only for tailgates and heartache. The very idea of Patrick Mahomes—or someone like him—seemed impossible.

It is our belief that Kansas City is the perfect embodiment of the midsize midwestern city and therefore the quintessential American town. It is, for better or worse, an Everywhere, USA, a heartland petri dish of every pioneering impulse and social disaster, a stand-in for every town and city that is not quite *somewhere*, the kind of place that creates the man who creates *Ted Lasso*. Kansas City's problems may not be unique, but if you want to understand what happened to the American city, you can start with the story of Kansas City.

The city, the writer Anthony Standen once wrote, did not have a trace of the East, and only a whiff of the West. It was not northern and it was not southern, but it was glorious and exhilarating and modest and "just plain central."

It rose from nothing on the prairie, not because of some abundance of natural resources, but rather the persistence of its residents. During its golden age, some one hundred years ago, it became a freewheelin' party capital, like Chicago and New Orleans, except the jazz clubs, numbering two hundred at the peak, stayed open later. It was, for a moment, the ultimate "open city," run by a political boss named Tom Pendergast, fueled by booze and beef, a haven for lawlessness, vice, and outsize dreams. ("I always loved Paris," said the renowned composer Virgil Thomson, "because Paris reminded me of Kansas City.")

When the poet Shaemas O'Sheel visited Kansas City for a piece for *The New Republic* in 1928, he labeled the city the "Crossroads of the Continent," not just in a physical sense but in the "diagram of national psychology." He wrote, "Every force and current and influence that has made, and is making, America flows and eddies here."

Then Kansas City brought America a different type of influence: the segregation methods of an eager developer, Nichols, whose neighborhoods were cut and pasted across the United States, long before anyone had heard of Levittown. When the trade publication *Builder* magazine counted down the one hundred most important figures for the US housing industry in the twentieth century, Nichols came in third, behind only Henry Ford and Franklin Delano Roosevelt. Transformed by Nichols's visions, Kansas City lost its jazz clubs and history and replaced the old with two monuments to a shriveling city: the "Troost Avenue Wall," the metaphorical dividing line between white and Black, and freeways—it held the dubious distinction of having more miles of freeway (per capita) than anywhere in the United States. Downtown was abandoned, hollowed out like a donut, a symbol of a city that had lost its way, plagued by white flight to the suburbs, a corporate exodus, and a more extreme version of the same cycle that afflicted cities across the country. "When I was in high school [in the 1990s]," said Jason Kander, a local nonprofit leader and former US Senate candidate, "people referred to downtown Kansas City as Belgrade."

By the final days of the twentieth century, Kansas City was mostly defined by its barbecue tradition and its ease of living, which could feel like a backhanded compliment: Well, the real estate *is* cheap, and the suburbs *are* plentiful. The one thing Kansas City had was sports—the last refuge of the midsize midwestern city—but by the mid-2000s, even that didn't mean much: the Royals hadn't been to the MLB playoffs in a generation, and the Chiefs were in the midst of a historic run of postseason ineptitude, eventually losing eight straight playoff games in a twenty-two-year span.

And then . . . Patrick Mahomes.

Which takes us back to the beginning of this decade, when the Chiefs won the Super Bowl, and the city started to reckon with its past.

All around Kansas City, people were thinking about the future: Could Mahomes and the Chiefs build a dynasty? Was Kansas City, once again, at a turn in the road?

Most importantly: What did Kansas City want to be?

PART I

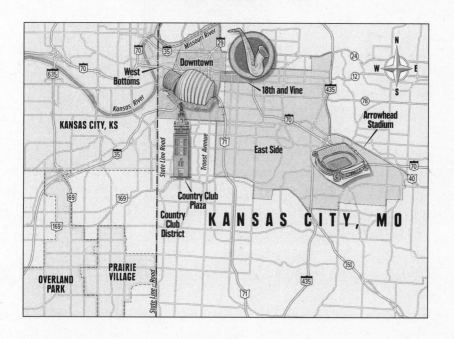

NO BOUNDARIES

Nobody knows where Kansas City is. This is because there are two Kansas Citys—though there is really only one *Kansas City*—and because the whole region sprawls across the border of two states.

But it's also because of a bar fight. At least, that's how it started.

It happened in November 1831 in Missouri, and the only person we know was there for certain was Gabriel Prudhomme. He lived on a plot of land in what would one day be the middle of the United States (the dead center, if you were measuring crudely), a heavily forested patch of bluffs along the Missouri River, one of the muddiest waterways on the continent.

Millions of years ago, much of North America was covered by glaciers. Mountains formed. The ice melted. The long process of glaciation left a labyrinth of rivers and tributaries crisscrossing the continent. Two of those rivers—eventually named the Kansas and the Missouri—would meet in the middle. Native American groups built what we now call Hopewell settlements, and tribes like the Osage, the Missouria, and the Kanza hunted bison and farmed in the region. The Kanza—or Kaw people—lived along the river that came to bear their name, building a village in the mid-eighteenth century forty miles northwest of what would become Prudhomme's land. The Osage, known for their skills as hunters, farmers, and warriors, built lodges with domed roofs in their Missouri settlements and facilitated trade through a wide swath of Missouri along a route called the Osage Trail. The tribes were forcibly removed from their home territories by the US government in the 1820s and '30s, around the same time more French Canadians moved in and built a few trading posts. Prud-homme was one of them, a blacksmith who purchased 257 acres from the federal government in 1831. His property contained what might've been the only valuable piece of land around: a rock outcropping that jutted into the river, ideal landing for ferries and steamboats.

Prudhomme started farming. He opened a grocery store and—fatefully, it seems—a tavern, where in the fall of 1831, a barroom brawl broke out, somebody drew a gun, and, according to an account from an early resident, Prudhomme ended up on the ground, his body in a pool of blood. The murderer was never caught.

Prudhomme left behind seven kids, a wife named Margaret, and a perfectly fine river landing, along with a legal mess that lasted seven years, until a group of fourteen men pooled their resources together and bought the land for $4,220 at an auction held on the coveted landing. One of the buyers, John McCoy, confessed years later that they were merely hoping for a quick profit. "None of them, he insisted, had any conception of town proprietorship, much less town building," wrote the historian Mildred C. Cox.

The only thing they knew was that a town needed a name. One grifter, Abraham Fonda, suggested they name the town after him, which didn't go over well. Others proposed Rabbitsville and Possum-trot. They settled on a name based on local geography. The French named the Kansas River after the Kanza tribe. The men were just miles from where the Kansas River flowed into the Missouri. They declared their new home the Town of Kansas, which would become the City of Kansas, and finally Kansas City. The new name didn't exactly feel like destiny. As McCoy said, they picked it "simply because nobody could think of anything better."

The men had no idea they had just ensured centuries of confusion.

SEVENTEEN years before the town founders gathered in a livestock pen for the auction, Missouri entered the union as the twenty-fourth state. It was a controversial selection. Missouri was designated a slave state and granted entry through a compromise—the Missouri Compromise—that admitted Maine as a free state and held that no Louisiana Purchase lands above Missouri's southern border would have slavery. It wouldn't last, but it wasn't the only issue. At that point, Missouri was also the westernmost state, and people were split about just how far west Missouri should go.

Missouri entered the United States as a territory in 1812 with a western border roughly twenty miles east of where the Kansas River collides with the Missouri River. It tried to become a state in 1817 with that original border, but Congress didn't believe Missouri was ready for statehood. The territory leaders tried again in 1818 with a border sixty miles farther west. Congress said no again, believing the territory would be too large.

This was all happening before Kansas City existed, and before the state of Kansas existed, *and* before anybody thought a town, much less a city, would rise up where the Kansas and Missouri Rivers met. In 1819, just as Missouri Territory leaders were negotiating again with Congress, the explorer Stephen H. Long journeyed across the middle of the country. Scoping out the vast plains aboard a steamboat with a prow designed like the head of a serpent—replete with nostrils that snorted steam—he and his expedition team described the area as uninhabitable. They helped inspire the naming of the region that stretched west of the Missouri River to the Rocky Mountains as the "Great American Desert." There was no grand promise for riches here.

What did it matter if the western border was twenty miles farther east or sixty miles farther west? Nobody wanted to build a great civilization on a cliff overlooking a giant desert anyway.

So Missouri came back in 1820, proposing the confluence of the

Kansas and Missouri Rivers as the boundary, and Congress accepted. The problem: The Kansas River travels east to west and does not provide a physical border, which meant Missouri ended at an imaginary straight line running north to south from the Kansas River's mouth.

It's impossible to know whether the Town of Kansas founders gave any thought to building a town at the edge of Missouri and calling it Kansas, a name that had been popping up on maps of the Midwest for years. (Given their general inability to plan anything, the answer is almost certainly no.) In their defense, they didn't know when another state might exist on the other side of the border, in the Great American Desert. Plus, in the 1830s, the land directly to the west was referred to as the Nebraska Territory, and that was still the case in 1853, when Town of Kansas was incorporated as City of Kansas. But a year later, Congress created the Kansas Territory—using the very popular name from all those maps—and now Kansas City was in a pickle. It was a city *in Missouri* with the same name as a new territory, a territory on the other side of an imaginary line following the mouth of a river that also shared the same name. Almost immediately, residents of the Kansas Territory falsely accused Kansas City of stealing their name, even though their territory had done the copying. Local leaders realized they were headed for a confusing disaster. In 1855, Robert Van Horn, an influential Kansas City newspaper publisher, sought the approval of the legislatures in Kansas and Missouri to move Kansas City, Missouri, into Kansas Territory. He could not have chosen a more complicated time.

- A year earlier, Congress had passed the Kansas-Nebraska Act, invalidating the Missouri Compromise. It stated that new territories, even those north of Missouri's southern border, would decide whether to allow slavery based on the popular vote.

- Thousands of Border Ruffians from Missouri swarmed into Kansas for an 1855 election, voting a proslavery legislature into office. Antislavery Kansans, many of whom had migrated from New England, formed their own government, but President Franklin Pierce recognized only the proslavery legislature.

- These proslavery lawmakers were open to Van Horn's idea, believing they could cement a voting majority to support entry to the union as a slave state if they annexed Kansas City and its growing population. Missouri's leaders wanted more slave states, too, so they agreed to give away their city.

Van Horn now only needed approval from Congress and he sent a buddy to Washington, DC, as an emissary to seal the deal. And then he waited. The story, recounted by a local judge, goes that Van Horn didn't hear anything from the politicians in the Capitol or from his buddy. Two years later, Van Horn's friend returned. Instead of lobbying Congress so that Kansas City could make sense, he had met a woman in DC, started an affair, and moved with her to Europe. By this time, any momentum for moving Kansas City into Kansas had dissipated in a torrent of violence. Kansas became a free state in 1861, spurred on by abolitionists and "Free-Soilers." The guerrilla warfare of "Bleeding Kansas" gave way to the Civil War. Missouri no longer considered giving anything to Kansas.

The fighting eventually abated and gave way to more confusion. After the Civil War, a city sprang up in Kansas's northeastern corner. It was inhabited by many former Kansas City residents who had spilled over, and it felt like a simple extension of Kansas City, so much so that the locals decided they should just call it Kansas City, too: Kansas City, Kansas. Kansas City was now a city in Missouri that shared a name with a different state that was separated from Missouri by an imaginary border running from the mouth of a river with the same name, and on the other side of that border was not only that other state but that other state's most prominent city, which had the *exact same name* as the state and the river. This proved to be way too much, and the Kansas City (Missouri) mayor lobbied for Kansas to annex Kansas City (Missouri) in 1879, weeks after *The Kansas City Times* released a poll showing strong support for annexation among the people of Kansas City (Missouri). "Half the people of the East," one respondent said, "think the city is in the state of Kansas." But the suggestion died on arrival in the Missouri State Capitol. The same border remained, as one Kansas official noted in the early 1900s, "cutting in almost equal parts the most interesting and promising city in the land." And today that imaginary line has a name: State Line Road.

THE weirdest part of State Line Road is a quarter-mile stretch in the West Bottoms neighborhood, an industrial hub that sits below downtown and, at various moments, was home to the Kansas City Stockyards, which were world-famous, and to the moribund NBA franchise that tormented the city from 1972 to 1985, the Kansas City Kings, who were not.

Before the Kansas River flows into the Missouri, it bends northwest for a mile and a half before winding back east and meeting the "Mighty Mo." The geography of the rivers creates a small peninsula that is west of the imaginary mouth of the Kansas River—the dividing line between states—but east of the Kansas River itself. If you are standing on State Line Road here, you can walk past a light pole and step onto a small patch of grass where you're no longer in Missouri. You're in Kansas. You don't have to cross a river, a major intersection, or even a median.

On this Kansas side of the light pole, you're still in the other Kansas City. Kansas City, Kansas, has its own mayor and police department and central business district, some of the best taco joints in the entire country, and the home stadium of the Sporting Kansas City Major League Soccer franchise. Everyone calls it KCK.

South of the West Bottoms, State Line Road keeps going. It turns into a bustling residential street, separating Kansas City, Missouri, from not only KCK but also leafy Kansas suburbs with names like Westwood, Prairie Village, and Leawood. Janelle Monáe, Paul Rudd, and Jason Sudeikis are among the famous people from the Kansas side of the metro. They and nearly everyone else from Kansas like to say they are from Kansas City, and nearly everyone on the Missouri side likes to remind them that, officially, they are not.

What if Congress had approved Missouri's original border, placing the entirety of the Kansas City metro in Kansas? What if the Town of Kansas founders had tried a little harder to come up with a name? What if Van Horn's friend had met his mistress *after* he stopped at the Capitol? Things would certainly be easier, and not just for Kansas City residents trying to explain where they live to their new roommates when they go away to college.

The division of Kansas City between two states has real political and economic consequences. Only once have Kansans and Missourians in the Kansas City metro united to pay taxes for a development project, the restoration of a dilapidated Union Station into a science museum in the late 1990s. The influence of a region of 2.3 million people is effectively split in half—and not by a mountain range or river. It's literally by a road.

But on an everyday basis, State Line Road serves as more of a unifier than a divider (just don't bring up abolitionist John Brown, Confederate William Quantrill, or college basketball). From the top of the Liberty Memorial, you can almost see the part of the West Bottoms that is actually Kansas. And in the blocks on either side of State Line Road, it feels like traditional directions and geography cease to exist. Wealthy Missourians drive to the Kansas City Country Club, located in the Kansas suburb of Mission Hills. University of Kansas Hospital nurses cross State Line Road to eat lunch in Missouri at a restaurant with "Louisiana" in its name. You pass between Kansas and Missouri and never notice, much less care, which state you are in. As the actor and tour guide Timothy "Speed" Levitch once put it, "Kansas City is, therefore, a capital city of boundary-disillusion; a place where the biggest border has almost no significance or visibility throughout the average day."

If a New York cabdriver were to ask Paul Rudd where he is from, he would simply say "Kansas City," and if the cabbie happened to know his geography and asked the pertinent follow-up . . . well, they might have a conversation on their hands. Kansas City is open and free and always in the middle of something: in the middle of two states, in the middle of the country. But the downside to having no boundaries means people often have questions or doubts. Nobody knows exactly where you are and what you are.

ARM TALENT

I n Kansas City, the first hint that something was about to change came in 2017. One summer day, in the middle of training camp, Brett Veach left practice and hustled back to Scanlon Hall on the campus of Missouri Western State University. Veach was used to moving fast; he was thirty-nine years old and in his first month as the Chiefs' general manager, which meant he had his alarm clock set before dawn and a million things on his plate. The list included an NFL roster to manage, an exceedingly abstruse salary cap to tame, and a staff of front-office lieutenants to lead, but as Veach zipped through the small campus in St. Joseph, Missouri, returning to the set of buildings that served as camp headquarters, he was consumed by something else: a clip from the "3s"—the Chiefs' third-string offense versus the third-string defense.

In most preseason camps, the general manager might wait to break down the third-string, the portion of the roster stocked with dreamers and future insurance salesmen, but up on the screen, amid the choreography of the offense and the chaos of the defense, was a twenty-one-year-old quarterback making another mesmerizing throw: strong, accurate, spun from an awkward angle on the run, the kind of toss that makes a football exec double-time it back to the dorms and then save the clip.

Brett Veach could not stop watching Patrick Mahomes.

It wasn't, of course, like Mahomes was some secret. The Chiefs had drafted him in the first round in April, trading up seventeen spots to grab him with the tenth overall pick. That alone made him an instant curio. But Mahomes was slated to spend his rookie season as an understudy to Alex Smith, the team's steady veteran. Most in Kansas City expected a slow transition: Smith would guide the offense after leading the Chiefs to three playoff appearances (and a 1-3 postseason record) in four seasons. Mahomes would spend the year learning the offense, refining his mechanics, and earning a graduate degree in quarterbacking under Professor Andy Reid, the Chiefs' head coach. But then training camp started, and Mahomes began working with the third-string—behind Alex Smith and Tyler Bray on the depth chart—and staffers and coaches kept rushing back to the dorms to watch film of the 3s, just to catch a glimpse of what they might've missed. One day, Veach pulled up the film and watched as Mahomes rolled to his right and slipped a no-look, sidearm flick between three defenders. If you looked closely, it didn't even really make sense. "It was like a phenomenon," Veach said.

Mahomes was unlike any football player Kansas City had seen: six feet three. Big arm. A quarterback with tantalizing promise. The son of a former major-league pitcher, Mahomes had grown up in East Texas and put up video-game numbers for Texas Tech, the Big 12 program famous for its Air Raid offense, a spread scheme that opened up the field and launched a revolution of no-huddle, breakneck passing attacks across college football. He was also something of a mystery. He had put up mind-blowing stats in college, though so did a lot of Texas Tech quarterbacks. His mechanics were a little raw. He was viewed as a "gunslinger," in the mold of former Packers great Brett Favre, but Reid—who had coached Favre in Green Bay—quickly pumped the brakes. "Brett's a Hall of Fame player, and this kid has got a long way to go before that," he said.

Mahomes could heave a football 70 yards on run, but it wasn't just arm strength. When he was at Texas Tech, he would study film of Saints quarterback Drew Brees and the Packers' Aaron Rodgers, who excelled at making what football people call "off-platform throws"—the catchall name for the off-balance, sidearm, freelance wizardry that was becoming en vogue at the position. At practice, Texas Tech coach Kliff Kingsbury forced Mahomes and the other quarterbacks to be creative, to seek out new throwing lanes with different arm angles, to *try shit*, even when it seemed unorthodox. "It was part of the development," recalled Emmett Jones, a former assistant.

When Mahomes first arrived on campus in 2014, he served as a backup to Davis Webb, one spot ahead of Nic Shimonek, a transfer QB from Iowa who was trying to get noticed. One day at practice, Shimonek tried to complete a short slant route without looking at his receiver, using a quick sidearm release. The move caught the eye of Kingsbury, who later pulled up the clip during a film session. "When did we start practicing this shit?" Kingsbury asked.

Shimonek figured Kingsbury was pissed, but his coach was actually intrigued. He liked ingenuity. Kingsbury, too, had been a star quarterback at Texas Tech before spending four seasons in the NFL—including a stint behind Tom Brady. As an offensive coordinator at Texas A&M, he had mentored Heisman Trophy winner Johnny Manziel, a six-foot jolt of electricity who marched to his own beat (and ultimately flamed out in the NFL). Kingsbury told the Texas Tech quarterbacks he didn't care how they got the ball out; it just needed to be complete. Nobody took the message more literally than Mahomes.

The very next practice, Mahomes faced a third-and-5 during a scrimmage. "Pat fucking throws a no-look pass," Shimonek remembered. "I'm like, OK, so now you're just going to try to steal my move." From then on, the throws became a game within a game, a daily football workshop, a laboratory in which Mahomes and Shimonek tried increasingly audacious experiments. Shimonek would complete a no-look pass on third-and-10. So Mahomes tried to uncork a 25-yard missile over the middle, no-look.

Still, as Mahomes won the starting role at Texas Tech, he mostly left the most audacious no-look exploits on the practice field. Until one game late in his junior year. The Red Raiders were playing on the road against Big 12 rival Oklahoma State, pushing hard to become bowl eligible. They trailed by a touchdown with only a few minutes left. Mahomes had just taken a 9-yard sack deep in his own territory. It was third-and-20. Time for something bold. On the next play, Mahomes dropped back into the pocket, glanced one way to freeze the defense, then launched a no-look strike on a deep crossing route, completing a 23-yard pass. On the sideline, Shimonek was standing next to Payne Sullins, a sophomore quarterback. "Bro," Sullins said. "He really just did that."

It was plays like that—the no-looks, the deep balls, everything *off-platform*—that caused NFL draft evaluators to lavish praise on Mahomes's "arm talent," which sounded like one of those annoyingly esoteric terms used by football scouts . . . until you watched him throw a football. "You knew you had something," Veach said.

And that was before Mahomes unleashed what might have been the most absurd throw in Chiefs history. It happened on August 31, 2017. The Chiefs were playing the Tennessee Titans in their final tune-up before the regular season. And the throw in question did not even count, because it was still preseason, and Mahomes was still twenty-one, and he was starting against the Titans only because Smith, the starter, was resting for Week 1. But it was a throw you do not forget: daring, athletic, basically impossible. Mahomes took the snap, dropped back, looked downfield, held the ball for another second, then took off on a dead sprint to his right. As he moved, he kept looking downfield, his eyes looking for an open receiver. When he finally realized a defender was bearing down, he planted his right foot in the ground, torqued his hips, and heaved the ball off his back foot. The football sailed 55 yards in the air and hit receiver Demarcus Robinson perfectly in stride.

When the play was over, Mahomes took a helmet to the chest, his body hitting the turf. He hopped up and put his arms in the air. "Quite a play," Andy Reid said afterward. In that moment, on a late-summer night, not one person across Kansas City understood just who had arrived in town. But one thing was clear: Arm talent was whatever Patrick Mahomes had.

"KANSAS CITY FROM NOW ON WILL BOOM"

On April 13, 1856, the steamboat *William Campbell* pulled up to Prudhomme's old landing after five nights churning through the Missouri River. To Sarah Chandler Coates, the journey felt endless. The wheel snapped in the choppy currents, and the stench of hundreds of mules filtered from the lower decks up to the luxury cabins. Some two weeks after departing the East Coast, she believed any destination would feel like a relief. But as the steep bluffs of Kansas City came into view, she had one thought: Why did I ever leave Philadelphia?

It wasn't that Sarah lacked courage. She hailed from an affluent Quaker family but rarely acted like an heiress. When the Chandlers vacationed in Nantucket, she planted her feet at the beach and collected seaweed to trace on greeting cards for her friends. She liked gardening and studying world history and translating French poets. Sarah had mastered arithmetic by the time she turned ten. At fourteen, she became an assistant teacher at her boarding school. At fifteen, she organized a school club dedicated to women's physiology—a deeply taboo subject at the time—so that her teenage peers could learn about their own bodies. She was curious and progressive, and what she wanted most out of life was to travel. "This world is so wide and beautiful," Sarah once wrote.

If you were to design her perfect match, it would have seemed that Kersey Coates was the one—a square-jawed Quaker abolitionist and an explorer of the New World. Despite having studied law under Thaddeus Stevens, a politician who would lead the congressional push for Reconstruction, Kersey chose the frontier over a legal career. They married the day before Valentine's Day in 1855. A year later he asked Sarah to join him in Kansas City. To see the world with him.

When Sarah dreamed of faraway lands as a teenager, she was almost certainly hoping for the sidewalk cafés of Paris or the serene coast of Marseille. Not "Gullytown," which is what people were derisively calling Kansas City in the mid-1850s. Cattle roamed freely between ramshackle houses, saloons, and gambling parlors. Buildings were erected into the sides of bluffs, their walls hugging dirt. The fourteen men who'd founded the city had done basically nothing since—it took a court order to get them to pay for their purchase.

And yet Kersey *chose* this place. He dreamed of business fortunes and promoting antislavery ideals. Unlike most abolitionists, who flooded into nearby Kansas, he went against the grain and settled in Missouri. (In 1860, white Kansas Citians held 166 enslaved persons while the county had around 4,000. There were 70 free African Americans in the county.) For Sarah, the downside was far greater. She was her family's only daughter. By moving to the middle of nowhere, she was abdicating the sheltered life they had planned for her. Sarah's sacrifice, her daughter later noted, was "perhaps the greatest she was capable of making."

After disembarking from the steamboat, Sarah and Kersey trudged up Main Street—a man-made canyon carved into the bluffs—to the Gillis House Hotel on the riverfront. They kept a Sharps rifle in the room and slept with a revolver under each pillow. There was no reason to think this was the right place for her, much less anybody. But her adventurous soul eventually kicked in. One of the first frontiersmen to exhibit the Kansas City Spirit was a woman.

"'Be Brave' said the spirit within me," Sarah recounted of her first day. "And instead of sitting down and weeping . . . I immediately went to work to investigate my new and strange surroundings."

YOU had to be insane to settle in a bedraggled little river town, and Sarah and Kersey Coates made plenty of relatively insane decisions in Kansas City.

When East Coast investors backing Kersey's real estate ventures immediately pulled out, lacking faith in Kansas City, he used his savings to buy $6,000 of land just southwest of Prudhomme's original plot. Locals weren't sure why he had done it; one Kansas newspaper described Kersey's bet as "the purchase of a crazy man." But Kersey had a vision. He began building a new development, requiring every building to be constructed with red brick. In 1857, they broke ground on a luxury hotel. They called the neighborhood "Quality Hill."

This was just the beginning. Kersey took Sarah for walks along Quality Hill's bluffs and pointed below at where the Kansas River collided with the Missouri. The silt and grass and dirt, he said, would soon become train tracks, warehouses, and heavy industry. Weirder, many of the other newcomers fed off their optimism. Excavators dug through the bluffs and leveled the hills. They crafted roads with names like Grand and Delaware. From 1854 to 1860 the population increased from a few hundred to more than four thousand. For every major holiday or anniversary, churches and immigrant societies would throw balls where people discussed impending libraries and opera houses, giving Kansas City a social scene before it had gridded neighborhoods. A journalist who visited from the East Coast in 1857 saw a striking contrast between Kansas City's dirty, hardscrabble streets and its confident—almost delusional—residents. They have an "unbounded, unquestioning faith," he wrote, "that here was the City of the Future."

That faith was put to the test by the Civil War. Cannon fire rang through the streets, three thousand men perished in the Battle of Westport, and Kansas City's population declined by a third. By 1866, the supposed "City of the Future" was war-torn, on its way to irrelevance, hoping for a miracle as railroad investors from Boston searched for a site for a railroad bridge that would span the Missouri River and function as a way station to the new American West.

The investors were eyeing Leavenworth, a city in Kansas that had a military fort and a population that boomed to twenty thousand. Importantly, Leavenworth did not have massive cliffs. What Leavenworth lacked, however, was the compulsive zeal and creative gamesmanship of Kansas City's leaders. Inside a Boston office that summer, the railroad investors told Kersey Coates they planned to sign a contract with Leavenworth. Kansas City had just enough time for a Hail Mary. Coates notified Robert Van Horn—now a congressman in Washington, DC—who leveraged professional friendships and leaned on the chair of the House Committee on Post Offices and Post Roads to secure approval for Kansas City's bridge.

It was a backroom master class. Coates's vision came true. Kansas City won the bridge. It didn't hurt that an official from the railroad company got a piece of land in the West Bottoms, which was about to explode in value. The Kansas City Spirit could manifest itself in mysterious ways.

On July 3, 1869, the day the first train traversed the bridge, Kansas City threw a parade. A hot-air balloon hovered in the sky. Fireworks popped. The bridge was draped in red, white, and blue. Some forty thousand turned out to celebrate. More people than in the entire town.

A local newspaper captured the giddiness in a headline: "Kansas City From Now on Will Boom."

IN the mid-1860s, not long before the Hannibal Bridge opened, James Dallas Bowser woke up in Kansas City just as his train pulled into a downtown station around midnight. He was in his early twenties; he had moved to Kansas City with his parents and a younger brother from Chillicothe, Ohio, where his father had been one of the town's first Black educators. After disembarking from the train, Bowser and his family wandered through downtown, turning down hilly streets that led nowhere. Like the Coateses they checked into the Gillis House, which was now outdated and, to Bowser, an "excuse for a hotel." In the daylight, he surveyed his surroundings: Main Street was the only paved road, a war trench was still dug into the ground in front of an auditorium, and the West Bottoms, a neighborhood below the bluffs of downtown, was a sycamore-covered hinterland.

Bowser, an outspoken, ambitious man, followed in his father's footsteps and accepted a teaching job at the Penn School, the first school west of the Mississippi opened exclusively for Black students. Penn School was nestled in an integrated working-class enclave about four miles south of downtown that came to be known as the Steptoe neighborhood. A year later, Bowser started teaching at Lincoln School, east of downtown. Most of his two hundred students were children, but he taught adults, too, and, a few years later, started his own secondary education program—science, English, the classics—after the state failed to help. Eventually, he served as principal at Lincoln and at Attucks School, worked for the federal government, invested in real estate, and edited *The Gate City Press*, a Black newspaper. (At one point, he nearly convinced vaunted journalist Ida B. Wells, whom he hosted during an education conference, to move to Kansas City and join the staff.) Bowser was, as journalist and author Charles E. Coulter would later describe, "Kansas City's leading Black intellectual." Like many of the three thousand African Americans who migrated to Kansas City in the late 1860s, Bowser believed the city offered the chance for "a fortune to be made."

Slowly at first, and then seemingly all at once, speculators, bankers, laborers, and cowboys piled in. The city's population shot up to 32,000 by 1870, an astounding gain, but nothing compared with the progress of the next ten years, when Kansas City more than doubled in size, to 55,000 by 1880 (with the Black population jumping to nearly 8,000), and still not even close to what happened over the next twenty years, when it hit 163,000 in 1900. More people led to more jobs and railroads and hotels and the city's first skyscraper, which begat more people still, and Kansas City reached a magnitude of development that almost matched the pipe dreams of its early boosters; in 1887 more buildings were constructed there than anywhere else in the United States besides Chicago and New York.

No part of Kansas City boomed like the West Bottoms, which transformed from a patch of sycamores into a thriving livestock center where thirty-four rail lines would soon cross. The Stockyards, a stunning (and sickening) sight, opened in the West Bottoms in 1871. By 1899, some eighteen thousand cattle a day arrived from Texas and the West. The cows were sized up and auctioned at the Live Stock Exchange and transported to an endless maze of muddy holding pens until they were slaughtered, butchered, and packed to be sold in Kansas City or sent east on another train.

The Stockyards work was excruciating, but anybody could get it. Black Southerners, in a migration known as the "Great Exodus," left in droves in 1879 for Kansas, glorifying its fertile land and reputation as the "Free State." Many who traveled north through Missouri stayed in Kansas City, finding jobs in the Stockyards and performing the grueling labor alongside immigrants from Ireland, Italy, Croatia, and Mexico. The city was mostly integrated, with Black residents living in every census-designated neighborhood in 1880, from Steptoe to the West Bottoms (although neighborhoods east of downtown featured the highest concentration of Black residents). Black and white Kansas Citians also shopped at many of the same clothing stores and stayed in the same boardinghouses and hotels, like the Gillis House.

But Kansas City was far from equal. Black workers toiled in the Stockyards because other industries would not hire them. Black students could not attend white schools. Kansas City police were known for brutalizing African Americans and failing to protect them. In the spring of 1882, a white mob of three hundred people lynched a man named Levi Harrington on a bridge in the West Bottoms after he was falsely accused of killing a police officer named Patrick Jones. Harrington was a young father of five who had moved from

Mississippi and found work as a plasterer and porter. One boss described him as "honest" and "industrious." He left behind a wife named Maria.

The city, noted Coulter, the journalist and author, represented to most members of the incipient Black community "two worlds," one offering the potential for advancement and another constrained by limitations. These were contradictions Bowser routinely pondered as an educator and editor. When Rudyard Kipling published the imperialist poem "The White Man's Burden" in 1899, Bowser penned a famous rebuttal, advising Kipling and the white community to make the Black man's "chances equal, / Give him the fairest test/ Then 'Hands Off' be your motto/ And he will do the rest."

WHEN Kersey Coates died in 1887, Sarah had a golden opportunity to return to the comforts of Philadelphia. She decided to stay. Her husband had backed up his abolitionist beliefs by donating the land for a Black Baptist church and Lincoln School. He sold to Black residents when many developers did not. At his funeral, a group of Black men insisted on carrying his casket.

Sarah continued to build up Kansas City. With her children, she demolished and rebuilt the Coates House Hotel, installing a Turkish bath, floral and bonnet shops, and marble floors. From her home on Quality Hill, she started more clubs, hosting the History Class of Kansas City, where locals met to discuss world history, and leading the Kansas City Women's Exchange and Equal Suffrage Association. Susan B. Anthony stayed with her in Quality Hill, speaking at a major suffrage conference in Kansas City in 1896. Sarah also founded an art club, thinking Kansas City could be as renowned for its culture as its cows. "It is something to have a nucleus of art, at least," she wrote, "and some of these days we may be the art center of the West. Who knows?"

For a little while, just after Sarah died in 1897, this prediction almost proved true. In 1899, the city opened Convention Hall, a twenty-thousand-person venue that was said to be the largest concert space in the country. Soon, civic leaders realized they could also use the hall to engage in their favorite pastime: proving Kansas City's relevance to the world. On a muggy July night, local merchants, hoteliers, and boosters gathered at Convention Hall to raise money for a long-shot attempt at hosting the next year's Democratic National Convention. In just thirty minutes attendees pledged thirty thousand dollars to bankroll the DNC. The rapid fund-raising impressed the Washington, DC, cognoscenti, and Kansas City won the bid. Then, in a stroke of poor luck, the whole thing burned to the ground three months before the convention.

Before the fire was out, city leaders were already discussing a rebuilding plan and negotiating with the Carnegie Company for steel trusses to provide the backbone for a new building. Construction crews rebuilt the hall in ninety days, William Jennings Bryan was nominated for president, and the secretary of the Democratic National Committee testified that Kansas City "contains a higher degree of public spirit than any other city in the United States." Less than fifty years after Sarah Coates's arrival, everybody was talking about Kansas City. And as journalists across the nation descended there, they noticed the locals strutting around town with special badges.

They read: "I live in Kansas City—ask me."

THE PINE CURTAIN SUPERSTAR

I n the spring of 1988, Major League Baseball scouts descended on East Texas to see a late bloomer with a golden arm. They passed a sign on the way to their destination. "Welcome to Lindale, Good Country Livin'."

Pat Mahomes lived with his parents just inside the Lindale city limits. With a population of 2,500 at the time, it was one of many suburbs outside Tyler, the largest city in East Texas, a pine-tree-shrouded region that felt more southern—and more isolated—than the rest of the state. Dallas was one hundred miles to the west, Houston was two hundred miles to the south, and Austin and San Antonio were even farther. The author Asher Price once described East Texas as having its own time zone: fifty years behind everyone else.

The Mahomes family had been in East Texas long before Pat ever picked up a baseball. Sometime after the Civil War, an Alabama-born man whose name appeared in records as Q Mahomes and Que Mahomes married Nellie Adkins, who was born in Texas in 1855, and they settled in Smith County, where Tyler and Lindale are located. Their son Wilber Mahomes grew up in Lindale, and so did William Mahomes, who was born in 1910 as one of Wilber and wife Ida's nine children. East Texas was a hostile place for them and other Black families. In Smith County, white residents voted by a 25-to-1 margin to secede on the eve of the Civil War, and many of them refused to accept that Black people could live freely in East Texas. In the first few decades after the Civil War, at least five African Americans were lynched in the Tyler area.

The Mahomes family navigated the constraints of the Jim Crow South. Wilber was a laborer, and William worked at the Tyler Pipe refinery. William's wife, Lucy, was mostly a homemaker, as well as a church volunteer. William had an eighth-grade education but a natural knack for math, recalled Johnny Mahomes, William's son. "Math kind of ran in my family," he said. Johnny was one of Lucy and William's three children, who came of age when Texas, after stiff resistance to court-ordered desegregation, was on the verge of change. William Mahomes Jr. graduated in 1965 from Bragg Morris High School, Lindale's Black school, and went to Texas A&M (becoming the first Black student to spend four years in the school's Corps of Cadets program) and the University of Texas Law School before embarking on a career as a corporate lawyer in Dallas. At Bragg Morris High, Johnny played baseball and basketball and served as the president of the Future Farmers of America Club and the Dramatic Club. He and William Jr. had started working in their early teens, canning peas, hauling watermelons, and picking blackberries. In 1966, Johnny graduated as valedictorian. Unlike his brother and sister, Marsha, who moved to California, he stayed in Lindale, marrying Cindy Norman. He liked it there. "It's pretty and people get along, for the most part," Johnny once said.

When he wasn't working for an oil company, Johnny played on a semipro baseball club and taught Pat the game at an early age. The expectation, set by Pat's father, his mother, and his uncle, was to stand out—and not just at baseball. At nearly everything, Pat drew inspiration from Cindy. When he was seven, she had been paralyzed from the neck down in a car accident, but gradually regained some of the movement she had lost and finished a psychology degree. To Pat, everything else seemed easy. By his senior year of high school, Pat was enrolled in college-level English, psychology, and sociology and was a member of the National Honor Society. He occasionally babysat for a cousin and her friend, the future country superstar Miranda Lambert. (The "Good Country Livin'" sign has since been replaced by a sign that says, "Lindale, Hometown of Miranda Lambert.") He was a popular student, too, rarely experiencing racial animosity despite being one of about a dozen Black students in the predominantly white school. "He gets along with everybody. He doesn't try to be better than anybody else or think he's somebody special. He just tries to be himself," a close friend said at the time. As Pat recalled, "A lot of it stemmed from me being so good in sports that I never had anything to worry about."

When Pat blossomed from a scrawny five-feet-six sophomore into a six-feet-one senior star at Lindale High School, his athletic career took off. He passed for 1,600 yards as a quarterback, averaged thirty points a game on the hardwood (earning runner-up for Texas's "Mr. Basketball" honor), leaped six feet six inches in the high jump, and batted over .600 in baseball. The only question was what he would do next. Per National Collegiate Athletic Association (NCAA) rules, Pat had five official college visits to use across every sport, so he knew he had to be selective. And at first he pursued football.

There was a dalliance with Louisiana Tech University and interest from Kansas State University, but the University of Southern Mississippi proved to be a serious suitor. The coaching staff asked Pat to come down for an official visit. On campus, he sat among a group of recruits who each shared their height, weight, and time in the 40-yard dash. He felt pretty good announcing that he was six-one and 175 pounds and could run a 4.6. But then the guy sitting next to him, a hulking defensive tackle, said that he was six-eight and 296 pounds—and he could run a 4.5. The Southern Miss coaches told Pat they still wanted him, insisting he could start the next year. But Pat was rightfully suspicious that they were engaging in the typical recruiting sweet talk. Southern Miss, after all, had a rising sophomore who had started ten games as a true freshman, a gunslinger named Brett Favre.

So, by the spring of 1988, Pat, who hated getting hit on the grid-iron, believed his most likely destination would be the University of Arkansas. The baseball team and the basketball team, reaching the heights of the "Forty Minutes of Hell" defense under coach Nolan Richardson, both wanted him. But the professional scouts kept on coming to the East Texas piney woods. Although the opportunity to play college basketball tantalized Pat, baseball had been his first love. And, perhaps as important, Johnny's mind was made up. He was sure that baseball was his son's best bet for success. In the 1988 MLB draft, the Minnesota Twins selected Pat in the sixth round. He signed five days later and reported to play for the team's rookie-league affiliate in Tennessee.

Pat Mahomes had made it: Over the next fifteen years he played for the Twins, the Boston Red Sox, the New York Mets, the Texas Rangers, the Chicago Cubs, and the Pittsburgh Pirates. East Texas remained a part of him. He kissed the ground when he came home from an early stint in the minors. After his first major-league victory, in 1992, he mailed the lineup card and game ball back to his parents. And Pat started a relationship with Randi Martin, who'd grown up in Troup, another small town outside Tyler. Martin, who had been a basketball player and honor roll student in high school, came from a family whose roots in East Texas also went back several generations.

When Pat and Randi got married in 1998, at Tyler's Colonial Hills Baptist Church, their first son hustled down the church aisle. Patrick Mahomes II, not quite three years old, was the ring bearer and the junior best man.

The first few years of Patrick's life were every young boy's dream. Pat gave him his own locker, dressed him in a baby Twins jersey, and took him on the turf of the Metrodome in Minneapolis. Patrick swung baseball bats with Alex Rodriguez and learned infield techniques from Derek Jeter. When his father's New York Mets made the World Series in 2000, he shagged balls in the Shea Stadium outfield during batting practice, battling with veteran pitcher Mike Hampton.

Mahomes was still very much a kid. The first time he met Mark Mc-Gwire, "he almost peed his pants," Pat Sr. recalled. But Pat noticed his son's baseball skills and the way he studied the practice habits of his major-league teammates, especially Rodriguez, and had the same revelation as Richard Williams and Earl Woods: He knew his child was going to be a professional athlete.

Pat spent his last season in the majors in 2003, then embarked on a long stint as a journeyman minor leaguer. Patrick settled in with his mother in East Texas. The parents split while Patrick was in elementary school, and Randi Martin raised Patrick and younger brother, Jackson, as a single mother, taking extra shifts and working weekends as an event planner at Hollytree Country Club to support their athletic pursuits. "Sometimes everybody focuses on my dad because he played sports," Patrick Mahomes later recalled, "but she was one of the main staples of my life."

There was no stopping a young Mahomes from playing sports. One time, a teammate of Pat's asked Randi how she got Patrick to do it, to run around the outfield and catch fly balls She was more concerned with another question about her hyperactive son: How did she get him not to do it?

WHEN Patrick Mahomes was in junior high, Reno Moore invited him to participate in a quarterback training program. To Moore, an assistant coach at Whitehouse High School, Mahomes was an average Texas boy, a close friend of a neighbor who often ended up at Moore's house, waiting on the curb with a towel with a bunch of other kids who were eager to swim in Moore's pool. But when Mahomes was out of the water, Moore saw him run around and play in the occasional backyard football game, and he was impressed. (You could say he liked the kid's "arm talent.") Like most everyone around Tyler, Moore was aware of Mahomes's athletic lineage and prodigious talents. The first conversation he had with Mahomes, he told him a story about playing against his father in high school baseball.

The days of hanging around major-league clubhouses were over for Mahomes. He was now in East Texas with his mother. Tyler and its suburbs were still isolated; they hadn't gotten any closer to Dallas since the '90s. But they were bigger and more modern, more flush with Whataburgers and more congested with afternoon traffic on Broadway Avenue.

To get to Whitehouse from Tyler, you drive south on Main Street and follow the rolling hills past one-story houses and look for a water tower emblazoned with a half-blue, half-red "W." On Friday nights in the fall, the lights from the high school football stadium glimmer for several blocks. Even on a bad night the stadium is three-quarters full, but by the time Mahomes settled in Whitehouse there weren't many bad nights. The area was undergoing an athletic renaissance. A.J. Minter, now a pitcher for the Atlanta Braves, worked out alongside Mahomes at athletic trainer Bobby Stroupe's Athlete Performance Enhancement Center facility. Tyus Bowser, who played for a high school in Tyler before getting drafted by the Baltimore Ravens, damn near looked like a bodybuilder as a teenager—and that's according to Dylan Cantrell, a high school teammate of Mahomes's who made it to the NFL, too.

Among this übertalented group, Mahomes stood out. In his first T-ball game, he fired a throw from shortstop to first base and smashed the first baseman's glasses, leading to Mahomes playing first base for the rest of the year. By middle school he was around six feet tall and weighed 165 pounds, making him roughly the size of Allen Iverson in his prime. Athleticism, however, was not his defining characteristic. People who knew him back then were drawn to his mature personality. He smiled all the time, and his favorite movie was a throwback, *Remember the Titans*. When he showed up at a Whitehouse High School summer camp as a fifth grader, he wore a backward baseball cap. Adam Cook, a Whitehouse coach, saw the fashion choice as a test. Was the son of a professional athlete cocky? Would he listen to the adults? He would. When Cook asked him to turn around the c?

Mahomes obliged. Just a few years after T-ball, Mahomes devised strategies alongside coach Chad Parker for a baseball team, Rose Capital East, which finished runner-up in the Junior League World Series in Michigan. He was also laid-back enough to go along with Parker's decision to bring the entire team to Arby's for a meal of two roast beef sandwiches and a large caffeinated soda before every game, the last time Mahomes can remember eating at an Arby's. And while Randi and Pat were convinced their son could be a professional athlete someday, sometimes Mahomes would half-seriously mention a backup plan to be a lawyer, perhaps after attending Duke, home to one of his favorite college teams. "People treated Patrick like he was a treasure, in a way," said Parker. "Not because they thought they were going to get anything—just because they were drawn to him."

One of the few activities he wasn't involved in was football. Aside from pickup games and a short Pop Warner stint as a linebacker (Mahomes disliked tackling), he didn't play in any organized fashion until middle school. At the start of the second semester of Mahomes's seventh-grade year, Moore took him, a close friend from the Little League team named Ryan Cheatham, and a few other prospective quarterbacks out of the school's athletic period—yes, there are sports during the school day in Texas—to give them a crash course on how to be a Whitehouse High School quarterback.

The lessons lasted several weeks. Moore had gotten the idea from Todd Dodge, a godfather figure among Texas high school football coaches who built a dynasty at Southlake Carroll. When most high school teams used the power-running game, Dodge introduced the spread—a high-flying, no-huddle, video-game offense in which as many as five wide receivers lined up on the field at a time. High school quarterbacks, previously game managers, were throwing the ball up to seventy times a game, which meant they had to memorize more plays and more formations and improvise on the fly. This is exactly what Mahomes was figuring out. The first two weeks of the program were in the classroom, where he studied a dizzying number of formations and pored over a manual filled with leadership tips from sources as varied as the Bible and Warren Buffett.

And then the football started. Moore placed a collection of five-foot-tall adjustable nets, each with three pockets big enough to catch a football, in a gymnasium. Mahomes faced a net, pretending his feet were planted in concrete, and threw. He faced away from a net, turning around when Moore said so, and threw. He lay flat on the gym floor, hurrying to his feet at the command of Moore, and threw.

Moore couldn't believe how quickly Mahomes released the ball. It was as though the leather were burning hot. And the kid could throw from every angle into the correct pocket of the nets. "Did I see better athletes through my years in junior high? Yes, I definitely saw better athletes," Moore said. "But I didn't ever see an athlete that could be . . . a quarterback [and] make decisions and do the things he was doing."

As Moore saw it, there was only one problem. Even within the flexible confines of the spread, in which coaches encourage experimentation, Mahomes's throwing mechanics were unorthodox. As Moore watched Mahomes, he'd tell the other coaches, "We've got to get his arm up."

Generations of quarterbacks had heard this command, mostly for good reasons. Funky throwing motions were fine if you were starting out, but quarterbacks who released the ball in any fashion besides the textbook L shape—a technique that supposedly harnesses maximum power and acceleration—were destined to find fewer college and professional coaches willing to give them a chance. NFL quarterbacks, at the time, were a bunch of L-shaped throwers. Some of the best were Peyton Manning and Tom Brady. Some of the worst played in Kansas City: Tyler Thigpen, Brodie Croyle, and Damon Huard rotated as starters in the 2008 season, when Mahomes began middle school, and only Thigpen threw more touchdowns than interceptions. L-shaped throwers were fairly robotic, but the good ones were consistent. And the NFL loves consistent.

Mahomes was anything but robotic. He had a three-quarter motion, something between the classic L and a sidearm. But that designation didn't quite suffice. His motion was fluid, adjusting slightly based on where the ball needed to go, not unlike a baseball infielder.

In fall 2009, Moore watched as Mahomes played for the Whitehouse eighth-grade team and was still bothered by his throwing motion. He kept telling the middle school coaches to work with him. To get that arm up. Then, during one game, Moore saw something he has a hard time believing to this day. Mahomes—who, just to remind you, was in the eighth grade—flung the ball sidearm into the air, and it spiraled and spiraled, and it seemed like it would never fall. Inevitably, it did, into the hands of a wide receiver. Moore is not sure of the distance, just that it should have been impossible for any young teenager, perhaps other than Patrick Mahomes.

Moore suddenly lost interest in changing Mahomes's throwing style. He told every coach not to screw this up. To let Mahomes be Mahomes. All of Mahomes's coaches—from his athletic trainer, Stroupe, to Texas Tech coach Kliff Kingsbury—learned the same lesson. Sure, they would hone something here or there. But they recognized the best thing they could do was unleash an unfiltered Mahomes into the world, and let the world enjoy the results.

Whitehouse High School sure did. In 2013, near the end of a high school senior year in which Mahomes threw for fifty touchdowns and rushed for fifteen touchdowns, he threw for 597 yards in a playoff game against Mesquite Poteet High School. Whitehouse lost a heartbreaker 65–60, and Mahomes's high school career was over. But it also provided the most ridiculous of ridiculous high school highlights. With the score tied at 7–7, Mahomes spun out of a tackle by Malik Jefferson, a future third-round NFL draft pick, and, before setting his feet, launched the ball some 50 yards down the field to wide receiver Jake Parker, who ran another 20 yards into the end zone.

The arm was, most definitely, not up.

IF you search for that Mesquite Poteet game on the internet, you'll find highlights from a Dallas TV station. The almost-sidearm sideline throw to Parker is the key moment, but otherwise the most noticeable part of the telecast is that the announcer mispronounces Mahomes as "Ma-homess."

"Ma-homess scrambles, spins out of a tackle, and then finds Parker," he says.

Mahomes was surprisingly unheralded as a high school football player. Not anonymous: He was chosen the Texas High School Player of the Year as a senior by the Associated Press. But it's no exaggeration to say that college football screwed up in evaluating his talent. Quarterbacks whose careers fizzled, like Keller Chryst and Rafe Peavey, earned four-star rankings for the class of 2014, while Mahomes was a three star, the number 29 pro-style quarterback in the country. A few months before his senior season Mahomes was ranked by one publication as the No. 55 player in Texas. "For the life of me I have no idea why people didn't recruit him out of high school," said Sonny Cumbie.

Cumbie, a former assistant coach at Texas Tech, actually *did* recruit him. But it took a decent amount of luck for him to start paying attention. In September 2012, he went to Whitehouse's homecoming game against Sulphur Springs High School to watch Mahomes's teammate Dylan Cantrell, a wide receiver. The conditions were less than ideal for good offense. Rain poured so hard that Cumbie snuck into the press box to stay dry. But the Mahomes-led offense scored at will. He scrambled away from the Sulphur Springs defense for three rushing touchdowns and connected with Cantrell on several long passes, many of them through tight windows just out of the reach of Sulphur Springs's secondary. Cumbie saw elusiveness and crisp passing angles. He thought he might have been watching the next Johnny Manziel, who had just begun a Heisman Trophy season at Texas A&M.

Cumbie shared his opinions of Mahomes with Kingsbury, who left a coordinator job at A&M to become Texas Tech's head coach in December 2012. All Kingsbury had seen of Mahomes was a highlight reel. The two started visiting Whitehouse as often as they could, coming away more impressed each time. Mahomes was a top student, came from a great family (Cumbie often chatted with Mahomes's maternal grandmother, who worked in the high school's front office), and had an impeccable talent for creating and learning game plans. One youth coach said that Mahomes had more sports IQ at age twelve than most adults have. Other people referred to this skill as his photographic memory. One time during basketball season, Kingsbury made a surprise visit and had a challenge for him. He had picked up a copy of the scouting report for an upcoming Whitehouse basketball game—so detailed that it included specific inbounds plays. Mahomes recited every word to Kingsbury.

Cumbie's only concern was that some blue-chip school, like the University of Texas or Louisiana State University, would come to its senses and nab Mahomes before Texas Tech signed him. But most schools were slow to notice his skills. Cumbie's best guess was that premier coaches thought Mahomes's unorthodox throwing motion was problematic, or they all believed he would rather play Major League Baseball, like his dad, or they just didn't feel like trekking through the Pine Curtain of East Texas. "There's no major airport," said coach David Bailiff, who offered Mahomes a scholarship to Rice as soon as he saw him on tape. "You gotta want to get there."

There was also the college football recruitment complex. Top programs typically home in on one prized quarterback in each recruiting cycle, picking teenagers they can watch at elite off-season camps. As a result, they have to pinpoint their chosen target early, often in the player's sophomore season.

Mahomes didn't do many camps. When he tried out for the Elite 11, the top quarterback competition in the country, he was snubbed. (He "didn't always spin the football perfectly," according to one account of his tryout.) And Mahomes was entirely off the radar as an under-classman. When he wasn't splitting time at QB on the freshman team, he served as a glorified secretary for the varsity, standing on the Whitehouse sideline next to Cook, the offensive coordinator, record-ing every minute detail—down and distance, the hash mark, the name of the play—onto a grid Cook had printed off Excel. He got called into action during the playoffs, but as a safety. He played the same position as a sophomore, earning all-district honors and putting himself on the radar of a certain state university renowned for its bumbling inability to make smart football decisions.

Yes, the University of Texas invited Mahomes to a camp sometime between his sophomore and junior seasons. This was supposed to be the beginning of a relationship. The one hundred or so kids who at-tended were considered recruiting targets—many would surely be playing in Austin in a couple of years. The coaching staff split the athletes into position groups, placing Mahomes with the safeties, and Pat Sr. was befuddled. Sure, his son had been named all-district as a safety, but a closer look would have revealed that Mahomes had no desire to play defense. It was obvious to Pat Sr. that the Texas coaches hadn't been paying attention. Despite their promise to switch Ma-homes to the quarterbacks group, Pat was not impressed. Father and son left. Sometime that summer, Pat remembered asking him, "What are we doing?" He told his son that better options abounded in base-ball, where Mahomes threw in the mid-90s and hit the cover off the ball, and basketball, the sport his godfather, LaTroy Hawkins, main-tains was his best. Football seemed an unnecessary distraction on the way to a professional career in either of those sports.

In the end, Mahomes decided to keep playing for one reason: His close friends would be out there on Friday nights, and he could not imagine watching them from the bleachers.

That fall, he faced the challenge of overtaking one of those good friends, Cheatham, for the Whitehouse starting-quarterback spot. Cheatham had pitched with Mahomes on the Little League team, thrown footballs into the same nets in middle school, and competed with him over who had the more accurate game log on the varsity sidelines as freshmen. The rainy game against Sulphur Springs, attended by Cumbie, was the first time Mahomes played an entire four quarters as varsity quarterback.

It was during that season Mahomes came to understand the magic of football, that being a quarterback provided a consistent challenge and unparalleled responsibility, that no matter how many high school no-hitters he threw at Whitehouse—his first came in the spring of his senior year—he was ready to forge his own way. "He liked being the guy that pulled the trigger and had the control," said Randy McFarlin, the head coach of Whitehouse for Mahomes's first three years.

By the time everything clicked, Mahomes's commitment was sealed with Texas Tech, the team that had wanted him all along, and it was too late for the biggest college football programs. Traditional powers like Notre Dame and Michigan eventually entered the sweepstakes, Pat Sr. recalled, sending stacks of letters. "Half of them, he never even opened," Pat Sr. said.

Their loss was most likely Mahomes's gain. When the four-star and five-star recruits preened for college scouts, he got to play basketball and baseball with his friends, honing skills and becoming addicted to competition. On the bus ride home from Whitehouse's playoff loss to Mesquite Poteet, he texted his basketball coach and asked if he could play in the team's game the next day.

It wasn't a typical decision for a future Division I quarterback who was seen as a Major League Baseball prospect. But it was something that would've happened in another era, which is what Mahomes's athletic career felt like. In his early years, he had generations of family watching him play baseball (great-grandmother Lucy Mahomes lived to be ninety-nine), and his grandfather and father, granted permission by Texas Rangers manager Johnny Oates to travel back from DFW to East Texas for Mahomes's summer games, coached some of his early teams. Then, as a high schooler, Mahomes got to live a fairly normal life. He ate at Sonic and Whataburger and cheered for the Texas Rangers and Dallas Cowboys, especially wide receiver Dez Bryant. He listened to the rapper Big Sean, made fun of Justin Bieber, gave up drinking Coke for a girl, and, like everyone else, was enraptured by Miley Cyrus's 2013 MTV Video Music Awards performance. He went on cruises with family and friends. He stayed up late to watch the reality-TV show *Duck Dynasty*. He sometimes made ketchup sandwiches as a snack. He woke up early to get dressed in a polo and attend Whitehouse High School prayer events called "See You at the Pole." (They began at 7:15 A.M. sharp.) He made good grades, mentored young basketball players in the Little Dribblers league, and served as social media officer of Whitehouse's National Honor Society. On Valentine's Day of his sophomore year, Mahomes gave a card and a rose to a junior soccer player. Her name was Brittany Matthews.

With the Texas Tech scholarship and the chance to play both football and baseball, Patrick figured he was college-bound, except for a moment on June 5, 2014, when his life could have drastically changed. As the Major League Baseball draft got underway and teams selected future stars like Kyle Schwarber and Trea Turner, he watched with his parents in Whitehouse. Sometime on that first day, as Pat Sr. remembers, the phone rang. The Arizona Diamondbacks were on the line and told Mahomes they wanted to draft him. They said they would pay him a $1.5 million bonus. The culmination of his childhood dream—of years spent emulating Alex Rodriguez—and a massive payday were within his grasp. And he said no. Mahomes got into his truck to leave for Texas Tech, where he had attended orientation the week before. Pat and Randi called their son and told him to return home. "And he came back, and I asked him, 'Are you sure?'" Pat Sr. said. "And he goes, 'I want to try this football thing. I really like it.'" According to a Diamondbacks official, the courtship wasn't quite as dramatic. An area scout visited Mahomes, his mother and father, and Brittany Matthews in the weeks leading up to the draft, and Mahomes and his family came up with the signing-bonus figure. The

Diamondbacks' interest was "strong," according to the official. Had Mahomes's interest in playing professional baseball been just as strong, the team would have selected him in one of the early rounds as a pitcher.

Either way, after the draft, Mahomes left Whitehouse and kept going, through the pines, past Dallas, all the way to the High Plains of West Texas. He planned to start summer classes on Monday.

THE BOSS AND THE DEVELOPER

Toward the end of 1894, a boulder-shaped man stepped off a train onto Union Avenue in the West Bottoms. He was impossible to miss: piercing eyes, handlebar mustache, bulging forearms from years on the baseball diamond, neck as wide as a tree trunk. Although later in life the man wore derby hats to cover his bald dome, at the time he still had a nice swath of brown hair. He was twenty-two, tired of kicking around the river town in northern Missouri where he'd grown up, and ready for some action in an untamed city. On Union Avenue, every bit as wild as the Bowery in New York, he jostled for space with cattle traders, prostitutes, and investors from as far away as Paris. Carnival barkers stood outside pawnshops, restaurants, and clothing stores, trying to sell everything from cheap suits and blouses to hotel rooms available in thirty-minute increments. Nearby on West Ninth Street—the "Wettest Block in the World"— there were twenty-four buildings and twenty-three of them were saloons.

It was exactly where Tom Pendergast wanted to be.

Pendergast's Irish American family basically owned the West Bottoms. His older brother Jim had been there since the late 1870s. At first, Jim settled into the dangerously mundane existence of a laborer for the A.J. Kelly Foundry, shoving iron ore into a hot smelter every day. The legend goes that Jim caught a huge break at the racetrack in 1881 and parlayed a winning bet on a long-shot Thoroughbred into opening his first bar. (For good measure, he named it after the horse:

Climax.) Soon, Jim had another bar, the American House, and then another, the Pendergast Brothers Saloon.

The West Bottoms sat figuratively and literally beneath Kansas City's main business district and the mansions of the well-to-do. Despite the Quaker-minded progressivism of Sarah Coates, a coterie of WASPs, spearheaded by *Kansas City Star* editor William Rockhill Nelson, had become the city's unofficial ruling class. They called themselves the Commercial Club, and they cared about two things: their own business interests and making Kansas City appear sophisticated to the rest of the country. They did have a point. Sophisticated cities had level streets and sewage systems and electricity, and Kansas City needed all these things.

In the 1890s, Nelson recruited renowned landscape architect George Kessler to make Kansas City the epicenter of the City Beautiful movement and turn many of its gridded streets into sweeping boulevards surrounded by parks. The project tied neighborhoods together—they were connected by an elaborate streetcar system— and created charming vistas. It was, as historians would note, a de facto zoning system ten years before zoning laws were enacted in Los Angeles and a prelude to urban renewal decades before interstate highways zipped through cities. The transformation came at great cost. The plan demolished homes near the Paseo, a Kessler-designed boulevard located east of downtown, and Penn Valley Park. The displaced residents packed into overcrowded slums. The Commercial Club cared little about extending city services or public welfare to Kansas City's working-class, immigrant, and Black populations toiling in the West Bottoms.

Where the Commercial Club saw the dregs of society, Jim Pendergast saw people who wanted jobs and the chance to unwind with a glass of whiskey and a card game. Jim used his saloon earnings to keep the police out of the West Bottoms and cashed the paychecks of packinghouse workers, who were denied service by reputable banks. Of course, it was opportunity, more than altruism, that drove Jim's relationships. He won election to the city council in 1892 and helped form the Jackson County Democratic Club, using his positions to dole out jobs and consolidate more power. "All there is to it," he once said, "is having friends, doing things for people, and then later on they'll do things for you."

Some say Tom Pendergast started out as a bouncer for Jim, and some say he was a bartender, but Tom always maintained he was a cashier. "I never sold as much as a glass of lemonade," he said. Jim also appointed his younger brother as precinct captain in the North End, giving Tom the job of drumming up support for the Pendergast machine in a neighborhood that bordered the West Bottoms and that was as rambunctious and as ethnically and racially diverse as any district in the city. Still, the Pendergasts wanted to extend their kingdom to the wealthier side of the tracks. They just needed a Trojan horse. And James Reed, a successful appeals lawyer, was their chosen mark.

With Reed, who was elected mayor in 1900, in their pocket, the Pendergasts crashed the distinguished halls of Kansas City power. And they took advantage. During his tenure as mayor, Reed hired 173 police officers. More than 70 percent were handpicked by Jim Pendergast, who now ran his political operation from a casino-saloon at 508 Main Street, where police had previously cracked down on gambling. Tom was appointed superintendent of the streets department, and he learned that most people were happy as long as the potholes got filled and the streetlights flickered on at night.

In 1910, Jim retired, and the younger Pendergast won the city council election to replace him. The West Bottoms and a portion of downtown belonged to him. But his ambition was for something greater. Pendergast was preparing to turn the whole of Kansas City into "Tom's Town."

FAR from the West Bottoms, on the other side of the state line, graduates from the Olathe High School class of 1897 gathered inside a packed Hayes Opera House. Olathe was the first organized settlement in Johnson County, Kansas, a community of orderly farms and green space where next-door neighbors lived a mile down the road. The Hayes Opera House, towering three stories above the plains, was the pride of the town. Locals reenacted shows they'd read about from New York and shared returns on election nights.

On this May evening, the walls were festooned in silver and gold to celebrate the graduates, a cohort deemed "unusually bright" by the local *Olathe News*. You could also describe them as deadly serious. Between piano and clarinet solos, almost half of the fourteen graduates took to the stage to give speeches that were drenched with epic themes and stuffy literary allusions. James Edson mourned over the Greek city-states lost to the "tempestuous tides of time." Not to be outdone, Cora Claytor referenced Galileo and the founding of the electron particle, plus Newton and the lamp of Aladdin.

And then the valedictorian, a doe-eyed sixteen-year-old with a mop of brown hair, took to the stage, prepared to recite a hot take for the ages, a speech titled "Is Peace a Dream?"

"The highest aspiration of the noblest soul," Jesse Clyde Nichols began, "whether for themselves, or for country, has ever been peace."

J.C. Nichols, known as Clyde at the time, was the son of Joanna and Jesse. She was a homemaker, and he was a prosperous farmer who also managed a general store. Nichols worked there every Saturday from seven o'clock in the morning until ten at night. Practically his entire life was based around work—his choice, because his family had more than enough money to get by. When Nichols was sixteen, he operated a "huckster route," loading up chickens, eggs, apples, and butter into a wagon and passing through nine towns on his way to Kansas City, where he sold the goods to markets and restaurants. The route was eighty-five miles round-trip, and Nichols tried covering it twice a week. Despite his various jobs, he earned a 99.2 percent grade average, the highest ever recorded at the school; organized Olathe High School's first football team and debate team; and began courting Jessie Eleanor Miller, daughter of the richest man in Olathe. Nichols rose to the top of his high school class over competitors who had far fewer responsibilities. "They did not run a 'cow route,'" he later noted, "did not work in stores on Saturday, did not spoon at night with girls."

As his valedictory oration went on, Nichols explained that world peace was coming, that wars were about to end forever, because technology had unified the world.

"The commingling of nations by the telegraph and the newspaper, by navigation and the locomotive is effecting the change of altruism for egoism."

Then, perhaps as an ominous sign that the first shots of the Spanish-American War would be fired in less than a year, the electricity powering the Hayes Opera House cut out. Technology had failed.

Undeterred, Nichols lectured in the dark.

After graduation, Nichols's parents offered tuition money to convince him to go to college immediately. Spurning their largesse, he took a gap year in Kansas City. He planned to work in the wholesale meat business and save enough money to pay his own way.

This was Nichols's first glimpse of life in any city, and he spent most of his waking hours in the Jim Pendergast–dominated underbelly. Every night at six, Nichols piloted a team of mules into the filthy heart of the West Bottoms just as the evening trains roared through Union Depot and roughnecks scrambled into brothels and saloons for a quick fix. Nichols procured meat and hauled it back to a storeroom he rented at Sixteenth and Grand downtown, where he packaged it for morning deliveries. The city he experienced was a chaotic puzzle. If the black soot didn't obscure your way, then the maze-like alleyways would, but Nichols found his footing. "I came to know the back entrance of every important restaurant and hotel in Kansas City," he wrote.

With enough money in his pocket, Nichols enrolled at the University of Kansas in fall 1898. On a bucolic campus at the top of a hill, he became every bit the overachiever he was in high school, dabbling in journalism as a stringer for *The Kansas City Star*, pledging Beta

Theta Pi, and organizing a letter-writing campaign to coax the state legislature to provide more funding for the university. His most prominent extracurricular activity was athletics. For one year, Nichols played third base on the baseball team. ("Always," he wrote, "hoping the ball would never come my way.") But he was vastly better off the field, coaching the baseball team another year and serving in a leadership position for the KU athletic department during a period when the football team had an undefeated season and the men's basketball team was coached by the inventor of basketball, James Naismith. The athletic department, which had been underwater for nine years, entered the black financially under his watch. Nichols was lauded in the media for his work, with *The Topeka State Journal* describing him in 1902 as "one of the most ardent workers for the rules which govern college athletics in the state."

Before his senior year, Nichols and a friend purchased fifteen-dollar bicycles and hopped aboard a Boston cattle ship bound for Europe. With clothes tucked into knapsacks, they toured Belgium, the Netherlands, Switzerland, Germany, and France. In Paris, they experienced what Nichols referred to, euphemistically, as "*rue* life."

The European cities were unlike anything Nichols had seen. Ancient and meticulously planned. Imposing and permanent. Their aesthetic stayed with him, latent through his last year at KU and onto Harvard, where Nichols was awarded a graduate school scholarship by the college's faculty. In Cambridge, he assumed he would study law. A course titled Economics 6 changed his mind. Standing in front of Nichols the first day of class was the distinguished Oliver Mitchell Wentworth Sprague, a slight man with an analytical mind. Sprague focused his curriculum that year on industrial economics theory, positing that the East Coast was overdeveloped and the United States' economic centers would shift west and southwest, where land values would skyrocket and investors would cash in.

Nichols was fascinated. As he formulated a thesis on the impact of development on the appreciation of raw land, he decided to give up on law. No longer set on being a self-made man, he left Harvard and hit up his Olathe contacts—including the wealthy father of Jessie Miller—for money to invest in the Southwest.

But real life was not as tidy as an academic dissertation. One day, Nichols was sitting in a Fort Worth hotel room, feeling like he had lost everything. "I was convinced I was a complete failure and there was no future for me whatsoever," he wrote. Nichols decided to flip a coin: Heads and he would return home. Tails and he would try a little harder in Texas. It came up tails—but he decided to go home anyway.

Back in Olathe, in June 1905, he married Miller, who had recently graduated from Vassar. The ceremony—a union of Jess(i)es—was at Miller's parents' home. Under a canopy of sweet peas, the couple recited their vows. Miller wore a white Paris muslin dress. "One of the notable social events in the history of the town," gushed the *Olathe News*.

Newly married, Nichols found it was time to grow up, but he wasn't ready to give up on his original dream of profiting off the land. Thinking again about Sprague's class at Harvard, he realized Kansas City's undeveloped areas were south of the city, between downtown and rural Johnson County. Once more, he reached out to his father and his deep-pocketed friends, and secured funds to purchase ten acres near Kansas City's southern limits, about a mile beyond the last streetcar line. Nichols intended to divide the land into lots and sell them to families, then build out streets and parks and schools and shopping centers around them, turning a collection of homes into an entire community. To promote the area, he built a house for his own family at 5030 Walnut.

There was only one complication: Jessie had agreed to marry him on the condition that they never live in Kansas City. But that was fine. Nichols was developing at the edge of the city limits, where he was poised to grow something else entirely: a sanitized, segregated model for American living.

THE COACH AND THE INTERN

O nce upon a time, before the passing revolution changed the NFL, before anyone in Kansas City had ever heard of Patrick Mahomes, there was a high school running back named Gary Brown. Listed at five-eleven and weighing 190 pounds, Brown starred at Williamsport High School in the 1980s, dancing under the lights on football fields across central Pennsylvania, a brilliant spectacle of speed and agility and raw power. As one local newspaper writer put it, Gary Brown was like "a bomb."

He was also the first football player that made Brett Veach fall in love.

One fall night in the mid-1980s, when Veach was no older than eight years old, his father took him to watch Brown play in a state playoff game. A crowd of more than ten thousand crammed into a small stadium under black skies. Brown took the ball and, like a powerful locomotive, ran all night. It was, Veach would say, the night he first understood just what football could mean.

Not that any of this was surprising. Veach grew up in Mount Carmel, Pennsylvania, a small borough of seven thousand people in the Susquehanna River Valley known mostly for two things: the rich deposits of anthracite coal once found buried under its soil and the Mount Carmel Red Tornadoes, the winningest high school football program in the state. Veach's father, Bob, played for Mount Carmel in the late 1960s. So did generations before him. The roots of the program dated back to 1893, when nine different coal mines were in operation and the town was churning out power to swaths of the country.

By the time Brett Veach was growing up in the 1980s, the coal boom had ended, the mines had closed, and the town's population had dwindled. The Red Tornadoes, however, were still rolling, so Veach made a pledge to himself: He wanted to be the best running back in the history of Mount Carmel. He wanted to be the Coal Region's Gary Brown.

It was a bold idea: Veach was boyish with dark hair and a slight, undersize build. Even after repeating the eighth grade—a common redshirt tactic in Mount Carmel—he stood barely five feet nine and appeared younger than many of his classmates. He didn't look much like a football star—until he started to run. One of the top track sprinters in the state, Veach was also elusive, possessing the kind of vision you only get from a childhood spent around the sport. As his high school coach, Dave "Whitey" Williams, put it: "He has moves I wish I had on the dance floor."

The second of three brothers, Veach led the school to state titles in 1994 and 1996. As a senior, with his father serving as an assistant coach, he rushed for 2,163 yards, becoming the leading rusher in school history. When a local reporter asked for his secret, Veach had a simple answer: He knew exactly where he was going.

"Wherever I find a hole, that's where I go."

It was during a 1996 Class AA state semifinal matchup against Bishop McDevitt—a powerhouse private school from Harrisburg—that Veach showed exactly what he meant. Mount Carmel was a consensus underdog, a small-town school from the Coal Region giving up an average of thirty pounds at each lineman spot. On the first two plays of the game, Veach was stuffed for short gains. Before the third play, Williams, the Mount Carmel coach, called "75 Go," and Veach split out wide to the right, making eye contact with his quarterback at the line of scrimmage—as if to say, *Yes, it's there*. Veach bolted from the line of scrimmage, ran past a defensive back, and hauled in a

65-yard touchdown. Mount Carmel pulled off an 18–7 victory on their way to a state title. The victory, Veach would say, was for every football player in the Coal Region.

When high school was over, Veach headed off to play at the University of Delaware, a top Division I-AA program not far from home. (He'd once dreamed of Notre Dame, but a young Irish assistant named Urban Meyer had shown up in Mount Carmel and told Williams that Veach was too small.) In college he returned kicks, switched to receiver, hauled in passes from a quarterback named Matt Nagy, and became the school's first academic All-American in six years. He also pondered his future. Teammates would notice how Veach seemed to know every college football player in the country—not just their name but also their high school and lineage—and how he'd spend his Friday nights calling home to his younger brother, Jon, asking for a postgame breakdown of Mount Carmel's latest game. "He really took the time to study and examine people," said Jerry Oravitz, a former Delaware football staffer and mentor. It seemed natural, Veach told others, that he'd be a football coach.

Veach stuck around Delaware as a graduate assistant, which led to a fortuitous series of events: Delaware hired a coach named Kirk Ciarrocca as the new offensive coordinator. Ciarrocca had a former colleague named James Urban, who had gone to work for the Philadelphia Eagles. In 2004, Urban was looking for summer interns for training camp. Ciarrocca figured the eager grad assistant was perfect. When Veach arrived at Eagles camp, one of his first assignments was particularly important, a first glimpse of the glamorous NFL life: He was asked to help find a new bed for receiver Terrell Owens.

Veach returned to Eagles camp again the next summer, and he ran errands, got coffee for the staff, and acted as a fly on the wall. Back at the University of Delaware, he'd ascended from graduate assistant to something bigger: supervisor of intercollegiate athletic events, one of those jobs where you show up to every event on campus, organize camps in the summer, and do a thousand little tasks each week. Veach executed each with a curious mind, but he also hit something of a crossroads. He was already twenty-eight years old and vacillating between possible paths: a career in coaching, a future in athletics administration, the unknown of the NFL. When his full-time job caused him to miss Eagles training camp in 2006, he figured his window to the NFL had closed.

Then one day in the winter of 2007, Veach was sitting in the cold at a Delaware lacrosse match when he received a phone call. It was Eagles coach Andy Reid, and he needed a new personal assistant.

Veach was so busy that he didn't even notice the call.

FOR the next three years, Brett Veach became Andy Reid's sidekick. If Reid arrived at the Eagles' practice facility at 4 A.M., Veach was there. When Reid bunked at the office on Sundays and Mondays, Veach did, too. His title was "assistant to the head coach." In reality, he was a professional gofer, a grunt who would enthusiastically pick up laundry or order cheeseburgers or change the oil in Reid's car. As one Eagles player put it: "If you saw Andy, you saw Brett Veach."

Not that Veach was one to mind. In some ways, it was like being back in grad school—studying, researching, pulling occasional all-nighters—except in this case his adviser was a football coach with a walrus mustache, the charming nickname "Big Red," and a knack for winning games. When Veach arrived in 2007, Reid had already been in Philadelphia for eight years. The Eagles had made the playoffs six times, played in four straight NFC Championship Games from 2001 to 2004, and lost to Tom Brady and the New England Patriots in Super Bowl XXXIX. There were questions, of course, mostly about his brusque style with the media, his clock management late in games, and his inability to win the *big one*, as a sports pundit might say, but somewhere along the way, between the yearly division titles and postseason runs, the Eagles had become a model organization—forward-thinking, innovative, analytically savvy masters of the salary cap—akin to a think tank for some of the best young minds in football.

At the center was Reid, quarterback whisperer and offensive mastermind, a head coach whose attention to detail was legendary, so much so that it had helped him land the job in the first place. When the Eagles were looking for a new coach after the 1998 season, team president Joe Banner started asking around the league: *Do you know any coaches who annoy players with the details?* When Reid, then a quarterback coach for the Packers, showed up for his interview with a five-inch binder full of plans and lists, Banner knew he had the right guy.

Reid was a stickler for the little things. He was known to teach young assistants how to properly hold a marker while drawing up plays. But he also relished empowering the staffers who made the football operation hum. So, not long after Veach arrived, Reid started handing him minor scouting assignments. *Look at this player. Watch this tape. What do you see?* In one case, Reid asked Veach to cross-check a list of college running backs heading into the 2009 draft. On the list was LeSean McCoy, a back from the University of Pittsburgh. McCoy was on the smaller side and lacked what football people might call the proper measurables. But Veach watched his tape, fell in love, then began hounding his boss about the back from Pitt. The Eagles took McCoy in the second round. He became an All-Pro.

Of course, there might have been another reason Veach latched on to McCoy: He'd gone to high school at Bishop McDevitt, Veach's old playoff rival at Mount Carmel.

With each scouting assignment, Reid came to trust his young protégé, and with each passing year—each training camp, each off-season, each draft—Veach came to know a little more about his boss. Reid was indeed a fascinating character. Born in 1958, he had grown up in the Los Feliz neighborhood of Los Angeles, not far from John Marshall High School (a filming location for *Grease*'s Rydell High—the classic American high school). His father, a scenic artist in Hollywood, created backdrops at the famed Dorothy Chandler Pavilion;

his mother was a radiologist. His worldview was formed by the intersection of art and science, his childhood infused with the Americana of Los Angeles: sunshine, drive-ins, Dodgers broadcaster Vin Scully on the radio.

There was also football, and when Reid was in the sixth grade, he was so gigantic that he looked like he could start for the John Marshall varsity. (When he found himself in a televised "Punt, Pass and Kick" competition during a Los Angeles Rams game, he towered cartoonishly over the other boys.) Reid did eventually play varsity football. According to one teammate, he offered the same halftime speech during close games: "We need to open a can of whup-ass!" He moved on to play offensive line at Glendale Community College—close enough to home that he could drive his family's 1928 Model A Ford to practice. One day, a graduate assistant from Brigham Young University named Mike Sheppard showed up to Glendale to recruit Reid's teammate Randy Tidwell. Soon enough, Sheppard wanted the big man next to Tidwell, too.

At BYU, Reid was a beloved teammate with an easygoing sense of humor who met his wife, Tammy, in a Fundamentals of Tennis class. One friend would describe Reid's practical disposition as "grandfatherly." Which made some sense, because Reid, at one point, was considering a very grandfatherly career path: He wanted to be a sports columnist. Inspired by the legendary *Los Angeles Times* columnist Jim Murray, Reid had grown up scouring the morning newspaper, reading *Sports Illustrated* and crafting his own prose. As he finished up at BYU, he scored a part-time gig at the *Daily Herald* in Provo, Utah, to write columns about BYU football that recalled an antiquated era of print. On October 29, 1981, for example, he published a column about BYU quarterback Jim McMahon, the future Bears cult hero, under the headline: "Sir James McMahon of Cougarhood."

Deep within the tunnel of time, in the greater area of Northern Ireland lies a large mystical castle. Inside this castle many magical potions brew stimulating royal minds with magical talents. The most talented of these royal minds is none other than Sir James McMahon, the most gallant knight ever to be.

Reid did not become the next Jim Murray. Before his senior year, BYU coach LaVell Edwards pulled him aside and asked if he had considered coaching. The question led to a graduate assistant role in 1982. But Reid did leave an impression on Marion Dunn, a longtime Utah sports columnist and the sports editor of the *Daily Herald*, who saw Reid as a "big, lovable and smart young man," always excited about his passions and studies, always thinking about the book he wanted to write. "If you can't like Andy Reid," Dunn said, "you can't like anyone."

The reputation suited Reid well as he started up the coaching ladder, from an entry-level position at San Francisco State to Northern Arizona to the University of Texas at El Paso to Missouri to a breakthrough stint on Mike Holmgren's staff with the Green Bay Packers. Along the way, Reid brushed up against everyone from Packers great Brett Favre to activist and leftist Angela Davis, with whom Reid shared a campus during his time at San Francisco State. Holmgren saw a sharp young coach who was going places. Friends noticed an imaginative and curious mind; sometimes Reid would be on the phone and he'd just start drawing, his artistic side coming out. So when Reid got his shot in Philadelphia in 1999, he tried to create an open environment that resembled a college campus, one in which unorthodox ideas were given respect and consideration, no matter where they came from. As John Harbaugh, one of Reid's assistants in Philly, once noticed, Reid even kept a note card behind his desk with a two-word mantra: "Don't judge."

THIS was the environment in which Brett Veach arrived in 2007. "I want to teach," Reid said. It wasn't unusual for the coach to hand out books or tell an assistant to go read *Find the Winning Edge*, a manifesto on coaching by legendary 49ers coach Bill Walsh. It wasn't unusual for him to assign homework that amounted to breaking down every offensive play from a given season. And because Reid had pro personnel duties in addition to coaching, it wasn't unusual for Veach to have odd jobs that dealt with both areas of the organization. For a young football junkie like Veach, it was heaven.

If the Eagles signed a player or restructured a contract, Veach would pop into the office of Joe Banner, the team president, and ask him about the intricate details of the NFL salary cap. *I saw we just did this deal. Why did we do that?* He quizzed executives about negotiating with agents or roster management. He asked Louis Riddick, then the Eagles' director of pro personnel, for the secret to finding talent at the margins. "It was the first time I started even thinking about him in a bigger role," Banner said, "because it was clear he just wanted to learn everything he could."

Veach had always been insanely competitive, even by the standards of professional football. As a low-level staffer at Delaware, he had once told the school's athletic director that the university should sponsor a race car in a nearby NASCAR race in Dover. To Veach, however, it wasn't just an idea; he even sketched out the design and presented it. When he joined the Eagles, he brought the same approach, overflowing with energy, falling so hard for football players that he would literally pound the table in support. "He was a maniac," said Nagy, his quarterback from Delaware, who joined Veach as an intern in Philly. Veach could be so passionate that, once, another member of the front office called him a "salesman," which was supposed to be a slight. Not to Andy Reid. He *needed* a salesman.

Veach spent three years as Reid's personal assistant, a job that often became a springboard into a coaching career. But at some point, Reid realized how much Veach loved football players, how every college player in each NFL draft had the chance to become his next personal Gary Brown. So he started pushing him into a different path: scouting.

In 2010, Veach became a full-time Eagles scout. Which is where he was when Reid was pushed out of Philadelphia in 2012, after his first losing season since 1999. Veach, however, was already thinking bigger. A few years earlier, when he was still Reid's assistant, he had run into his old high school coach from Mount Carmel at training camp. Dave "Whitey" Williams liked to tease Veach about his status as an NFL errand boy. This time, he asked if he planned to be a gofer his whole life. A moment later, Veach looked back at Williams.

Coach, someday I'm gonna be a GM.

PART II

A J.C. Nichols sign from around 1912 in Kansas City.

CONCRETE AND THE COUNT

William James Basie wasn't sure how he got to the hospital. He had felt fine just a few weeks earlier. On Independence Day in 1927, he played a sold-out show at Kansas City's Lincoln Theatre with Gonzelle White and Her Big Jazz Jamboree. Comedians joked, dancers sashayed, and White smiled constantly, revealing a glimmering diamond in one of her front teeth. Basie, a converted drummer, set the tone for the festivities from the orchestra pit, propping up one of his legs on a piano and playing with his back to the keys. He was only twenty-two but a highly adept player, having literally learned at the feet of the renowned Fats Waller during his childhood in New York and New Jersey. A visiting critic from Chicago was impressed by the show, hailing it, in a column titled "In Old Kaysee," as "far superior" to the average vaudeville act. It seemed that Basie, a balding, gregarious ladies' man, was going places.

But the run at the Lincoln ended, and Basie discovered the tour company hadn't scheduled any shows beyond Kansas City, nor had it budgeted for a return trip to the East Coast. That left Basie stranded and broke. Then a brush with viral meningitis put him in the hospital for a month, leaving him staggered and even more broke.

There are no good places to be stranded and in medical debt. But if you were an entertainer in the 1920s and '30s, there were worse places than the Eighteenth and Vine district of Kansas City's East Side, which is where Basie knew he had to go.

Eighteenth and Vine was the nexus of Black culture and commerce, an area where the community developed a sustainable economy apart from white Kansas City and carved out spaces and institutions where its leaders could organize against the city's injustices. Apartments sat atop restaurants, dry cleaners, and hair salons—a majority of the businesses Black-owned, with others run by Jewish Kansas Citians and white immigrants. Houses were sprinkled in between, occupied by teachers and laborers and lawyers. Nearby churches shook with joy on Sundays. At 1510 East Eighteenth Street, Ella and Reuben Street operated the Street Hotel, where prominent Black visitors stayed, and Satchel Paige, Buck O'Neil, and other teammates on the Kansas City Monarchs Negro Leagues baseball team played pool. (Later, Jackie Robinson lived at the Street Hotel during his lone season with the Monarchs.) Two blocks to the east, journalists penned stories and columns for *The Kansas City Call*, a nationally known Black newspaper, and a block to the south, Homer B. Roberts opened what was one of the first Black-owned car dealerships in the country, renting extra office space to doctors and dentists. Roberts's neighbor, at Nineteenth and Vine, was Henry Perry. Perry smoked beef over oak and hickory inside an old trolley barn, packaging the meat in newspaper and selling it for twenty-five cents. (He would later sell his business to Charlie Bryant, who would pass the restaurant on to his brother Arthur, who would one day operate a joint that *Playboy* magazine would call "possibly the single best restaurant in the world.")

When Basie fell ill, somebody took him to General Hospital No. 2, a public hospital that served the Black working class and poor. The community held the hospital in high regard despite political corruption and racist policies stunting its development. Its all-Black administration and staff were a first for a municipal hospital in the United States, and the hospital's training programs were nationally recognized. Around one-third to one-half of the country's Black medical school graduates in the 1920s found internships in Kansas City and St. Louis. Nursing students came from all over, too, and the annual graduation ceremony turned into a community celebration.

While Basie recuperated at the hospital, the doctors and nurses asked him to play piano in the recreation room. It was a test to see if the meningitis had any long-term effects. He passed.

Fully recovered, Basie got a job scoring films at the Eblon Theater. But the real work started when his shift ended at 10:30, when Eighteenth Street was bathed in neon. Basie handed out business cards printed with the moniker "Count Basie"—a nickname he claimed he had awarded himself, figuring the upper echelon of jazz stars all seemed to go by Duke, King, or something royal—and searched for a piano with an empty bench. There were around two hundred jazz clubs to pick from in Kansas City, fifty of them scattered between Eighteenth and Vine and Twelfth Street, another major corridor for nightlife. There was jazz below the street at the Subway Club. There was jazz situated in both Kansas and Missouri at the State Line Tavern, where a white line down the middle of the bar marked the official border of the two states. At one point, Basie thought, "That was all Kansas City was made up of, was clubs."

Because of the city's centralized location—in the heart of America—jazz musicians from around the country ended up in town for one reason or another and found musical influences melding together. Like Basie, they stayed, mingling with the local talent, including the Sunset Club's singing bartender, the rock-and-roll pioneer Big Joe Turner. Mary Lou Williams, the queen of Kansas City jazz, stuck around for a dozen years. One night, she found a young Thelonious Monk on tour with a Christian evangelist and took him under her wing. Under her mentorship, Monk would tell his son that Kansas City had changed his playing forever.

The reason why had plenty to do with Basie. He got recruited by Bennie Moten, a Kansas City native. Alongside bandmates like Lester Young and Hot Lips Page, the musicians discarded song sheets and played from memory and by improvisation. During their songs, the band melded freestyle riffs into a steady, distinct harmony while one artist engaged in a solo, building off the riffs and taking the song in a new direction. The sound brought swing, blues, and big band together. Mainly, the sound was unpredictable—faster and looser than anything you'd hear in New York or Chicago and better for dancing. One music critic described Kansas City jazz as putting "wheels on all four bars of the beat."

At his peak in Kansas City, in the mid-1930s, Basie led an orchestra at the Reno, a seamy hole-in-the-wall on Twelfth Street. His breakfast shows were the best. They happened on Mondays, *starting* at 4 a.m. The sessions were kind of like pickup basketball games: Newcomers could hop in, but they were expected to live up to the high standards set by the regulars. In the summer of 1936, Charlie Parker, a fifteen-year-old who had started playing the sax at the Penn School in fifth grade, didn't cut it. After Parker stumbled along to a rendition of "Honeysuckle Rose," drummer Jo Jones hurled a cymbal at his feet when the kid wouldn't leave the stage. Parker grabbed his instrument and exited, a little more determined to make it.

Sarah Coates had been right. Kansas City was something of an arts capital. The city had not invented jazz—that was New Orleans—and it wasn't the preferred destination for the country's greatest artists, which was New York. But, like Atlanta with hip-hop in the 1990s, Kansas City produced a distinct, innovative style that soon became inseparable from the entire genre. Kansas City, the musician Jesse Stone once said, "did more for jazz, Black music, than any other influence at all."

The artists had cultivated the sound in small, daring steps, experimenting here and there in forgotten, untraceable moments of revolution. But the new style also served a practical need. The Kansas City sound—danceable for the listeners and continuously fresh for the musicians—was made for endless nights. And in Tom Pendergast's town, the nights were always endless.

EVERY so often, police raided the Sunset Club. They'd nab employees and clientele—anyone could have been doling out the illegal liquor and drugs—and haul them to the police station. But by the time they arrived, as Big Joe Turner later explained, "the boss-man would have his bondsman down at the police station. . . . We'd walk in, sign our names, and walk right out." They'd go back to the club and party until dawn.

Yes, Pendergast was a musician's friend. Not that he was shaking hands with Basie or Moten: He was usually in bed before the clubs started hopping, the better so he could be at his office early in the morning.

Some twenty blocks west of Vine, in a modest brick building on Main Street, Pendergast held court at the Jackson County Democratic Club. Above the Southwest Linen Company, he hosted fifty to sixty people who were gathered in a single-file line stretching out to the sidewalk. Women skipped to the front; everyone else waited, whether they were job seekers, gangsters, or senators. Technically, Pendergast's job was to identify and assist local Democratic candidates. In reality, he was managing nearly every aspect of life in Kansas City. Political insiders referred to Pendergast's Main Street office as the "Missouri State Capitol."

No favor was too small or too large, but Pendergast's assistance always required a favor in return. Elected officials who asked for help in turning out the vote handed out patronage jobs in departments ranging from sanitation, to police, to the board of elections. The people who got the jobs were expected to be loyal voters of the Pendergast ticket.

By the 1920s and '30s, much of the city was indebted and obedient to Pendergast. He used his sway to monopolize the sex, drug, and entertainment industries fueling the all-night club scene. Gangsters ran many of the jazz joints, paying musicians double what they made anywhere else and funneling a cut of their gambling and alcohol revenues back to Pendergast, who also owned a portion of a wholesale liquor company. It didn't matter if a Kansas City business was legitimate or crooked. A business that made big profits owed a Pendergast tax said to be higher than any levied by the state or city. His take from gambling, drugs, and prostitution was once estimated at $32 million a year. (Al Capone supposedly made $100 million, but Capone's Chicago had nearly ten times the population.)

Chicago had always been front of mind to civic leaders, who wanted to grow faster and transport more and more cows through the Stockyards, but the Windy City was perhaps too tame for Pendergast's Kansas City. Exotic foreign capitals made better comparisons. "If you want to see some sin," wrote Edward Morrow in the *Omaha World-Herald*, "forget Paris and go to Kansas City." It wasn't just a case of small-timers from Omaha being blinded by the lights, either. The far more famous Edward R. Murrow compared Kansas City to Singapore and Port Said. Sure, you could grab a drink during Prohibition in plenty of cities, but Kansas City stood out for its blatant disregard of federal law. Most of the bars weren't even speakeasies. At the Chesterfield Club in downtown, naked waitresses—with their pubic hair shaved to represent diamonds, hearts, clubs, or spades—served cocktails to distinguished businessmen. The bar was just down the street from a courthouse.

The only thing in town more prevalent than illicit cocktails was cement, and Pendergast was running a business for that, too: Ready-Mixed Concrete, a company filled with no-show jobs and flagrant corruption. As the Great Depression ravaged the country, Pendergast teamed up with his highest-ranking crony, city manager Henry McElroy, whose position had, ironically, been created to dilute Pendergast's power. They devised a long-range plan to improve the city's infrastructure and fill the skyline, designed in an opulent art deco style. On May 26, 1931, voters went to the polls and overwhelmingly approved the Ten-Year Plan, a $32 million bond program that functioned as a localized New Deal existing before FDR's own. Along with untold profits for Pendergast, the project resulted in a new twenty-nine-story city hall, the Jackson County Courthouse, and Municipal Auditorium, an art deco venue on Thirteenth Street that would host nine NCAA Final Fours, along with untold profits for Pendergast.

As America suffered from the Depression, Kansas City soared, thanks to the Ten-Year Plan. "In Kansas City," said Conrad Mann, the president of the chamber of commerce, "we are building the greatest inland city the world has ever seen." New skyscrapers sprouted from the ground every year, and jazz clubs rollicked into the morning, at a time when, as one agent put it, the rest of the country "couldn't afford three dollars a night for a musician."

Pendergast liked to think generosity was at the core of his power. When a British parliamentarian named Marjorie Graves visited his Main Street office in 1933, he told her he helped "the poor through our organizations." It was true that Tom's Town was built on undervalued workers—immigrants, Black labor, the poor. "The Boss" hosted a fancy dinner for the needy every Christmas and kept quarters in his pockets for the homeless. By the early 1930s, with police brutality against the Black community on the rise, Pendergast seized control of the Kansas City Police Department, taking it back from the state of Missouri, which had assumed leadership in the Civil War era. Pendergast assigned staffing oversight to "Brother John" Lazia, the leader of the Fifth Democratic Ward and a charismatic crime boss, and when dozens more loyal Pendergast supporters were appointed to the force, *The Kansas City Call* reported that police brutality had declined. But Pendergast's Ten-Year Plan funds rarely made it to Black communities, and the occasional gifts from his patronage system masked the need for lasting racial reforms.

The city had never been more corrupt, with local government by fiat and the threat of political violence never far away, and, strangely, it had never been more relevant. Under the watchful eye of Pendergast, Walt Disney opened Laugh-O-Gram Studios near Thirty-First and Troost Avenue. Cub reporter Ernest Hemingway wrote short, declarative sentences at *The Kansas City Star* (abiding by the paper's house style). Nell Donnelly popularized gingham for American mothers and built a fashion empire. Baseball stars Paige and O'Neil turned the Kansas City Monarchs into a Negro Leagues powerhouse. Homer B. Roberts invested profits to open another car dealership in Chicago. Even Pendergast's detractors fed off his power. During his reign, local boosters were crazy enough to talk about Kansas City becoming a city of one million people, more than double its size.

It still felt like the city could turn into something great, following the trajectory of the many jazz musicians who passed through. Basie stuck around for nine years. Kansas City, in his eyes, was "a cracker town but a happy town."

THE SIGN

Patrick Mahomes had fun at Texas Tech. He passed for more than 11,000 yards in three seasons, studied marketing, spent one spring playing baseball, and on a windy day in Lubbock hit a Wiffle ball over a three-story campus dormitory. Friends maintain it traveled four hundred feet. Mostly, he wasn't afraid to try new things. When Mahomes was a freshman, he bought Rollerblades with teammates Hunter Rittimann and Coleman Patterson; he used them to navigate the sprawling campus. The friends skated to chemistry class and rode directly into the classroom, and for once in his life, Mahomes wasn't a natural. "I have a picture of it," Patterson said.

On the football field, the Red Raiders weren't the best team, either. They went 16-21 during Mahomes's three seasons, thanks to a porous defense, but nearly every game was a show. On October 22, 2016, Mahomes threw for 734 yards, the NCAA record, in a 66–59 loss to Oklahoma even though he was playing with a sprained shoulder in his throwing arm and broke his left wrist *during the game*. "We're just really deep with receivers," Mahomes explained afterward.

But everything Kansas City ever needed to know about Mahomes happened a couple of years earlier, on September 30, 2014, just a few weeks into the first semester of his freshman year.

Kansas City was having a collective heart attack. The Royals were appearing in their first playoff game in twenty-nine years, a winner-take-all wild-card game at Kauffman Stadium, and they fell into an early 2–0 hole before coming back to lead 3–2. Then Oakland hit a

77

three-run homer off a rookie starting pitcher and added another two runs, but Kansas City came back again, tying the game 7–7 with a sacrifice fly in the bottom of the ninth inning.

In the eleventh inning, as the clock ticked past 11 P.M., the score was still 7–7. Mahomes was in Lubbock, probably in the athletic dorms, having fun watching baseball. He pulled out his iPhone and typed a message. It was 11:11, the time for good luck, for when you make a wish.

"I really want the Royals to win," Mahomes tweeted. He added two smiling emoji for good measure.

The next inning, Oakland took an 8–7 lead. The heart attack turned into a full-on coronary. With three outs before elimination from the postseason, Lorenzo Cain grounded out. The city basically flatlined. But then Eric Hosmer fouled off a million pitches and hit the ball off the outfield wall, then raced all the way to third base. He scored when Christian Colón slapped an infield single. With two outs, Salvador Pérez stepped to the plate. He was hitless in five at bats and fell behind in the count. Colón stole second. Now it was so close. Pérez reached for a pitch on the outside of the plate, and he laced the ball just past third, and Colón scored, and Kansas City partied like it hadn't partied in three decades.

It was meant to be.

THE COUNTRY CLUB AND
THE COVENANTS

On March 31, 1909, J.C. Nichols took an oath for one of his new neighborhoods. Peering at a certified notary through a pair of rimless eyeglasses, he looked nothing like the high school boy who had predicted world peace. His mop of hair was gone, for one thing, and his waist had expanded a couple of sizes. He wore a tailored suit, although it would be a stretch to say he was dressed to impress. Despite his increasing wealth, Nichols didn't like to spring for dry cleaning and sported suits that were stained with ash, the result of his penchant for lighting his next cigarette with the cigarette he already had in his mouth.

What he lacked in sartorial expertise, he made up for with business acumen. Spurred by the investments from his farmer friends, Nichols had purchased some one thousand acres of hog lots, farms, and swampy prairie south of downtown. In 1908, he began advertising lots for homes in neighborhoods he christened Rockhill Park, Country Side, and Sunset Hill. These were the earliest subdivisions of the Country Club District, the grand experiment of Nichols's theory that the best way to live in a city was . . . to build a world apart from the city. The land that brought him in front of the notary was yet another addition. He wanted to go farther south and farther west, and, same as with Rockhill Park, Country Side, and Sunset Hill, Nichols wanted everything he touched to stay bucolic and pristine forever.

He had learned from his first subdivision that forever didn't come easily. The young families who followed him into his first development in 1905 lived for a long time without running water, electricity, or gas. A nearby brickyard, which he thought would shutter, kept spewing soot. They had to sell their homes below their original purchase prices.

The fiasco became Nichols's origin story: After stewing for a while, he reoriented his real estate company around preserving what he referred to as the "character of residential neighborhoods." He coined an pretentious motto, "Planning for Permanence."

How could a neighborhood be permanent? The problem with his first development, Nichols realized, was a lack of control. Cities were unpredictable. Apartments could rise next to houses. Grocery stores could pop up on street corners. A new neighbor might raise chickens. As a subdivider and community builder, Nichols pretty much had power over only the first sale of a lot to a homeowner, who could build just about any type of house they wanted on their land. Then that person could sell to anyone, who could sell to somebody else, who could sell to somebody else. There was no telling who might buy a house in the future, and there were limitless ways for a neighborhood to evolve at the whims of Pendergast's Kansas City, which even by the standards of an American city was wild and chaotic, particularly in the eyes of a farm boy who preferred lush green lawns and songbirds to jazz, booze, and concrete.

Inside the notary's office, Nichols presented a document that contained his idea for maintaining control. The document, which had a numbered list running about a page in length, was part of the plat for the new subdivision and would bind every single home that would go up on the subdivision's land. Nichols had included similar instructions for Rockhill Park, Country Side, and Sunset Hill. The first parts of the list included restrictions for the types of houses that could go on the property and the types of adjustments that could be made to the land. There were a minimum construction price, a required amount of free space on the sides of every home, a ban on apartments, and explicit directions for where sewer lines and electricity poles could go.

There were seven restrictions in all, but the last one stood out. It had nothing to do with pricing, spacing, or dimensions. "No part of the property during the period aforesaid shall be conveyed to, owned, used, or occupied by negroes as owners or tenants," it read.

The notary asked Nichols, who was white, if the document was a true representation—the "free act and deed"—of his company. He said that it was.

THERE was a tidy legal term for what Nichols was doing. The restrictions were known as covenants. They had been around since the end of the nineteenth century—setting rules for various uses of land—but increased in usage as Nichols came of age. That was especially the case for racial covenants, which barred African Americans in Nichols's neighborhoods, and, in many cases across the Kansas City area and the country, kept out Jewish, Asian, and Hispanic people. Some developers were using racial covenants on the East Coast by the early 1900s. Nichols was among the first to use them in and around Kansas City.

The timing was no accident. Many of the tens of thousands of Black people who migrated north to Kansas City had arrived on the basis on the Free State reputation of Kansas and crossed over the Kansas River to find good jobs—albeit lower-paying jobs than whites got—and a more hospitable atmosphere than in the South. Black and white people lived together in nearly every section of the city during these first few decades. Most neighborhoods actually had racial compositions that reflected the demographics of Kansas City as a whole.

Things started to change around 1900. When the construction of several grand parks and boulevards as part of the City Beautiful movement forced many poor Black and white Kansas Citians out of their homes, white residents became more acutely aware of the growing Black population, especially of the many displaced Black residents who went to the East Side, near Lincoln High School and Black churches. As progress continued on the City Beautiful plan, the parks and boulevards went up around new racial enclaves, turning into tree-lined, manicured buffers to separate Black from white.

Walls went up elsewhere, too. In 1904, Black teachers were ordered to sit in a separate section at district-wide meetings. Cemeteries with white owners declined to serve Black families, and white-owned meeting halls refused Black customers. Soon, about the only part of public life left integrated was the streetcar.

In March 1908, around the time Nichols was making the first lots of the Country Club District available, a white Kansas City clerk wrote in a letter to *The Kansas City Post* about a Black family who had purchased a home next door. The man said he was concerned about the safety of his teenage daughters and railed about Kansas City being on a slippery slope that encouraged Black people "to believe in racial equality and then they buy homes near us." That fear was gone in a Nichols neighborhood. The racial covenants were an official bulwark, stronger than any strategically placed park, and perfectly legal, unlike segregated housing ordinances set by cities like Baltimore and Louisville, which were knocked down by the Supreme Court in 1917.

Nichols spread the word about his all-white neighborhoods on billboards and in newspaper advertisements. "Have you seen the Country Club District? 1,000 acres restricted. For those who want protection," read one of his first ads, in 1908. Another boasted that Nichols's restrictions blocked "all undesirable encroachments." Rockhill Park was described by Nichols as the "best protected and safeguarded" residence district in Kansas City: "Complete uniformity is here assured."

The only problem with assuring uniformity, Nichols figured, was the covenants' expiration dates. Courts had been iffy about whether they could be set in perpetuity, but he devised a work-around that soon spread around the country, creating subdivision-wide covenants lasting for periods of twenty-five to forty years and inserting language that stipulated an automatic renewal five years before the expiration date. The only way out of the covenants was if a majority of a subdivision's homeowners voted to remove them. And that essentially meant they lasted forever, because Nichols had a plan for this, too. He was one of the country's first developers to establish homeowner associations, which had a primary goal of preserving the status quo and wielded the power to take legal action against anyone who did not follow the covenants. If somebody dared sell a home to a Black family, they faced the legal wrath of the association.

Nichols wasn't the only developer in the United States using restrictive covenants or forming HOAs to enforce them. But he stood out by making them self-perpetuating and implementing them at such a wide scale, tying dozens of planned neighborhoods together, melding them with parks and golf courses and schools into self-sufficient, homogenous outposts surrounding the city center.

The Country Club District became a sensation. Its roads naturally wandered around curves and up wooded hills, just like in the country. It had no alleys; Nichols eliminated them in favor of driveways and garages connected to the house. Deep setbacks from the street made the homes feel secluded and imposing and stripped the neighborhoods of noise, replacing pedestrians and street chatter with massive landscaped gardens and bubbling fountains. In Sunset Hill, where Nichols bought a house for his own family in the Country Club District, a visiting writer from *The New Republic* saw roses cascading over walls and sensed Nichols had created neighborhoods that were a symbol of the "American's domestic ideal," a reward for those who had worked hard and succeeded.

Even Pendergast, whom Nichols depended on for permits and favors, saw the Country Club District as his dreamworld. He bought his first house in the district in 1915. The developer liked to engage the Boss in games of poker. According to family lore, Nichols was the superior card player but let Pendergast win to obtain more favors for his business. In the late 1920s, Pendergast plunked down $5,000 to buy another Nichols lot. There, at 5650 Ward Parkway, Pendergast hired a Nichols architect to design him an ostentatious mansion that was near equal parts French Regency, Italian Renaissance, and American Prairie.

Somehow, that wasn't the most surprising infusion of European influences. In 1923, Nichols gambled by opening the Country Club Plaza, a posh shopping district designed in a Spanish Colonial Revival aesthetic, replete with a 138-foot-tall bell tower and original artwork by the Florentine sculptor Raffaello Romanelli. The development cost him $5 million. Around half the land was used for parking lots and roads. In time, the Plaza would be recognized for what it was: the first planned shopping center in America, a forerunner to suburban malls— and certainly the first shopping center designed for the automobile. But critics believed Nichols had lost a step. They labeled the Plaza "Nichols's folly." Why waste so much space for cars and build a few miles from the heart of Kansas City's population? There were tons of stores downtown and many more off the streetcar line.

But the developer was right again. Nichols, who saw the future promise of the automobile firsthand while visiting Henry Ford in Detroit, had realized the Plaza offered the full package: People who lived in his neighborhoods could now avoid downtown. They could avoid the streetcar. (In 1908, fewer than four hundred automobiles were registered in all of Kansas City. Ten years later, Nichols was paving his asphalt streets with a special twelve-inch base, and the number of cars had spiked by nearly 5,000 percent.) Thousands of people patronized the Plaza almost immediately. In 1925, one merchant hung Christmas lights outside his store, jump-starting a preeminent holiday tradition for the city. The Plaza became the center of attention, a fashionable new downtown.

Sometimes, on weekends, Nichols showed off the Plaza to architects who visited from as far away as Sweden and India. Other times, he patrolled his neighborhoods in a car, marking infractions in a little black book—a garage door open here, a trash can left out there—and listening for birds. Nichols believed an abundance of chirping made his subdivisions more homey and cheerful, so he mailed out fifteen thousand bird pamphlets to citizens, and—after testing the efficacy of one birdhouse in his backyard—he purchased hundreds more from a manufacturer and sold them at cost to residents of the Country Club District. His "bird census" estimated that the district had one thousand songbirds from fifty species.

Between the birds, the HOAs, the shopping center, and the self-perpetuating covenants, no one had seen anything like the Country Club District. It "stood head and shoulders above all other subdivisions in America," praised prominent Minneapolis real estate man Samuel S. Thorpe. "If Webster was asked to provide another synonym for city planning," wrote one New York City journalist in 1925, "his answer would be Jesse Clyde Nichols, Kansas City, Mo." By 1926, the district even had the attention of President Calvin Coolidge, who nominated him to the National Capital Park and Planning Commission. Herbert Hoover was an even bigger fan. He visited the Nichols home in Sunset Hill, an eighteen-room mansion where guests could lounge on a sun porch and pull a chain to alert a butler to carry out drinks on a silver tray. Nichols and his wife, Jessie, entertained guests all the time, but she used special "Hoover china" for the president.

The Country Club District was a leafy wonderland, a vision for a new American way of life, a model easily followed in cities across the country, if only they had a developer who understood the right methods. "Not another spot in the world nor another man have done so much to bring beauty and comfort into everyday life," said Charles Reade, a famed city planner in England who became a regular visitor to the neighborhood.

Nichols was always willing to share his secrets. Local and national real estate organizations handed him leadership positions, and major conferences sought him as a featured speaker. In 1912, standing before distinguished architects and civic leaders at an annual convention of one real estate association, Nichols told his audience he was once afraid to suggest covenants. "Now," he continued, "I cannot sell a lot without them."

Nichols's ideas were starting to take hold, to reshape his city and America writ large, and he was adamant about his influence, about the ability of just a few private developers to impact massive populations for years and years to come. "Cities are handmade," he said. "And the men who build the city today are responsible for the heritage posterity receives."

BIG RED'S ARRIVAL

On the afternoon of October 28, 2012, a tiny, unidentified object appeared in the sky above Kansas City. It was, upon closer inspection, an airplane—small, compact, certainly not a commercial jet—and it was headed toward Arrowhead Stadium, where the Chiefs were hosting the Oakland Raiders in a Week 8 matchup.

If you happened to be tailgating in the stadium parking lot that day, you would have seen the aircraft come into focus just above the horizon, through the traditional Sunday haze of barbecue smoke. If you looked a little closer, you would have noticed something else: a long banner flying behind the plane, its message spelled out in large block letters and flapping in the breeze.

RETURN HOPE—FIRE PIOLI—SAVEOURCHIEFS.COM

The fall of 2012 was absolute hell for the Kansas City Chiefs. The team—which hadn't won a playoff game in nearly nineteen years—opened the season with a 1-10 record, including six losses by at least seventeen points. Its head coach was Romeo Crennel, a jolly, empathetic former defensive coordinator who had taken over the previous season and always seemed genial but overmatched. Its starting quarterback was Matt Cassel, a dark-haired, good-looking former backup from the New England Patriots whose lack of conventional arm strength was surpassed only by his propensity to toss the ball to the other team. (He had twelve interceptions in eight starts before a head injury forced Brady Quinn, a dark-haired, good-looking current backup, into action.) The main target of the banner, however, was Scott Pioli, the Chiefs' general manager, who had arrived from New England in 2009 to rebuild a franchise after three embarrassing seasons. Pioli, a disciple of legendary Patriots coach Bill Belichick, had brought with him a gang of friends from New England, including Crennel and Cassel, all steeled in the so-called Patriot Way, and the crew had cobbled together an AFC West Championship in 2010. But by 2012, everything had fallen apart.

The list of calamities included (but were not limited to) the following:

Four days before he was fired in late 2011, Todd Haley, the Chiefs' head coach, implied to *Kansas City Star* reporter Kent Babb that he believed rooms at the team facility were bugged and that his phone had (possibly) been tampered with. (The Chiefs denied this.) Paranoia reigned. In one infamous incident, Pioli came across a discarded candy wrapper in a stairwell, waited a week to see if anyone would pick it up, then placed it in a plain envelope, which was then presented at a meeting of higher-ups. To be fair to Pioli, it was the kind of militant, almost fanatical attention to detail that is the coin of the realm in the National Football League, and had the Chiefs been winning, maybe it would have gone over better. The Chiefs, however, were not winning.

One reason was the quarterback: Just one QB in franchise history had led the team to the Super Bowl, and Len Dawson—"Lenny the Cool"—was now a seventy-seven-year-old broadcaster. Cassel was clearly not the answer. He was playing so badly, in fact, that in October he'd been knocked out of a game and the fans—not knowing the severity of his injury—had let out an instinctive cheer, causing lineman Eric Winston to bark back. ("This is not the Roman Coliseum!") Then, the same day the "FIRE PIOLI" banner appeared above Arrowhead, the Chiefs lost to the Raiders 26–16; Cassel and Quinn combined for four turnovers; and Jamaal Charles—the team's All-Pro running back—finished with just five carries, which was utterly confusing to everyone, even head coach Romeo Crennel. ("I'm not exactly sure either," he said.)

The banner was part of an organized fan revolt—branded as "Save Our Chiefs"—that included more crowdfunded banners and a planned "Blackout," in which fans were encouraged to wear black to a November 18 game against the Cincinnati Bengals. (It didn't take much to join in; at one point, tickets were appearing on StubHub for $3.99.)

The message was intended for one person: Chiefs chairman Clark Hunt, the son of franchise founder Lamar Hunt, who had died in 2006. The younger Hunt was a former Southern Methodist University soccer player and Goldman Sachs analyst, an NFL heir trained in the family business who had ascended to Chiefs chairman at the age of forty in 2005—and who was now dealing with a restless fan base.

The franchise was adrift, beleaguered by a culture of angst and secrecy, with no hope at quarterback or head coach and no reason to think that things might get better.

And then everything got much, much worse.

ON the first Saturday morning of December, Scott Pioli was in the parking lot of the Chiefs' practice facility when he came across Jovan Belcher, a twenty-five-year-old linebacker who had just pulled up in a black Bentley Continental GT. Belcher had grown up on Long Island. He graduated from West Babylon High, a suburban high school in a leafy hamlet. He starred on the wrestling team and led the football team and—although he wasn't heavily recruited—earned a scholarship to the University of Maine, where he grew into an unlikely NFL prospect. He went unselected in all seven rounds of the 2009 draft, but the Chiefs gave him a chance as an undrafted free agent. By 2010, he was a starter at linebacker. After the 2011 season, he earned a one-year, $1.9 million contract. On that Saturday morning, December 1,

2012, he was standing in an NFL parking lot, holding a .40-caliber Beretta handgun to his head. "I'm sorry, Scott," he told Pioli. "I've done a bad thing to my girlfriend already."

The night before, Belcher had stayed out late in downtown Kansas City, partying with another woman while his girlfriend, Kasandra Perkins, attended a concert a few miles away. He left downtown at 12:45 A.M.—leaving the bustle of the Power and Light District for the quiet avenues of Midtown—then said good night to the other woman, fell asleep in his Bentley outside her building, and woke up to the sound of cops about two hours later. The officers—who were called by a concerned neighbor—did not notice any visible signs of impairment, and when Belcher could not reach the other woman, he was taken in by some friendly Samaritans, who would later say that Belcher seemed a little drunk and "in good spirits." Finally, around 6:30 A.M., after catching a few hours of sleep, he returned to his home on Crysler Avenue, where he and Perkins continued an argument that had been simmering for some time.

It will never be known exactly what was said in those final moments. (Belcher's mother, who had been staying with her son, heard shouting from a nearby room but did not immediately intervene.) Nor will it be known just what was happening inside the mind of Jovan Belcher. An autopsy would later show he was under the influence of alcohol, while another doctor would later find evidence that Belcher's brain showed signs of chronic traumatic encephalopathy, a neurodegenerative disease caused by repeated blows to the head and associated with dementia and depression. What is known is that Belcher grabbed a gun and shot Perkins nine times; then he kneeled down to say he was sorry. Before he left, he kissed their three-month-old daughter and said goodbye to his mother. Then he drove his Bentley to the practice facility, where he saw Pioli. He requested to see Romeo Crennel and linebackers coach Gary Gibbs, expressed thanks for the chance to play football, and asked that the team watch after his daughter. Then he walked behind a car, knelt down, made the sign of the cross, and shot himself in the head.

The tragedy left Kansas City reeling. Two families devastated, one child orphaned. If football was the city's cultural glue—the one thing that kept people together—for a moment it didn't seem to matter. The Chiefs played a home game the next day and won. They held a moment of silence for victims of domestic violence. They didn't mention Belcher. The mood, on the whole, was somber and subdued—the arguments about the quarterback and play calling replaced by debates about concussions, domestic violence, and guns. The Chiefs finished out the season 2-14, tied for the worst record in franchise history, the kind of season you'll never forget, for better or worse, and if the evidence wasn't already ample, one thing was clear enough: Everyone needed a fresh start.

THE day after the final Sunday of the NFL regular season is known as "Black Monday." It is, to put it gently, a twenty-four-hour interval of pink slips, trips to HR, front-office resets, and so much general upheaval that if you happen to be an NFL owner making a call in the middle of the storm, you're probably expecting voice mail. Which was the first thing that surprised Clark Hunt. Andy Reid answered.

It was New Year's Eve 2012, and Reid had just walked out of a farewell party in Philadelphia, where the Eagles had officially fired him after a 4-12 record in his fourteenth season. Reid had cried when he met with his players. He then stood before a group of team employees and mustered a smile and a few jokes. "Sometimes change is good," he said. Then he received a call from Hunt, who was curious if Reid still wanted to coach. Reid was fifty-four, prime age for an NFL head coach, but he'd been through his own year from hell. In August, his oldest son, Garrett, twenty-nine, was found dead in a dorm room at Lehigh University while assisting the staff at Eagles training camp. A coroner determined that he died of an accidental heroin overdose.

He had struggled through a "long-standing battle with addiction," the family said, and his related criminal exploits—along with those of his younger brother Britt—had blown open publicly in 2007, becoming fodder for the tabloids in Philly. Reid, however, kept going to work. It was easy to wonder if he needed a break. But if someone asked, Reid had a simple response: "This is what I do."

Reid's final seasons in Philly had been a slog, but when viewed from twenty thousand feet, he was the best coach on the market. Which meant others were interested, too. At 4:29 P.M. the next day, ESPN's Adam Schefter—the dean of NFL breaking news—reported on Twitter that an anonymous league source said he was "95 percent" certain that Reid would wind up as the head coach of the Arizona Cardinals. The Cardinals had quarterback Kevin Kolb (an underachiever who had played for Reid in Philly) and they had receiver Larry Fitzgerald (one of the best of his generation) and they had been in the Super Bowl four years earlier, and although they did not have the tradition of the Chiefs (and they certainly did not have a die-hard fan base), they did have plans to officially interview Reid later in the week. Until Hunt made sure that never happened. Hunt and a crew from the Chiefs' front office flew to Philadelphia and, the next day, interviewed Reid inside a room at the airport. It was supposed to be a three-hour meeting. It lasted nine. The group ordered food from a sports bar. Nobody touched it. Hunt knew Reid's reputation as a builder of football teams; he didn't expect they'd hit it off so quickly, that the detail-oriented football man could seem so . . . warm. The meeting dragged on so long that a limousine—slated to connect Reid with a flight to Arizona—showed up at the Reid home and startled his wife, Tammy. At one point, Reid looked at Hunt and pointed to a plane outside. "I was supposed to get on that," he said. He never did.

Two days later, Reid arrived in Kansas City so that his wife could see the city. They dined at the Capital Grille on J.C. Nichols's Country Club Plaza, where some fans gathered outside. A news helicopter followed him around town. "You got this feeling," Reid said, "that this is the right thing to do." Reid needed to assemble a staff and help fill out a front office, and he brought just one member from the Eagles' player personnel and scouting department: his old assistant Brett Veach.

The bigger question was at quarterback. At his first press conference, Reid wore a red tie and promised to dig in, to really "build that thing."

"I've got to find the next Len Dawson, doggone it," he said.

THE BATTLE FOR LINWOOD

R oy Wilkins moved to Kansas City just as the bombings picked back up.

It was 1923 and he was a fresh graduate of the University of Minnesota, a slender man with a thin mustache. He had visited Kansas City a few months earlier for a race-relations conference hosted by the NAACP. Ten thousand people gathered to see George Washington Carver receive a scientific achievement award and listen to W.E.B. Du Bois challenge the accommodationist rhetoric of Booker T. Washington. When NAACP leader James Weldon Johnson offered a sharp rebuttal to an emissary of the Missouri governor, telling him the crowd of people was in "a fight to the death" to attain the rights guaranteed to them by the Constitution, Wilkins believed he had found his cause. Weeks later, when *The Kansas City Call* hired him as a news editor, he had also found his city.

At *The Call*'s offices, a low-slung brick building, he felt right at home. But only around Eighteenth and Vine. One day, Wilkins told his coworkers he was going to watch a Kansas City Blues minor-league baseball game, and they looked at him funny. He realized why when he got to Muehlebach Field (later rechristened Municipal Stadium). The only seating for African Americans was the last row of the bleachers in right field. At the Orpheum Theater, Wilkins could barely see Ethel Barrymore onstage after climbing to a section so high he was at eye level with the skylights. The same type of second-class balcony was reserved for any Black person who wanted to see Count

Basie at the Reno. Even the integrated spaces were hostile. On the streetcar, an elderly white woman called Wilkins a racial slur when he offered her his seat. Kansas City was geographically closer to Chicago than to the Deep South. But Wilkins felt like he resided in a cross between Memphis and Gulfport, Mississippi—in a "Jim Crow town that nearly ate my heart out."

Never was Jim Crow more prevalent to Wilkins than when he reported on real estate. The constant fight for Black Kansas Citians to find livable housing provided a grim backdrop to the flourishing of Eighteenth and Vine. When Wilkins moved to town, Black residents were mostly forced to live in the core of the East Side, constrained to areas east of Troost Avenue and north of Twenty-Seventh Street. (Some neighborhoods outside these boundaries continued to be Black enclaves, such as Steptoe, where Charlie Parker attended school.) The most established members of the Black community bought stately homes near the Paseo, in neighborhoods like Beacon Hill. James Dallas Bowser, the pioneering educator who lived until 1923, owned a house at 2400 the Paseo with a fireplace and spacious library. He hosted parties with his wife and shared what he had learned at NAACP conferences, making his home, one Kansas Citian believed, a "social and cultural center of Negro life."

But the supply of quality housing—to rent or buy—was limited. It wasn't unusual for two to three Black families to inhabit a single home, residing in attics and basements. The reason for the overcrowding was obvious to Thomas A. Webster, the president of the Greater Kansas City Urban League. "There is little area for expansion of the increased Negro population because of the use of restrictive covenants," he wrote in a letter to the city council. The Urban League estimated that private developers built just fifteen houses in areas for Kansas City Black families between 1925 and 1940. *The Call* reported that the older, crumbling housing stock often cost a Black family twice what a white family would pay. "It seems impossible to get anything decent," one woman told *The Call*.

Across town, as the 1920s and '30s beat on, Nichols's Country Club District expanded from one thousand acres to five thousand acres, adding dozens of upper-class and middle-class subdivisions stretching all the way into Kansas. The development featured at least six thousand homes, seventeen schools, fifteen churches, five golf courses, and between thirty thousand and fifty thousand people. "The good life" is how *Time* magazine put it in a story lavishing praise on Nichols. Copycat developers and neighborhood associations introduced restrictions, too. The result: Around 76 percent of subdivisions that went up in the Kansas City area between 1930 to 1947 were tied up in racial covenants, becoming off-limits to Black residents. The segregation compounded, as a new cycle emerged:

1. White and upper-class Kansas Citians, protective of their enclaves, exported city dumps and grimy industrial buildings to the crowded core of the East Side.

2. Residents came to notice the atmosphere on the East Side was opposite of what they experienced in their spacious subdivisions, which happened to be nearly all white. In time, they began to associate overcrowding, dilapidated houses, and industrial waste with Black neighborhoods and Black residents.

As the Kansas City historian Sherry Schirmer later reflected, "To be white and middle class now meant to be an ordinary person. Being Black came to mean being something less than ordinary." The racial stereotypes heightened by segregated housing prompted white Kansas Citians to seek *more* segregation, which meant they had to rely on Nichols and the real estate industry, which continued to emphasize white-only neighborhoods as the ticket for generating wealth and status. The cycle made Nichols's neighborhoods ever more valuable and neighborhoods with any infusion of Black residents more reviled.

Nichols and developers across the country created a market for segregation—spurred on by restrictive covenants and homeowner associations. It led the builders to see racially homogenous neighborhoods as a "professional duty," said Kevin Fox Gotham, an author and expert on national housing policy.

Wilkins followed the rise of homeowner associations in non-Nichols neighborhoods. These older, mostly white neighborhoods envied Nichols's restrictions and rushed to form their own committees and sign belated racial covenants on their individual homes. (One East Side notary told *The Call* that entire neighborhoods were coming to his office.) But covenants that were introduced for older houses were easier to break than Nichols's covenants, so when Black residents started moving into white areas the neighbors resorted to unofficial means to promote segregation. Like bombings.

By this point, bombings were already an ugly Kansas City tradition. In 1910 and 1911, angry white neighbors threw dynamite at six Black-owned properties on the East Side near Twenty-Fifth and Montgall. Many of that area's residents were teachers, like Hezekiah Walden, whose home was severely damaged. Nobody was gravely injured, and the violence did not deter his family or others affected from living on Montgall. When the mayor and police failed to investigate, Walden and his neighbors sought assistance from the NAACP. Despite a push from the organization's legal department, the police never took the violence seriously. In the same area in 1918, two white men bombed Priscilla Quarles's house, destroying her porch. She was a widow whose sons were stationed in France, serving the United States in World War I. The same men were suspected of throwing dynamite at another house a couple of miles away, this one owned by Wade Langley, shattering his windows. *The Kansas City Sun*, a Black paper like *The Call*, noticed a pattern among the Langley and Quarles incidents. They were Black middle-class aspirants who had recently purchased quality homes and wanted "to live under better conditions than have heretofore been enjoyed upon the back streets and side alleys." There were up to seven bombings a year between 1921 and 1928. In 1923, teacher Ida Williams's house on Twenty-First Street, where she lived with her sister, was bombed for the third time. When a Realtor tried to buy her home for less than market value, she declined. Williams said she and her sister planned to stay "until the Lord moves us."

To Wilkins, these were some of the most important news stories of the time. "There didn't seem to be any limit," Wilkins said, "to what the white people would do to keep Blacks from moving up."

The struggle reached a crescendo in Linwood, a neighborhood between Twenty-Eighth and Thirty-First streets from Flora to Brooklyn, about a mile south of where the Monarchs and Blues played at Muehlebach Field. It had a history of bombings, but by the mid-1920s was still seeing Black buyers and renters cross Twenty-Seventh Street and move in, prompting a group of white neighbors to retaliate through the Linwood Improvement Association. Its leader, John Bowman, rallied support from churches and community leaders to convince residents to enter into racially restrictive covenants. The association's next step was to petition the Kansas City parks department to add more green space between Troost Lake Park, just south of Twenty-Seventh and Vine, and Spring Valley Park "on account of the encroachment of negroes." The park would have created a stronger barrier to the heart of the East Side and would have necessitated the demolition of sixty homes occupied by Black families, some who had lived there for ten years. As the parks department debated, some thirteen hundred Linwood residents signed a petition saying they would pay for the park.

At every juncture, Wilkins fought the Linwood Improvement Association. When a Linwood resident proposed a new area where Black people affected by the park plan could move, Wilkins reported that it was filled with shanty houses owned by slumlords allied with the association. When the same resident proposed another area where new homes could be constructed, Wilkins showed that zoning rules meant warehouses and manufacturing facilities could spring up between houses. When mobs circulated around Linwood, he reported on that, too.

Eventually, the plans for the park were denied. In Kansas City, that counted as a victory.

And it wasn't the only one for Black Kansas Citians. Rev. D.A. Holmes, who presided over the Vine Street Baptist Church, condemned the Linwood Improvement Association, too, and sermonized against the favor-for-a-favor excesses of Pendergast. To separate jazz from Pendergast's rackets, Bennie Moten played at venues like the Paseo Hall, giving concerts for Black crowds who got dressed up in formal attire and didn't allow alcohol. Despite being overcrowded, Lincoln High School and other Black elementary schools were "much better than they had any right to be," Wilkins said, because the teachers could have easily been college professors and because Kansas City's "Negro parents and children simply refused to be licked by segregation."

But the wins were rarely complete. Amid their reporting on the Linwood Improvement Association, *The Call* received a threatening letter from Linwood neighbors stating that the sixty Black occupied homes would be turned into a park even "if we are compelled to blow every one of them up." The experience made it hard for Wilkins to live in Kansas City. "Anyone who could feel comfortable in his home or optimistic about the future when those Linwood snakes were at work was a bigger fool than I was prepared to be," he wrote. Wilkins left in the early 1930s and eventually became executive director of the NAACP.

Like that of many visitors and chamber of commerce–style boosters, Wilkins's time in Kansas City left him convinced that the city was a symbol of the entire United States. The difference was he saw the country's worst influences flowing inward and outward, making Kansas City deserving of a different nickname: "The Hard Heart of America."

THE DRAFT

When Brett Veach followed Andy Reid to the Kansas City Chiefs in 2013, he accepted a position as the team's "pro and college personnel analyst," a vague, undefined front-office role that doubled as a blank canvas, a dream job for an upwardly mobile football scout. Veach worked under general manager John Dorsey, an archetypal football grunt with a general's baritone voice and a habit of wearing the same gray sweatshirt, and Chris Ballard, a handsome, well-coiffed director of pro personnel with a bright future. Veach did a little of everything—college scouting, pro personnel work; the job description was basically *Let's see what you got*—but above all else, he watched tape of football players.

If you think you understand how much tape football scouts consume in a given year, you're almost certainly wrong. It is an astonishing, astounding, almost sickening amount. When Dorsey came to Kansas City, the organization's scouts spent the seventeen days before the NFL Scouting Combine watching tape of college players—marathon sessions that began at 5 A.M. and sometimes lasted late into the evening, like a training camp for scouts. Dorsey was the type of football man who believed that salvation could be found through film work, that if you couldn't discern an answer about a player on tape, it probably didn't exist. In the old scout's view, the only way to find talent—the only way to build a championship roster that could win a Super Bowl—was to grind tape, three, four, five games at a time, so much tape that if you looked up at the clock and realized five hours had passed and your brain wasn't completely numb, well, maybe you were onto something. This is what happened to Brett Veach one day in early 2016.

Veach no longer held a vague title. He'd been promoted to codirector of player personnel, and he was looking at an offensive lineman from Texas Tech who was projected to go in the NFL draft that spring. Among the first games he watched was Texas Tech's 56–27 loss to LSU in the Texas Bowl on December 29, 2015. It wasn't much of a game. LSU had All-American running back Leonard Fournette and NFL talent all over the field. But as Veach watched, he kept finding himself drawn to the quarterback from Texas Tech, who was slinging sidearm passes and scrambling around and fighting like hell to keep his overmatched team in the game. Veach once joked with colleagues that he has an internal "excito-meter" that surfaces when he watches football players, a crude measurement system that existed in his mind and his gut. On the day he first witnessed Patrick Mahomes, the system overloaded.

Mahomes had just finished his sophomore season—just two years removed from Whitehouse High. He'd thrown for 4,653 yards as a sophomore and put up big numbers in the Red Raiders' Air Raid offense, as most Texas Tech quarterbacks did, but owing to his quiet college recruitment and the fact he wasn't eligible for the draft for another year, he wasn't exactly on NFL radars. "Who is this guy?" Veach thought.

To Veach, the question became an obsession. Who was Patrick Mahomes? What was his story? Why was he at Texas Tech? Did he have the right size? How old was he? Would he be in the draft next year? It eventually led Veach down a rabbit hole—more tape and more ridiculous throws and more questions—and one day that spring, as he later recalled, he was grinding Mahomes tape on a quiet weekend inside the Chiefs' offices when Andy Reid happened by. Reid was curious about what Veach was up to. Veach had a simple answer: He was watching the next quarterback of the Kansas City Chiefs.

———

VEACH was not the only person interested in Patrick Mahomes. Fifteen hundred miles away, Leigh Steinberg sat inside the offices of Steinberg Sports and Entertainment in Newport Beach, California, his desk overlooking the blue waters of Newport Bay. Steinberg was sixty-seven and one of the godfathers of the sports agent business, a sandy-haired, blue-eyed entrepreneur who still wore mesh basketball shorts to work and who had once allowed director Cameron Crowe to follow him around in the early 1990s. (The result was *Jerry Maguire*, the 1996 Tom Cruise hit that earned Cuba Gooding Jr. an Oscar for repeatedly saying the phrase "Show me the money.")

Steinberg, in fact, was in many ways more fascinating than the Hollywood version. He had grown up in Los Angeles in the early 1960s and come of age at the University of California during the height of the counterculture, an idealistic liberal who shared a dorm with Steve Wozniak (before he founded Apple with Steve Jobs) and learned about negotiation tactics during the bloody battle for Berkeley's People's Park in May 1969, when police, at the direction of Governor Ronald Reagan, clashed with activists who had transformed a derelict university construction site into a DIY public space. Police opened fire during the mayhem, wounding dozens with buckshot and killing one bystander. Five students from Steinberg's dorm were shot, he told a local newspaper a year later. He carried one to the hospital. In response, he formed a campus political organization—the Nonviolent Action Party—and was elected student body president the next year, winning as a moderate antiwar voice among a sea of campus radicalism. "If someone wanted to end the war in Vietnam, the right way to do it would be to go to the middle of America and convince them," he told a reporter.

Steinberg stayed in Berkeley for law school, envisioning a future in politics. But that changed when he met another Steve on campus: Steve Bartkowski, the No. 1 overall pick in the 1975 NFL draft. The modern conception of a sports agent didn't really exist in 1975, but

Bartkowski asked Steinberg to help him with his contract negotiation. When they scored the largest rookie contract in NFL history, Steinberg came to realize the resonance of sports—and the quarterback spot in particular. Over the next two decades, he became one of the most powerful agents in the NFL, representing Troy Aikman, Steve Young, Warren Moon, and a long list of NFL stars. Money poured in. Media attention followed. Tom Cruise and Cameron Crowe came next. Steinberg was cast as a different kind of football superagent—thoughtful, compassionate, a little eccentric and crunchy in that California kind of way. And then came the free fall: a tailspin in the 2000s that included alcoholism and divorce and bitter legal battles with former colleagues and two sons afflicted with a brutal eye disease. His reputation soiled, Steinberg got sober and decided to start over. In 2013, he opened a new agency. He hired a young entertainment attorney from the Philadelphia area named Chris Cabott. In 2016, they landed a first-round quarterback—Paxton Lynch from the University of Memphis. But by the summer of 2016, they were still after the Next Big Thing, a player that could change their lives. Steinberg and Cabott believed it was Patrick Mahomes.

Steinberg had first heard the name while visiting his friend Earl Campbell—the NFL legend and East Texas native—at a dinner in Tyler. (The mayor's wife bragged about the local product, but she still thought he'd play baseball.) Cabott was already on the hunt. On the day Texas Tech played LSU in the Texas Bowl, he told a board member at the agency to tune in if he wanted to see the top quarterback in next year's draft class. "What he had," Steinberg said, "was miraculous." First, though, they had to find a way in, to make inroads before Mahomes played his junior season. The agency tried a cold message to a social media account. They called Pat Mahomes Sr. Nobody responded. Cabott unearthed an email address for Mahomes's mother, Randi. It bounced back. Finally, Cabott took a shot, cold-calling Randi at work in Texas and leaving a message. A few weeks later, she called back.

The first meeting was at a restaurant in Grapevine, Texas. As they ordered brunch, Pat and Randi wanted Steinberg and Cabott to know that their son had once considered going to law school, that he didn't fit the typical mold of a football star, that he cared about family and his friends in Whitehouse and he had a broader sense of the world around him. Steinberg and Cabott listened. They presented their pitch, offering their own vision, one that almost nobody in football yet shared: Mahomes, they said, could be a Hall of Fame quarterback.

"The whole key is to underpromise and overdeliver," Steinberg said later. "But it was hard to remember another quarterback who passed like that. And then when you spent time with him and you realized: He was going to do all the work. And he had a strategic mind. He thought about things from the standpoint of a technician."

Steinberg just had to wonder: Would NFL teams agree?

ONCE Brett Veach found Patrick Mahomes, he couldn't shake him. There was something about the way Mahomes's body worked, how his right arm could unleash thunderbolts from the most awkward angles, how he was built sturdy like a running back—with a backside that once helped him earn the nickname "Fatrick" at Texas Tech. Veach had less than a decade of scouting experience since joining Reid in Philly, but the more he watched, the more he was certain: Mahomes was the best football player he'd ever seen. He had spent the fall of 2016 combing through Texas Tech film, culling clips and sending them to Reid. He used his salesman's touch to lobby Dorsey, who would have final say on the Draft. At one point, late in the fall, Veach put together around ten Mahomes highlights and flooded Reid's phone. *OK*, Reid texted back, *that was enough. Wait until the season is over.*

The Chiefs finished 12-4 and won their first AFC West title since 2010—before another crushing home playoff loss to the Steelers in January. But at some point in the new year, Reid came across one of the first media mock drafts for the upcoming 2017 NFL draft. He texted Veach to come to his office, where he had a printout of the first round. Did he realize Mahomes wasn't even listed?

The doubters saw a "system quarterback"—a description reserved for college quarterbacks who were said to benefit from playing in a high-powered or innovative spread-passing attack. It was an epithet that dated back to at least the early 1990s, when the University of Houston had multiple quarterbacks put up historic numbers in a run-and-shoot passing attack, and it followed all Air Raid QBs, too, especially after a series of Texas Tech quarterbacks had failed in the NFL. The doubters also saw a project that had adventurous footwork and questionable decision-making. ESPN draft analyst Todd McShay wrote that Mahomes "misses entirely on too many open targets because his mechanics are all over the place." The NFL Network's Mike Mayock had Mahomes ranked as the fourth-best quarterback in the draft, behind Notre Dame's DeShone Kizer, Clemson's Deshaun Watson (who had just quarterbacked the Tigers to a national championship), and North Carolina's Mitch Trubisky. When Mahomes heard back from the NFL Draft Advisory Board, a panel of executives and scouting experts who assign grades to prospective players, he was told he was, at best, a second-round pick. When *Sports Illustrated* profiled Mahomes in early March, the headline read: "The Draft's Rorschach Test."

IF you looked closer, or stared harder at the inkblot, you might have noticed there were explanations for the flaws: Mahomes had been playing quarterback for only five years, and he'd been a full-time football player for only one. It wasn't even until after his sophomore season, following a talk with Texas Tech coach Kliff Kingsbury, that he realized he had a chance to play in the NFL. "I think if you focus on football for one off-season, that you'll get drafted," Mahomes recalled Kingsbury saying. So he quit baseball for good. Mahomes did have sloppy footwork. That was obvious. Sometimes he'd just drift backward and throw off his back foot for no reason in particular. Other times, he'd chuck a ball up for grabs, like he was playing the children's game 500. "There's some dumb throws," Mahomes said that spring. But the backyard mechanics made his 65 percent completion percentage all the more impressive.

To fully appreciate Mahomes, you just had to watch him, the way he would feather an accurate throw in the strangest of situations, the way his mind could make split-second calculations on the field, so a reckless throw was actually a well-considered risk. There was one clip from his junior season, from a nonconference game against Louisiana Tech, where Mahomes scrambled to his left near midfield, planted his right foot in the ground, and flicked a ball 50 yards in the air—despite never turning his body or squaring his shoulders to the target to gain power on the throw. It was, Mahomes would say, a nod to his days as a baseball shortstop.

The 2017 NFL draft was set to begin April 27 in Philadelphia. Mahomes had three and a half months to prove himself and move up draft boards. So in January, Steinberg and Cabott sent the quarterback to the Exos training facility in Carlsbad, California, where he began daily workouts with former NFL quarterback coach Mike Sheppard—the same Mike Sheppard who had once recruited Andy Reid to BYU.

On a field two miles from the Pacific Ocean, Sheppard ran Mahomes through drills to refine his technique: They worked on taking snaps under center. Sheppard emphasized holding the ball higher during five- and seven-step drops. Mahomes was a willing sponge. On one of their first days together at Exos, Mahomes wanted to take his shirt off and soak in the sun. When Sheppard protested, Mahomes respectfully acquiesced, slipping his shirt back on. "He was a likable dude," Sheppard said. Mostly, though, Sheppard wanted to teach Mahomes what the NFL sounded like, so they zeroed in on the different languages of NFL schemes. They went over the verbiage of the West Coast offense, pioneered by Bill Walsh. They studied the "number system" of the "Air Coryell" offense, the vertical passing attack made famous by the San Diego Chargers and their head coach Don Coryell. They covered so much ground that Sheppard came to realize that Mahomes was more than a big arm. "He was smarter than maybe anybody knew," he said.

Mahomes had earned a 3.71 grade point average at Texas Tech, but when Steinberg and Cabott first met him, they learned of his photographic memory—the same eidetic recall he'd used in travel baseball and high school football. "Does that mean you can remember every play you've ever played?" Steinberg asked. "Yes," Mahomes said. "Somehow." If NFL teams were concerned that Mahomes was a system quarterback—specifically one from a simplified scheme that almost exclusively used the shotgun formation—Steinberg believed they just needed to see how his mind worked. When Mahomes met with the Arizona Cardinals before the draft, Cardinals head coach Bruce Arians put his memory to a test. On a board, he drew up six plays and two or three pass-protection schemes; then he showed Mahomes video of some blitz packages and offered audible calls that would allow him to switch the protection, depending on the look. Just two hours later, Mahomes was out on the field, and Arians blurted out a protection-and-blitz package. "Rightie! Rightie!" Mahomes said, fixing the protection. "Holy cow," Arians thought. Then he did it again. Mahomes had already mastered something that might take another quarterback a year.

The secret was starting to get out. The Cardinals (who had the thirteenth pick) liked Mahomes. So did Buffalo Bills owner Terry Pegula, who sought to give his front office complete autonomy to make their own choice at No. 10. The New Orleans Saints, who picked one spot after the Bills, were thinking quarterback, too, and when Saints coach Sean Payton traveled to Lubbock, Texas, he was taken by Mahomes's talent—and his smile: "Man," Payton thought, "this is the best quarterback I've ever evaluated." The Chiefs, meanwhile, were picking twenty-seventh and still hadn't picked a quarterback in the first round since 1983, when they drafted Todd Blackledge seventh overall out of Penn State—after John Elway and ahead of Hall of Famers Jim Kelly and Dan Marino. Blackledge was famously a bust, the black sheep of the Class of 1983, never starting a full season and finishing with more interceptions than touchdowns, and for the next generation the Chiefs more or less stopped taking chances on young QBs.

Back in Kansas City, however, Dorsey and the front office were starting to plot. On January 17, Veach had run into Cabott at the NFLPA Collegiate Bowl—a predraft scouting event—and revealed a secret: He loved Mahomes. The conversation started a daily back channel of texts and updates that lasted for another three months. Steinberg and Cabott saw Kansas City as an ideal landing spot. Steinberg had known Chiefs owner Clark Hunt since Hunt was a ball boy. Andy Reid was renowned for his work with quarterbacks. The Chiefs had a good starter in Alex Smith, but even the Mahomes family believed he might benefit from a year of development on the bench. And then there was the city: Steinberg saw Kansas City as a "scalable" town for a kid from Tyler, Texas—a place where Mahomes might fit into the culture and connect with a fervent fan base. Steinberg thought of the cliché "Midwest nice." It fit Patrick Mahomes. "It's a city where you know the fan base loves football," Mahomes said. "You want to be a part of a city that's just all in for you."

Of course, just as Steinberg and Cabott believed, Mahomes was moving up. If the Chiefs were going to land him, they couldn't wait until the twenty-seventh pick, so as the draft approached, the front office looped in Hunt. First, they brought him to the team's war room to look at Mahomes's film. ("I don't watch tape on many players," Hunt said. "But that was a special situation.") Then, about six weeks before the draft, Hunt joined Reid, Dorsey, and Veach on a conference call. All throughout the process, Veach had been consumed by the thought of *what if?* What if Mahomes could learn from Andy Reid? What if he could utilize his skills in a West Coast offense?

What if you surrounded him with speed and skill? What if the Chiefs finally drafted a quarterback? On the call, another question came into focus: What if the Chiefs traded up with another team to get Patrick Mahomes? The front office laid out the various trade scenarios for Hunt. ("The hot zones," Veach said later.).

Around the same time, as the calendar pressed toward April, Andy Reid picked up a phone and called Mike Sheppard, his old friend from BYU. In seconds, Sheppard understood what Reid was after. Reid deemed it a "due diligence" call. The Chiefs liked Mahomes, he said; he just had some questions. Of course, that kind of call usually lasts about fifteen minutes, and when Reid was still on the phone close to an hour later, still asking questions about Mahomes, Sheppard sensed something different.

"This is more than just a due-diligence call, isn't it?" he asked.

Yes, it was.

"I think he's Brett Favre," Reid said.

ON the morning of the NFL draft, as Veach headed off to work, his wife, Allison, wished him good luck and handed off a small note, a message scribbled by their six-year-old daughter, Ella.

Pat No Matter What.

The note was a reference to the 2014 film *Draft Day*, which stars Kevin Costner as an NFL executive navigating the emotional twists of the first round while trying to land a future star named Vontae Mack. If you've seen the movie, you know that it wasn't a perfect analog to the Chiefs' predicament—nor was it a particularly good movie—but the note offered the kind of good vibes that Veach needed. "Go, Chiefs," his wife said.

The same morning, John Dorsey was calling Doug Whaley, the general manager of the Buffalo Bills. Their communication had started months earlier, around the NFL Scouting Combine, and just days earlier they had agreed to the basics of a possible trade, in which the Chiefs would package the twenty-seventh pick, a third-round pick, and their first-round pick in 2018 to move up to the Bills' spot at No. 10. Now Dorsey wanted to keep the lines open. "Don't get scared now," he told Whaley.

The NFL draft can feel like an impenetrable black box. Teams protect their intel like diplomatic cables. Smoke screens are everywhere. Dorsey, for instance, had invited the top five quarterback prospects to visit Kansas City before the draft, just so Mahomes would not stand out, and he kept dropping the name of Alabama linebacker Reuben Foster into conversations with other executives. But this meant that nobody in the Chiefs front office could be certain how it would go. The Saints lurked at No. 11, and Dorsey was certain they wanted Mahomes. The Cleveland Browns (always in need of a quarterback) had the first pick and the twelfth. Nobody seemed to know anything about the Chicago Bears at No. 3. But if the Chiefs could move up to No. 10, Dorsey was really worried only about the Chargers at No. 7—who could stash Mahomes behind an aging Philip Rivers.

Veach, meanwhile, worried that the Saints and the Cardinals, picking at No. 13, had the draft picks to trade up higher than No. 10, if they were so motivated. But there was one piece of NFL fine print working in the Chiefs' favor. NFL contracts for rookies contain a team option for a fifth season, and it just so happened that the slotted money for the fifth-year option fell off substantially from the tenth pick to the eleventh. Thus, it made financial sense for the Saints and Cardinals to sit tight and not trade up. The Chiefs, Veach thought, could catch the entire league by surprise.

Back in Texas, Mahomes was still hopeful about Kansas City. He had left his predraft meeting with the Bears convinced they might take him, and he heard similar sentiments from other coaches, but as the draft approached, he had his agents deliver a message to the Chiefs front office, using the inside info they'd gathered from other teams: If the Chiefs wanted to draft Mahomes, they needed to move up to at least twelfth. It wasn't perfect intel—Mahomes didn't know how much the Saints coveted him—but it was a confirmation of sorts for the Chiefs: "I wanted to be here," he said later.

On draft day, Mahomes skipped an invite to sit in the green room at the draft in Philadelphia and instead held a party for his family and friends at Lago del Pino, a stylish Tex-Mex restaurant tucked into an idyllic backdrop of pine trees on Lost Pine Lake in Tyler. As the draft began, Mahomes took a seat on a sofa on the second floor of the restaurant. Steinberg clutched a piece of paper with possible scenarios. Cabott looked at his phone and saw a text message from Veach. It was the Texas Tech logo.

The draft began as expected: The Browns took defensive end Myles Garrett. But then came a surprise: The Chicago Bears traded up one spot to take North Carolina quarterback Mitch Trubisky at No. 2, which astounded executives across the league. Trubisky had started just one season at North Carolina, and the Bears had flattered Mahomes in their meeting. Bears GM Ryan Pace would say one difference was Trubisky's perceived ability to process information, which he compared with that of the Saints' Drew Brees.

Back in Texas, the selection of Trubisky rippled through the party. As Adam Cook, Mahomes's high school coach, would later recall, it was at that moment that Texas Tech coach Kliff Kingsbury made a prediction: "Watch them Chiefs," he said. The Chiefs, too, were hopeful when Trubisky went off the board. But they still had to worry about the Chargers at No. 7. That could throw a wrench in the entire plan. They also still had a trade to finalize, and when the Chargers opted for Clemson receiver Mike Williams, Dorsey went to work, sorting through the trade details with Whaley one more time. The deal, in principle, was done, and when the Bills went on the clock at No. 10, Dorsey called back.

"Let's get it done," he said.

Whaley still wanted to wait on other offers before turning in the trade to the league. Inside the Chiefs' draft room, they could only wait. One minute, then two, then three. Finally, Whaley called back. Veach tapped out a second text to Cabott, who looked at his phone at the party in Texas. It was another Texas Tech logo. Pat Sr. began to cry.

In the final moments before NFL commissioner Roger Goodell announced the pick, Reid rushed to call Alex Smith, and Mahomes sat on a sofa at Lago del Pino, flanked by his mother and Steinberg. Nothing would ever be the same, not for Mahomes or the Chiefs or Kansas City. At one point that night, Mahomes got a text from Brett Veach.

It was a photo of a note.

Pat No Matter What.

NICHOLS AND THE NATION

Nobody ever found out who killed Johnny Lazia. He was gunned down at 3 A.M. on a steamy July morning in the summer of 1934, wounded eight times in a blistering hail of gunfire, left for dead in the circle drive of Park Central Hotel on East Armour Boulevard, where he lived in a tony penthouse apartment with his wife, Marie.

Lazia, the head of the North Side Democratic Club, never saw it coming. On the morning he was assassinated, he was returning from his resort home at Lake Lotawana, some twenty-five miles away. His driver, a wise guy named Charlie Carrollo, maneuvered a sedan into the front drive, and Lazia emerged to open the door for his wife. It was then that the shots began. It's believed that one assailant had a submachine gun and another a shotgun. According to one neighbor, there were rumors the stray bullets recovered at the scene were soaked in garlic.

When Lazia arrived at St. Joseph Hospital on Linwood Boulevard, doctors worked for eleven hours to save his life. At one point, according to an account in that evening's *Kansas City Star*, he looked up at one and started to speak. "Doc, what I can't understand is why anybody would do this to me," he cried. "Why to me, to Johnny Lazia, who has been the friend of everybody?" Moments later, the doctor dialed up one of those friends: Tom Pendergast.

Lazia was not just the head of a local Democratic club. He was the flamboyant front man of the Kansas City underworld. Born in

Brooklyn in the late 1890s, he had arrived in Kansas City's Little Italy as a child, earned an eighth-grade education, and embarked on the hoodlum life, which resulted in an arrest for armed robbery and a subsequent prison sentence. When he got out, he returned to the North End. In 1928, he executed a coup d'état to topple Michael Ross—an Irishman who controlled the ward that included Little Italy—exerting his power with kidnappings of Ross's underlings, and soon enough, he was one of Pendergast's chief lieutenants, free to run the rackets and hold sway over the police. Such was the power of the Italian voting bloc. In 1929, Lazia represented Kansas City at the Atlantic City Council, where Meyer Lansky, Al Capone, and mob leaders from around the country met to discuss the future.

For Pendergast, the 1930s were poised to be big. The machine controlled the rackets *and* the cops. Its liquor business could capitalize on the end of Prohibition. Construction projects exploded as Kansas City's Ten-Year Plan went into effect. And two months before assassins ambushed Lazia, it had launched the campaign of another politician on his way to the US Senate: Harry S. Truman of Independence, Missouri, a once failed haberdasher whose career had been rescued twelve years earlier when the Pendergasts suggested he run to be a local county court judge.

If you looked closer, however, there were cracks. Many were filled with blood. One year earlier, in the summer of 1933, a helter-skelter, bloodstained shootout outside Union Station had left four lawmen and the fugitive Frank Nash dead. The incident—which would be known as the Union Station Massacre—shocked the public and put national scrutiny on the city. (One gangster, Michael James "Jimmy Needles" LaCapra, would tell the feds that Lazia was aware of the plan to spring Nash before it happened, though it remains uncertain if he was telling the truth.) And then more bloodshed: In the spring of 1934, a local primary election erupted into so much mayhem—four people shot, voters intimidated, and the ballot box stuffed—that newspapers across the country ran boldface headlines, like the one in the *New York Daily News*:

TERROR REIGN MARKS KANSAS CITY VOTING

The murder of Johnny Lazia didn't help the PR problem. So even as the machine triumphed—by a curious vote ratio of 1,469 to 1 in one ward, according to a US attorney—it felt as if the Pendergast way was unraveling. Money problems made everything worse. Pendergast still loved to bet the horses, and he didn't have the same luck as his older brother: He lost some $600,000 (more than $12 million today) during a monthlong bender at the New York racetracks in 1935. With his deep reserves of dirty money, everybody knew Pendergast could cover the losses. The problem was his tax returns, which gave federal investigators an opening to give Pendergast the Al Capone treatment.

The IRS zeroed in on a suspicious six-figure payment Pendergast had received as part of a state insurance settlement. As rumors swirled, friends of Pendergast turned. Missouri governor Lloyd Stark visited Franklin Roosevelt in the White House to share his knowledge of the sketchy insurance dealings. While Roosevelt didn't throw the weight of his administration behind the investigation, he didn't stop it, nor did he grant Truman's desperate request to remove the Missouri US attorney who was hot on Pendergast's trail. On April 7, 1939, the Feds handed down an indictment for tax evasion. It was Good Friday, and as Pendergast prepared to dab his fingertips in ink at his arraignment, he told the assembled crowd that he felt like Jesus Christ, betrayed and persecuted.

He pleaded guilty.

Pendergast got a fifteen-month prison sentence. Few friends struck around. His wife left him. Others, like Lazia, were dead. Harry Truman stayed loyal, saying to Pendergast's last day, "He has always been my friend, and I have always been his." So, too, did J.C. Nichols, his poker buddy. He was one of a handful of signatories of a petition asking a judge to give Pendergast lighter probation terms and to forward a request for clemency to the Justice Department. It was all to no avail.

Pendergast, reeling from heart and stomach issues and unable to climb stairs, spent his last few years cooped up behind the wrought-iron door of his Nichols mansion, sometimes leaving to ride in a car on the newly paved roads of the city he once ran. But he could never get far. Based on his probationary terms, Pendergast couldn't cross the state line.

THE petition was a nice gesture. Nobody needed Pendergast anymore, least of all Nichols, whose influence had surpassed Boss Tom's in Kansas City and just about everywhere else. As the 1930s pushed on, he became a mainstay in Washington, DC, commuting every other month, proposing designs and zoning for the National Capital Park, and making inroads with the Beltway elite. Nichols counted FDR's uncle F.A. Delano as his "dear friend." President Herbert Hoover, his dinner guest, was his "good friend." He worked alongside Ulysses S. Grant III.

The connections opened doors. Real estate was as depressed as anything during the Depression—about half of all homeowners had defaulted on their mortgages, and building and loan associations failed. Something had to be done. So Nichols and two fellow leaders from the National Association of Real Estate Boards cozied up to their Washington friends in 1933, circulating a memorandum that suggested the federal government should become involved with home loans to resuscitate the housing industry.

The National Association of Real Estate Boards' work built toward hearings with the House Committee on Banking and Currency in 1934. After several days of listening to the real estate suits, Congress passed House Resolution 9620—known as the National Housing Act of 1934—and FDR signed it in late June. The key part of the bill was the creation of the Federal Housing Administration, a government-sanctioned clearinghouse for insuring home mortgages. The insurance would make it easier for builders to obtain funding, for average Americans to get cleared for a mortgage, and for lenders to sleep at night, knowing they'd be covered if somebody's payments dried up. Lenders started offering buyers mortgages with friendlier rates—10 or 20 percent down and a fifteen- to thirty-year repayment period, similar to the terms we still have today—because they trusted the FHA. It was the type of entity Nichols and the real estate industry desired.

The FHA, staffed with real estate industry heavyweights, saw the highest potential for profit by following the cardinal tenets of Nichols's developments: zealous attention to building standards, the shunning of apartments, and racially restrictive covenants. (Somehow, however, they omitted the need for a songbird census.) The organization's Bible-thick manual set criteria for properties to be eligible for government-secured mortgages and stressed the false belief that it was necessary for neighborhoods to "be occupied by the same social and racial classes" for them to retain any value. As one way of ensuring segregation, the FHA drew up maps grading the safety of mortgages in areas throughout US cities, assigning the lowest grades to neighborhoods with Black and Hispanic people, immigrants, or poor white people. The FHA deemed these areas too risky for its mortgage insurance and—in broad terms—insured only mortgages in newer, all-white neighborhoods, helping to prompt and subsidize a great migration out of America's cities and into the suburbs. The process was called redlining. And the FHA didn't stop there: To make sure these suburbs stayed exclusively filled with white people, the organization's manual called for racially restrictive covenants that kept out "adverse influences" and "undesirable encroachment."

What was once a practice of private builders was now institutionalized by the FHA, which was one of the most prolific organizations to come out of the New Deal, backing three of every five homes bought in the United States from the mid-1930s until 1959. (As Kevin

Fox Gotham, the national housing policy expert, later described, the FHA "adopted [Nichols's] methods and practices almost verbatim.") The federal government copied the DNA of Sunset Hill, Mission Hills, and Armour Hills and incentivized developers to paste replicas—in huge quantities at huge profits—at the edges of major metros across the country.

With segregation patterns already in place from Nichols's and other developers' covenants, the FHA likely would have had an easy time shading the areas of the metro it believed to be risky and picking what the agency considered safe spots in the suburbs, or in the distant neighborhoods that Kansas City desperately annexed in Missouri, some 250 square miles of new land, quintupling the city's geographical size to make it feel as suburban as possible. (The city's population still stagnated while suburbs proliferated.) Because the FHA purposefully destroyed its redlining maps on the heels of a lawsuit in 1969— the Nixon administration apparently thought it was smart to store tapes but not maps—it's impossible to know the exact areas barred from secured mortgages, only that the mortgage insurance almost never went to people who weren't white. The FHA backed some seventy-seven thousand mortgages in the Kansas City area from 1934 to 1962, and just 1 percent of them were for Black families, who also struggled to receive loan approval for home repairs, further disadvantaging Black neighborhoods. Roy Wilkins, then in a leadership position with the NAACP, wrote to the head of the FHA in 1939 to express his view of the situation: The agency, he believed, was using "public tax money to restrict instead of extend opportunities for home ownership" and to "enforce patterns of racial segregation."

Another federal agency, the Home Owners' Loan Corporation, made *another* set of maps in the 1930s that gave a snapshot of areas inhabited by Black people and poorer white people, the types of neighborhoods the FHA and most private developers would have considered too racially and economically mixed. The heart of the East Side, as described by the HOLC, was a "typical colored area, ragged in every respect." It labeled the area "hazardous" and shaded it in red. A "noticeable infiltration of Jews" was an issue in another area, which the HOLC tagged as "definitely declining," shading it in yellow. Green-shaded neighborhoods were still favorable, and a common trait linked many of them. "This area," the map's description read, "embraces the best of the far-flung, nationally known J.C. Nichols exclusive subdivisions."

All told, the Kansas City metro, including the Missouri and Kansas sides, had 52 percent of its geographic area shaded in red by the HOLC, twice as high of a share as, for example, Philadelphia or Detroit. Out of the biggest cities in the country—those with more than three hundred thousand residents—Kansas City was redder than any other, aside from the borough of Manhattan.

The HOLC maps displayed what pockets of Kansas City had become under the early influence of Nichols and racially restrictive covenants, and the FHA accelerated Kansas City's transformation into what it would be for many decades: increasingly neglected and poor in the middle, and increasingly sprawled, segregated, and comfortable on the edges.

IN the summer humidity of 1941, a crew of construction workers lugged wooden joists, brick, and stone to a grass clearing on the Kansas side of the state line, carrying the building blocks of Nichols's next profitable venture. First, the workers set the foundation and next came the walls and the shingled roofs. Then they hauled in the modern features: sparkling mirrors, all-steel cabinets, a General Electric range to give "the woman carefree time for other things." It all happened so fast.

The first home looked terribly out of place, like a redwood in the desert. But then came another and another, an old Kansas dairy farm transformed into a modest subdivision, twenty-five Cape Cod–style homes adorned with shutters, brick chimneys, and garages, the latter a necessity in a Nichols neighborhood far from the din of the city. The

J.C. Nichols Company gave the new subdivision the most Kansas-sounding name you could imagine: Prairie Village. "Nothing quite like it . . . anywhere!" proclaimed an ad announcing the new subdivision.

This was true. Prairie Village was modern, mass-produced suburbia—an assembly-line version of Nichols's Country Club District—platted and planned six years before the developer William Levitt laid out his "Levittown" on the potato farms of Long Island, New York. (Levittown would become famous for defining America's postwar suburbs, but when the newspaper *Newsday* chided Levitt for naming the development for himself, it mentioned that Nichols was already "a pioneer in the housing development business," never committed that sin.) Prairie Village, however, wasn't just Levittown before Levittown. It was an expansion of Nichols Land, a charming creation where saplings were planted in rows along the curbline, where European statues were placed at the end of each street, where no two homes would be the same, as the company claimed. But unlike many houses in the ritzier Nichols developments nearby, they were still affordable, manufactured for the everyman—a young engineer, returning GI, or local high school principal such as Howard McEachen, who bought a house on Sixty-Ninth Street when he arrived in town in 1944. The first batch of houses could be had for a small down payment and $39.16 a month. The total cost, "under [an] FHA long-term payment plan," was less than $5,000. And, of course, the neighborhood barred Black residents. "Best of all," noted the Nichols announcement for Prairie Village, it had the same "protective restrictions and safeguards" as the Country Club District.

Prairie Village was an instant hit. In 1942, one of the subdivision's first homes—snapped up in one day—was featured in the January issue of *Better Homes and Gardens.* By 1949, the subdivision was named the best planned community in the United States by the National Association of Home Builders. And when the prime minister of Pakistan, Liaquat Ali Khan, toured the United States with his wife in

1950, they requested to see a typical midwestern home. They stopped in Prairie Village.

Those first twenty-five homes bloomed into something greater than a subdivision. Prairie Village became an entire city, home to twenty thousand people, with a fire station, a police force, and schools all its own. To the men who gathered in a family basement on Sixty-Eighth Street for the first city council meetings, Prairie Village was their own wonderland of Americana, the name shorthand for a suburban aesthetic. Said Ralph Brenizer, the city's first mayor: "The main thinking was that it helped preserve your identity." Nichols shared a similar view. "When you rear children in a good neighborhood," he told a reporter in 1947, "they will go out and fight communism."

Prairie Village was as homogenous and affordable as anything the Kansas City area ever saw—although the Nichols Company's covenants were losing momentum. In December 1945, a group of Black residents met at Centennial Methodist Church to discuss initiating what *The Call* described as an "all-out fight" against restrictive covenants. Multiple court cases ensued, including one brought in 1947 by Carl R. Johnson, a pioneering Black attorney in Kansas City. Johnson represented Winfrey and Margaret Bridgewater, whose purchase of a deed-restricted house near Thirtieth Street was challenged by white neighbors. He tested out a couple of innovative legal theories, arguing that racial covenants created and perpetuated hazardous living conditions that went against the nation's interests and that they violated the Equal Protection Clause of the Fourteenth Amendment. A local judge ruled against him. But, around the same time, lawyers were using similar legal arguments for a St. Louis couple in a case that went to the Supreme Court. In 1948, the Supreme Court ruled it unconstitutional for courts to enforce racially restrictive housing covenants in *Shelley v. Kraemer*, a case argued by civil rights icon Thurgood Marshall. In the wake of the decision—and after facing years of pressure from Marshall, the NAACP, and local groups like those in Kansas City—the FHA reluctantly decided to be less explicitly discriminatory. It scrapped covenants as part of its criteria and, in late 1949, announced it would no longer secure mortgages on subdivisions that featured racial restrictions. The new conditions would go into effect on February 15, 1950.

As the clock ran out, some developers panicked. The daughter of a Kansas builder who used Nichols's counsel to ban anyone except for "the Aryan race" in his neighborhood was now concerned she wouldn't be able to obtain FHA financing for additions to the subdivision. A VP for Nichols calmed her fears, telling her in a letter that she could still get the FHA backing so long as the racial restrictions were filed before the February 15 deadline. "As a matter of fact," the VP wrote, "we are planning to have certain areas, which we contemplate developing very soon, [platted] now and have such restrictions filed prior to that February 15th date."

The Nichols Company knew a racial covenant—which it casually referred to as a "Negro clause," in company records—could not be enforced by courts. But it could still be an informal deterrent for keeping neighborhoods segregated. So the company imposed restrictions on at least fourteen areas of yet-to-be developed land. On February 11, the Nichols Company filed a covenant for the subdivision Bunker Hill. It did the same for Indian Hills on February 9. For the rapidly growing Prairie Village, it acted faster, filing a covenant on February 4, 1950, to bar Black people for forty years, with the potential for renewal.

When the Supreme Court handed down its decision on covenants, the Urban League of Greater Kansas City pondered whether any real changes were coming: "Does it mean Negroes in the Country Club District?" the organization asked in its members' newsletter. "The answer is no, not hardly."

NICHOLS fell ill with cancer during the last few months of 1949. He died on February 16, 1950, the day after the FHA had, at least in the official sense, discouraged racial covenants. President Harry

Truman wrote a letter to Jessie, Nichols's widow, describing him as a "distinguished public servant." In Washington, lawmakers eulogized Nichols on the Senate floor. "There are few cities of large size in the United States that in one way or another have not felt his genius," praised James Kem, a Missouri senator.

Kansas City had wanted to leave an imprint on the world—to feel just a little bigger, a little more vital—and as it turned out, Nichols had been its most prominent vessel to achieve those ends, showing the United States how to soften the wild, glorious fixtures of a city and remake them into a languid, formulaic compound of segregation and suburbia.

At a church in the Country Club District, his casket was covered in red roses. Some two thousand people, overflowing from the pews into the foyer, attended the funeral. The pastor spoke of Nichols as a man who had accomplished his dream, as somebody who developed a remedy—"fine homes" for "contented peoples"—that blocked forces of destruction afflicting the world.

It may have seemed like the end of a chapter for Kansas City: a final goodbye to an influential leader. But Nichols's hold on the city was far from over.

PART III

Patrick Mahomes and Andy Reid at training camp in 2018.

MAHOMES THE APPRENTICE

On a mild Thanksgiving night in 2017, Gary Lezak, a gregarious meteorologist who loved to overshare stories about his dogs (named Windy, Stormy, Breezy, and Sunny), hosted an annual event that makes no sense to anyone not from Kansas City. In front of him, tens of thousands of people clogged the J.C. Nichols–designed streets of the Country Club Plaza, waiting for the Christmas lights to turn on, at which point—the shopping center fully illuminated—a middle-aged band called the Elders would play Irish songs.

"Is Kansas City ready?" Lezak asked.

Next to him stood Chiefs quarterback Alex Smith, linebacker Derrick Johnson, and a lucky kid named Daniel. They were going to flip the switch to light up the Plaza in hues of red, white, green, and yellow—the holiday tradition started in 1925 by Charles Pitrat, a Nichols Company maintenance man.

"Is Alex Smith ready?" Lezak bellowed, with a touch more enthusiasm. Smith, wearing khakis and a dark jacket, gave a half-smile and laughed, and then he got serious. "I think it's amazing to be a part of a custom like this," he said. "This doesn't happen anywhere else."

At thirty-three, Smith was having the best season of his career, topping the NFL in quarterback rating, and by leading the city in its Thanksgiving tradition, silly as it may seem, he was joining a list of famous athletes, comics, and musicians who mattered to Kansas City (George Brett, Kate Spade, and Paul Rudd had all turned on the lights in previous years). Yet Smith still knew, barring some type of miracle, it would be his last as a Chief—his last in a town that had grown to like him—all because of the phenom waiting behind him on the bench. When the Chiefs had drafted Mahomes seven months earlier, Smith was realistic about his fate, saying, "I get it, right."

If there was one way to describe Alex Smith—one aspect that nearly everyone could agree on—it was that he was the kind of person who *got it*, an NFL quarterback who graduated from college in two years, listened to NPR in the car, read *The Wall Street Journal*, and sometimes arrived at the team facility touting a research study he'd heard about. When Donald Trump was elected president in 2016, Smith showed up to a press conference with a safety pin on his shirt, a quiet symbol of support for marginalized groups that he'd learned about from his son's school. "Just kind of everything to do with tolerance," he said. If the latter move surprised anyone, it was only because Smith was rarely opinionated; he was a thoughtful teammate who gave off the vibe of a steady, buttoned-down CFO. As Johnson, a veteran linebacker, later put it: "Alex goes by the book."

The overachiever rep was born at Helix High near San Diego, where Smith's father, Doug, was the principal. Smith quarterbacked the football team (mostly handing off to famed teammate Reggie Bush), served as senior class president, and took so many advanced placement classes that he was working on a master's degree in econ by his third year at the University of Utah. His mother, Pam, sensing his academic potential, had pushed him to think Ivy League, while his father forced him to sign up for a competitive speech class—which is how Smith became a regular at local Rotary Club speech contests, delivering an original oration he'd crafted himself. The topic: overpaid professional athletes.

Nobody figured Smith had much of a chance to be one. His only major scholarship offers came from Utah and Louisville, where his uncle was the head coach. But Smith chose Utah, where he helped revolutionize college football, pioneering the run-pass option (RPO) in Urban Meyer's influential spread offense. The accidental discovery came one day at practice, when a receiver forgot his blocking assignment and Smith adjusted by pulling the handoff back from the running back and flipping a pass to the receiver. In the next decade, the RPO would infiltrate the NFL and make its way to Reid's offense in Kansas City. But first, Smith became an improbable star and the No. 1 pick of the San Francisco 49ers in the 2005 NFL draft, a quarterback whose greatest gift was his discernment. "Unless he knows exactly what's going on, he won't throw it," Meyer said. "He won't just try to guess and take a shot."

Smith spent eight years with the 49ers, which turned into a clown car of regime changes, offensive coordinators, injuries, and labels. He was seen as a bust, a game manager, a survivor, the quarterback forever selected twenty-three picks before Aaron Rodgers. And then in 2011—reborn under new coach Jim Harbaugh—he was suddenly very, very good. He outdueled Drew Brees in the divisional round of the playoffs and led San Francisco to the NFC Championship Game. The next year, the 49ers were once again Super Bowl contenders, and Smith was having the finest season of his career—third in the NFL in passer rating, first in completion percentage—until Rams linebacker Jo-Lonn Dunbar lowered his head and delivered a vicious hit during a short run in Week 10. Smith was concussed, surrendered his job to Colin Kaepernick, and never got it back. Kaepernick, not yet the central figure in a culture war, took over and led the 49ers to the Super Bowl, where they lost to the Baltimore Ravens. Smith was on the field only for the coin toss.

Three weeks later, the 49ers traded him to Kansas City, where Andy Reid was just settling in. The Chiefs desperately needed competence. Smith, ever the accursed QB, needed a home. "We'd love to stick it to everybody who thought we couldn't do it," he said. In the next four years Smith guided the Chiefs to four winning seasons, three postseason appearances, and the franchise's first playoff victory in twenty-two years. He couldn't shake his rep as "Captain

Checkdown," the moniker that conveyed his conservative style. Nor could he win in the playoffs. But unlike most of the retread QBs from San Francisco who had defined the Chiefs for a generation, Alex Smith was something different: He won a lot of games. He was a nice guy. He got it.

If he hadn't, he probably would have been embittered when Reid told him that the Chiefs were drafting Mahomes. The NFL, after all, is full of awkward quarterback-succession plans and icy relationships. For someone like Smith, it felt especially cruel. He had lost his job once, and now he might again. But something funny happened as the 2017 season began and Mahomes prepped for a year as the backup. Reid told Smith to have the best season of his career. Smith met Mahomes and felt like they were "natural friends." He decided he'd do whatever he could to help. He'd be the same person he'd always been.

As Mahomes's godfather, LaTroy Hawkins, would later put it, Alex Smith was "a gift from God."

THE 2017 season was, in most ways, the last one Patrick Mahomes ever had to himself. Most mornings started at 7:15, when he arrived at the facility and met with Mike Kafka, a young, entry-level assistant coach. The official quarterback meetings didn't start for at least another hour, but Mahomes desired extra study, so the two would sit and go over everything: the upcoming game plan, identifying coverages and fronts, the nomenclature and verbiage of Reid's offense. If Mahomes had more questions, he just watched Smith. The relationship had begun in training camp, which is when the competition began, too. Not for the starting job. Everyone knew that was Smith's. But in the minutes between workouts or walk-throughs, the Chiefs' quarterback room would split into teams of two and hold an accuracy challenge—a game in which players would stand at the 5-yard line and attempt to hit the crossbar of the uprights with a throw.

Once you and your partner hit the bar, you'd move back to the 10, then the 15, and so on, and most days Mahomes paired with fellow reserve quarterback Joel Stave while Smith teamed with Tyler Bray. Then one day they found a Frisbee in the facility, and Mahomes stood at the 5-yard line, whipping the Frisbee at the bar in that familiar sidearm style. The thing about Mahomes, of course, is that even when he's tossing a football, he can look like he's throwing a forehand Frisbee; his arm lowers, and the ball comes out sidearm, and it's like he's back in Texas, playing shortstop or third base.

One day during camp, Mahomes, Stave, and rookie receiver Gehrig Dieter headed out to polish their Frisbee skills at a local disc golf course. None of them were that good, but there was something about the way Mahomes's arm worked, the way he made a little progress every day, the way he could conceive of throws that other quarterbacks wouldn't even see. In one drill during camp, the quarterbacks were supposed to scramble to their left, toward the sideline, before flipping their hips, throwing across their body, and backpedaling out of the play. It was an awkward drill. Mahomes made it look easy. "Every day in practice," Stave recalled. "There'd be three or four throws where you'd kind of step back and say, 'I don't know if I make that one.'"

When Mahomes started running the scout team during the regular season, he started pulling out his no-look repertoire on quick slant passes. The only other person Smith could remember doing anything like that was Brett Favre. "I'd be standing off to the right and Coach Reid would just be sitting there," said Matt Nagy, the Chiefs' offensive coordinator. "After a play, he'd just look to his left and kind of smile." The thing about scout-team quarterbacks is they're not really supposed to win. They execute a script of the upcoming opponent's plays. The defense knows what's coming. It's an orchestrated rehearsal, designed to give the defense reps, and the usual result is a lot of interceptions and ugly plays, mostly because the receivers are practice squad guys and backups and nobody is ever open. But then Mahomes started running scout teams and the no-look passes started, and the Chiefs' defense started getting pissed. *Can you even fucking do that?* "He used to torch us at times," Johnson said. "We used to get in trouble."

One day, Mahomes was mimicking an RPO used by a mobile quarterback. Bob Sutton, the Chiefs' defensive coordinator, told the defense what was coming. Johnson, playing inside linebacker, had a slot receiver to his side. Mahomes was supposed to read Johnson. If the linebacker sat in space, he'd hand the ball to the running back. If he didn't, he'd pull it back and look to pass. Johnson knew this, which meant he planned to sit in space for a quick second, baiting Mahomes to hand it off; then he'd attack the running lane. He just didn't want Mahomes to pass. Except Mahomes did pull the ball. He ignored the read and unleashed a dart to the slot. Johnson should have been in perfect position to defend the play, but the pass was too quick, too good. It whistled past his shoulder, into the arms of the receiver. "I told you the RPO was coming!" a coach yelled. Johnson couldn't believe how quickly the ball had come out.

"I can remember Coach Sutton cussing at us, 'Hey, we gotta get right!'" Johnson said. "It was like: 'OK, Coach, I get it. We gotta stop this quarterback, and we gotta stop their plays. We are stopping their plays, but we can't stop this quarterback.'"

Sometimes Mahomes made no sense. His play was so experimental and free-form that Justin Houston, the Chiefs' star pass rusher, would yell at Sutton, *He can't do that to us!* Not that Reid was concerned. He had an old adage, one he used to tell quarterback Donovan McNabb when he was in Philly: "Keep shooting, buddy." *Just keep firing.* Reid would tell his players to think of the field as a workshop, a place to generate ideas and subvert the rules of the game. "Let your mind go. Expand. Who said we can't do something?" Which was perfect, because Mahomes just happened to be a quarterback who thought he could do anything. "Those at-risk throws at training camp were all green-lit," said Brad Childress, the Chiefs' assistant head coach that season. "Typically in a seven-on-seven [period] you can always throw underneath, and you can always throw the checkdown. Andy didn't want to see that shit. He wanted to see him take chances."

When Mahomes and Smith sat together in the quarterback room,

Childress would often watch as a coach pulled up a film clip and let the quarterbacks break down the opposing defense. While Mahomes loved to color outside the lines, Smith had grown into an experienced, disciplined quarterback who stayed within the box. If Mahomes had an idea, Smith might politely point out what he did not see. It was an organic bond. Smith appreciated that Mahomes was sincere and deferential; Mahomes admired how confident and professional Smith was. If Smith was conflicted about mentoring his replacement, he never let it show. He just kept letting Mahomes in.

Of course, sometimes Mahomes could seem like he was in a world of his own, which was not so much a judgment of his disposition but a reflection of his talent. One day during a meeting, a coach put a play up on the screen and asked the quarterbacks to break down the coverage reads and decide which receiver to target. *Would you hit the "over" or the "under" here?* The "over" would have been an 18-yard throw to a receiver; the "under" might have been something like 4 yards. Mahomes looked at the screen, considered the different factors, then came to a decision. "'Shit,'" Childress recalled him saying. "'I'd throw the post.'"

"I'd look at him like, 'Fucking what?'" Childress said.

The post was the third option—a deep ball over the middle, way out over the top of everything—and when Childress looked closer, peering at the screen, he realized it was indeed open. The quarter safety was standing flat-footed. The receiver had a step. It just required a quarterback who could put it on the money from 65 yards out. "A huck," as Smith would put it.

Soon enough, everyone understood: Mahomes would always let his personality show.

ONE month after the ceremony on the Plaza, on December 24, 2017, Alex Smith helped the Chiefs clinch the AFC West title in the penultimate game of the season. The victory over the Miami Dolphins locked the Chiefs into the No. 4 seed in the AFC playoffs, which meant that the final game of the season didn't really matter. So Reid opted to rest Smith and give Kansas City the perfect Christmas present: Mahomes would make his first career start in Week 17 against the Broncos.

On a freezing Sunday in Denver, Pat Mahomes Sr., wife Trisha, and some friends arrived and found refuge and warmth in a bar at Sports Authority Field, where another fan recognized Pat Sr. and invited the group to spend the game in a suite. It was from that vantage point that Pat Sr. watched his son jog onto the field for the Chiefs' first drive, take control of the huddle, and—three plays later—hit tight end Demetrius Harris over the middle on third-and-10 for a gain of 51 yards.

Nobody in Kansas City had seen Mahomes play since training camp, which meant nobody had seen the scout-team magic, but even then, some of the Chiefs' veterans weren't sure how Mahomes would fare. His practice reps were still somewhat limited. They were playing a bitter rival on the road. No quarterback drafted by the Chiefs had won a game since 1987. But then Mahomes started to play, and it was like a glimpse into the future, a crystal ball of possibilities: On third-and-14 early in the second quarter, he evaded a blitz in the pocket—slipping out of the grasp of defensive back Will Parks—and fired a strike to receiver Albert Wilson for 17 yards. On the sideline, punter Dustin Colquitt started to realize what he was watching. "That's when I knew," he said later. "I was like '*God, this kid is special.*'"

Mahomes showed touch and poise and accuracy and schoolyard genius. He threw a bad interception in the first quarter, but then turned around and helped the Chiefs take a 24–10 lead. He exited the game in the fourth quarter, allowing third-string quarterback Tyler Bray to get some reps. But the lead quickly disappeared, and the coaches sent him back in with 2:45 left and the game tied at 24–24.

It was moments later, with 1:44 left, that Kansas City witnessed the witchcraft that had pissed Justin Houston off all year. On first-and-10 from the 32, Mahomes took a snap in the shotgun, saw the pocket start to collapse, and started to drift back to his right, away from the advancing defenders and all the way back to his own 17. If you had never heard of Patrick Mahomes and had just started watching the game at that precise moment, it might have looked like one of the most idiotic plays of the year. But as he approached the sideline, he planted his right foot in the ground, executed a little jump off one leg, and (OH MY GOD!) heaved a pass that traveled 27 yards and hit receiver Demarcus Robinson in the chest along the sideline. "The quarterback of the future," said Von Miller, the Broncos' star linebacker.

The Chiefs finished off the drive and left town with a 27–24 victory. Mahomes piled up 284 yards passing. The next week, Smith returned to the field for the playoffs, and the Chiefs fell to the Tennessee Titans in the AFC Wild Card round, squandering a 21–3 lead at Arrowhead Stadium, a civic tease before a familiar comedown. The next day, the city was in mourning: angry, exhausted, coming to grips with a sixth straight playoff loss at Arrowhead Stadium, the latest heartbreaking moment in a long and miserable playoff history, and in the afterglow of defeat, Brett Veach met with Andy Reid.

It was time to let the kid do his thing.

THERE are endless ways for a young quarterback to charm a city: Patrick Mahomes started with jorts and a cutoff baseball jersey. It was May 18, 2018, nearly four months after the Chiefs agreed to trade Alex Smith to Washington for a third-round pick and defensive back Kendall Fuller, and Mahomes had been invited to the KC Masterpiece 400 at the Kansas Speedway in Kansas City, Kansas.

To that point, even after the Broncos game, Mahomes was still more of a conceptual idea than a real phenom. He had been in town for nearly a year, but people didn't know, for instance, that Mahomes's culinary guilty pleasure was ketchup or that he was an unabashed sports nerd. They weren't yet fascinated with the contours and influences of his raspy, twangy Kermit the Frog voice. What Kansas City was learning, though, was that Mahomes has a way of connecting with his audience. He possessed the most important gift for any superstar athlete: People like him.

So on a spring day in 2018, as NASCAR arrived in Kansas City and Mahomes prepared to join the party, he planned out the easiest way to fit in: He put on a pair of jean shorts and a cutoff jersey of the Kansas City T-Bones, a small-time independent-league baseball team that played its home games in a ballpark adjacent to the Kansas Speedway. It was a little like wearing the T-shirt of a barely beloved (and pretty shitty) local indie band.

Mahomes could have stopped there, but the coolest athletes in sports understand how to accessorize, so Mahomes added sunglasses and a FootJoy visor.

The city was smitten.

THE GAMBLER'S SON

On the day after Christmas 1962, Lamar Hunt arrived in Kansas City, walked outside the Hotel Muehlebach, and waited for his ride. He was there on a double-secret mission, one complete with code names, covert intel, and clandestine recon, but before he could even worry about being noticed, a big blue limousine pulled up to the curb. Inside was a three-hundred-pound man in his early sixties with pale and jowly cheeks, slicked-back hair, and a thunderous baritone voice enhanced only by the twenty cigars he smoked each day. His name was H. Roe Bartle, the mayor of Kansas City, and he wanted to show Hunt around.

The ground rules: Nobody could know. Hunt was the thirty-year-old owner of the Dallas Texans and the precocious cofounder of the American Football League, the fledgling arriviste of professional football—the upstart challenger to the National Football League. Just three days earlier, Hunt's Dallas Texans had won the AFL Championship, beating the Houston Oilers in a double-overtime thriller watched by 56 million viewers on ABC. To many, the audience signaled the arrival of the three-year-old league. But Hunt had realized something else: The Texans needed to move.

In 1962, the city of Dallas was not yet a sprawling megalopolis with a global brand—J.R. Ewing, futuristic skyline, Troy Aikman—but it was a city with a rich future, propped up by oil wealth, Texas Instruments, and a deepening love affair with football. In truth, Dallas would have seemed like the ideal place on earth to market professional

137

football, which was still trying to catch up with the tradition-rich college game. The problem was, it had one team too many.

Like the Texans, the Dallas Cowboys were three years old. They owed their very existence to Lamar Hunt, who had tried to bring an NFL team to Dallas, only to be rebuffed by the provincial lords of the NFL, who were mostly clustered on the East Coast and weren't interested in expansion in Dallas. Hunt turned his focus to creating a rival league, cobbling together a group of billionaires—forever known as the "Foolish Club"—and starting the AFL in 1960. The NFL, realizing its mistake, responded by putting the expansion Cowboys in Dallas. The ensuing feud between the Texans and the Cowboys (and all the lawsuits and billable hours that followed) was bitter and costly.

The feud lent Lamar Hunt a brash persona. He was really one of the most practical, penny-pinching rich kids imaginable, the kind of mild-mannered intellectual who would double-check every restaurant receipt and show up to AFL meetings with only one of his dress shoes properly repaired. He wasn't *actually* foolish. So when the NFL's television contracts kept swelling, giving the Cowboys the upper hand, and the Texans still struggled financially in 1962—the year they won the championship—he knew he needed a new home.

Bartle, the cartoonishly large and ebullient mayor of Kansas City, had heard all the rumors. To Bartle, this was great news. Earlier that year, he had wined and dined a wealthy man from Maryland named Warren Lockwood, who planned to make a formal application to bring an AFL team to Kansas City. ("I like the public spirit of the people here," Lockwood told reporters.) Lockwood wanted to sell stock in the team to local citizens, à la the Green Bay Packers. Bartle threw his public support behind the bid, which went up against groups from New Orleans and Atlanta. But then the AFL—and its guiding force, Lamar Hunt—did an about-face, pushing expansion into the future. In reality, Bartle realized the best way to land an NFL team was to get to Hunt. So in the fall of 1962, he made a surprise trip to Dallas to introduce himself.

There was no telling what Hunt would think of Kansas City in the winter of 1962. Twelfth Street, the beating heart of the city's jazz club scene, had atrophied into a seedier red-light district. (The nearby Folly Theater was hosting an exotic burlesque show starring "April Flowers" and "Bubbles Champagne.") The Stockyards had been decimated by a cataclysmic flood in 1951. The Missouri River had swelled over forty-foot-tall levees, engulfing the Livestock Exchange Building, railroads, warehouses, and cattle pens in twenty feet of water, leaving a rancid aroma of mud, debris, and animal remains that had lingered in the summer heat for weeks. The event marked the beginning of the collapse of Kansas City's livestock industry. A mile up the bluffs in downtown, shoppers still flocked to Petticoat Lane, an assemblage of mid-rise department stores and jewelry shops adorned with gaudy signage along Eleventh Street, but the crowds on the sidewalks were thinning. Mighty Italianate Renaissance and terra-cotta skyscrapers had begun to show their wear. "Downtown buildings are grimy, drab," noted an influential real estate agent. The city, which had been the twentieth biggest in the country in 1950—population 456,000— was now just the twenty-seventh biggest, its population plateauing at 475,000 in 1960.

Nichols Land and the rest of the suburbs were growing rapidly, and the city had attracted the Kansas City Athletics in 1955, pulling the bottom-feeder from its previous home in Philadelphia. But it wasn't clear if Lamar Hunt cared about any of that.

HUNT was, at his core, a Texan, the son of Haroldson Lafayette Hunt, one of the most successful and richest wildcatters in American history. The elder Hunt had started out in the cotton business before parlaying some poker winnings into an entrée to the oil business. He then struck it rich in East Texas in 1930, after borrowing $30,000 in cash to acquire an enormous portion of the East Texas Oil Field from Columbus Marion "Dad" Joiner, who had discovered black gold on the farm of a woman named Daisy Bradford. Joiner, a self-taught promoter, didn't realize what he had. The elder Hunt promised an additional $1.3 million if enough oil was found. The deal yielded the largest petroleum reserve in the history of the contiguous United States.

When Lamar Hunt came along two years later, the family had settled in Tyler, Texas, where they lived in a big white house on Charnwood Street, just a short drive across town from where Patrick Mahomes would learn to throw a football. When the family relocated to Dallas in the late 1930s, Lamar Hunt witnessed his first football game at the Cotton Bowl. The marquee draw was Texas Tech University.

The undefeated Red Raiders were upset by St. Mary's—a small program cast as David—and Hunt was hooked. He spent his childhood scouring box scores in the local newspaper and listening to games. He rode the bench at SMU. He was studious and cerebral and so consumed by the very conception of sports that he later deemed it an unexplainable creative impulse within. He was not an artist. Nor did he write. He had another outlet. "I make up games," he said.

The other thing about Lamar Hunt was that he didn't drink. Which is about the only thing he had in common with Roe Bartle. Well, except for the fact that Hunt needed a city for his football team, and Bartle was desperate for one.

ROE Bartle was inaugurated as the forty-seventh mayor in Kansas City history on Monday, April 11, 1955. The day before, *The Kansas City Star* had splashed an all-caps headline across its front page: "WE GO BIG LEAGUE TUESDAY!" Bartle didn't have much to do with it. He had been elected in late March, just weeks before the Philadelphia Athletics officially moved to Kansas City and opened their first baseball season at a remodeled Municipal Stadium.

The headlines ignored the Kansas City Monarchs—the Negro Leagues powerhouse that had once been among the most talented baseball teams in the world with players like Satchel Paige and Jackie

Robinson—but they reflected an emerging divide in American life: There were cities that had professional sports, and there were those that didn't. People in Kansas City had understood this for years. Once upon a time, you could build a boulevard system, host a political convention, or erect a monument to build civic clout. Kansas City had tried all of those. By the early 1950s, there was another way: You needed sports.

The city's latest crusade had begun in earnest in 1953, when local newspapers and civic leaders took up the cause. The breakthrough came two years later, when the city lured the struggling Philadelphia Athletics. To satisfy their new team, the city built an upper deck on what was then called Blues Stadium, where the *Kansas City Call* editor Roy Wilkins had once sat in segregated seating. That it could pull it off in ninety days, locals said, was just further proof of the city's spirit.

Into the picture stepped Mayor Roe Bartle, who spent his first full day in office at a baseball game, witnessing the city revel in the A's home-opener victory over the Detroit Tigers. If ever there were a mayor who understood the power of branding, it was Bartle, a former college football player who had grown up in Virginia, gone into law, and found his way in the 1920s to Kansas City, where he carved a career out of two passions: the Boys Scouts of America (a movement taking root in a nation becoming less agrarian) and speaking very loudly. Bartle had become chief area executive of the Boy Scouts in 1928. Inspired by an earlier scouting experience in Wyoming—and his encounters with the local Arapaho tribe—he founded a Boy Scouts honor society (the Tribe of Mic-O-Say), which co-opted the culture and customs of Native tribes and turned them into scouting cosplay. Scouts would attend camps and earn the rank of "Brave" or "Warrior." Bartle took the nickname "Chief Lone Bear," which came, he claimed, from a relationship with an Arapaho chieftain of the same name. After a while, everyone just called him Chief. (He later ended his inaugural address by giving the Boy Scout Oath.)

When he wasn't growing the Boy Scouts, Bartle excelled on the public speaking circuit. He was—as one journalist wrote—an "orator of the old breed," charming and buoyant, with a salesman's delivery and a psychologist's ability to read a room. He owned a home in Nichols's Armour Hills. He liked to work in his office with his tie off and the top three buttons of his dress shirt splayed open. Every year, he reread Hugo's *Les Misérables* as an act of concentration. When he ran for mayor in 1955, he rolled to victory on a platform to move away from the machine factions that controlled city hall.

Bartle's two terms offered the usual mix of good local government (economic expansion, desegregation of city hospitals) and bad (he tended to focus more on speeches than on policy). He was, however, the ideal mayor to hard-sell Lamar Hunt and the Texans. He introduced Hunt to business leaders. He obeyed the rules of secrecy, offering code names to both Hunt ("Mr. Lamar") and Texans executive Jack Steadman ("Jack X.") And when Bartle finally brought Hunt to meet the city council, he wasn't shy about how much he wanted professional football.

In an account of the meeting by *Sports Illustrated*'s Dan Jenkins in 1963, Bartle told the council: "Gentleman, you have known me a long time and you have never known me to make love to another man. But Mr. Hunt, I have courted you and wooed you like a princess, have I not?"

IN the end, Kansas City got its football team by acting like Kansas City: It threw everything it had at the project. The city offered the use of Municipal Stadium for just two dollars for the first two seasons of a seven-year lease. It promised to build more seats, a team office building, and a new practice facility. And it provided a sweetener: The deal would not become official unless the city sold twenty-five thousand season tickets by May 15, 1963—a goal that was more than double the previous AFL record for season tickets and three times the league average. "At first, we were cool on the proposition," Hunt said, "but we have had reason to change our minds."

The chamber of commerce headed up a ticket drive. Fifty-two local companies would purchase at least fifty season tickets. Ray Evans, a former Kansas All-American and president of Traders National Bank, sent his children door-to-door hawking tickets in J.C. Nichols's old neighborhoods. The local boosters would stall out at under fifteen thousand tickets, but Hunt had seen enough. The Texans were headed to Kansas City. Their quarterback, a former Purdue star named Len Dawson, wondered why. Wasn't it a cow town?

The only thing left was the name, and Hunt, at first, wanted to keep "Texans." He figured the Lakers did not change their name when they moved from Minneapolis to Los Angeles. Same with the Brooklyn Dodgers. The Texans had just won a championship, too.

Considering all the geographic shenanigans that had dogged the city since its founding, perhaps it wasn't the craziest idea to put a professional football team in Missouri and name them the Kansas City Texans. But Hunt relented. The local newspaper cosponsored a naming contest, and submissions included the Mules, Royals, Steers, Plainsmen, and Mo-Kans. Hunt liked Chiefs, a tribute to Roe Bartle.

"It has local significance," Hunt told reporters. "The Kansas City area was once a dwelling place for at least four different Indian tribes. It has class and is short to appear in headlines."

It was not the last time the city considered the name of its football team.

THE FREEWAY

Municipal Stadium was surrounded by homes: Victorians and Colonials and Shirtwaist houses with limestone porches. You could see them from the bleachers. A few fortunate fans who drove to games nabbed spots in a parking lot (there wasn't room for thousands of spaces in a residential neighborhood), and everybody else parked their cars on the street or on somebody's front lawn. Where Diane Charity lived, about five blocks south of Municipal Stadium, they charged for the space. Her parents had plunked down $11,000 for a home with gorgeous bay windows in 1962, the year before the Chiefs' first season in Kansas City.

Charity was twelve, a voracious reader and a Girl Scout. She and her friends often wandered by Municipal Stadium, listening to the sounds of baseball, football, and, on one September night in 1964, a Beatles concert. Afterward they would scurry along Vine Street, still the anchor of the neighborhood. There were local grocery stores and drugstores and some of the last jazz clubs to survive the end of the open-city era, like the Mardi Gras. Arthur Bryant's, the legendary barbecue spot where Chiefs players would join fans in line for ribs, was around the corner on Brooklyn Avenue. Charity's grandmother, who had been taking her to canvass for elections since she could walk, lived nearby at Twenty-Fifth and Flora, and her Catholic school, Annunciation, was just up the street. "We didn't have to go out of the neighborhood for anything," Charity said.

Of course, they were also boxed in. FHA-backed loans, blockbusting, white flight, and gerrymandered school boundaries redrawn so white families could avoid integration had added permanent ink to the redlining of J.C. Nichols and other developers, turning Kansas City into two distinct cities divided by Troost Avenue, a street named for prominent physician and slave owner Benoist Troost. The mostly white, prosperous side, developed by Nichols, was to the west of Troost. The mostly Black side, underserved by the city and the school district, encompassed Troost and everything to the east. *The Star* emphasized the border in classified listings, advertising apartments and houses from the J.C. Nichols Company and other real estate firms as "West of Troost." Between 1950 and 1970 nearly one hundred thousand white people left the East Side, while more than sixty thousand Black residents moved in, including Charity's family.

The migration patterns meant that a large portion of the white population would never go downtown or to the nearby core neighborhoods, aside perhaps from commuting for work or attending a sporting event at Municipal Stadium. City leaders realized they needed to move quickly to accommodate the spread, which was why, almost as soon as Charity moved to Kansas City, she heard neighbors sharing an ominous refrain: "The freeway's coming through. The freeway's coming through."

J.C. Nichols had an epiphany before he died. He expressed concern that American cities were falling apart. How could a Kansas City—a Chicago, a Baltimore—survive with hundreds of thousands of taxpayers fleeing to the next town over? Nichols was still the young man who visited Europe and came home enthralled by Paris's "*rue* life," believing the core of every city should be left alone, bypassed by major highways and hooked up to quality public transportation. But he also saw how his suburban developments had shifted Americans' habits. Perhaps, he reasoned in a speech in New York City, "planning for permanence" should mean preparing a city for a wave of drive-through commuters, making it "reasonably easy for such customers to reach our downtown areas."

To sort out these issues, Nichols cofounded the Urban Land Institute, yet another powerful real estate lobbying group, and guided it in the early 1940s. The Urban Land Institute's developers used the term "decentralization," which came to describe the exodus to the suburbs, and they blamed the cities themselves, believing blighted neighborhoods adjacent to downtown were fueling the migration. They failed to admit the overcrowded conditions and run-down homes of many neighborhoods stemmed from their industry's government-subsidized promotion of restricted suburbs and neglect of the city. "Blight" was a nebulous term to define, anyway. There wasn't a textbook example. (New York City identified Greenwich Village as blighted.) "Blighted" more or less came to mean areas that didn't resemble the restricted developments promulgated by developers like Nichols. Some of these areas featured homes that were nearly falling apart. Others featured a mix of races and social classes, grocery stores built on the same streets as row houses, and delis and jazz bars within spitting distance of warehouses. They were a lot like what you would've found around Eighteenth and Vine, around Municipal Stadium.

In late spring 1942, the Urban Land Institute disseminated a paper proposing the elimination of blighted areas as its solution for saving the American city. The idea was for the federal government to subsidize the destruction and let cities and private developers work in tandem to plan new buildings. It proved persuasive. Harry Truman signed the Housing Act of 1949, ushering in the era of urban renewal. Related policies soon led to cities knocking down the old neighborhoods and replacing them with public housing and freeways. The federal government even offered to kick in 90 percent of highway construction costs as part of the Federal Highway Act of 1956.

To leaders across the country, the only way to save cities was clear: eliminate blight, rebuild new housing and businesses, and offer high-speed routes into downtown from the suburbs. Doomed as this all sounds, the concept of public housing held promise. It was originally envisioned as temporary housing for families on the cusp of the middle class, a way to drive upward mobility and future homeownership. It was seen as a potential fresh start for millions of Americans by a wide range of activists and politicians. But success stories were rare. Local governments usually followed the wishes of real estate lobbyists and made public housing a last resort for the poorest Americans. They also segregated the public housing by race and typically isolated it from middle-class neighborhoods and jobs. Many of the new homes were inadequate from the start, and not nearly enough were constructed, leaving displaced people with nowhere to go. By one estimate, roughly one unit of low-income housing went up for every four units demolished. James Baldwin was interviewed for a PBS documentary in 1963, and he offered a famous definition of "urban renewal." "It means Negro removal," Baldwin said. "That is what it means."

Kansas City was ready for urban renewal long before the ink from Truman's pen dried. In 1940, the city hired L.P. Cookingham, later hailed as the "dean" of big-city managers. Nicknamed "Spike," Cookingham had been a bruising all-state lineman and tailback in high school—he might have suited up as a college athlete if not for World War I. To observers, he had the same athletic build as Tom Pendergast. But he had opposite goals for the city. He immediately cut two thousand jobs from the machine's bloated payroll and balanced the city's budget. He quintupled the geographical area of the city through annexations and broke ground on an international airport. He foresaw the potential of urban renewal, delineating several neighborhoods as slums in 1946—nearly half of them featuring large numbers of Black residents at a time when Black people made up 12 percent of the city's population—and starting to design a comprehensive highway plan in 1947, years before the Feds offered to pony up for the cement. Cookingham's new-look Kansas City would have two highways that both severed the heart of downtown and encircled it like a giant concrete fence. With new roads and interstates, officials saw no use for the streetcar, and the city shuttered the last line in 1957.

Cookingham's first project was something called the Intercity Freeway. (Today it's known as the North Loop of I-70.) In a narrow strip north of downtown, bulldozers toppled boarding homes, warehouses, and mom-and-pop shops, leaving ashen rubble in the wake: the Dresden of the Plains. "The stranger visiting Kansas City for the first time," wrote one reporter, "blinks as soon as he crosses the airport bridge and heads south on Delaware. Is this London? Had the German bombers passed the night before?" When the highway was finished, in 1957, a crowd of curious onlookers and a few wealthy luminaries, including William Zeckendorf, the developer of the United Nations headquarters in New York City, watched eleven government officials snip a golden ribbon—using golden scissors—to open the freeway to an onrush of cars.

Zeckendorf believed Kansas City was among a class of "more enlightened cities" primed for "a great urban renaissance." The American Institute of Architects gave the city a citation of honor in 1959 for its urban renewal highway and housing plans (a prize awarded just fifteen times in one-hundred-plus years). But inside the affected neighborhoods, community leaders saw what was coming before the first wrecking balls hit. Black residents protested the location of the public housing throughout the 1950s, fearing they'd get short shrift. They were right. Wayne Miner Court, one of the largest new housing complexes for Black Kansas Citians, was plagued by lax security and maintenance and never more than 60 percent occupied. Two elevators got stuck the day it was dedicated in 1960.

Wayne Miner went up a few blocks from Twelfth Street and Vine. Eight years earlier, Los Angeles songwriters Jerry Leiber and Mike Stoller, who had never been to Kansas City but geeked out over Charlie Parker and Count Basie records, immortalized the intersection in the song "Kansas City." Wilbert Harrison released the most famous version of the song in 1959, as Twelfth and Vine's clubs and businesses crumbled under urban renewal. At Eighteenth and Vine, many old clubs and juke joints were destroyed, replaced by heavy industry. "There are plenty of musicians to keep Kansas City jumping like the old days," lamented a longtime trumpet player in 1965. "But there's no place left to jump."

The wave of destruction spread. Thousands of Kansas City families were displaced for urban renewal and highway building in the 1950s and early '60s, from the Italian and Irish American North End to the Mexican American Westside, damaged so badly by the Southwest Trafficway and the I-35 that the federal government described the area as "no longer a viable residential community."

To complete the Downtown Loop, Kansas City even plowed near the edge of West Terrace Park, a lush hillside punctuated by red-roofed observation towers—an al fresco Italian villa in the heart of America. It was near the location where Sarah and Kersey Coates went for Sunday walks and dreamed of the city of the future.

BOXING off the entirety of downtown with highways wasn't enough for Kansas City. As national leaders like Baldwin and Jane Jacobs questioned the merits of urban renewal and freeway building, the city's leaders kept pushing for a final interstate, an artery that would puncture Kansas City like no other. This was the road Diane Charity and her neighbors kept hearing rumors about.

Known as the South Midtown Freeway, it had been featured in Cookingham's original 1951 highway plan as a way to extend US Highway 71 into the city. It was supposed to stretch as wide as eight lanes, traversing from the southern suburbs to downtown, blazing a path through the East Side along the way. The thought of yet another highway seemed like a cruel joke. So many people had already been displaced by the city's years of construction on the East Side, and lots of middle-class Black families were just starting to feel at home, finally breaking south past Twenty-Seventh Street to more spacious, comfortable houses. Where would they go, given the illicit real estate practices cordoning off much of the city, if another highway went up?

But the South Midtown Freeway wasn't a done deal. On the other side of Troost, talks heated up about an entirely different highway: the Country Club Freeway.

The city trotted out the idea as an alternative. It would run six lanes across and trace an old streetcar route that zipped through the center of Nichols Land. Exit ramps would deposit cars next to the Plaza and a shopping center near Armour Hills. The benefits were evident. The Country Club route would pass by more growing suburbs and outlying city neighborhoods than the South Midtown. Officials were split on which route would handle the most traffic and best serve the city, but the Country Club route required less destruction. The South Midtown route would need to plow over block after block of houses and shops. In the Country Club District, houses were already set back from the old streetcar route, leaving more undeveloped land for a submerged freeway. The city council learned from an engineer that houses could be saved along most of the route: The people living nearby would have a noisier neighborhood, but they would still have their homes.

Ironically, in a move that would have flummoxed J.C. Nichols, the Nichols Company expressed support for the freeway. Company president Miller Nichols, J.C.'s elder son, thought a Country Club District highway would benefit the developing suburbs, and he believed the "consequences of not providing adequate traffic arteries for our city would be far worse and more damaging to the overall area than would be any harmful effects" to the Country Club District. The boosterism tracked with the rallying cry of urban renewal, of highway building writ large, which was community and interconnection, destruction that portended a grander future—a phoenix *sprawling* from the ashes.

But these communal benefits were hardly on the minds of the district's residents. In June 1961, they sauntered into a downtown

courtroom, stretching its capacity to the limit, and they were represented by enough legal minds to fill an NFL roster—some fifty attorneys paid to argue that their clients should be compensated for a
future loss in property values because of a highway that hadn't yet
been built. The judge was not sympathetic, but the dispute engendered more support for the Country Club District residents. During
the next few years, they hired professional spokespersons to speak at
city council hearings and used their attorneys to brainstorm more legal objections and voice their fears that a freeway would divide the
area in two and place their children in peril. *Wednesday Magazine*, a
Country Club District publication, pondered why the city would "destroy the cultural value of a beautiful part of the city for this purpose,
especially when a freeway could be located . . . in areas where property
values are not so high."

In 1964, the state highway commission approved both routes.
Still, most politicians were leaning toward building a highway as far
to the east as possible, to avoid, as one city councilman put it, echoing
the chorus of Country Club District residents, "demoralizing effects
on property values." As talks went down to the wire, a key regional
planner warned Kansas City leaders that the South Midtown Freeway
would have the same effect as a catastrophic flood, potentially displacing six thousand families. He later said city officials refused to respond
to his list of objections, and then waited until he was out of town to
make their decision official. That decision, made in the fall of 1965,
was to pick the South Midtown. The freeway *was* coming through the
East Side. Like the Country Club District residents, the East Side
community pushed back. They didn't have fifty lawyers, but they filed
a petition at city hall.

The politicians who voted for the South Midtown Freeway talked
about complications with budgets—the cost estimate of the South
Midtown route was cheaper by about $15 million—and with a legal
ruling that spoiled the city's chances to use eminent domain to secure
the route along the old streetcar tracks. But to many observers, the

justifications didn't add up. The cost of the South Midtown route quickly ballooned past the estimate for the Country Club Freeway, and the city could have purchased the old streetcar route from a local transit agency in the early 1960s. (Eventually the transit agency regained control, and the streetcar route was converted into a running trail.) Bruce R. Watkins, who cofounded the civil rights organization Freedom Inc. in 1961 and became the first Black man elected to the Kansas City Council, gave a blunt assessment of what swayed the decision-makers to nix the Country Club Freeway: "The affluent people of that area protested and the route was moved eastward."

In 1966, state surveyors descended on the East Side with notebooks and tape measures. They inspected houses, crunched numbers, and made lowball offers, explaining that they would eventually seize the property—might as well sell now. After a couple of years, the picture that came into focus was a Prairie Village in reverse: developed middle-class neighborhoods transformed into dirt. Houses became craters. Weeds burst through roads and sidewalks. Some seventeen churches, three schools, eighty-seven businesses, 1,500 houses, 250 duplexes, and 700 apartments were razed. "We had a beautiful neighborhood," recalled Carmaletta Williams, whose grandparents cut hair for neighbors and hosted gatherings on the porch of a Fifty-Fifth Street home in the freeway's path. "And then they came through, displaced all those people."

Left behind was a gash that ran for miles in length and was as wide as a football field, the emptiness interrupted every so often by someone who held on until the bitter end. Adell Outley, who had been displaced by the construction of the Downtown Loop, fought for her new house at Thirty-Second and Michigan—"for my rights"—into the 1970s, for as long as she could. Alvin Brooks, a young civil rights leader who headed the city's Department of Human Relations, viewed the damage from a police helicopter. To him, it looked like "an area under siege."

The NAACP estimated some ten thousand people would lose their homes because of the South Midtown Freeway (slightly more than the state's estimate of 7,400), most of them African Americans, who numbered around 80,000 at the start of the 1960s in Kansas City. Some middle-class Black residents, barred from going west of Troost or to many suburbs, were forced into substandard housing and made to sell their homes for less than half their appraised value. "Many of the properties," Watkins said at the time, "have been stolen."

THE highway route missed the house where Diane Charity lived by half a mile. Many other residents, including Charity's grandmother, Comer Elizabeth White, weren't as lucky. White's Flora Avenue block, where everybody knew everybody, was destroyed. She had spent the last few months of her life wondering whether her home could be saved, and the state bought it a few weeks after she died, in December 1967. Charity carried away vinyl albums—Thelonious Monk and Ramsey Lewis and Miles Davis—before the bulldozers came.

It was one of several experiences Charity had dealing with injustice in her childhood, and she had learned a certain way to react. When a nun at school incorrectly accused her of stealing a pair of gloves, Charity decided that she would never take the blame for anything that wasn't her fault. When she and her mother, Edna Mae Stiggers, who was a member of the NAACP, learned that many Kansas City restaurants wouldn't serve African Americans, they protested. And when somebody deposited leaflets out of a plane warning the residents of her neighborhood not to align with Martin Luther King Jr., she brushed off their threat.

The way Charity saw it, you could face injustice and bullying and be overcome by fear, or you could fight and "really raise more hell." Charity vowed to choose the latter.

EVOLUTION

At some point in his life, Patrick Mahomes realized he was not fast. He could heave a football 65 yards from his knees, he had a feathery jumper on the basketball court, and he swung a golf club with such a delirious mix of clubhead speed and coordination that he once nearly reached the green on the tenth hole at Hollytree Country Club in Tyler from 310 yards away (the ball instead landed on a golf cart belonging to the next group). But no, Mahomes was not fast—at least not by the standards of the world-class speedsters who zoom across an NFL field. When he worked out at the NFL Scouting Combine in 2017, he ran the 40-yard dash in 4.8 seconds, the same time once recorded by Peyton Manning, a six-feet-five pocket passer known for his statuesque athleticism, and slower than one clocked by retired NFL quarterback Michael Vick as he approached his forty-first birthday.

Mahomes, in time, came to accept (and even poke fun at) his perceived lack of elite speed. Like Achilles, the hero of the Trojan War, he had one glaring imperfection, a kinetic foible that could perhaps be blamed on his "elongated calves," a muscular shape he noticed and could never quite seem to change.

The amazing thing about Mahomes's lack of speed, however, was not that he could still play quarterback at such a high level. Plenty of classic QBs—like Manning—fell into the genre of big and plodding. No, it was that Mahomes's design flaw became the catalyst for an evolutionary adaptation, akin to how a blind man might thrive on his other senses. Somehow, Mahomes turned his "slowness" into a superpower.

As the 2018 NFL season approached in Kansas City, there was so much hype on Mahomes that nobody was thinking about any of this. The focus was on his arm, not his feet. But when the Chiefs opened the season against the Los Angeles Chargers on September 9, 2018, something happened that cannot be fully explained, much in the same way that quantum mechanics cannot describe what happened after the big bang, in the earliest moments of the known universe. It was like a football explosion—a singularity, really—a blast of energy that sent shock waves across the NFL. In the first game of his first full season, Mahomes tossed four touchdown passes in a 38–28 victory, and coaches and executives across the league perked up: Uh-oh.

The next Sunday, on the day before his twenty-third birthday, Mahomes threw another six touchdown passes on the road in Pittsburgh, tying Len Dawson's single-game franchise record. In his third game, he threw for 314 yards and three touchdowns (including one missile on a mad scramble) as the Chiefs stayed perfect against San Francisco. But it was during Mahomes's fourth game—a return trip to Denver to face the Broncos on *Monday Night Football*—that people started to ponder whether the quarterback position would ever be the same.

The Denver–Kansas City rivalry, a bitter and heated exercise, dates back to the early days of the AFL. But in the previous twenty-five years, the Broncos had taken the upper hand, winning three Super Bowls and appearing in another four while the Chiefs won four playoff games in total. From 1983 (the year the Broncos drafted John Elway and Kansas City got Todd Blackledge) to 2017, the Chiefs had won just eight times in thirty-four trips to Denver, a record due mostly to the discrepancy at quarterback. No player has lived rent-free in the heads of Kansas Citians like Elway. But after Mahomes's heroics in his first career start the previous December, it seemed something was starting to shift.

As the game began in Denver, Mahomes gave the Chiefs a 10–3 lead on an 8-yard rushing touchdown early in the second quarter. But the Broncos settled in and hit back, building a 23–13 lead with under thirteen minutes left. The Chiefs needed points to stay alive, and Mahomes completed ten passes on a fourteen-play touchdown drive that sliced the deficit to 23–20 with six and a half minutes left. The Chiefs defense quickly forced a punt, giving the ball back to the offense with 4:35 left, and two plays later, it faced a third-and-5 from its own 45-yard line.

Mahomes dropped back to pass, and the Broncos came with a "fire zone" blitz, a defensive pressure designed to cause confusion by sending five men after the quarterback while dropping at least one defensive lineman into zone coverage, taking away the quarterback's "hot" read (his safety valve against a blitz). Mahomes did not see it coming and didn't set the right protection, which meant the pocket almost collapsed immediately. The play had gone to hell.

Mahomes knew he had to buy time, so he hurried to his left, looping backward away from the pressure and hoping something might open up downfield. But just as he did, Von Miller, a pass rusher who had once run a 40-yard dash in 4.4, came flying in free from the backside, chasing him from behind. In a split second, it became clear: Mahomes was not going to outrun Miller. As he scrambled, however, he did spot Tyreek Hill about 11 yards downfield, streaking toward the sideline and looking for the ball. So as Miller dived at his legs, wrapping his mitts around those elongated calves, Mahomes did the only thing that made sense: He moved the ball into his left hand and pushed the ball 10 yards down the field, like a left-handed shot put. Somehow, it landed softly in the arms of Hill, who quickly burst upfield for the first down.

On the sideline, Eric Bieniemy, the Chiefs' offensive coordinator, looked over at Andy Reid. "Did he just throw that with his left hand?" he asked. Reid quickly screamed at Bieniemy to call the next play. ("When you slow it down," Bieniemy later said, "you just look at it and say, 'Damn, how did he do that?'") Four plays later, Mahomes hit tight end Demetrius Harris for 35 yards. The Chiefs took the lead for good with 1:43 left. If you stood inside the Broncos locker room in the moments after the Kansas City victory, you would have heard one thing: "Two fucking plays, man. Fuck!"

For Mahomes, it was pretty simple. He wasn't always fast enough to escape a pass rusher, so he relied on everything else: his spatial awareness, his balance, his creative mind, his years playing baseball and basketball and golf, his year-round workouts with a personal trainer, which trained his body to be a finely tuned machine of coordination, touch, and feel. He was a quarterback who could force the game to be played at his speed. As Chiefs offensive tackle Mitchell Schwartz would put it, "His ability to manipulate the speed and tempo of the game within a single play is insane." Which in that moment, four games into his first season as a starter, made it fair to ask:

Had there ever been a quarterback like this?

IN the beginning, there were no quarterbacks like Patrick Mahomes, in part because the quarterback could not pass or run . . . or really do anything. As American football came into being in the 1870s and 1880s—evolving from the English games of rugby and soccer, and pushed along by the visionary Yalie Walter Camp—the quarterback (or "quarter-back") was still a middle manager, a powerless corporate cog whose only role was to receive the "snap-back" and deliver the ball to teammates. Which, frankly, made the position kind of lame. It wasn't until the first decade of the twentieth century that a national crisis caused everything to change. In the early days, the sport was almost inconceivably violent. In 1905 alone, at least nineteen people died while playing football—many of them on college campuses. The *Chicago Tribune* documented the carnage in a muckraking story titled "Football Year's Death Harvest." The public backlash prompted calls to abolish the game—and an intervention led by President Theodore Roosevelt, whose son played at Harvard (and who wished to preserve some rough play for young men). "I demand that football change its rules or be abolished," Roosevelt said, gathering a group of college officials at the White House. "Brutality and foul play should receive the same summary punishment given to a man who cheats at cards! Change the game or forsake it."

To college football's leaders, the solution came via a set of reforms designed to open up the game, none more radical than the legalization of the forward pass. The original rule, implemented in 1906, was primitive: Quarterbacks had to throw from at least 5 yards behind the line of scrimmage, and if a pass was not touched before it hit the ground, it resulted in a turnover. But the most surprising thing was that nobody seemed to understand just how profoundly the rule change would change football. As *The New York Times* wrote in September 1906, "There has been no team that has proved that the forward pass is anything but a doubtful, dangerous play to be used only in the last extremity." Except that wasn't entirely correct. There was one team, and one player, and it would pain any loyal Kansas Citian to know that a crude version of the quarterback position, as we know it today, was actually born in St. Louis.

Bradbury Robinson was a midwestern boy who came of age in Wisconsin and started his college career in Madison in 1903 before finding his way to Saint Louis University, where he studied medicine, joined the football team, and made a groundbreaking discovery—one Mahomes would confirm a century later. When the forward pass became legal in 1906, nobody knew exactly how to execute it. The football of the era was shaped more like a watermelon, fatter and rounder, commonly referred to as "a blimp"—and how exactly were you supposed to throw it? Should you toss it end over end like an option pitch? Wing it submarine-style? Or use two hands as in a basketball chest pass? Robinson believed the answer was obvious: In the years before the pass was legal, when it was still just a novelty—a hypothetical tactic discussed by football's thought leaders—Robinson saw a teammate throw a football overhand and started messing around with different grips and techniques. He found he could throw a football with the same basic mechanics he would use to throw a baseball.

With Robinson on the roster, and Saint Louis head coach Eddie Cochems embracing what he called the "overhead projectile spiral pass," the team sequestered itself in Lake Beulah, Wisconsin, for a preseason camp, then unleashed its "air attack" offense on schools throughout the Midwest, outscoring opponents 407–11 as it finished a perfect 11-0. It worked so well that Cochems couldn't figure out why others weren't doing the same. The Saint Louis receivers (or "ends") ran choreographed routes. Robinson threw an accurate ball. When the school played host to unbeaten Kansas on November 3, 1906, Robinson completed an 87-yard touchdown pass that, according to one account, carried 40 yards in the air. "One would have thought that so effective a play would be instantly copied and become the vogue," wrote Knute Rockne, the legendary Notre Dame coach. "The East, however, had not learned much or cared much about Mid West and Western football."

Soon enough, though, the sport would catch up to Bradbury Robinson. Rockne and company popularized the pass at Notre Dame. A series of rules changes made the ball skinnier, allowing for easier throwing. Benny Friedman, the son of a tailor from Cleveland, brought the idea of the *big-armed QB* to the NFL in the late 1920s. The quarterback became the field general, the signal caller, the matinee idol, the role evolving into the preeminent figure in all American sports: not just a title but an archetype, the embodiment of a certain kind of American boy, clean-cut, popular, everybody's All-American, from Otto Graham ("Automatic Otto") to Johnny Unitas (the crew-cut legend) to Roger Staubach (the navy man on America's Team).

What Robinson and Cochems proved would, in time, become football's natural law: The smartest play in football was one where the ball was in the air. The only strange thing was how long this took. It wasn't until 1982 that NFL teams, on average, attempted more passes than runs. It wasn't until 2007 that a team (in this case, Tom Brady's

New England Patriots) ran a majority of their plays out of the shotgun—the formation most conducive to spread offenses and high-flying theatrics. The evolution wasn't completely linear: It was Lamar Hunt's American Football League that first went airborne, producing Sid Gillman's "Vertical Stretch" scheme with the Chargers in the 1960s. But once a Bengals assistant coach named Bill Walsh borrowed from Gillman and fashioned his West Coast offense—preferring shorter, horizontal passing routes to vertical bombs—the NFL was ready to fly. Rule changes. Coaching innovations. Analytics. Everything pointed to one thing: passing. And soon enough, the most valuable commodity in football was the man who could throw a football.

In 1979, the two highest-paid NFL players were running backs O.J. Simpson and Walter Payton, the latter making $450,000—or $50,000 more than Bob Griese, the league's best-paid quarterback. Leigh Steinberg, then a young sports agent barely removed from his Berkeley days, thought the pay scale was grossly out-of-date, so he started promoting a term to help market the value of the position: the "franchise quarterback." By 1990, Joe Montana was running Walsh's offense in San Francisco, collecting Super Bowls and making at least six times what Griese did a decade earlier. There was no going back. Montana. Elway. Marino. Young. Manning. Brady. The only way to win big was to find the next one.

But then something fascinating happened. As offenses kept spreading out, adopting concepts from mad-scientist college coaches, and as defenses became more complex, quarterbacks mostly fit the same mold they always had. The standard-bearers still looked like Tom Brady and Peyton Manning: tall, strapping men who would sit back in the pocket and fling the ball over the defensive line. So everyone kept looking for the next Manning. It was as if NFL coaches couldn't see the revolution happening right in front of them.

"I think Peyton Manning set quarterback play back," said Bobby Stroupe, Mahomes's longtime personal trainer, "because everybody wanted a guy that could sit back there and throw darts. And what they didn't realize was that Peyton was incredibly unique. Even his brother couldn't do what he did."

Then Mahomes arrived in 2018, and pushed the sport into the future, revealing skills that nobody realized a quarterback needed. The talent pool opened up as teams became less concerned with height or style or classic mechanics. The NFL's history of prejudice against Black QBs—which had softened in recent decades but was a part of its past—seemed to further recede from the sport. The most exciting NFL quarterbacks were suddenly more athletic, with more diverse body types and bigger arms and the audacity to throw from angles previously considered too wild or risky. They were men like Mahomes, who didn't just bend the laws of physics with his right arm. Sometimes he did it with his left.

TWO days after the Chiefs' comeback in Denver, the Missouri Department of Transportation created an official illustration that doubled as a meme tribute to Patrick Mahomes. It showed two cars on a highway—one with a Chiefs decal—and offered a reminder to drivers: Pass on your left. Four days later, on the next Sunday, Mahomes threw for another 313 yards and (gasp) his first two interceptions in a 30–14 clubbing of the Jaguars. Five games into his first season, he had fourteen touchdown passes and the Chiefs were 5-0. It shouldn't have been so easy—nothing in Kansas City was ever this easy, not since Kersey Coates had started erecting houses in the mud—but this was, and it wasn't just Mahomes's 112.7 passer rating or the team's perfect record. The experience of watching Mahomes play quarterback took on an almost metaphysical quality, like falling in love for the first time, as one Kansas Citian put it.

It wasn't that Mahomes was perfecting the quarterback position—though it was hard to imagine someone playing at a higher level. It was that he was subverting the art, crafting a wholesale reinvention. Aaron Rodgers, the inscrutable Packers star, may have been the closest figure on the evolutionary chart. He had spent much of the last decade mastering off-platform throws. (The emergence of the industry term seemed to coincide with his best seasons.) Rodgers was the master of the "pop step" (or foot pop), a clever mechanical innovation in which he would step into his throw and execute a little hop-skip on his front foot as he released his hips and delivered the ball. The maneuver was quick and mesmerizing, especially on the run, as if Rodgers were jumping into his throws, launching himself forward and levitating for a split second as his body created maximum torque.

It allowed for increasingly acrobatic throws. It also looked kind of weird. But Rodgers was awesome, so others started to follow.

Mahomes had started studying Rodgers when he was a teenager. On January 16, 2016, when he was still at Texas Tech and Rodgers threw an absurd Hail Mary to send a game to overtime, he sent out a tweet: "Rodgers this is why you are my idol." It wasn't just the foot pop. In Rodgers, Mahomes found a permission structure—a license to be a different kind of quarterback, one who could tap into his natural athletic gifts. When the Chiefs incorporated the RPO out of the shotgun in 2018, Mahomes came up with his own spin. Whereas most quarterbacks had to reset their feet and square their body to throw if they elected to pull the handoff back from the running back, Mahomes's arm was loose enough that he could unleash a pass with his feet still in the handoff position, speeding up the play.

It was the kind of move that looked like instinct. But really, it was by design. When Mahomes was in the fourth grade, his father had introduced him to Stroupe, a local performance coach in Tyler. What started as group workout sessions for local kids eventually became a decades-long partnership. Stroupe taught the concepts of "movement literacy" and "locomotive patterns," which distill the essence of quarterback play into an assortment of one-legged skips, asymmetric shuffles, awkward-looking jumps, baseball swings, and sprints—all of which might help Mahomes stay balanced during a madcap scramble, his perceived weakness turning into a strength.

Most world-class athletes can run backward at 75 percent of their max speed and move in circle patterns at 80 percent; Mahomes runs backward at nearly 90 percent of his max sprint speed and (incredibly) he can run faster in curvilinear patterns than when he's running straight. As Stroupe came to see it, his client *was* fast. He registers in-game speeds that few quarterbacks can reach. He possesses a sort of instinctive athletic genius—body control, balance, imagination—nearly unseen in NFL history. (Stroupe likens Mahomes to NBA star Luka Dončić, another unconventionally gifted athlete without a shredded physique.)

If you saw Mahomes play high school basketball back at White-house, he did not look particularly explosive then, either, but he excelled at baiting opponents into throwing passes, then bounding forward to steal the ball. To witness Mahomes play quarterback in 2018 was to see the same contradictions: There he was outside the pocket, spinning past defenders, juking linebackers, finding Hill and tight end Travis Kelce downfield, literally running circles around his opponents, always seemingly one step ahead. To Stroupe, it all made sense: "Game speed" is an expression, not a time, and nobody can express themselves on a football field like Patrick Mahomes. Or as former 49ers quarterback Steve Young put it: "The game changed, and then in came Patrick to that new environment, and he was capable of taking it to its full measure."

Young was once something like a proto-Mahomes, a mobile quarterback in a West Coast offense with a keen eye for improv and making plays on the run. The difference was that football in the 1980s and '90s was still a closed system, a rigid, disciplined enterprise with less freedom and self-expression. When Mahomes arrived in 2018, he found a system evolved, finally primed for someone like him. To Young, there was one word that came to mind. "It's a dream," he said.

In Kansas City, there was only one question: How long could the dream last?

THE BALLAD OF LLOYD WELLS

Nobody wanted Len Dawson to stare at them. His blue-eyed gaze was steely and stern and so cold "you could feel it in your bones," Chiefs tight end Fred Arbanas once told a reporter. Teammates typically encountered the stare when something bad happened. A dropped pass. A missed block. A sack. When an opposing defense brought Dawson to the turf, he would bounce back into the Chiefs' famed choir huddle—an unorthodox formation in which the players faced Dawson like he was a conductor—and stare down the guilty offensive lineman for what felt like an eternity. Even in the 1960s, when it seemed like the league banned passes longer than 12 yards, the quarterback was still the prime position on the field and the most important leader in the locker room. Some quarterbacks, like Joe Namath of the New York Jets, were brash and loud. But Dawson was different. As Arbanas put it, Dawson "led you by the force of his presence." With his eyes.

Dawson was never supposed to play for the Chiefs. Before anyone cared enough about the NFL draft to use the term "bust," he was . . . a bust. Selected fifth overall by the Pittsburgh Steelers after an All-American career at Purdue in 1957—one spot ahead of iconic running back Jim Brown—Dawson languished on the bench behind Hall of Famer Bobby Layne. He was traded to the Cleveland Browns, where he failed to beat out quarterback Milt Plum. In his first five seasons, Dawson completed twenty-one passes.

Lamar Hunt signed him to the Dallas Texans in 1962, on a lark, as a favor to Hank Stram, who had bonded with Dawson as an assistant coach at Purdue. Hunt believed Dawson would be cut by the time training camp ended. Dawson knew this because during one of his first practices, as he was still shaking off the cobwebs from his years on the bench, he overheard the owner say he would never make the team. But Dawson survived, winning the starting job and leading the NFL in touchdown passes that first season with the Texans. In Kansas City, he wowed fans in his first game at Municipal Stadium by throwing four touchdowns. The Chiefs had their franchise quarterback.

Off the field, Dawson was eloquent, later embarking on a distinguished broadcasting career. But on it, he still communicated desires with his eyes. Stram and Hunt learned to interpret the different meanings of his stares, and like the Chiefs' offensive line, they did not want to be on the receiving end of an icy, disappointed glare.

To keep their star quarterback happy, Stram and Hunt knew they needed to surround him with talent. Each was well prepared for the job: Stram had deep connections to college programs from his days in the NCAA, and Hunt was more than willing to outspend rivals. But the smartest thing the franchise did to shape the roster was hire a Texan named Lloyd Wells, who was the first full-time Black scout in professional football.

Wells was a former Marine sergeant who worked as a photographer and newspaper editor in Houston, using his spare time to mentor young Black athletes and help them find opportunities to play football, often at historically Black colleges and universities (HBCUs). For many Black athletes, he was their best chance. College football teams in the Southeastern Conference, Atlantic Coast Conference, and Southwest Conference were still all white in the early 1960s. Despite the NFL being desegregated since 1946, its white owners and general managers favored those elite southern leagues and limited African American participation through unofficial quotas and unwritten rules. Coaches, who were skeptical of the leadership skills of Black athletes, essentially barred them from positions like quarterback and middle linebacker. Basically, the NFL functioned a lot like Kansas City and other American cities at the time. Official segregation might have been on its way out, but there were numerous excuses used to restrict African Americans.

In Kansas City, Hunt was never confused for a progressive. He was, however, a strident capitalist, an AFL outsider trying to disrupt the establishment NFL, which meant scouring for inefficiencies in the market, and there was no easier way to gain an edge than to sign over-looked Black football players from HBCUs. So Hunt hired Wells. The relationship came to change the fortunes of the Kansas City Chiefs—and alter the face of professional football. "The best thing that ever happened in the NFL," said Chiefs linebacker Bobby Bell, an early Black star, "is that Lamar Hunt started the AFL."

Wells was something of a football raconteur—charming, intelligent, a smooth salesman. Stram liked to call him "Outta Sight," because Wells had a habit of telling Stram, "Coach, you got to see this guy. He's outta sight." Running back Mike Garrett thought of him as a Hollywood agent (and Wells later became a close confidant of Muhammad Ali). Jim Kearney, a Chiefs safety from Texas, summed him up thusly: "The Man."

To most, though, Wells had one name: Judge. He absolutely knew how to evaluate talent.

In 1963, Wells scouted Bell, a versatile linebacker from the University of Minnesota who could have played any position on the field, and hulking defensive tackle Buck Buchanan, a Grambling College product. Buchanan was drafted by the Chiefs first overall, marking the first time an NFL or AFL team had selected a Black player at No. 1. The next year, Wells targeted Otis Taylor of Prairie View A&M. Unlike many HBCU players, Taylor was no secret. He was a prototype for the future of the wide receiver position: long, fast, and adept at chasing deep balls, yet physical enough to jostle against defensive backs for the short-yardage plays favored by coaches at the time.

Naturally, the Dallas Cowboys loved him. Two days before the AFL draft in November 1964, the Cowboys stashed Taylor in a Holiday Inn, hoping to keep AFL teams from negotiating with him. Hunt called Wells with a simple directive: Go get Otis Taylor. So Wells drove to Dallas. The full story remains hazy: It might have involved calls to Prairie View A&M, girlfriend informants, and bellboy double agents. Maybe that was Wells telling tales. What is true: Wells posed as a journalist to get into the hotel and escorted Taylor out a back door, shepherding him to Kansas City in the darkness of the night.

By the mid-1960s, Kansas City had become the prime landing spot for HBCU football players, signing and developing more Black talent than any other team in the AFL or NFL. The Chiefs became a force—blinding speed on defense, offensive fireworks, a balanced and cohesive roster that was among the most forward-thinking in football. Dawson was still the anchor, of course, but the influx of players like Bell, Taylor, and Buchanan—undervalued because of the color of their skin—gave the team an opportunity to become great.

On the field, the team was a real meritocracy. Willie Lanier, a linebacker drafted out of Morgan State College in 1967, became the first full-time Black middle linebacker in pro football. And the locker room was mostly free of racial tension, a fact that Lanier credited to Hunt. "The reality of their understanding of race and where it fit into the mindset of America was one that was as pure as it could be," he later said.

The outlook of Kansas City was more complicated.

ON a crisp March morning in 1966, Mike Garrett boarded a 5:45 flight out of Los Angeles, headed to a place he knew nearly nothing about.

Garrett was a reserved but driven man. At the University of Southern California, he had proved wrong the doubters who challenged his diminutive five-nine height and won the 1965 Heisman Trophy. But some professional scouts still thought he was too short, which was part of the reason he was leaving his hometown of Los Angeles. The Rams drafted him into the NFL, but they wouldn't budge on contract terms. The Chiefs made the better offer and sent Hunt and executive Don Klosterman to the West Coast to recruit him. Garrett signed on, even though his knowledge of Kansas City was limited to one thing: the Wilbert Harrison song that referenced the intersection at Twelfth and Vine, which, by 1966, had been decimated. When Garrett's University of Southern California teammates asked him if Kansas City had horses and buggies, he could not say for sure.

The plane touched down in the early afternoon. Garrett, dressed in a blazer adorned with a Chiefs logo, chatted with reporters alongside Stram. He met with Hunt and stayed at the Hotel Muehlebach. He toured the Swope Park practice facility, a modest rectangular building with the team's front offices and locker rooms, adjacent to a green practice field. Kansas City felt smaller than Los Angeles, but he liked what he saw (including the lack of buggies). The city was going to be his home, and Garrett decided to look for places around the Plaza.

Garrett had grown up in the Maravilla housing projects, tagging along with a big brother who taught him how to play sandlot football against older kids. His family wasn't well-off, but there was usually enough food on the table. During his teenage years, his family moved to Boyle Heights, a diverse working-class neighborhood in East LA, and he starred at Roosevelt High School before attending USC. His fellow college students looked at him as a gifted athlete and nice person, someone who was going places and was sure of it. But Garrett looked at himself as a late bloomer, always grinding to "be at the right place at the right time to capture the moment."

In Los Angeles, he saw the benefits for people who moved up in the world. The city had redlining and segregation, but it had opportunities for ascendant Black professionals to progress into larger houses and luxury neighborhoods, like near Wilshire Boulevard. Garrett was now progressing to a new stage in his life, and he believed the Plaza, with a newly installed fountain named after J.C. Nichols, could be his version of Wilshire.

Garrett and the Plaza should have been an obvious match: He had secured a lucrative contract, and the Plaza had some of the nicest apartments around. Garrett saw plenty with signs displaying rooms for rent. Yet, at every one of them, a property manager told him the signs were incorrect. Nothing was available—not for a Black man. "I was hoping that Kansas City was more progressive than that," Garrett recalled.

Black Kansas Citians had fought for many advancements the previous twenty years. One day in 1950, four Black men—in an act of athletic disobedience—quietly teed off on Swope Park's whites-only golf course, setting off a cascade of Black players who came over the next few months, pushing ahead as white golfers slashed their tires in the parking lot. Around the same time, Thurgood Marshall litigated the integration of Swope Park's public swimming pool. Downtown, some of the most prominent department stores declined to let Black customers in their cafeterias until protesters picketed on their sidewalks for several weeks in the winter of1959, braving temperatures as low as seven degrees and snowfall totals as high as ten inches. Their boycott was covered extensively by Lucile Bluford, who both chronicled the civil rights movement and initiated change in Kansas City after taking over from Roy Wilkins as *The Call*'s editor, shaming other media outlets into reporting on the Black community. The summer of 1963—when Black Chiefs players arrived in town and were denied service at bars—was another turning point. The city had witnessed protests at stores and an amusement park, and heard public pressure from Black leaders like Bluford, Bruce Watkins, and Alvin Brooks. That fall, the Kansas City Council passed an ordinance barring discrimination at most public places.

Plenty of restaurants and stores still weren't welcoming (and the

Black community had to hold off a John Birch Society–led referendum on the ordinance), but changes were noticeable. Garrett would go to the Plaza for steaks at Plaza III and indulge, nearly nightly, at the district's Baskin-Robbins. But housing was still a different story. Not even Chiefs players could penetrate the Troost Wall.

Bobby Bell, already a homeowner in Minnesota, wanted a house in that great wonderland of Americana: a Nichols suburb. He looked at some two hundred houses in the mid-1960s, always without success. A real estate agent would notify Bell that the house he wanted had just been sold, or a banker, pressured to bar Black people by a subdivision's residents, would refuse to underwrite the mortgage. The assistance of Stram, who lived in Prairie Village and made calls on Bell's behalf, had no impact. Bell later recalled that being a football star didn't make any difference. "If you were Black you didn't need to be out there. That was the thinking of the people."

Garrett shared the backfield with Curtis McClinton, a University of Kansas graduate who had regularly visited Eighteenth and Vine during college. McClinton scored the Chiefs' first-ever touchdown in 1963 on a 73-yard run in the preseason. At the time, he was living in a one-bedroom basement apartment that rented for seven dollars a week. "I had to ask myself, 'What is the problem? Why can't I find a place to stay'"? he recalled later. "And it boiled down to the fact that I represented the Black element." The situation shocked McClinton. He wondered how Kansas City could attract talented Black professionals of any occupation if it kept refusing to invest on the East Side and integrate neighborhoods west of Troost. He knew the Chiefs, despite their reputation for scouting and developing the best Black players in the country, were being undermined by the city. Future Hall of Famer Gale Sayers, who, like McClinton, grew up in Wichita and starred at the University of Kansas, was drafted in 1964 by the Chiefs in the AFL and the Chicago Bears in the NFL. The Bears were a middle-of-the-pack team headed nowhere, and everybody knew the Chiefs were loaded. Yet Sayers picked Chicago. A few months later,

McClinton shared one of the reasons why: "He knew Kansas City; he knew what the housing situation was."

Outside of football, McClinton worked four days a week as a loan officer at Black-owned Douglass State Bank in Kansas City, Kansas. He was a baritone singer who loved classical music. Once a week, he hosted a radio show on KPRS, the first Black-owned and -operated station west of the Mississippi. He looked up to Paul Robeson, the former college football star turned singer and political activist, and met with the likes of Jim Brown, Muhammad Ali, and Bill Russell at the Cleveland Summit, where they discussed Ali's refusal to serve in Vietnam as a conscientious objector because he opposed the war on the basis of his Islamic religion. The men decided to back Ali's decision, leading journalist William C. Rhoden to later describe the event as the first time that "so many African-American athletes at that level came together to support a controversial cause."

McClinton was unwilling to accept the status quo of Kansas City. In 1965, he formed a corporation to develop McClinton Courts, an integrated thirty-three-unit apartment complex on the west side of Swope Park on Fifty-Sixth Street. McClinton Courts was set to feature built-in appliances, a recreation area, a swimming pool shaped like a football, and central air and heat. At the time, McClinton said, Kansas City had just one apartment complex with central heating and A/C open to Black people. It had been developed by another athlete, A's pitcher John Wyatt. McClinton got Wyatt on board as an investor, along with teammates Bell, Alphonse Dotson, Fred Williamson, and Buck Buchanan. Bruce Watkins, the city council member, attempted to curry favor with local politicians.

In the end, the city refused McClinton's proposal. The area was zoned for single-family homes and duplexes, and the city council voted 7–6 against the development. It was a loss for McClinton, for the whole city, but hardly the end of his activism. He joined Watkins in his political and civil rights organization, Freedom Inc., and started a local chapter of the Black Economic Union, offering classes, investing in Black start-ups, and connecting Black businesses to Kansas City's white corporations. "In this community, they were before their time," Alvin Brooks remembered.

McClinton's reach would not have been nearly as wide if not for football. Along with Bell, Buchanan, and Taylor, he was a pillar of the Black community in the team's earliest years. In 1966, McClinton got even better when he was paired with Garrett in the backfield. They combined for 1,801 all-purpose yards, and both made the Pro Bowl. The Chiefs put everything together: Taylor averaged 22.4 yards per catch, the defense intercepted thirty-three passes, and the team went three months without a loss. On January 15, 1967, they played the Green Bay Packers in the first AFL-NFL championship, a game that Hunt would later be credited for naming the "Super Bowl." The Chiefs tied the game at 7–7 on a touchdown pass from Dawson to McClinton, and then nothing went right. They lost 35–10.

After the disappointment, McClinton got back to work on his greatest off-field priority. The denial of the McClinton Courts apartment complex had helped catalyze a housing movement, drawing in Watkins, Brooks, Freedom Inc., and other activist groups. For the past year McClinton had spoken at rallies across the metro area, hoping to change laws in six counties. At Watson Memorial Methodist Church in Independence, Missouri—down the street from the home of Harry Truman—McClinton addressed a crowd of 120, sharing the story of his basement apartment and how he had to buy a home far from the Chiefs' practice facility. "No one likes to be directed to a particular area of the city to live, but wants to choose where he will live," he exclaimed. The pressure picked up, even in the face of hostile opposition from the local real estate industry. On July 21, 1967, six months after the Super Bowl, Kansas City passed a fair-housing law.

THE city had changed, ever so slightly, in ways Garrett realized the next time he went apartment hunting. His first year, he ended up living at the Hilltop House apartments near Forty-Seventh and the

Paseo. He had a short drive to practice at Swope Park and games at Municipal Stadium; and the University of Missouri–Kansas City, where he took sociology courses, was a few blocks away. But Garrett yearned for the area that had drawn his attention when he arrived in Kansas City. In 1968, with the city falling for a franchise that was getting better and better and the fair-housing ordinance in effect, Garrett returned to the Plaza, searching for vacancy signs. This time, somebody rented him an apartment.

The housing reforms that McClinton pushed for took longer to reach Nichols's suburbs. Prairie Village passed a fair-housing ordinance in May 1968, forced into action after President Lyndon Johnson signed a national fair-housing act. Prairie Village mayor Carl Schliffke said the town really didn't need the ordinance. "We've never questioned the right of anybody to move to Prairie Village," he told a reporter. Bobby Bell wasn't so sure.

The same year Prairie Village passed the fair-housing law, Bell finally did get the house his family sorely needed: a four-bedroom Colonial on Delmar Street that had been for sale for a year. Bell bought it with the help of a friendly white man who had heard about Bell's situation. The man bought the house and then rented it to Bell until Bell could find a willing mortgage underwriter.

Bell's family was one of just a handful of Black families to have integrated Prairie Village or other Nichols suburbs. As Bell recalled, the man who sold him the house was "blackballed," ostracized by the community. And on the day that Bell's family moved in, somebody knocked on the door. The subdivision was holding an emergency meeting that night. They were organizing a protest of their new Black neighbor.

But Bell wasn't going anywhere. And soon, teammates Willie Lanier and Buck Buchanan joined him in nearby subdivisions.

IF the realities of Kansas City were complicated for Mike Garrett and Curtis McClinton and Bobby Bell, there was one aspect of life that was not: football. Lamar Hunt and Lloyd Wells had assembled a kick-ass group of football players—explosive and committed and smart—and three years after the disappointment against the Green Bay Packers, the Chiefs returned to Super Bowl IV in New Orleans on January 11, 1970.

The Minnesota Vikings were the heavy favorites to win the game. It was still assumed the NFL was the superior league. But the Chiefs—leaning on Dawson and a stout defense—built a 9–0 lead and were driving again in the second quarter. Then Hank Stram had an idea.

Sixty-Five Toss Power Trap was a deep cut, a banger buried in the back of the playbook. The Chiefs hadn't practiced it in three weeks. When Stram sent the play in with wide receiver Gloster Richardson, a Lloyd Wells signee from Jackson State College, Dawson was taken aback. "Are you sure?" Dawson asked Richardson. Stram was sure. The play, he thought, might "pop wide open."

Garrett, who would be receiving the handoff, was excited but slightly worried. The play worked great if the defense fell for the fake toss. If not, a Minnesota linebacker would be right there to drill him in the chest. They didn't have time to debate.

Dawson, playing for months on an injured knee, lined up under center E.J. Holub for the snap. One lineman, Ed Budde, plowed straight ahead for a block. Another lineman, Mo Moorman, pulled from his position to seal off a defender on the left side. Meanwhile, Dawson handed the ball to Garrett, who cut left. Garrett saw the linebacker was two steps behind and immediately thought, "I got it." He darted through the giant hole into the end zone, almost untouched.

Some ninety minutes later, with the Chiefs' 23–7 victory official, the locker room was bedlam. Some players yelled. Taylor bawled. Dawson stood on a table, embracing his eleven-year-old son. Garrett, in a TV interview with CBS, pulled Wells into the frame to give him credit.

The next afternoon, the team landed at the brand-new Kansas City International Airport for a parade. Immediately, players realized the enormity of the city's support: Hundreds of people had parked their cars along the highway to greet them on the route to downtown. Truckers blew their horns. At Broadway and Grand Avenue, a crowd numbering as high as 175,000 enveloped the streets, tossing confetti at the motorcade. The last stop was the Liberty Memorial. Standing below the concrete tower, Dawson exclaimed, "This is the greatest football and sports town in the world."

To Garrett, the glow in Kansas City seemed to last for months, a point of civic pride the city could hold over Los Angeles, New York, Denver, and everywhere else. For a city hollowing out its downtown and for an East Side figuring out how to resist being carved up by the South Midtown Freeway, the victory provided a welcome respite. It was therapeutic for Garrett, too. "You still had the redlining and all that," he recalled, and none of those problems were going away. But, he believed, the Super Bowl transcended life and "you could, for a period of time, forget."

PRIME TIME

On a quiet spring morning in 1972, a committee of Kansas City boosters held a press conference on the forty-second floor of the Socony-Mobil Building in New York City. They decorated the swanky Pinnacle Club with color photos of Kansas City. They invited representatives from *The New York Times*, *Life* magazine, *Reader's Digest*, and any news outlet that would come. They premiered a promotional short film, served expensive cocktails, and tried to sell *the idea* of Kansas City to the coast. In the middle of the presentation, Nichols Company president Miller Nichols stood before a crowd of nearly sixty people. "Our Chiefs have made it twice to the Super Bowl," he said. "And our Royals, a baseball expansion team, in three years have moved up to second place in their division."

The lavish Manhattan press conference was the brainchild of the Prime Time Committee, a group of businessmen and civic leaders who hoped to rebrand the image of Kansas City, distancing it from its frontier-cow-town roots. Along with Miller Nichols, the committee included Charles B. Wheeler, the city's mayor; Ilus W. Davis, the former mayor; and Donald Hall, the forty-three-year-old president of Hallmark Cards, who stood inside the Pinnacle Club and tried to pitch dozens of New York journalists on a version of Kansas City that would become America's inland capital. "We are viewed as flat and dusty with wheat piled in the streets by those who have never visited our area," Hall told the audience. "Yet we live amid sizable hills, in a forest, with ample water and enjoy the nation's finest park system."

The Prime Time Committee hired a New York public relations firm—Carl Byoir and Associates—to spread the word to the country. It enlisted a local firm to craft a new, practical slogan for the city: "Kansas City, one of the few liveable cities left." The message was splashed on billboards, placed in newspaper ads, and became the tagline for a television commercial, complete with picturesque scenes of the city and a dramatic narration from old Hollywood actor Barry Sullivan.

Narrator: "There's a city with more public green space than San Francisco, including the second largest urban park in America. With more fountains than any place but Rome, more Boulevard miles than Paris, and cleaner air than Honolulu. Kansas City: One of the few liveable cities left."

The advertising campaign was a hit, in the sense that it got Kansas City talking. (The trade publication *Advertising Age* named the commercial one of the top 100 in 1974.) Not that it was completely factual. The city was losing the war with the suburbs, on its way to shedding more than 10 percent of its population in the decade. Downtown had been sliced up by highways and covered by parking lots. The Nichols Company was continuing its inexorable march south into Johnson County, Kansas, where farmland was plentiful and cheap and fresh subdivisions could be laid out and marketed to the next generation of homeowners. Kansas City *was* losing some of its cow town ties. That was true. The proliferation of long-haul trucks and the creation of highways had allowed the cattle trade to spread anywhere. No longer did you need a centralized distribution center, so livestock pens in the West Bottoms rotted, trains stopped coming through, and packinghouses migrated to smaller midwestern cities. But "one of the few liveable cities left"? The claim was invented when some local advertising execs discovered that Kansas City had a lot of parks and the ninth-best air quality in the country, worse than Seattle's but better than Honolulu's. "That's fairly livable," the exec said.

"More Boulevard miles than Paris"? Actually, yes. "More fountains than any place but Rome"? That was a guess. And when the Midwest Research Institute, headquartered in Kansas City, crunched the numbers on a variety of other livability factors, the organization found that Kansas City actually ranked pretty far down on the list, noting its deep-rooted segregation.

One story the Prime Time Committee could sell was that of a building boom, a construction frenzy unseen since the days of Pendergast, pushed along by hopes that Trans World Airlines would make the city a main hub for supersonic air travel. TWA had been headquartered in Kansas City from 1931 until 1964, when it picked up and left for New York, but it still kept a presence downtown, and if airlines were going to be shuttling customers around the world on futuristic aircraft at supersonic speeds, the dead center of the continental United States seemed like an ideal place to build a gateway to the world. The city spent $250 million to build Kansas City International Airport, which opened in 1972 and, at the direction of TWA, featured three horseshoe-shaped terminals, allowing people to pull up to the curb outside their gate and hop on a flight in minutes, sort of like a drive-in airport. The design immediately became obsolete, when the hijacking of Southern Airways Flight 49 (and the subsequent threat of a crash into a nuclear reactor in Tennessee) made national headlines and caused the industry to reconsider security. The era of supersonic flight never happened, either. But Kansas City kept building.

It approved a $102 million bond issue to construct the Harry S. Truman Sports Complex, a twin-stadium concept on land nine miles southeast of downtown that resulted in Arrowhead Stadium, a thematic nod to the Chiefs' name, and Royals Stadium, a new baseball venue. (It nearly included a futuristic rolling roof sliding between the venues.) The city eventually named a new convention center for old mayor Roe Bartle, who landed the Chiefs, and built Kemper Arena, a modern sports venue, in the West Bottoms, not far from the old Stockyards, each structure designed by postmodern architect Helmut

Jahn. But the most ambitious project—and certainly the most 1970s-looking one—was Crown Center, the grand vision of Hallmark Cards, a $200 million development built across eighty-five acres in an area known as "Signboard Hill," just east of the Liberty Memorial. Billed as a "City Within a City," and compared to New York's Rockefeller Center, Crown Center was essentially a privately financed urban renewal project, a massive undertaking with all the aesthetics and architectural influences of the '70s: a million feet of glass-paned office space, apartments for eight thousand people, underground parking for seven thousand cars, an indoor shopping center, a central square with an ice rink, and, according to the project's backers, "the only hotel in the world with a six-story tropical garden . . . and a 300 million year old limestone outcrop inside its lobby." To Donald Hall and his father, Joyce—the legendary founder of Hallmark—the real objective of Crown Center was to conceive and create a "downtown suburb." If Kansas City couldn't compete with J.C. Nichols's meticulously curated neighborhoods, it could bring the pleasant suburban life to the heart of the city.

The Crown Center expansion pressed on through the decade, even as the American economy wobbled and the suburbs exploded, as the Prime Time era brought the 1976 Republican Convention to Kemper Arena. By 1980, Crown Center added a second luxury hotel; this one was forty stories high with a revolving restaurant (Skies) on top, a four-story lobby atrium inspired by the Galleria in Milan, Italy, and enough cachet to host the Philadelphia Phillies when they arrived for the 1980 World Series. But perhaps most impressive were the three futuristic walkways that spanned 120 feet across the giant atrium—one each on the second, third, and fourth floors—designed to look as if they were floating above the lobby.

In time, they became known as the Hyatt skywalks.

MICHAEL Rudd moved his family to Kansas City in the mid-1970s, back when the Prime Time commercials were still on the air and

TWA was realizing that supersonic flight might not work. Rudd was a TWA sales manager, a corporate cog who had moved up the ladder from New Jersey to Kansas and on to Southern California. When the Rudd family moved back to the Kansas City area for good, they settled into life in a Kansas suburb called Lenexa, nine miles west of State Line Road. Michael had been born in Great Britain. He came to the United States and served in the navy in the Vietnam era. He obsessed over the story of the *Titanic* and liked to write letters to *The Kansas City Star*. (His targets included Nazi physician Josef Mengele and animal abuse at the famed American Royal.) His wife, Gloria, was also born and educated in England. In the quaint confines of Nichols Land, they could have been outsiders, but like most families in the area, they came to love Johnson County. Their children settled into the Shawnee Mission School District, the top public district in Kansas. Their only son, Paul, attended Shawnee Mission West High School, where he was elected student council president, worked as a DJ for the school's radio and television station, and served as a Viking yell leader. (His StuCo efforts included pushing for a candy machine in the cafeteria to keep up with rival district Blue Valley.) His most formative experience, however, came in Sally Shipley's forensics class, where he donned a beret, sang songs, acted out skits, and honed the craft of competitive speech, including one of his specialties: humorous interpretation. "I don't know if I'll make it as a comedian," Rudd said then, when a local reporter showed up to write about the school's powerhouse forensics program. "But whatever, I know I'll do it better because of this class."

When Paul Rudd wasn't at Shawnee Mission West, he (like most other kids in Johnson County) was often spending time at Oak Park Mall, where he scored a part-time job. If there was a monument to Nichols Land suburbia, it was Oak Park Mall, a climate-controlled, 1.2-million-square-foot shrine with specialty shops, extravagant fountain displays, glistening tile floors, artificial plants, arcade games, and a food court with a beloved fast-food taco shop: Taco Via. (The local myth was that the taco sauce could clean the rust off a penny.) Oak Park Mall wasn't all that different from the rest of the suburban shopping malls that came to define American life in the 1980s. In fact, it was such a classic version that when CBS went searching for an American mall to help chronicle the rise of mall culture for a 1982 documentary, the network chose Oak Park Mall. "If you want to find America today," CBS correspondent Charles Kuralt told viewers, in perfect network-news cadence, "this is where you have to look."

Oak Park Mall had sprung up in 1975, on an old dairy farm in Overland Park, not far from a hot new development of two-story homes and cul-de-sacs named Oak Park Manor, which, of course, was being developed by the Nichols Company. If the Country Club District was the model, and Prairie Village was the mass-produced boutique version, Overland Park was suburbia perfected, a giant pocket of land that grew fourfold in area between 1960 and 1995. Each of its dozens of subdivisions had a pastoral yet dignified-sounding name (Nottingham Forest, Shannon Valley, Pinehurst Estates), and every homeowner coveted a finished basement outfitted with a big-screen cable TV (parents of the lucky kids would spring for the "B-side" premium subscription with MTV). Oak Park Mall was Overland Park's de facto capital. Rudd landed a job at Imagery, a trendy men's clothing store on the second level, not far from Montgomery Ward, next to Cheesecakes by Jill, Coffee Connection, a custom T-shirt shop called Shirtman, and Skyflyers, which sold balloons, kites, and other novelty inflatables. He was like many '80s kids. He listened to Depeche Mode; he made jokey videos that channeled David Letterman's for the school TV station; he came to love the Royals and the Chiefs, the comforting ease of Johnson County, and the familiar contradiction the place engendered: It really was a bubble of sorts, if you noticed that sort of thing, but for people privileged to live there, it was a wonderful place to be, with surprising bits of art and culture, like in

Rudd's high school forensics class, where a few years later a Shawnee Mission West basketball player named Jason Sudeikis would also be inspired by Sally Shipley. "I think there's something kind of good about growing up in a place you know is not the cool place to be," Rudd would say. "I think it's good for your head."

Paul Rudd left home for the University of Kansas, a stopover on his way to a career in acting, but as he grew older and moved to the coast, as he returned home again and again to visit his parents, he came to develop some theories about Kansas City. One theory: At any moment of any day, he could always find George Thorogood's 1982 song "Bad to the Bone" playing on FM radio. A second one concerned the Royals and the Chiefs: No matter where he lived, no matter his age, no matter how much time passed, he realized his hometown seemed to care more about sports than anywhere else.

ON the evening of July 17, 1981, Eugene and Karen Jeter arrived at the Hyatt Regency at Crown Center for a night of dancing. It was a summer Friday, the temperature touching ninety degrees in the late afternoon. The Chiefs were finishing their first week of training camp at William Jewell College, where quarterback Steve Fuller was trying to beat out Bill Kenney. The Royals' season was still halted by a fifty-one-day players' strike, which robbed the city of baseball. Mayor Richard L. Berkley and Councilman Emanuel Cleaver were clashing over an upcoming election concerning a proposed capital improvement sales tax. As Eugene and Karen entered the hotel and stepped inside the giant four-story atrium, a banner outside advertised the night's event:

TEA DANCING TONIGHT AND
EVERY FRIDAY NIGHT 5–8.

Eugene and Karen were newlyweds, coworkers at the same insurance firm. Sixteen days earlier, they had been married near the Rose

Garden Fountain in Loose Park, in the heart of the Country Club District. They went on a honeymoon, returned home, and decided to spend the third weekend in July at the Hyatt, which was hosting one of the newest parties in Kansas City: a Friday-night tea dance. The event had launched in late May as a way to attract locals to the new forty-story hotel and nod to the city's jazz and big band traditions. The Steve Miller Orchestra played classic numbers by Tommy Dorsey, Glenn Miller, and Count Basie. The lobby bar served glasses of champagne for one dollar. Attendees presided over a dance contest. Eugene and Karen loved to dance.

If you looked closely at the crowd of middle-aged suburbanites flocking back to Crown Center to dance to big band music, it wasn't hard to see the symbolism. The Crown Center development had brought some life to Crown Center, but it hadn't done much for the rest of downtown, still a squalid ghost town after 5 P.M. The malaise and neglect, locals believed, spread through the city as a whole. In January 1978, an early-morning four-alarm fire in Quality Hill had killed twenty people at the Coates House Hotel, which had once hosted presidents when Kersey and Sarah Coates owned the place. But it had declined in recent years and was then a home for short-term, transient guests. The next year, a violent storm caused the roof of the Helmut Jahn–designed sports arena to cave in, causing millions in damages, not to mention a loss in morale. (Bizarrely, the roof collapse came as the American Institute of Architects and Jahn gathered in town for its annual convention. When word of the collapse reached the conference, Jahn rushed to the West Bottoms to survey the wreckage.)

And then, in the summer of 1980, as the Hyatt marked its opening on July 1, Kansas City withstood the start of a brutal heat wave that resulted in at least 176 heat-related deaths in the metro area (and 137 in the city alone), numbers made worse by deteriorating conditions throughout the city. By the summer of 1981, *The Kansas City Star* published a blunt editorial that stated what everyone understood:

"The core of Kansas City is often dingy, sometimes ugly." To stand inside the Hyatt, owned by a subsidiary of storied local company Hallmark, and witness a crowd dancing to Tommy Dorsey's "I'm Getting Sentimental over You," a staple from the 1930s, was to imagine a city nostalgic for the past.

As Eugene and Karen Jeter hit the dance floor at the Hyatt, the evening sun was still shining, the glow reflected through the atrium's windows. Eugene wore a dark coat and tie, Karen a white dress. Balloons of all colors decorated the lobby. As they locked hands and smiled, the couple danced past Dave Forstate, a television cameraman from KMBC-TV (channel 9). Forstate had come to the Hyatt with Micheal Mahoney, a twenty-seven-year-old reporter on the station's lifestyle beat who had moved to Kansas City the previous year and was doing his latest feature on the tea dance trend. It was a light story. Forstate would shoot some B-roll footage. Mahoney would deliver the words. Just a pleasant, unremarkable Friday night.

At just before 7 P.M., two hours into the dance, the atrium inside the Hyatt was packed. The Steve Miller Orchestra was playing. Drinks were flowing. On the second-floor skywalk, a crowd of partygoers had gathered to watch. More people stood directly above on the fourth-floor skywalk. On the other side of the atrium, Forstate and Mahoney took an escalator up to the Terrace Restaurant on a mezzanine, directly across from the skywalks. At 7:05 P.M., as the orchestra played a song by Duke Ellington called "Satin Doll," Mahoney leaned down to pull a new battery out of Forstate's bag. That was when he heard it.

Pop! Pop!

FIFTEEN miles away from the Hyatt, Brent Wright was at Oak Park Mall, working a shift on the loading docks at Macy's. Four days shy of his eighteenth birthday, he had just graduated from Shawnee Mission Northwest High School. In the fall, he would start his freshman year at the University of Kansas. As he worked on the dock, he had a radio on, which was how he heard a voice mention a developing story at the Hyatt Regency. Wright continued to work. He didn't know his mother and stepfather, Karen and Eugene Jeter, had gone down to Crown Center. He didn't know that at 7:05 P.M. the skywalks on the second and fourth floors had buckled, more than seventy tons of steel, glass, and concrete pancaking onto each other and collapsing onto hundreds of people in the lobby. He didn't know about the carnage that ensued: the moments of eerie quiet after the collapse, before anyone knew what had happened; the water line that was severed, causing the lobby to fill with blood-soaked water; the eleven-year-old boy from Prairie Village who was trapped underneath the wreckage with his mom, each alive and waiting for help; the police chief who was so shaken he compared the scene to an image from the Korean War. Wright did not know that his mother and stepfather were two of the 114 people who would not survive what became the deadliest structural collapse, to that point, in American history.

Inside the Hyatt, in the moments after the skywalks fell, the air was filled with white dust. Nobody had had any warning. People who had been standing in line for the bar were killed instantly or suddenly trapped under the mangled wreckage. Sometimes a foot made the difference. One man walked around the lobby, searching for his missing wife. Doctors and first responders arrived and set up a makeshift triage center. A doctor used a chainsaw to amputate a leg; the man did not survive. The authorities would use heavy machinery to smash through the hotel entrance and bring in cranes to try to hoist the wreckage. A temporary morgue was set up near the lobby.

The youngest victim was an eleven-year-old girl from Leavenworth, Kansas, who died alongside her father. The oldest was an eighty-year-old musician and retired insurance salesman from Portland, Oregon, who was back in town to visit his brother. It seemed like everyone in Kansas City knew someone who was there. The reason for the collapse was a design flaw that none of the engineers had detected. The skywalks on the second and fourth floor were supposed to be suspended from the ceiling of the atrium by six long hanger rods that would run through box beams on each skywalk, but at some point during the construction process, the plan changed and the engineering firm Gillum-Colaco had used twelve shorter rods. The second-floor skywalk was essentially hanging from the one on the fourth floor. The box beams on the fourth-floor skywalk could not handle the extra load.

For a long time, nobody in Kansas City could process how it had happened.

On the morning after the collapse, Wright still had not heard about his mother, so he returned to work at Oak Park Mall. His father called and asked him to find his sister, Shelly, and come home. In the days that followed, Wright picked up his mother's car from Crown Center. He collected a bloodied purse and makeup bag. He attended his mother's funeral and realized that the last time he saw her was on the Country Club Plaza, where they had taken a tennis lesson at the Plaza's courts and then headed to a local diner called Winstead's for steakburgers. At some point, he cleaned out their apartment a few blocks away, where he found birthday gifts his mother had bought—a gold chain, a nice shirt—and a birthday card with a check for $18.

He never cashed it.

THE VILLAIN'S NAME WAS TOM

atrick Mahomes's first loss came against Tom Brady. Even in the moment, it felt narratively symbolic. On October 14, 2018, the Chiefs visited the Patriots, and the quarterbacks—born eighteen years apart—engaged in a prime-time duel in New England, a clash of eras and styles and generations, a fifteen-round donnybrook in which Mahomes threw for 352 yards, four touchdowns, and two interceptions, and Brady held tightly to the heavyweight belt. With three minutes left, the Chiefs erased a 24–9 halftime deficit and knotted the game at 40–40 on Mahomes's 75-yard touchdown pass to Tyreek Hill.

But the Kansas City defense could not stop Brady. That made the defensive unit similar to hundreds of others in NFL history, but it was also an apt summation for the season. Mahomes would finish the season with 5,095 yards passing and fifty touchdown passes—tied with Brady for the second most ever—which made him the youngest league MVP in thirty-four years. He guided the Chiefs to the third-most points in NFL history, a 12-4 record, and the top seed in the AFC playoffs. And when Mahomes and the Chiefs blitzed the Colts in the AFC divisional round—giving Kansas City its first home playoff victory in twenty-five years—they prepared to welcome Brady and the Patriots to Arrowhead Stadium for a rematch in the AFC Championship Game on January 20, 2019.

On a frigid night in Kansas City, the game followed a familiar script: The Patriots built a 14–0 halftime lead and led 17–7 entering the fourth quarter, which is when Mahomes started to produce his magic. He led three touchdown drives in the fourth quarter, extending plays, finding throwing lanes, and hitting receiver Sammy Watkins for 38 yards with three minutes left to set up a touchdown that gave the Chiefs a 28–24 lead. On the next drive, Brady threw high to tight end Rob Gronkowski, who tipped the ball into the arms of Chiefs cornerback Charvarius Ward, which should have sent the Chiefs to the Super Bowl, but the play was wiped out by a penalty on linebacker Dee Ford, who was lined up offside. The Patriots took a 31–28 lead on the drive; Mahomes led a furious drive to set up a game-tying field goal. The Patriots won the coin toss in overtime and clinched the game with a 75-yard touchdown drive. The Chiefs could not stop Tom Brady.

"You have to take in the hurt," Mahomes would say. "You have to accept that it hurts. It's supposed to hurt."

In the minutes after the game, the home locker room was catatonic. Ford faced his locker and picked at his belongings. Teammates hugged. Andy Reid stopped to share a message with defensive tackle Chris Jones. "It leaves an odd feeling in your heart," Jones said. Outside the locker room, in a crowded foyer, Mahomes left a press conference and walked a few paces in front of owner Clark Hunt. Nobody was prepared for a debut season like this, and nobody was prepared for the end, but in the moments after the loss, Mahomes found himself in a quiet nook of the locker room, where Brady appeared through a back door.

Brady had missed Mahomes on the field after the game, so he sought out an official to arrange a meeting. He told Mahomes to keep going, that he was doing it the right way. Most of all, Brady seemed to recognize what everyone else did: Mahomes was the future, and the future was coming fast.

THE MARTYBALL '90S

When a lot of people were leaving Kansas City, Quincy Bennett wanted back in. A single mother of three, she slipped a mechanic a few hundred dollars for repairs to her 1979 Ford Thunderbird. The car was a classic, a lowrider coupe with a hood as long as the passenger cabin, but in the summer of 1992, the T-Bird sputtered as much as it purred. That was OK with Bennett, who just needed the car to survive a two-hundred-mile journey and get herself, her two daughters, and her son, Quinton Lucas, to Kansas City.

Lucas was in third grade, but he seemed like a mini adult. He spent many Sunday mornings watching Tim Russert on *Meet the Press* with his mother. He read the newspaper—and not just the sports section. He once sketched out a model city on a scroll of paper, buildings, roads, hospitals, and all. Lucas envisioned Kansas City as something like that: a grand metropolis. He was born there, but had lived in Hutchinson, Kansas, the last few years and knew the place only from his older sisters' stories about the fountains at Royals baseball games and the roller coasters at the amusement park Worlds of Fun. Even the cockroaches were larger, they said.

Lucas's first views of Kansas City outside the T-Bird's windows validated the images he'd built up in his mind: Two-story homes with gabled roofs and three-car garages, as neatly ordered and bountiful as the sorghum crop in Central Kansas, appeared on the side of the highway. Lucas had never seen homes so large. His mother kept driving the Thunderbird north, and then to the east. The houses, he realized, didn't stay "big and giant and new." Those massive homes, with immaculately landscaped yards, were in Johnson County, at the southern edges of Nichols Land. Lucas and his mother were going to the East Side of Kansas City.

That first summer, Lucas lived in a nursing home with his great-aunt Pinkie. Later he resided with Bennett at the Crown Lodge motel, in a single-family home on Indiana Avenue, and in an apartment on Troost. From a duplex on Meyer Boulevard, Lucas could ride his bike about half a mile before butting into the construction of the South Midtown Freeway. The highway had displaced some of his older relatives, and he saw it as an odd-looking intruder among so many homes. Wherever Lucas lived, there was plenty of family around, and plenty of people who believed in him, but Bennett, who worked as a secretary at the accounting firm KPMG and elsewhere, remembers they didn't have much else. Sometimes, they didn't have enough to cover their expenses. They were evicted more than once.

For several hours on weekdays, however, Lucas experienced a very different life. His mother drove him to Barstow Academy, a prestigious K–12 school on the Missouri side of State Line Road, where he had earned a scholarship. They passed Prospect and Troost Avenues, and then the houses started getting bigger, and then they started getting palatial. When Hallbrook, a private golf course and country club, came into view, Lucas knew they had arrived at Barstow. The vast majority of his classmates were affluent and white—he was one of the few Black students, one of the few students who didn't come from means, and probably the only student wearing Malcolm X T-shirts to school. "He certainly moved within two worlds," Bennett recalled. Lucas's neighborhood friends liked playing basketball and video games, and the kids at Barstow played video games, too, but they also hung out at plush new bowling alleys in the farthest reaches of the suburbs and invited him on ski trips to Colorado. The routine of passing a "clean divide" of class and race made Lucas constantly question why the system—the city and its schools and services—was constantly failing those in his community. "Why does it gotta be like that?" he wondered. He ended up writing his college essay on how the world changed on his ride to school every morning.

Between Barstow and the East Side, there was at least one interest that rose above all the differences: the Chiefs. Lucas saw that "poor people love the Chiefs, Black people love the Chiefs, white people, rich people. The doctor kids I went to school with but also the dudes in the barbershop."

"They were," he believed, "this great equalizer."

LUCAS usually watched the Chiefs on TV. Once, however, Bennett snagged a pair of tickets to a preseason game. The seats were at the top of the stadium, so far up that she and Lucas could barely see the players' numbers. It didn't matter. The Chiefs always instilled a sense of pride in Lucas, whether it was from watching them in the nosebleeds, from hearing Kansas senator Bob Dole argue with Russert about the team's supremacy on *Meet the Press*, or from seeing Len Dawson host the nationally televised *Inside the NFL*. To Lucas, the Chiefs made Kansas City—and everyone in it—matter just a little more.

His favorite player was Christian Okoye, a Nigerian-born running back who didn't play football until he was twenty-three. Lucas saw in Okoye somebody who also came from another world and thrived. Okoye, whose shoulders were so broad, it looked like his pads rose higher than his helmet, possessed an absurd combination of speed and strength that nobody in the NFL—at least this side of Bo Jackson—could match. Kansas Citians took to calling him the "Nigerian Nightmare," a nickname Okoye trademarked.

Okoye was the platonic ideal for Martyball, the bruising but ultimately flawed style of play that came to define the Chiefs in the '90s, an era that would torment a generation of kids, like Lucas, who were growing up in Kansas City.

Marty was Marty Schottenheimer, a bespectacled football professor who stuck his play sheet in his pants and quoted Alfred, Lord Tennyson to motivate his players. ("There's a gleam, men. There's a gleam. Let's get the gleam.") Newbie general manager Carl Peterson hired him ahead of the 1989 season. Together they resuscitated a Chiefs franchise that had bottomed out in the 1980s, and transformed a stale and directionless outfit into a perennial playoff team, built on equal parts entertainment and substance. Peterson, a well-coiffed Angeleno with three degrees from UCLA, took care of the entertainment. He first glimpsed Arrowhead Stadium on a clandestine invite from Hunt and saw a "beautiful, magnificent 78,000-seat facility" and a parking lot that was roughly the size of Monaco. Both were desolate on Sundays in the 1980s. Peterson, having seen football at the University of Missouri and the University of Kansas, had learned one thing about the heartland: Give folks enough space to park their Chevy Suburbans and prop a charcoal grill next to a pony keg, and they'll be entertained for several alcohol-fueled hours. So, to stimulate interest, Peterson opened the parking lot for Chiefs games at 9 A.M. and allowed fans to go to their cars for a beer (or three) at halftime. By 1990, Peterson's second season, nearly every game was a sellout, and barbecue smoke and car exhaust swirled for miles.

Schottenheimer's smashmouth football was as delectable for the tailgating masses as a slab of baby back ribs. Okoye slammed through linebackers. Defensive end Neil Smith swung an invisible baseball bat after big tackles. Albert Lewis stuck to opposing receivers like adhesive (Jerry Rice described him as the toughest cornerback he ever faced). Linebacker Derrick Thomas once recorded seven sacks in a single game. The fans, meanwhile, covered their bodies in red paint. They got louder as the weather got colder, as the prime-time lights shone brighter, pushing the decibels to levels previously unheard at NFL games, making the Arrowhead experience a slightly frightening one for small children and opponents alike. (John Elway once asked the referee to tell the crowd to take it down a notch.)

Martyball was 13–7 final scores and the I formation. Martyball was medium-well steaks, beer funnels, and the Rolling Stones' 1981 hit "Start Me Up" blaring before kickoff. But, just as prominently, Martyball was a failure in the postseason. Under Schottenheimer, the Chiefs almost always won more games than they lost. In his best years, they were almost dominant. No matter what, they lost in the playoffs in heartbreaking fashion, done in, usually, by an opposing franchise quarterback who found a seam in the stout defense and by a hyperpredictable offense led by the Chiefs' San Francisco leftover du jour at quarterback, from an uninspiring Steve DeBerg to an aging Joe Montana to a boring Steve Bono.

The litany of failures went something like this:

- 1990: The Miami Dolphins' Dan Marino engineers two second-half touchdown drives in the Chiefs' 17–16 loss.

- 1991: Jim Kelly and the Bills throttle the Chiefs.

- 1992: The Chiefs get shut out by the Chargers, a team they beat twice in the regular season.

- 1993: Joe Montana suffers a concussion in the AFC Championship Game, and the Bills prevail.

- 1994: Dan Marino engineers another comeback in the Chiefs' 27–17 loss.

- 1995: In subzero windchill, Lin Elliott misses three field goals and Steve Bono throws three interceptions in a 10–7 loss to the inferior Colts.

As the losses piled up, Kansas Citians came to feel as tortured as the melancholic figures who abounded in the poetry Schottenheimer knew so well. They were the type of tragedies that drove people to express their own feelings on the page: "Offense was its usual medio-cre style," Lucas wrote after a game in 1996.

Some Barstow teachers convinced Lucas to track the national sporting scene, so he started a journal, "The Quinton Lucas Sports Journal," in which he wrote about the corporate influence of big brands in athletics, reposted a school essay on the danger of concussions, and critiqued local TV stations' coverage of the retirement of Chiefs running back Marcus Allen ("KMBC: Okay, left too soon for Jerry Springer."). But mostly he commented on the ups and downs of being a fan of a snakebit team. In the aftermath of a brutal loss to the Steelers, Lucas imagined an absurdist scenario in which the Chiefs' offensive coordinator, Paul Hackett, endorsed a strategy to have Bono throw passes directly at the Steelers' defense, believing the football would bounce off their chests and into the arms of a Chiefs receiver. Lucas, like everyone else in town, had zero patience with Bono, who once said, half-jokingly, that the "worst restaurant in San Francisco" was "better than the best restaurant in Kansas City." During the 1996 season, Lucas pondered whether he should skip the TV show *Chiefs Update* and instead watch *Knots Landing* reruns. "Donna Mills vs. Steve Bono getting picked off!" Lucas wrote. "What would you pick?"

But Lucas started to get excited in 1997. Bono was gone. He was replaced—as was seemingly written in the city charter—by yet another San Francisco backup, Elvis Grbac, but then Grbac injured his collarbone, so backup Rich Gannon assumed the starting-quarterback position. Behind the stability of Gannon, the Chiefs went 5-1 and finished the season 13-3, landing the top seed in the AFC and entering the playoffs as favorites to (finally!) make the Super Bowl for the first time since 1970. Then Grbac healed, and Kansas City found itself in the throes of a quarterback controversy as the playoffs began. Schottenheimer, as usual, chose predictability and went with Grbac. (In one of the weirder stories in sports history, the Grbac-Gannon controversy eventually led to a hilarious miscommunication in which *People* magazine accidentally named Grbac as its "Sexiest Athlete

Alive," when an editor had actually meant Gannon.) It was a tragi-comedy all around. Facing the Broncos in their first playoff game, the Chiefs trailed 14–10 with two minutes left. Grbac led the team into Broncos territory, but he heaved an errant throw into the end zone on fourth down, and the Chiefs once again failed in the postseason.

Lucas was numb. "For the second time in three years," he wrote, "the Chiefs, the number one seed, were knocked out of the playoffs by a wildcard seed." In that spiral notebook, he summed up the feeling of everyone who watched the Chiefs of the '90s in one rhetorical question: "Why do I have to be a fan of this flip-flop team?"

In time, the losses and the heartbreak manifested themselves in a hard-earned perspective, a worldview, a passion that grew out of the pain. "You got this kind of vibe . . . ," Lucas said, "that we'll make it someday."

Lucas carried this mantra as an undergrad at Washington University in St. Louis and through his law school days at Cornell University, when he listened to Chiefs games on his laptop in the library. When he finished at Cornell, he was offered a lucrative associate position with WilmerHale, a white-shoe East Coast law firm. Lucas was torn. He felt deep pride for his hometown but also pressure to live up to a standard where making it big meant carving out a niche in a more glamorous city. Before he started at WilmerHale, he clerked for a federal judge who had moved back to Missouri after he graduated from Yale Law School. The judge, Duane Benton, asked Lucas: Would he rather be the millionth lawyer in Washington, DC, or make a real impact in Missouri?

THE VOICE

Perhaps the most bizarre thing about Patrick Mahomes—other than his ability to throw a football without looking—is his voice. It's a strange brew of East Texas twang, rocky gravel, and Jim Henson Muppet. In press conferences, he tends to speak quickly and at high volume, which makes it stand out even more. The first time he stepped into a huddle and started to bark out a play call, tight end Travis Kelce started laughing. Mahomes was so rattled, he couldn't even finish.

Kelce was not the first teammate to be confounded by the pitch and intonations of Mahomes's speaking voice. Tyreek Hill likened the sound to Kermit the Frog. Anthony Sherman, the Chiefs' fullback, was just confused. "What's going on?" he thought. Andy Reid was so amused that he started crafting a pitch-perfect imitation.

If there was clear evidence that Mahomes was a genial teammate, the kind of young quarterback who could win over his elders in the cutthroat confines of an NFL locker room, it was his ability to take the teasing in stride. It wasn't like it was new. Adam Cook, Mahomes's high school coach at Whitehouse, recalled that one coach as far back as middle school had used the "Kermit" moniker. Mahomes just embraced it. "I've heard it since I was in, like, seventh grade," he said.

On July 8, 2019, 169 days after the AFC Championship loss to the Patriots, Mahomes happened to be thinking about his voice. It felt a little croaky. He had spent the weekend in Nashville at a childhood friend's bachelor party, wearing a cowboy hat to blend into the crowds, then turned around and flew to Los Angeles on Monday morning to be a guest on *Jimmy Kimmel Live!* When Kimmel mentioned the Nashville trip, Mahomes referenced the collateral damage from the festivities. "The voice, which is already kind of hoarse, is kind of going back and forth with me," he said.

It had been one hell of an off-season. He jetted around the country and added endorsements—including a lucrative deal with Oakley sunglasses and another with Essentia water. He earned the coveted cover spot on *Madden NFL 20*, the latest video game from EA Sports. He flew to Minneapolis to cheer on the Texas Tech basketball team in the Final Four. In the aftermath of his MVP season, he was enjoying the fruits of NFL stardom, and he wanted to bring his teammates along for the ride. So about a month earlier, on May 31, Mahomes had sent a text to Dustin Colquitt, the Chiefs' veteran punter, who had joined the organization in 2005, when Mahomes was nine. *Hey, we're headed to a Stanley Cup hockey game. Do you want to come?*

The game in question was actually game 3 of the 2019 Stanley Cup finals. The St. Louis Blues were set to host the Boston Bruins, and Colquitt quickly realized something: Wasn't the game tomorrow? Mahomes said he'd text him with details. Colquitt offered to drive the four hours to St. Louis. The next day, Mahomes provided a rendezvous point. It was shortly after that, as Colquitt left his home on the Kansas side of State Line Road, that he noticed he was headed to the small airport near downtown: Mahomes had arranged a private jet. The traveling party included Mahomes's girlfriend, Brittany Matthews, and Kelce. When they arrived in St. Louis, a big SUV was waiting. When they rolled up to the arena, Colquitt checked his watch. "We just got to a game in St. Louis in, like, forty-two minutes," he said.

Mahomes stepped onto a crosswalk and put his hood up. The group entered the arena and walked into the NHL commissioner's suite. Mahomes started chatting with someone—some sports executive in a suit—he certainly did not know. It was around this point that Colquitt had an epiphany, the kind of moment that everyone in Mahomes's orbit—from his high school best friends to his Chiefs teammates—was starting to experience. Mahomes was a superstar, and he belonged to an even rarer class of professional athlete, the kind who doesn't just fly around in private jets but who would soon become the brand ambassador for an entire private jet company in Kansas City, an athlete who was growing into a Fortune 500 business unto himself: choreographed public appearances, a charitable foundation, publicists, premanaged appearances on the late-night-television circuit, a brand that would soon be known around the globe.

If Mahomes was burdened by all this, he had an uncanny ability to seem perpetually unbothered, to generally say the right thing at the right moment, to retain a general wholesomeness while being just authentic enough. After Colquitt watched him hold a conversation with a stranger for much longer than he needed to, Mahomes sat down to watch the hockey game, finding a seat at the front of the box, which was soon shown on the arena jumbotron. The crowd began to cheer. Mahomes, wearing a Blues sweater, obliged by chugging the rest of his Coors Light.

SOMEWHERE back inside the suite in St. Louis, Travis Kelce was in the middle of a conversation, doing a little dance to the music in the arena while munching on chicken fingers. He wore a Wayne Gretzky throwback jersey and a red Supreme hat. He was having a great time. Travis Kelce usually seemed to be having a great time. If you could design the perfect road-dog companion for Mahomes, it would probably be someone like Kelce: six feet five, 250 pounds, a badass NFL tight end who had grown up in Cleveland Heights, Ohio, followed his older brother, Jason, to the University of Cincinnati, and been drafted by the Chiefs in the third round in 2013, just months after Reid had arrived in Kansas City. Kelce was not only excellent at catching passes; he exuded a certain type of football player je ne sais quoi, an irresistible mix of energy and cool, the kind of person who wears designer outfits and has an encyclopedic knowledge of '90s references. Once, during practice, Kelce stopped for a moment and quizzed a young player: "Are you old enough to know who Tim 'the Tool Man' Taylor is?"

Kelce also had a hard-earned perspective on second chances: As a sophomore at Cincinnati, he had been kicked off the team for smoking marijuana. His football career in jeopardy, his college life on hold, he moved into his brother Jason's off-campus house and, after taking a job as a health care telemarketer for eight dollars per hour, encouraged the residents of southern Ohio and northern Kentucky to sign up for Obamacare. "I was just getting yelled at every single day," he said.

As he punched the clock and cold-called strangers, Kelce wondered whether he'd wasted his talent and messed up his life. But Jason, a senior offensive lineman, found his brother a place to work out, kept him well fed, and convinced the Cincinnati coaches to take him back. Kelce returned to the program the next year and grew into a tight end with NFL potential. But the labels—immature and tempestuous, to name two—lingered as he arrived in Kansas City in 2013.

Of course he was a little wild. Kelce drew one fine in 2014 for an obscene gesture directed at Von Miller—he appeared to use the universal symbol for wanker—and was ejected in 2016 when he protested a call by throwing a towel at an official. He didn't help his case by starring in a reality dating show (*Catching Kelce*) on E! Entertainment Television in early 2016, when he had made only one Pro Bowl. But perhaps he was just forward-thinking. Because Kelce not only grew into a star, he soon became one of the most prolific tight ends in NFL history, a physical specimen with sure hands, proficient routes, the ability to shred defenses after the catch, and sensational comedic timing.

On the field, Kelce was a quarterback's best friend: always open, a wrecking ball in the field, hauling in eighty receptions per year in Alex Smith's last three seasons in Kansas City. But when Mahomes took over in 2018, his career really took off. It was slightly ironic because Kelce, a passionate defender of Smith, once showed some mild skepticism about Mahomes. When news broke of the trade that sent Smith to Washington, Kelce was at the Super Bowl in Minneapolis and sat down for an interview with radio host Dan Patrick. He seemed confused by the move.

"What's Mahomes give you that Alex Smith does not?" Patrick asked.

"That is something I haven't seen yet," Kelce said.

In truth, a bond between Mahomes and Kelce had already started to form. After the Chiefs' final preseason game in 2017, Mahomes and some other rookies decided to take advantage of an open weekend and go out on a Saturday night, as the only team responsibilities on Sunday were a short morning walk-through. When they bumped into Kelce at a bar, he invited the rookies over to his table, and the excitement picked up. As usual, Kelce was having a great time. When Mahomes got home, he set a series of alarms on his phone but forgot to plug it into a charger. He woke up late, sped off to the team facility, and felt mortified as he sat in the locker room, waiting to be handed a team-issued reprimand. He still wasn't ready for the first question from a Chiefs staff member: Were you with Travis?

Kelce had been late, too.

Mahomes and Kelce would clean up the tardiness and develop a potent chemistry, and when Kelce caught a career-high 103 passes for 1,336 yards in 2018, the tag-team connection was established. They would fly off to the Stanley Cup finals, blend their old friend groups from back home, and compete in celebrity golf tournaments, two friends sharing cold beers and creating a credo for their adventures: "Man, we didn't come here to lay up."

As Mahomes sat on the television set with Jimmy Kimmel, he was living up to the mission statement. In addition to his exhaustive travels, he was spending his off-season sweating through workouts with his trainer Bobby Stroupe, increasing the flexibility and body control that allowed him to perform magic on the field, and focusing on shedding some of the "baby fat" still noticeable from his college days. Everyone in Kansas City was thinking about the Super Bowl. The loss to the Patriots provided all kinds of motivation.

"Do you love Kansas City?" Kimmel asked.

"I love it," Mahomes said. "I honestly do."

Mahomes and Kimmel would spend part of the next four minutes discussing the intricacies of the "Z-Man," the famous brisket sandwich from Joe's Kansas City, a barbecue spot connected to a gas station just a mile or so from Nichols's Country Club Plaza. Mahomes had developed a habit of ordering the sandwich from Postmates, which wasn't ideal for his off-season fitness routine. But before Mahomes could offer a personal review, Kimmel pointed to a fan in the crowd, a transplant from Kansas City named David Leach, who stood up in the audience, turned around, and lifted his Mahomes T-shirt to reveal a huge Mahomes tattoo on his lower back. According to Leach, it had taken every bit of sixteen hours to complete, and even though Mahomes had started just one season in the NFL, and even though he had not yet played in a Super Bowl, two words were inked underneath a depiction of Mahomes throwing a football:

"Champ Stamp."

The only question, it seemed, was, *When?*

REVENGE OF THE COW

As if things couldn't get worse after the Elvis Grbac debacle, one day in Kansas City near the turn of the new millennium, a cow disappeared. The cow, of course, wasn't real, but that made the situation more peculiar. A real cow in a real pasture could wander away from the herd. This cow was a statue, and how could a cow statue, an inanimate hunk of fiberglass displayed in downtown Kansas City, vanish?

The statue was, specifically, *The Hereford Bull*. Some locals knew it colloquially as "BOB," an acronym for "bull on building." The thing was gargantuan: twenty feet long, twelve feet tall, and four feet wide. It weighed 5,500 pounds, almost as much as a killer whale and more than twice as much as an extraordinarily heavy actual bull. But, perhaps because it was attached to the top of a ninety-foot pylon, some people swore BOB was even larger, standing two stories tall and spanning the width of a highway.

BOB was once a big deal for Kansas City. In October 1953, just two years after the disastrous flood depleted the city's famed Stockyards, the American Hereford Association debuted a new headquarters in Quality Hill. It was a whole production, aimed to symbolize the revival of the cattle trade and celebrate the opening weekend of the American Royal horse and stock show, an annual tradition since 1899. President Dwight Eisenhower flew in for the building's dedication. Behind a podium decorated with bunting and stars, he addressed a crowd of seven thousand, made a few insidery cow jokes—people *absolutely lost it* when he mentioned the Black Angus and the Galloway breeds—and unveiled a plaque that described the headquarters as a tribute to the city's pioneers.

But the headquarters lacked something: an earnest representation of the American Hereford Association's mission. So a year later, the association got BOB. He was brown and white, modeled on a Hereford named Hillcrest Larry IV, and sculpted by Paul Decker and fabricated by Rochette and Parzini, who turned over the prototype to workers at the Colonial Plastics and Colonial Neon companies. They pulled out all the stops. Maybe too many: They stuffed the statue's scrotum with cold-cathode fluorescent tubing so the bull could glow a brownish red at night. Laser red lights were mounted to its stern to flash a warning to pilots.

The bull statue got its own dedication ceremony. Although this time Eisenhower was absent, the president did send along a simple prerecorded message. "I now request that the lights be turned on," he said.

And with that, *The Hereford Bull* became part of the skyline, towering over many mid-rise buildings because of its location near the top of a hill. "The people of Kansas City," wrote the *Star*'s editorial board, "will take pride in the fact that the animal is there."

And then the bull statue disappeared. It may have happened in 2000 or 2001. The date is lost to history, because Kansas City did not seem to notice when BOB went missing. His absence might have passed without any fanfare if a cattle-obsessed visitor from New York had not been alerted by a high school friend. Calvin Trillin, the humorist and journalist (and to Kansas Citians, a local boy done good), experienced the Stockyards when they were busy and pungent. "I can still imagine the smell," Trillin said. "Not a good smell." He made it his mission to educate the country on the benefits of Kansas City, convincing the East Coast elite that barbecue, especially Arthur Bryant's slow-cooked meats, was haute cuisine. Trillin lamented Kansas City's disavowal of its cow town image. He was puzzled when he opened an airline magazine one day to find an advertisement for Kansas City containing the tagline "Cowtown No More."

Cows did speak to the city's past. The Stockyards had transformed Kansas City into a competitor of Chicago, and the maze of railroad tracks emptying out in the West Bottoms had made Kansas City an easy destination for traveling musicians, for the likes of Mary Lou Williams and Thelonious Monk to visit, stay, and build a jazz and nightlife mecca.

While investigating the statue's removal on a trip to Kansas City in 2001, Trillin found that BOB had plenty of supporters. ("I love that bull," said the director of the Nelson-Atkins Museum of Art.) But as it turned out, the new tenant of the Hereford Association's building, the architecture and engineering firm HNTB, didn't think a giant cow fit its image. So BOB was gone, lassoed into a subterranean business park fashioned out of limestone caves just north of downtown. The city assumed ownership of the statue and planned for a new home inside a park. BOB would be back, but he would not be part of the skyline.

Kansas City was no longer a cow town. But it also clearly was not the city of the future, or the rip-roaring town of Tom Pendergast and Count Basie, or, for a huge portion of its residents, all that livable.

What was it, then?

IF you viewed Kansas City from the all-seeing eyes of BOB, up high in the animal's old resting spot, you could tell the city didn't stand for much at all. As the 1990s and early 2000s rolled on, pretty much all you would be able to see was Kansas City continuing to get beat up.

Some of these losses were kind of silly, like when corporate overlords dismantled the Zambezi Zinger, a roller coaster as prized as the Coney Island Cyclone in Brooklyn or Space Mountain at Disneyland, and shipped it to Montenegro, Colombia. But some of the losses were catastrophic. It was in 2001 that the South Midtown Freeway, the stretch of US Highway 71 that carved up the East Side, was

completed after years of resistance. The stretch of highway was renamed Bruce R. Watkins Drive, after the late councilman and civil
rights leader. Although Watkins opposed the project, he had worked
for concessions that reshaped its construction, and his family supported the dedication to Watkins. Still, the highway brought noise
and fumes and dangerous intersections to neighborhoods that had
already dealt with having a miles-long scar in the middle of them for
decades. And it was in 1995 that the US Supreme Court canceled
court-ordered remedies sought by Kansas City school district students
as an attempt to correct segregation patterns, achieve more diversity,
and reduce the gap in achievement between city and suburban
schools. (One law journal described the case, which started in 1977,
as "the beginning of the end for desegregation" in America.)

Then there was the disappointment emanating from beneath the
bull statue. The heart of Kansas City still had no pulse. Around six
thousand people lived downtown, a decline from thirty-two thousand
in the middle of the twentieth century. The skyscrapers were beset by
high vacancy rates, and the sidewalks were devoid of pedestrians. The
area, plainly, was not suitable for human life: In a four-block zone
considered to be the core of downtown, parking garages and parking
lots (seven) outnumbered apartment buildings, restaurants, bars, and
hotels (zero). "Downtown was an eyesore," recalled Sylvester "Sly"
James, a prominent attorney, at the time.

James needed cheap rent for his new firm in 2002 and moved to
office space downtown, hanging up a shingle amid a jumble of mas-
sage parlors and empty parking lots cordoned off by rusty chains.
Inspired by the *Mad Max* desolation, James bet another attorney he
could walk naked across the street at 6 P.M. So, one evening in the
early 2000s, Kansas City notched another entry in the city's rich urban lore when James stripped out of his suit and won the bet. "I did
it," he claimed.

It's not that other American cities were doing much better in the
downtown department. But at least Cleveland had a new downtown

baseball stadium and the Rock and Roll Hall of Fame, and other cities, like Baltimore and Denver, made people believe that downtown comebacks were possible. Kansas City could never put together a revival plan. Its attempts had ended with tragedy in the case of the Hyatt or with apathy for everything else. In the late '90s, theater magnate Stanley Durwood proposed an elaborate entertainment zone nicknamed, regrettably, the Centertainment District. Political bickering, red tape, and an inability to secure any tenants for the developments pushed the project further and further from reality. In 1999, Durwood died. Without his prodding, Centertainment fell apart. The door was slammed shut on the project in a unanimous city council vote. Gone, in the words of one councilman, was the "last, best hope" for downtown.

After the meeting, Kansas City's new mayor, Kay Barnes, applied some spin to the defeat, suggesting she had a more expansive, albeit convoluted, plan. Barnes wanted to build an arena, a shiny new complex for basketball and hockey and concerts. There was just one catch: Kansas City had no tenant to fill it.

TO get into politics, Barnes infiltrated boys' clubs. And to infiltrate boys' clubs, Barnes often talked about sports.

She'd grown up just north of Kansas City, the daughter of a high school football coach who showed her the Xs and Os of the plays he ran on Friday nights. Barnes was twenty-five when the Chiefs came to town. She attended the first exhibition game, bought season tickets, and spent many fall Sundays piling into a car and partying with friends outside Municipal Stadium. She was at a friend's house when the Chiefs won the Super Bowl and, at halftime, Barnes noticed funky water levels in the restroom. Later, she heard the same story throughout the region. People were getting up to use the bathroom at the exact same time, the city moving in sync with its team.

In 1999, when Barnes was inaugurated as Kansas City's first woman mayor, a time when both the city and the football team were mired in slumps, she tried channeling JFK—"it isn't enough for me to hear what your city is not doing for you"—and telling residents it was time to think differently. While it would be considerably longer before the Chiefs tried something new and drafted a franchise quarterback, Barnes decided a downtown arena would be her way of showing people she intended to be different, albeit by attempting the same style of revitalization trotted out by Cleveland and others. There was more to her idea than the arena (incentives for new housing, a performing arts center, renovations for Eighteenth and Vine), but she expected the arena to be the equivalent of planting a flag, of posting on the window a neon sign that says, "Yes, we're a real city."

Barnes laid out the specifics in May 2004. Private developers agreed to pay around 40 percent of the $250 million cost, and Sprint pledged to sign a naming-rights contract. But that meant the arena, the Sprint Center as it would become known, hinged on the public for the other 60 percent. Barnes had an idea for this, too. The city would simply jack up fees for hotel rooms and rental cars to cover a large share of the expense.

A ballot question was set for the August 4 primary election. The roughly ninety-day period between Barnes's announcement and Election Day was roughly the same amount of time it took the city to rebuild a state-of-the-art convention hall in 1900. But the Kansas City Spirit of 1900 was fresh. It had not yet been crushed by the play calling of Paul Hackett. So in ninety days, Barnes had arguably just as grueling a task. She had to convince people to have faith in a city that had let them down for decades.

The odds didn't look great. "A dream sequence in a bad sitcom," said one columnist after Barnes shared the plan for the first time. "A mistake," crowed another. And that was just for the concept of the arena. The likelihood of getting an NBA team was more remote. "I've learned not to say never" was all NBA commissioner David Stern promised. There was so much doubt Kansas City could pull it together that the Kansas suburb Olathe sought funding to float its own arena. Johnson County, said one elected official, was the "economic engine" of the Kansas City metro. Not downtown.

The opposition came to a head in July. A collection of odd bedfellows—including a city councilwoman, a rich guy who happened to own land in the West Bottoms near Kansas City's old Kemper Arena, and a rubber stamp and seal company—formed an anti-arena cabal. The group's unquestioned leader, though, was Enterprise, the rental-car colossus headquartered in St. Louis. Enterprise didn't want the extra fees and spent heavily to convince Kansas City that the arena would be just another boondoggle.

As the summer humidity ratcheted up, so did the coalition's intensity. They aired TV ads and hired a professor from the Chicago suburbs to explain why arenas spelled economic disaster. Across from the Golden Ox, an historic steak house, they unveiled a bizarre mural of a storm cloud raining dollar bills above the words "Tax Money down the Drain." Sometimes they said that Kansas Citians would actually foot 50 percent of the rental car tax, and other times they claimed 65 percent. The messages felt inconsistent and a little outsidery, because they were.

Enterprise happened to be from a city with a rooting interest against Kansas City, which gave Barnes an idea. "I'm not going to let some company from St. Louis come in here," she announced at a press conference, "and tell us we cannot have a future."

In essence, Enterprise let Barnes turn the election into something Kansas City found more entertaining than a spat over taxes or the merits of constructing a $250 million building that might never get a pro sports team. Something Barnes knew quite well: a sports-adjacent competition. The haughty St. Louis outsiders versus the underdog Kansas Citians.

In other words, the arena became secondary to pride.

A varied group of supporters coalesced in the run-up to the election. Everyone from Freedom Inc. to local sports radio hosts wanted to fight back. When a professor in San Francisco—a city that had tormented Kansas City for far too long—claimed the Chiefs' fan base would erode because people would be so attached to the new arena and the hypothetical NBA or NHL team that might someday come, Lamar Hunt voiced his support for the Sprint Center. "It's important for Kansas City to show progress," he said.

Barnes still had nerves on Election Day. She left voters with a simple message—"we can stop St. Louis"—but she wasn't sure if they would turn out. And Enterprise, like a classic villain, had not given up. The company bused in dozens of volunteers to stand outside polling locations and harp on the irresponsibility of the downtown plan. Meanwhile, Barnes rode around town. What she encountered was not your usual display of democracy. Throughout the city, scores of people showed up wearing Chiefs gear, and the red-and-gold-clad fans voted yes and hassled the Enterprise volunteers—"almost accosting these poor people," Barnes recalled. Kansas City had been swept up in a tide of old-fashioned boosterism.

When the polls closed, supporters gathered in an empty lot at Fourteenth and Grand for a tailgate, just like at football games. Somebody brought pool chairs, and they grilled out and shot baskets on a miniature hoop. The sun began to fade behind the city skyscrapers. Was Kansas City on the precipice of a new day, or waiting for another defeat to symbolize its sustained obsolescence?

The returns filtered in. Nearly 60 percent of Kansas Citians wanted the arena. It wasn't even all that close.

Shovels went in the ground less than a year later. A supergroup of Kansas City architects renowned for their work on sports facilities—including HNTB, gaining redemption for its sin of unloading the bull statue—molded the Sprint Center into something that resembled a spaceship, a hulking jewel encased with more than two thousand glass panels that gleam day and night.

There were still plenty of questions. So many other gambles, from convention hotels to a massive indoor shopping center, had been trotted out for decades in Kansas City, a civic version of keeping up with the Joneses, which Trillin referred to as "domeism." They had all underwhelmed. But this appeared different, Barnes thought, as if downtown had been lifted to a new plane. An entertainment venue called the Power & Light District opened across the street from the Sprint Center. Similar establishments had popped up around the country. They seemed to all feature some rendition of an Irish pub, an obnoxious piano bar, and a whiskey joint with a mechanical bull. But Kansas City's came with an enormous open courtyard in the middle, which drew a near-fanatical gathering of people for every major sporting event.

There was more change at the southern edge of downtown in the Crossroads neighborhood. It happened slowly at first: an art gallery here. A refurbished loft there. Bars and eateries followed, and a sandwich shop erected a stage in its backyard and packed in three thousand people to see Wilco. First Fridays got so popular that some gallery owners hosted Third Fridays. One entrepreneur decided to celebrate the past that Kansas City had done its best work to eradicate and opened a speakeasy. A sign in the bathroom read, "Al Capone pissed here."

The NBA didn't call, and neither did the NHL. But Kansas Citians didn't much care when the Sprint Center held an open house upon its completion in October 2007. For nearly twelve hours, anybody could tour the city's new downtown addition. Barnes expected two to three thousand people might show up. The actual number, she recalled, was closer to twenty-five thousand. Twenty-five thousand people to ride escalators, critique sight lines, scan menus of unopened concession stands, and use restrooms.

Three days later, Elton John performed at the Sprint Center for a sellout crowd. His first track, a breakup song about a person forced to search for a better way, brought to mind a city that had altered its direction.

THE ELECTION

His first year back home from the East Coast, Quinton Lucas spent his Sundays going to Arthur Bryant's, where he would grab a sandwich and return to his apartment near Eighteenth and Vine, then fall asleep to the incompetent offense of Chiefs coach Todd Haley. He eventually bought season tickets in the nosebleeds and tailgated with a mix of local attorneys and childhood friends, far from the stadium in Lot N. There were cheap beers and pee bags—which are exactly what they sound like—so nobody had to endure the long lines at the portable toilets. It always felt twenty degrees colder than the forecasted low.

After his clerkship with the federal judge, Lucas started at the law firm German May and joined the law school faculty at the University of Kansas in 2012. He dipped his toe into politics, winning a city council seat in 2015 at the age of thirty. His campaign message focused on bridging the gaps between the neighborhoods he represented on the East Side and the tony Nichols neighborhoods on the other side of the city. A year into the job, Lucas proposed a bill to limit incentives for developers. He helped pursue revival plans for the Eighteenth and Vine district. He sponsored legislation that gave a citywide definition for affordable housing, targeting it for people with extremely low incomes. A local political columnist wrote a gushing piece that invoked the name Barack Obama, an audacious comparison, especially since Lucas was barely known beyond the local scene. When he announced his decision to enter a crowded 2019 race for mayor at a local business on Troost Avenue, the kickoff event was modest. The buzz around town surrounded Jason Kander, a former Senate candidate and emerging national darling whose presence in the race threatened to swamp the field. (Kander, a former army intelligence officer, later dropped out to seek treatment for PTSD and depression.)

Kansas City had become a more vibrant city in the last twenty years, but it wanted something new out of the next mayor. Debates and forums indicated Kansas Citians were concerned with violent crime, affordable housing, and a lack of economic development in neighborhoods outside downtown. In a runoff, Lucas faced councilwoman Jolie Justus, a better-funded candidate who had endorsements from previous mayors Kay Barnes and Sly James. Justus discussed plans to make Kansas City more equitable, but Lucas had a compelling advantage: He knew what it was like to be evicted, to grow up in forgotten neighborhoods, to draft legislation for affordable housing. When his campaign knocked on doors—some sixty thousand, purportedly the most by any mayoral campaign in the history of the city—the narrative resonated.

On June 18, 2019, he was elected mayor of Kansas City with nearly 59 percent of the vote. He was thirty-four years old, one of the youngest mayors in America and the youngest in Kansas City in more than a century. He still possessed his copy of "The Quinton Lucas Sports Journal."

IF you needed an example of the Chiefs' unusual hold on Kansas City, you could find it at Lucas's own election-night victory party, where a few hundred people gathered at a venue in a converted Wonder Bread factory on Troost. At some point, a DJ put on the "war chant" track that usually accompanies the "tomahawk chop," the arm-waving motion popular at Arrowhead Stadium (and associated with Florida State University and the Atlanta Braves). Sensing the cringe factor, a Lucas campaign official ran over to the DJ and asked him to change the song.

The tomahawk chop could certainly be an awkward topic in Kansas City. In 2019, it was still a fixture at Arrowhead Stadium, where Native American imagery abounded at every home game: a celebrity guest who banged a drum before kickoff; a horse mascot named Warpaint; fans who wore Native American headdresses. In recent years, Chiefs ownership had convened an American Indian Working Group and altered some of the traditions, blessing the drum with the support of Native American representatives, for instance (and eventually banning headdresses altogether). But aside from distancing itself from the worst instances of cultural appropriation, the team had not seriously considered the future of its name, even as the NFL's Washington Redskins remained under fire (and ultimately dropped the name in 2020).

Kansas Citians could point out that the name "Chiefs" honored former mayor H. Roe Bartle, who was white and who swayed Lamar Hunt to bring the franchise to Kansas City. They could note that "Chiefs," unlike "Redskins" or "Cleveland Indians," was not a slur or a historically inaccurate epithet with its own baggage. It was, broadly speaking, a rank—a term used across the business and political worlds. Of course, others could respond that Bartle's "Chief" nickname stemmed from his role in creating an inauthentic Native American cosplay group with the Boy Scouts, while the franchise's original logo from the 1960s featured a cartoonish "Chief"—holding a tomahawk and a football—running across a map of the Great Plains. Since the mid-2000s, Not In Our Honor, a coalition of American Indians from the Kansas City area, had protested the team's name, the chop, and the drum in the Arrowhead parking lot. They were not included in the Chiefs' working group.

One of the activists was Rhonda LeValdo, an Acoma Pueblo woman and an educator at Haskell Indian Nations University. LeValdo said she loved Kansas City and its diversity, but she worried that the chop and the Chiefs name were traditions that would find an audience with young people across the region, perpetuating hurtful stereotypes while ignoring the history of genocide and oppression against Native people—a story erased from many public schools. In a series of columns that outlined why she thought the chop was disrespectful and done in "a bastardized context," she wrote that "too many people don't care about Native Americans unless they can use our likeness for their companies, cars, or costumes." She added: "We don't need to be reminded that general American society is so disinterested in, and disrespectful of, our culture that they choose to perform nonsense chants."

Among other locals, opinions were mixed—and intense. In Kansas City, the chop itself had become such a commonplace institution—a signifier for communal celebration—that it wasn't odd to see it done at weddings, concerts, or in grocery store ads. So many residents were accustomed to engaging in a cartoonish stereotype that many people believed mocked Native American culture. It even happened on Election Night. The Chiefs had tried to phase it out in the early '90s, when Native American groups voiced their objections, but that changed when fans complained. "If no offense is intended," the team wrote in a newspaper ad in 1992, "why then must offense be taken?" Nearly three decades later, not much had changed. The tradition remained controversial enough that when Lucas became mayor, he was asked for his thoughts. He did not partake in the chop, he said, but he did not want to tell fans how to cheer.

As Lucas took office, his days would soon become consumed by the minutiae of public policy: a zero-fare transit initiative, marijuana decriminalization at the city level, punishment reforms for simple parking tickets. But he took seriously the impact of football on Kansas City. As mayor, he attended most home games, socializing at tamer tailgates that were much closer to the stadium than in his prepolitical days (and much less likely to feature pee bags). At one winter game, Lucas, wearing a black overcoat and a Chiefs scarf and sipping an

IPA, was stopped in the parking lot several times for handshakes. Others just yelled, *"Mayor!"* and kept on walking. Some were old friends, but most were strangers—an older man in a cowboy hat who wanted an autograph, a group of young women who wanted a picture. The tailgating scene reminded Lucas that everybody cared about the Chiefs, just as he had growing up on the East Side.

And yet, as Lucas looked back at his old notebook entries, he realized he had a slightly different relationship with his childhood team: If everyone was going to take pride in the football team and Mahomes, he also wanted them to start thinking about the city's blemishes.

JET CHIP WASP

Every year, Kansas City surveys a random sample of its residents to determine, among other things, how happy they are. The Resident Satisfaction Survey, as it is known, collects anonymous data each fiscal quarter on everything from the approval rating of city services to citizens' top priorities, creating something akin to a civic happiness quotient—a local vibe check. When Sly James, the attorney who claims to have crossed a downtown street in the nude, took office as mayor in 2011, he made a keen observation about the surveys: They really needed to start sending them out after big Chiefs wins.

Every fall, as the leaves change on the Country Club Plaza and the days grow shorter in the heartland, Kansas City becomes its truest self, a city whose outlook is almost wholly dependent on the results of a Sunday football game. This may sound bleak to a certain segment of society, and perhaps hyperbolic to others, but it is at least 98 percent true. "It affects the way the city sees itself," said Jason Kander, the former US Senate candidate who pondered a mayoral run in 2018. It changes the civic calendar, too. Every Friday during NFL season in Kansas City is "Red Friday," an unofficial holiday that dates back to 1992, when a local businessman pitched Chiefs owner Lamar Hunt on a weekly pep rally, complete with a special Chiefs edition of the newspaper, the proceeds going to charity. And if this sounds like some quaint tradition that might happen in a college town, that was the idea. The city adorns streetlamps on the Plaza and downtown with Chiefs logos. The exterior lights at Union Station glow red. Kids wear their

Chiefs jerseys to school. Even local baristas put on trendy KC T-shirts from Charlie Hustle—a local brand famous for its heart-themed design—and serve lattes to customers wearing the same thing. Whether you live on the East Side, not far from Eighteenth and Vine, or in some far-flung suburb in Nichols Land, the Chiefs Kingdom flags are up.

As Kansas City marked its first Red Friday in 2019, the vibes were particularly sunny. Patrick Mahomes was the reigning MVP. The defense had added safety Tyrann Mathieu (nickname: the Honey Badger). The Chiefs were Super Bowl contenders (+600 preseason odds in Vegas, trailing only the Patriots), which meant Kansas City was still adjusting to a bizarre new reality, an identity crisis of sorts, because it possessed the franchise quarterback who made the unimaginable seem feasible—not the least of which was making a city feel good about itself. If the mood of the city was determined by the Chiefs, though, one thing was certain:

October 17, 2019, was almost one of the worst days in Kansas City history.

It all happened on a Thursday night in Denver, the seventh game of the 2019 season, when Mahomes lay on the grass near the Broncos' 3-yard line, his right kneecap twisted so far from its anatomically correct position that it appeared to be located somewhere on the outside of his leg. "It's out," Mahomes said, his voice loud enough for teammates to hear. "It's out." Mahomes had run a quarterback sneak on fourth-and-1 from the 5-yard line early in the second quarter, barreling forward into the jaws of the line. When the pile of bodies cleared, he was still at the bottom, awkwardly lying on his left side, on the back of center Austin Reiter, who didn't realize what was happening. "Stay still," a voice told him. From the start, everyone feared the worst. Mahomes pointed at his knee, unsnapped his chin strap, removed his helmet, and covered his face with his hands, his eyes revealing a dazed look of panic. The Chiefs' training staff rushed onto the field. If you looked closely, as Travis Kelce did, you would have noticed that Mahomes's patella—the medical term for the kneecap—had popped out of the trochlear groove, where it usually sits, which meant that inside the knee joint all manner of tendons and ligaments were being stressed and stretched and possibly catastrophically damaged. His knee, Kelce thought, didn't even look like a knee. ("You think, like, hopefully he can play football again," Kelce would say.)

The Chiefs were 4-2, opening the season with four straight wins before home losses to the Colts and Texans, which was not quite the dominance they expected. But if an October slump was worrisome, this new problem was the Kansas City equivalent of DEFCON 2. If Mahomes's major ligaments were shredded, his season was in jeopardy. If his season was over, the Chiefs' Super Bowl hopes were dead. Out on the field in Denver, J. Paul Schroeppel, a Chiefs team doctor, crouched down and cradled Mahomes's right leg with his hands, straightening it out with his right hand, then gently pushing his patella back into place with his left. *Click.* Mahomes came to his feet and refused a cart; he wanted to walk to the sideline. He kept saying he was fine, that he wanted to go back in, though later he would admit that he, too, was worried his season was done. He returned to the visitors' locker room, where an X-ray showed no significant damage, which was a relief, but only a magnetic resonance imaging exam—an MRI—the next day would reveal the true extent of the injury. As Mahomes sat inside the locker room, watching the rest of the Chiefs' 30–6 victory on a television, he was joined by general manager Brett Veach; girlfriend, Brittany; and his father, who hadn't planned on being in Denver until he had a premonition that his son might get hurt. "It's in my bones," he told his wife. At some point, as visitors came and went, and Mahomes watched the game, Veach considered the upside. It was going to be a crazy story to tell after they won the Super Bowl.

Which is how the greatest comeback story in Chiefs history began.

OF all Mahomes's athletic superpowers, there was one that nobody knew existed. His ligaments and joints were apparently very pliable. This was not an accident. Every week during the season, Mahomes would meet with Bobby Stroupe for a series of workouts, a routine separate from his duties with the Chiefs. On Mondays, they executed their "A" workout, a regimen that consisted of twelve different squat positions, sixteen lunge positions, twenty movement patterns, and a full-on gymnastics routine, which could last two hours. The goal was resiliency. Stroupe likened the work to the art of motorcycle maintenance, a philosophy of daily practice. "If you're always working on your Jet Ski or motorcycle," Stroupe said, "it's not broke."

In order for Mahomes to engage in the impossible, he first had to put his body to the test. Mahomes sometimes hated the flexibility-workout circuit, but perhaps he hated it less when his MRI revealed no major structural damage to his right knee, when he was running on an underwater treadmill two days later, when he was back at practice that week stretching with his teammates, when he missed only two games, the Chiefs going 1-1 with backup QB Matt Moore. Mahomes returned on November 10, just twenty-four days after dislocating his kneecap, in a road game in Tennessee. He threw for 446 yards and three touchdowns in a 35–32 loss to the Titans, which dropped the Chiefs to 6-4, but most importantly, they were still in first place in the AFC West.

Mahomes's recovery wasn't literally miraculous. It could be explained using medical science, modern rehab methods, and sheer luck. (His father would claim his son was double-jointed, a genetic gift he received from his mother.) But it seemed to enforce something that people in Kansas City believed: Mahomes was different, not just in his virtuosic play or his intangible leadership qualities, but in his literal physiological makeup—including the ligaments inside his knee. He was, as Kelce would put it years later, the "Houdini of our era."

The week after the Titans loss, the Chiefs beat the Chargers in Los Angeles. Then they routed the Raiders at home and went on the road to New England, where they defeated the Patriots 23–16, clinching a fourth straight AFC West title and becoming the first road team to win in Foxborough, Massachusetts, in more than two years. Mahomes hurt his hand in the victory, though X-rays came back negative again, and it didn't seem to linger. (He threw for 340 yards and two touchdowns the next week.) The Chiefs closed the season with six straight wins, which was enough to edge the Patriots for the No. 2 seed in the AFC playoffs after Ryan Fitzpatrick—a.k.a., "Fitzmagic," the bearded, Harvard-educated quarterback of the Miami Dolphins— engineered a truly miraculous upset of New England in Week 17, giving Kansas City a crucial first-round bye.

But that was all prologue to the AFC divisional round against the Houston Texans, when Mahomes conjured his most death-defying act to date. With 10:58 to go in the second quarter and the Chiefs trailing 24–0—the result of disastrous special teams and a million drops—Mahomes stood before his offensive teammates on the sideline and started to raise his voice. "They're playing man coverage," he said, gesturing with his hands. "We catch the ball and make one person miss, it's a touchdown. Let's do something special. Let's do something special. They're already counting us the fuck out!"

Arrowhead Stadium was quiet, the postseason ghosts circling above, the demons so familiar that a thirty-one-year-old postal worker named Charles Penn, believing he was a jinx, stood up and left. Then it all changed so fast, a wave of free-form offense so note-for-note perfect that it seemed hard to process. Mahomes led touchdown drives on the next seven possessions, a postseason record that included four touchdown passes in the final ten minutes of the first half. And not only did the Chiefs win, rolling to a 51–31 victory, but they held the lead by halftime. "Thank God we've got Pat Mahomes," defensive end Frank Clark said.

The next Sunday, the Chiefs hosted the AFC Championship

Game against the No. 6 seed Tennessee Titans, who had handed Mahomes a loss in his first game back from his knee injury. The Titans did not seem like a particularly good matchup. They had beaten the Patriots during wild-card weekend before knocking out the No. 1 seed Baltimore Ravens in the divisional round, and they had running back Derrick Henry, a six-feet-three, 250-pound, modern-day Jim Brown. And sure enough, the Titans jumped out to a 10–0 lead. This time, Mahomes didn't need to use his voice; he needed only his legs, pulling off a scrambling, juking, spinning touchdown run just before halftime that was officially a 27-yard touchdown run down the sideline but had covered close to 64 yards of turf, causing CBS broadcaster Jim Nantz to scream into his microphone: "Out of this world!"

The Chiefs finished out a 35–24 victory, and Mahomes held up the Lamar Hunt Trophy—named for the franchise founder and given to the AFC champion. Kansas City was in the Super Bowl for the first time in a half century, which meant that Resident Satisfaction Survey levels were off the charts, and for a moment it felt like a dream. The Chiefs would play in Super Bowl LIV at Hard Rock Stadium in Miami against the San Francisco 49ers, the team that had once supplied to Kansas City a generation's worth of backup quarterbacks— the game managers and also-rans who had defined an era. But this time, the Chiefs had something special. Patrick Mahomes.

"DO we have time to run Wasp?"

Mahomes was standing near his sideline midway through the fourth quarter of Super Bowl LIV, with 7:13 left on the clock, the Chiefs trailing the San Francisco 49ers 20–10, and a crowd of 62,417 crammed inside Hard Rock Stadium on a perfect February night in South Florida. Eric Bieniemy looked up at the quarterback from a play sheet.

"You like Wasp?" Bieniemy said.

On the previous play, second-and-15 from the Chiefs' own 35, Mahomes had stepped into pressure and flung an underthrown pass over the middle to Tyreek Hill, who adjusted his route and attempted to dive back to the football. At first, it was ruled a catch, which gave the Chiefs a first down just past midfield, but 49ers coach Kyle Shanahan tossed a challenge flag, summoning referee Bill Vinovich to the San Francisco sideline.

"What do we got?" Vinovich asked. "Incomplete?"

"Yeah," Shanahan said.

Shanahan was correct. Hill had let the ball touch the ground before completing the catch. But as Vinovich left to go check the replay, Mahomes had time to wander over to confer with Bieniemy, which led to a question: Did they have time to run Wasp? Mahomes wasn't talking about the game clock. Seven minutes remained, so the Chiefs had plenty of literal time to run Wasp, one play in Andy Reid's dictionary-size playbook. But Mahomes wondered if they would have the requisite protection for Wasp—a slow-developing deep shot to Hill—before the 49ers' fearsome pass rush destroyed the pocket, as it had done all game. To that moment, Mahomes had played arguably the lousiest game of his career, which was relative, of course, and also a direct reflection of the San Francisco defense, a unit that ranked among the NFL's best. In the regular season, the 49ers had surrendered the fewest passing yards in the league and led all teams in yards-per-play allowed. Their pass rush—a balanced force that featured Pro Bowl defensive tackle DeForest Buckner, top rookie Nick Bosa, and former Chief Dee Ford—led the league in quarterback hurries on a per-play basis, and when San Francisco wasn't harassing opposing quarterbacks, it was suffocating receivers and snuffing out the big play. The 49ers, amazingly, had allowed just eight completions on passes thrown at least 20 yards in the air, the lowest number in the past fourteen years.

For three and a half quarters in the Super Bowl, the 49ers had forced Mahomes to run for his life. Shifting between Cover 3 (a zone defense where three defensive backs are responsible for the deep third) and "Quarters" (where four defenders each guard a quarter of the field), San Francisco neutralized Mahomes's most dangerous weapon: the deep ball. At times, the 49ers supplemented the zone look with a "Robber" coverage: One safety in their Cover 3 scheme would slide down and take away crossing routes in the middle of the field. But mostly, they turned up the heat. Late in the first quarter, on a third-and-long from the San Francisco 15-yard line, Mahomes had scrambled to his right and taken off sprinting toward the end zone, only to be blasted inside the 5 by safety Jimmie Ward, who sent the football flying out of bounds. "That's a good-ass hit," Mahomes told Ward, as he picked himself up. On fourth-and-short, the Chiefs kept the drive alive with a play called "Shift to Rose Bowl Right Parade," complete with presnap choreography that resembled a boy band's and a direct snap to running back Damien Williams, and Mahomes finished the drive with a touchdown on a 1-yard run around the edge, giving the Chiefs a 7–3 lead.

From there, though, the 49ers' defense seized control, blowing up plays at the line of scrimmage, squeezing the life out of the Chiefs' offense, forcing Mahomes into interceptions on back-to-back drives in the third and fourth quarters as the deficit swelled to 20–10. In the moments after the first interception, Andy Reid found Mahomes on the sideline. Reid had been an NFL head coach for twenty-one seasons, but he still thought of himself as a teacher first, so he offered Mahomes an old piece of advice, the words he used to tell Donovan McNabb and pretty much every quarterback he'd ever coached: "Listen," he said, "you just keep firing." But when a pass intended for Hill on the next drive was a few inches behind its target, it tipped off the receiver's hands and ended up in the arms of San Francisco safety Tarvarius Moore, who corralled the interception, then bolted for the corner of the stadium, where the 49ers defense gathered for a candid celebration, as if posing for a victory photo. On the sideline, Mahomes found a seat on a bench and held a tablet in his hands, until backup quarterback Matt Moore wandered over and tried to lift his spirits: It's never over, Moore told him. "I got you, baby," Mahomes said, his voice rising an octave, almost defiantly. "I'm believing."

What Mahomes wanted most was the ball back in his hands, to put seven on the board and push the 49ers to respond, to see if they might break. "Make 'em tighten up!" he yelled. When the defense did its job, Mahomes stepped back into the huddle, and six plays later, as the officials reviewed Hill's bobble, the Chiefs faced third-and-15 from their own 35-yard line.

"DO we have time to run Wasp?"

The name itself was not a cypher. It derived from a batch of play names inspired by insects, a shorthand trick to simplify the confusing language of the West Coast offense, another creation from the beautiful mind of Reid. The full name was "Gun Trey Right 3 Jet Chip Wasp Y Funnel," which included the formation, the protection call, and the route concept. The formation called for trips—three receivers—to line up to the left side of Mahomes and another tight end to the right. The outside receiver on the left was Sammy Watkins, who would run a deep ninety-degree "in" route (sometimes called a drag or dig). The inside receiver was Travis Kelce, who would run a Stutter Cross across the field. In between them was Hill, the Wasp, who would run a double move, feigning a deep post to freeze the safety in the middle of the field before turning back to the corner of the field.

A football play, at its most basic level, is an act of deceit. There is a reason why a coach refers to their offense as a "scheme," a description not far removed from a scam, a sleight of hand to make a defense believe one truth over another. The Chiefs had run Wasp in the 2018 AFC title game, when Tom Brady had bested Mahomes at Arrowhead Stadium, and the key was not just the blinding speed of Tyreek Hill. It was the acting job of Watkins, who was supposed to run his route with precision and vigor and attract the defensive back responsible for the outer third of the field, where Hill was headed. The play had worked against the Patriots, and Hill had done a little celebratory jig on a cold night in Kansas City, but that was not the beginning of the Wasp. A football play is a living, breathing organism, not unlike a city, always evolving, a reaction to what has come before. In the 2018 preseason, before Mahomes had electrified the NFL, the Chiefs had run a variation of the Wasp concept against the Atlanta Falcons, where Hill lined up in trips to the left and ran a deep post across the middle of the field, hauling in a 69-yard bomb from Mahomes. The touchdown did not count in the official ledger of NFL statistics, but in a small way, it might have changed NFL history, because at that moment, everyone in the league knew: If Mahomes and Hill were on the field together, you could never stop worrying about something as simple as a deep post.

Back on the sideline, Bieniemy held a play-call sheet in his hands as he conducted two conversations at once. On his headset, he was communicating with Reid, who needed to sign off on the call. In front of him was Mahomes.

"What down and distance do you like it?" Bieniemy asked.

"If it's first-and-10, Wasp," Mahomes answered. Then he added, "Any down and distance."

For a second, it felt as if Mahomes was back on a Little League baseball field in Whitehouse, Texas, where he would turn to his coach, Chad Parker, and suggest a move or in-game strategy. He always saw sports through a different lens than his peers did, thinking two plays ahead, recognizing patterns and trends, following in the footsteps of his father, who, before the Super Bowl, had sent his son a text message: *Players make plays, and I love you.* As Vinovich announced the incompletion inside Hard Rock Stadium, Mahomes was convinced he had the right play. He returned to the huddle, where he told his teammates the call, and then turned to his receivers. He told Hill and Kelce to get open and pointed at Watkins, the decoy. "You be working!" As the Chiefs broke the huddle and lined up, Watkins was covered by cornerback Emmanuel Moseley, who was responsible for the outer third of the field in the Cover 3 zone. Jimmie Ward, the safety who'd battered Mahomes in the first quarter, had the middle third. If Watkins could force Moseley to bite on his deep in route, if only for a second, Hill would have an opening. Would Mahomes have the time?

HE lined up in the shotgun. DeForest Buckner, Nick Bosa, and the rest of San Francisco's pass rush crouched at the line of scrimmage. Nearly everyone at Hard Rock Stadium was standing. In Kansas City, more than 97 percent of televisions turned on were tuned into the game, from the East Side to Nichols Land to the Power and Light District downtown, where thousands of fans nervously watched on a giant screen.

Mahomes took the snap and dropped back nearly nine steps, an extraordinary drop out of the shotgun, giving Hill time to get downfield. But even with the extra depth, the 49ers created an instant push, and Buckner, the defensive tackle, came free around the outside. As Buckner closed in, Mahomes made a decision: Hill was going to be open. He just needed to put it out there, so he planted his feet, leaned ever so slightly away from the rush, and created enough torque with his body to wing the ball as far as he could. *A huck.* For a second, it hung in the air, sailing 57 yards through the night sky, creating a parabola high above Hard Rock Stadium, until the picture came into focus: There was Hill, all alone, settling under the pass, cradling the ball like a baby at the 23-yard line. It was officially a 44-yard completion—and a first down and much more. Moments later, Mahomes hit Kelce for a touchdown and went running to the sideline.

"This shit ain't over," he yelled, to anyone who would listen. "Let's go get it!"

Once again, Mahomes was right. Jet Chip Wasp had changed the game—a "65 Toss Power Trap" for a new Kansas City. The Chiefs' defense forced a three-and-out, and Mahomes marched the offense down the field, leading a 65-yard drive that culminated in a go-ahead touchdown pass to Damien Williams with 2:44 left. It was far from over, but it more or less was. The Chiefs led 24–20. They had Patrick Mahomes, and when the defense made another stop and Williams got loose for a 38-yard touchdown run, Kansas City was the Super Bowl champion for the first time in fifty years.

In the moments after the victory, as the confetti dropped and the party began back in Kansas City, Reid found Mahomes and gave him a kiss on the cheek. Mahomes was twenty-four, the youngest quarterback in history to win Super Bowl MVP, and as he kept moving about the celebration, he finally found his mother and his father, who was bawling. "We did it, baby," Mahomes said, enveloping his father in a bear hug. "We did it. I love you."

All around Hard Rock Stadium were people from Kansas City: Bobby Bell, the Chiefs legend who had had to fight to buy a home in the suburbs in the 1960s and then stayed in Kansas City the rest of his life; Quinton Lucas, the thirty-five-year-old mayor who as a boy had found solace in the franchise; Paul Rudd, the child of the suburbs who hugged his son, Jack, as the celebration began. "It feels like I'm seeing colors for the first time in my life," he told a reporter.

There was Brett Veach, the personal assistant turned general manager; there was Andy Reid, the head coach who finally got his ring; there was Mahomes, who wore a gray championship T-shirt over his shoulder pads and wove his way through the crowd on the field, back to the Chiefs' locker room, where the offensive line was posing with the Super Bowl trophy and teammates were talking about Mahomes's dislocated kneecap, just as Veach had predicted. Near the front of the room, defensive tackle Chris Jones was surrounded by a group of reporters. He was shouting. "We gonna build a fucking dynasty in Kansas City!" he said. "We're like the Golden State Warriors, baby."

Back in Kansas City, it felt like the beginning.

PART IV

Diane Charity speaks at a rally in 2022 in downtown Kansas City.

A FOUNTAIN AND A RECKONING

The demonstrators met on May 31 at the J.C. Nichols Memorial Fountain, which was in the southern end of a park that ran adjacent to J.C. Nichols Parkway, the road bordering the Country Club Plaza. It was a little more than one hundred days after the Super Bowl parade, and more than a thousand people packed into the park to sway and chant and protest. Lots of them carried signs that said "Black Lives Matter." At least one person dressed in a Patrick Mahomes jersey. There were people from downtown and the North End and the East Side. There were people from Kansas and Missouri suburbs. There were so many people that when organizer Justice Horn looked at the crowd assembled in the park, he could have sworn they were undulating like some sort of wave. "It looked like an ocean," he recalled.

Six days earlier, police officer Derek Chauvin had murdered George Floyd. Protests in Minneapolis spread to Memphis and Los Angeles, and the unrest reached Kansas City on Friday, May 29, when a few dozen protesters gathered near the Plaza. More people showed up the next day, and the atmosphere grew tense at night. Some of the police fired tear gas and projectiles on the crowd, and some of the protesters vandalized and graffitied stores on the Plaza and set a police car ablaze. Meanwhile, Horn, an LGBTQ rights activist and recent graduate of the University of Missouri–Kansas City, where he had served as student body president, had been circulating a Facebook event for a Sunday rally with other activists. The RSVP list went from a few dozen to more than a hundred after a day, and then the attention spread rapidly, multiplying to several thousand.

Just after 2 P.M., the ocean of people shouted, "Power to the people," and the rally began. The fountain was surrounded with water bottles, first-aid kits, and containers of milk (in case police used tear gas). Several speakers addressed the crowd, including Horn, longtime activist Sheryl Ferguson, and the parents of young Black men who had been killed by the police. An older man, dressed in a Kansas City Royals polo, took to the microphone.

Emanuel Cleaver II, a civil rights leader, Kansas City's first Black mayor, and a congressman for the past fifteen years, had been here a lifetime ago. Next to the J.C. Nichols Memorial Fountain in 1972, he organized "Resurrection City" as his first demonstration in Kansas City. Cleaver and other leaders hung a tarp among oak trees, and some 150 people without homes stayed in the encampment for six days, resisting a city ordinance banning overnight sleeping in public parks, and showing Kansas City's most powerful people they were insulated from the city's deepest issues. "Protest is righteous," Cleaver told the crowd, reflecting on the experience. Cleaver had been surprised by the response to Resurrection City back then—only a few people stopped by to heckle, and plenty of Plaza residents asked how they could help. But nearly fifty years later, he was moved by what he was witnessing in the park. "This is about as beautiful a representation of the great rainbow of humanity that I have ever seen . . . Black, white, and brown sitting on the ground. This is America."

After the speeches, the protesters left the park and marched through Midtown. When they returned in the early evening, the police formed a wall along J.C. Nichols Parkway, blocking people from marching on the Plaza. The city had set a curfew for 8 P.M. The police arrested people who attempted to cross into the Plaza and, again, launched tear gas. (They claimed protesters threw water bottles at officers.) Horn noticed what felt like a swipe to his eyes. They started to itch and burn and then his vision clouded up. As fellow protesters rushed to wash his eyes out with milk, a thought entered Horn's mind, one that had undoubtedly dawned on others: "We were there standing in solidarity [for Floyd], but we have a problem in our own home."

The city had progressed a lot since the days when Curtis McClinton and Mike Garrett were denied quality housing options. Countless local activists had fought to usher in an era when African Americans could win election as mayor and to the city council, serve in the chamber of commerce, and reside in any neighborhood. Troost Avenue itself had been rejuvenated by local businesses. But the legacy of redlining endured in 2020, Kansas City standing out as a stark example of America's entrenched segregation. A few blocks west of Troost were stately mansions, dozens of banks, and office buildings occupied by physicians and doctors and specialists for all types of ailments. A few blocks to the east were rental homes, scant places to obtain a loan or start a savings account, and zip codes where the life expectancy was fifteen years lower than the city average. The East Side was still predominantly Black, and, on average, Black Kansas Citians were more likely than white Kansas Citians to be enrolled in underperforming schools, live far from economic opportunities (and have more difficulty finding transportation to them), face higher unemployment rates, and be vulnerable to rapidly increasing rents. It was Black Kansas Citians who shared stories of police brutality and being severely punished for minor infractions. The region's infamous sprawl, meanwhile, meant Kansas Citians with means could keep gobbling up the open space, moving far enough to never encounter these problems, or interact with anyone who did.

Horn saw the protests as a lightning bolt, a rare moment when otherwise disparate Kansas Citians got together. It was, therefore, a time to examine Kansas City's problems.

Days later, outside police headquarters, the protesters got the city to agree to a list of demands, including to fund body cameras for the police and to prioritize wresting control of the police department from the state of Missouri, a practice that had continued since the Civil War era—aside from a few years under Pendergast—and that kept Kansas City from making key decisions on how to operate its own police department.

The demonstrations continued for days. More marching, chanting, and demanding. Sometimes the protesters met downtown, but they mostly chose the Plaza area, back at the fountain.

THE J.C. Nichols Memorial Fountain, as it became known, arrived in Kansas City in 1951, a Nichols family purchase from the Long Island estate of a New York financier. It was refurbished and installed on the Plaza in 1960. The fountain, which was adorned with four bronze horsemen that represented the four rivers from which life had sprung, turned into an enduring symbol of the developer. But if one wanted to see a monument to Nichols, as the pastor who eulogized him suggested upon the community builder's death, in 1950, all one needed to do was "look around."

Nichols's monuments were the Plaza, Kansas City's distinguished Nelson-Atkins Museum of Art, and the Liberty Memorial. His monuments were the Troost Wall, an eroded city core, and the racial covenants, unenforceable but never stricken from most of his neighborhoods' deeds. His monuments were curvy, tree-lined vistas, spacious cul-de-sacs, and strong neighborhood associations that fought tooth and nail against change. His monuments were inequity, like the fact that some middle-class houses east of Troost, which cost the same amount as similar homes west of Troost in the middle of the twentieth century, were now worth roughly one-fifth as much as the housing to the west, preventing many Black Kansas Citians from earning generational wealth. In 2019, a report from the Urban League of Greater Kansas City showed the median net worth of a Black family in Kansas City was 10 percent of the median net worth of a white family.

Nichols's legacy was a fraught coupling: It was "Beauty," as his daughter-in-law Martha Nichols said in a 2006 PBS documentary, and it was devastation—how he "took the model of redlining in Kansas City, and it went national," said Pastor Ron Lindsay, who remembered learning about Nichols in a civics course at Southeast High School in the 1970s.

Over the years, one side clearly won out. As Gabe Coppage, an activist and artist who grew up on the East Side in the 2000s, recalled, "I definitely knew the Troost line was a dividing line, but I didn't necessarily know how much work it took to make it that way." Said the author Whitney Terrell, "You did not discuss why the city was arranged the way it was. You just didn't talk about it."

Terrell had an inside glimpse into Nichols Land. He grew up in one of the developer's neighborhoods in the 1980s and '90s, and one of his aunts married Miller Nichols, leading to the occasional dinner at Miller's home, a palatial estate with a cupola on the roof and a front yard that Terrell remembered as doubling as a burial site for an old racehorse. Friends and neighbors filled their homes with paintings of the Plaza and other tchotchkes that brought to mind the Nichols family. "They were incredibly popular," Terrell said. "They were really, really highly thought of. There's, like, the Royals, and the Chiefs were terrible, and then there was J.C. Nichols, who invented all this great stuff."

Later, as Terrell brainstormed ideas for his second novel, another aunt showed him a racial covenant for her subdivision. It felt to Terrell like he had found a secret that explained why downtown was abandoned and why so many white people like him and his family had moved to the outlying neighborhoods of Kansas City, Missouri, or the Kansas side of the metro.

In 2005, Terrell released his novel *The King of Kings County*. It wasn't exactly a roman à clef, but the novel did feature a prominent developer with the last name Bowen and a decorated shopping center called the Campanile with an annual Christmas-lights tradition. The book told of covenants and blockbusting, of urban renewal and highway building, of unfettered suburban growth and downtown disinvestment.

Terrell's book sold well locally and nationally. It was well reviewed by critics. But also: Kansas City sort of missed the point. People were reading the book, Terrell recalled, and hailing it as a tale about the American dream rather than systemic racism. Some local reviewers didn't even mention the Nichols family. Eventually, however, the message filtered out in book clubs and on social media. The Kansas City Public Library hosted events with Terrell and civil rights leaders. Historians who spoke about Nichols would be approached by Black residents living in the Country Club District who would show them a document with their subdivision's restrictions, still imprinted with a racial covenant. At one point, Cleaver described the covenants as a "national embarrassment," and professors at the University of Missouri–Kansas City inserted lessons on Nichols into the curriculum. Terrell thought the city had perhaps reached a tipping point when he heard Soren Petro, a Kansas City sports radio host on local station 810 WHB, talk about the covenants on the air. "And I was like, 'Holy shit, we finally got this all the way to 810.' That means it's become a commonly known thing in the city."

People were finally doing what Kansas Citians had been allergic to doing for decades: talking about the shape of their city. And in June 2020 many of them happened to be gathering en masse in the same park next to the Plaza.

CHRIS Goode, a Kansas City Parks and Recreation commissioner at the time and an entrepreneur, lived with his family on Forty-Sixth Street, across from the fountain. He saw the protesters march on Main Street and a TV news vehicle go up in flames. Outside his apartment he stepped on a police officer's tear gas canister. Having been racially profiled and mistreated by police in the past, Goode related to the protesters' pain and felt called to do something.

Goode had grown up on the East Side in the 1980s and '90s, attending a daycare on Troost Avenue. To him, the street that many Kansas Citians perceived as a dividing line was where he got dropped off by a bus every morning and shopped at a day-old bread store. "It was just home," Goode recalled. He opened Ruby Jean's, a healthy juice and food establishment, in 2017 on Troost. The street, the entire East Side, had never seen anything like it. Goode set up a long communal table in the center of the store to enhance the chances of customers conversing with strangers, and Ruby Jean's saw a near-even mix of Black and white customers and people coming in from both sides of Troost. A community mural was painted on the exterior, a vibrant mix of people from different cultures and races—a vision of what Goode considered the true reality of Troost Avenue, instead of what it had become known for under the influence of Nichols and segregation.

With a fountain and parkway named after Nichols, Goode saw Kansas City honoring hate and division in a highly visible area. The J.C. Nichols Memorial Fountain was on postcards. Television producers shared images of its four horsemen, sometimes spraying red-colored water, when they returned from commercial breaks during Chiefs broadcasts. On June 4, Goode typed up the "Unity Memo," a short letter presenting the need to strike Nichols's name from the fountain and parkway and to stop allowing "racism to take center stage in our most photographed, valued, and visited destination in Kansas City." Just before he hit send, circulating the memo to the mayor's office and parks department leadership, Goode prayed.

The idea of removing Nichols's name from the fountain and parkway had been floated before but never gained traction. Steve Kraske, a host on local NPR station KCUR, suggested a name change in 2017. Artist Chico Sierra started a renaming petition in 2019. Kansas City had a decidedly mixed record regarding the people it honored. There were Emanuel Cleaver II Boulevard and Mary Lou Williams Lane for the jazz legend, and the Liberty Memorial reminded everyone of the soldiers who fought in World War I. But Troost Avenue was named for a slave owner, and Kansas City had also achieved infamy as one of the only major cities in the country lacking a street honoring Martin

Luther King Jr. In 2019, the city council voted to rename the Paseo—
the historic boulevard on the East Side—as MLK Boulevard. Yet the
decision turned into a fiasco when the predominantly Black population
who lived on the street felt their voices were not included in the decision, and nearly two-thirds of the city voted to restore the Paseo name.

To avoid similar backlash, Goode partnered with Roosevelt Lyons, a deputy director for the parks department, to set up public listening sessions and a formal process for removing the Nichols name.
He spoke with Whitney Terrell about Nichols's legacy. He contacted
Justice Horn to ask him to spread the word about the opportunity for
public input.

Over the next few weeks on Zoom, because Zoom was where you
met in 2020, Kansas City discussed Nichols. One person said it was
"high time" for removing the developer's name. Somebody shared
that they were now finally realizing why they had always glorified living west of Troost. Another speaker said Kansas City could not continue with the nickname "City of Fountains" if it celebrated J.C.
Nichols on the most prominent one. Even those who wanted the name
to stay acknowledged the pain Nichols had inflicted as he shaped
Kansas City. On June 30, the Kansas City parks board made the removal of Nichols's name official in a unanimous vote.

The next day, a construction crew headed for the Plaza and removed a plaque that bore Nichols's name and described him as a
dreamer. "Few men," it read, "can have so variously and profoundly
influenced the development of any American community." The workers filled the void with fresh concrete.

During the renaming process, when Goode went on the radio or
gave interviews to local journalists, he made clear that stripping away
Nichols's name would not undo the legacy of redlining, that it would
not fix the myriad problems plaguing Kansas City. But Goode was
certain that this counted as a disruption of the status quo, forcing
Kansas City to contemplate the full extent of Nichols's influence and
start conversations it had avoided for years.

A QUARTERBACK'S HOME

When he moved to Kansas City, Patrick Mahomes did what many young professionals and transplants do: He looked for a place to live near the Plaza. A few months after the 2017 NFL draft, he bought a penthouse in a boutique condominium with a rooftop deck, not far from the glow of the holiday lights. Just over a year later, after an MVP season assured a long future in Kansas City, Mahomes sought something more permanent, a slice of the American dream for himself and girlfriend, Brittany Matthews.

They eyed a showstopper in Sunset Hill, a Nichols subdivision just south of the Plaza where J.C. Nichols had lived for decades before his death. The home was at the edge of State Line Road—in Kansas City but almost close enough to throw a football into Kansas. It was an old ranch house, modernized with French doors, mahogany-framed windows, a floating fireplace, and raised ten-foot ceilings. When the couple moved in, they personalized their new space, carving out a shoe room stocked with Mahomes's Pharrell Williams x Adidas NMDs and the *Game of Thrones* x Adidas Night's Watch Ultra Boosts—180 pairs in total. The house was something he and Matthews could grow into—"a big step in our life," Mahomes said.

The previous owners operated a well-known floral and design studio. Before them, a distinguished Kansas City attorney had lived in the house, and before her, it had belonged to a doctor, who had purchased it from a married real estate agent couple. The first people to live there were the Wolfermans, a famous Kansas City family that owned a chain of grocery stores.

And not long before them, there was no house, just farmland owned by Seth Ward, whose sons, Hugh and John, enlisted the services of J.C. Nichols. Nichols divided the farm into lots and helped develop and market the new subdivision as Sunset Hill, one of the early jewels of his Country Club District. The properties were shaded by enormous trees and connected to curvy roads that led to the future site of the Plaza. Golf courses bordered each side of the neighborhood. Three private schools were nearby. Nichols knew he had struck gold and was not shy in saying so. "No residence district in America equals or even approaches it. Sunset Hill is truly making Kansas City America's most beautiful residence city," proclaimed an ad from the Nichols Company.

The subdivision was also an exemplar for Nichols's infamous covenants. To help sell lots there, as well as in adjacent Mission Hills, Nichols hired the comptroller of a prominent insurance company to boast about the neighborhoods' covenants. The restrictions took up sixteen pages, covering everything from the prohibition of billboards and the limitation of land use, to the requirement for single-family homes—no apartments allowed—to the specifications for building vestibules and stairway landings and porches. On page fifteen, there was the familiar all-caps clause, "OWNERSHIP BY NEGROES PROHIBITED." Underneath, a short paragraph explained, "None of said lots shall be conveyed to, used, owned, nor occupied by negroes as owners or tenants." The restrictions were self-perpetuating; after twenty-five years they would be extended unless a majority of the subdivision's residents voted otherwise. The comptroller's endorsement stated that Nichols "had solved the problem of changing neighborhoods," and Nichols blasted out the praise in his ads. Others took notice. The restrictions for Sunset Hill and Mission Hills were "copied by developers in more than 50 cities in 1920," according to the Nichols Company advertisement.

When the Wolferman family moved into Sunset Hill—and for decades after—someone like Patrick Mahomes would not have been allowed to live there. But as he closed on the house in 2019, he didn't have to worry about that. He had more than enough money to afford a home in Sunset Hill, so he bought one. All throughout Kansas City, Mahomes's move caused a big stir. Not because anybody was thinking about the legacy of J.C. Nichols, or the meaning of a superstar Black quarterback buying in one of his neighborhoods. It was because a local television station had published the new address and the city freaked out about the invasion of privacy.

Everyone wanted to make sure Mahomes loved his new neighborhood and felt safe and comfortable there.

FOR the next year, Mahomes settled into the Country Club District. He played golf at Mission Hills Country Club. He won a Super Bowl. He partied with Post Malone and Paul Rudd on the night of the championship parade. (Post Malone got a tattoo of Mahomes's autograph after a backstage beer-pong bet went awry.) It wasn't until the spring of 2020, three months into a pandemic, that his relative calm was disturbed. The Kansas City protests had erupted on the Plaza, a couple of miles from Mahomes's house. When he sat down to watch the video of police officer Derek Chauvin kneeling on the neck of George Floyd for more than nine minutes, he couldn't bring himself to finish it. "It hurts me too much to my soul to see him and feel like I can't help," he said. Mahomes wanted to do something, though, and soon enough, he heard from New Orleans Saints wide receiver Michael Thomas, who asked if he would lend his voice to a player-driven initiative, a video that would call attention to systemic racism and demand the NFL apologize for its treatment of players who kneeled during the national anthem to protest police brutality.

The protests during the anthem, which originated in 2016 with the 49ers' Colin Kaepernick, had, by that point, become a political lightning rod, another front in a culture war, inflamed in 2017 when

President Donald Trump called for the firing of any "son of a bitch" who kneeled. One of those players was Marcus Peters, an All-Pro Chiefs cornerback whose protests during the anthem had divided sentiments in Kansas City. Chiefs owner Clark Hunt said he preferred that players stand (though he didn't demand it). One local pastor and civil rights leader said he was inspired. When the 2017 season was over, the Chiefs traded Peters to the Los Angeles Rams.

The Peters situation was complicated, stretching beyond the protests—at various moments he threw a penalty flag into the stands, reportedly had a spat with a coach, and received a one-game suspension—but the arc of his tenure left some wondering: Why was Peters traded? The story was still fresh when Michael Thomas reached out. First, Mahomes wanted to listen.

He had been largely sheltered from racism growing up—or at the least, unburdened by it. The white and Black sides of his families gathered at cookouts and baseball games. His grandparents from each side had become good friends and even sat next to each other at the 2020 Super Bowl. "We were probably as close as anybody," recalled Johnny Mahomes, Mahomes's paternal grandfather. Whitehouse was small, too. People who didn't personally know Mahomes knew him as the son of a decorated professional athlete and a budding high school star. He never had "the talk" that many young Black men have with their fathers about dealing with unjust treatment from the police, the justice system, or anybody else. In that way, Mahomes considered himself blessed. "I never was put in a situation where I felt like I was not getting the same privileges as someone else," he said.

When Mahomes arrived at Texas Tech, however, he started having conversations with Black teammates who came from far different backgrounds. They told him about the discomfort they felt after being pulled over, about the segregated sections of their hometowns. He heard the same stories in Kansas City, and, after Thomas contacted him, Mahomes reached out to NFL players across the league. He also spoke to his godfather, the former MLB pitcher LaTroy Hawkins, who had grown up in Gary, Indiana, a decaying industrial center, and a world away from Whitehouse. To Mahomes, the conversations made it clear that George Floyd or Ahmaud Arbery could have been one of his family members. He decided to be in Thomas's video.

It came out on June 4. Looking into a camera, Mahomes said, "Black Lives Matter." The next day, NFL commissioner Roger Goodell released his own eighty-one-second response: The league would support the rights of players to protest. "We were wrong," he said. Mahomes wasn't the only NFL star who read lines in the video. In addition to Thomas, there was Giants running back Saquon Barkley and Cowboys running back Ezekiel Elliott, top talents in two of the league's biggest markets. Mahomes, though, was something different, a franchise quarterback unlike any in NFL history: twenty-four years old, the Super Bowl MVP, and Black, a set of facts that had never been said together. Across the league, it was clear: Goodell could not ignore Mahomes.

Which was ironic, because at one point, all the NFL had done was ignore Black quarterbacks. Fifty years before Mahomes debuted for the Chiefs in 2017, there were zero Black starting quarterbacks in professional football. Why? It was a great question. So in the spring of 1968, the *Los Angeles Times* journalist Charles Maher started putting it to prominent people in the NFL.

"I can't remember a real great Negro quarterback in college ball," Packers coach Vince Lombardi said. "I mean, so far as what the pros are looking for. I can say this: I wouldn't give a damn what color a man was if he could throw the ball."

"Up to now there hasn't been a Negro quarterback with pro ability," Chargers coach Sid Gillman said. "I'm speaking honestly now."

Gillman mentioned Eldridge Dickey, a top collegiate quarterback from Tennessee State. "This is truly one of the great athletes in college football," he said. "But if I wanted a quarterback, I couldn't use his arm. You could put him at end, put him anywhere else . . . but he's not a quarterback."

Said a coach who asked for anonymity: "I don't know quite how to describe it, but the Negro is often sort of loosey-goosey. He seems to throw the ball a little differently."

There were concerns that a Black quarterback could not command a huddle of white teammates. Others questioned if they had the intelligence, or the arm. Even if a Black quarterback played the position in high school or college, like Bobby Bell, the future Chiefs linebacker, they were always pushed to another spot. "They said you couldn't even play," Bell said.

The first breakthrough came later in 1968, when Marlin Briscoe, a quarterback from Omaha University, got an opportunity for the Denver Broncos after starter Steve Tensi got hurt. Listed at five feet eleven, Briscoe lacked traditional size, but he was elusive as a scrambler and possessed a big arm, the kind of cannon that caused one scout to declare that Briscoe had "the greatest arm I have ever seen on any quarterback—college or pro." He made five starts at quarterback in 1968, throwing fourteen touchdown passes and thirteen interceptions and rushing for 308 yards on forty-one attempts, leading the Broncos to two of their five wins. Chiefs coach Hank Stram said facing Briscoe was like playing against twelve men. But the next year, he was not invited back to play quarterback. He became a Pro Bowl receiver instead.

The NFL wasn't ready for a quarterback like Marlin Briscoe, but his story inspired James "Shack" Harris, who led the Rams to the playoffs in 1974, and Harris did the same for the next generation. Even still, progress was shockingly slow. Warren Moon, a college star at the University of Washington, had to switch positions or start his career in Canada. Doug Williams, the first Black quarterback to win a Super Bowl, needed an injury to get his chance. Charlie Ward, a Heisman Trophy winner at Florida State, had to choose a basketball career in the NBA. Into the 1990s, the position remained predominantly white, even as attitudes changed and offenses evolved, even as quarterbacks like Moon and Randall Cunningham excelled.

As the years passed, and Moon retired, he could recognize the same stereotypes and tropes, the same systematic bias in scouting departments, the coded words that dogged him when he left Washington in 1978. "If it has to do with race, they're gonna make excuses," Moon said. "They're gonna say things like, 'Oh, he's not tall enough, or his arm isn't strong enough, or he didn't come out of a pro-style offense.' Those are things that I was hearing about me coming out of school."

When Mahomes arrived in the NFL, the landscape had changed. Steve McNair and Donovan McNabb had played in Super Bowls. Michael Vick changed the sport, if not without controversy. Russell Wilson guided the Seahawks to a Super Bowl championship in 2014. But until Mahomes came along, nobody could state that the consensus top quarterback in the NFL was Black. Now you could. And it delighted Marlin Briscoe. Before he died in 2022 at the age of seventy-six, he told journalist Jason Reid how much joy he got from watching Mahomes play.

"This kid . . ." Briscoe said. "There's just really something about him."

AFTER the video came out, Mahomes did not stop there. A few weeks later, the Kansas City parks department heard from his charitable foundation. Mahomes wanted to team up to revitalize Martin Luther King Jr. Park, a dilapidated green space on the East Side that had been dedicated in 1978 and spanned both sides of Brush Creek. In the dispute over naming a street after King, the park's deteriorating quality became an embarrassment, an example of the effects of redlining. For the previous few years, the parks department, the health department, and the Urban Land Institute had been studying the city's green spaces. Most of the parks system in Kansas City's core areas had been built out before 1920, in the era of the City Beautiful movement, when, as the Urban Land Institute explained, many of the parks were developed to create barriers between the "white elites . . . and African-American communities."

The result, decades later, was a parks system that served as a microcosm of the city's inequities—pristine green space West of Troost and outdated playgrounds and overgrown grass on the East Side, the map echoing the old ones from the HOLC. To enjoy the parks system, people on the East Side often had to drive long distances to somewhere like Loose Park, the gem of the Country Club District. But soon, MLK Park had a new playground and a plan for a pedestrian bridge so that people could walk from nearby homes and schools. Mahomes's contribution, about $1 million, targeted just a sliver of what ailed Kansas City, but then something unexpected happened: The city received several more donations to spruce up MLK Park.

The parks department announced Mahomes's contribution just ahead of the Chiefs' 2020 season opener, a Thursday-night matchup with the Houston Texans that kicked off the NFL season. On a cool September night at Arrowhead Stadium, as the pandemic limited the number of fans, and the crowd featured cutouts of Ruth Bader Ginsburg and Dorothy from *The Wizard of Oz*, Mahomes walked to the middle of the field and locked arms with Texans quarterback Deshaun Watson, a ceremonial "Moment of Unity," with a script on the scoreboard that included the phrases

WE SUPPORT EQUALITY.

WE MUST END RACISM.

WE MUST END POLICE BRUTALITY.

WE CHOOSE UNCONDITIONAL LOVE.

WE BELIEVE BLACK LIVES MATTER.

It was, after the summer of 2020, a fairly ambiguous and conventional response, two teams standing together for equality and unity, which made it all the more confusing when NBC cameras picked up what sounded like isolated booing from the crowd. For the next day in Kansas City, as the moment went viral, cell phone footage from Arrowhead Stadium was replayed like the Zapruder film, and people tried to reckon with the boos. *It was only a few. It was directed at the Texans. It was fans enunciating "CHIEEEEEFS," which can sound like boos.* "No," said Quinton Lucas, the city's mayor, who attended the game, "there were people who booed." In the days after the game, as Lucas processed the reaction, he reached out to the Chiefs and set up a call with Mahomes and safety Tyrann Mathieu. He wanted to thank the players for speaking out over the last few months. As he hung up the phone, he left them with a message: Be strong, he said. Be loud.

The question, after a summer of protests, after a public debate over J.C. Nichols, was whether enough people would continue listening and working for change. Nothing brought Kansas City together like the Chiefs. But Kansas City was still a complicated place. "So often here in Kansas City," social justice advocate Nicole Price told local TV station KSHB, "many good people remain silent and that's part of the reason we hear the boos."

THE CRASH

In a perfect world, the rest of this book would chronicle a simple narrative: A team becomes an instant dynasty—a winner of multiple Super Bowls, the wholesome heartland version of the New England Patriots—and a city rapidly transforms into something more cosmopolitan and, at the same time, fairer, safer, and more unified. The ultimate comeback comes easy. Rome is built in a day.

But most of the time it is not.

In early 2021, the Chiefs were on the verge of something dynastic, favored to repeat as champions, a feat accomplished just eight times in NFL history, and not since 2005. They adopted a bold slogan—"Run It Back"—and dominated the regular season: 14-2, with one loss to the Chargers because the starters sat out in a meaningless end-of-season game, and the other to the Raiders, which Mahomes avenged with a last-minute comeback in their second meeting. In Super Bowl LV, they faced (somehow, again) Tom Brady: the GOAT vs. the Baby GOAT.

In an unusual scenario, Chiefs players and staff were in Kansas City during the week. For most Super Bowls, the teams spend an entire week at their destination, churning through a gauntlet of media availability and special events. But COVID-19 precautions rejiggered the schedule, and the Chiefs remained in Kansas City until the day before the game, which meant they were still prepping at Arrowhead Stadium on February 4. It was that night, three days before Super Bowl LV, that assistant coach Britt Reid consumed alcohol—likely at a team facility—got behind the wheel of his Dodge Ram, and put a local family through hell.

The crash happened around 9 P.M., on the highways near Arrowhead. Decades earlier, when city leaders and Chiefs brass planned the stadium, they prioritized cost and car access above anything else, engaging in what one official termed "positive, rational business methods," for the site selection. The resulting Truman Sports Complex stood at the lightly populated eastern edge of the city, connected to two of the region's most important highways: I-435, a loop that encircled the bulk of the metro area, and I-70, the interstate that sliced up downtown—displacing residents—on its way into Kansas. It was, people claimed, a sports facility in the middle of nowhere, devoid of life in the fall and winter except for games on Sunday afternoons and the occasional Monday night. But that wasn't quite true. A different type of bustle hummed in the vicinity of Arrowhead at all hours: the ebb and flow of commuters. The Chiefs might have practiced in isolation, but beyond the parking lots were roads that, as District Attorney Jean Peters Baker would say later, were used by everyone. "It's the only way to get around," she said.

That night, Alfredo Vasquez needed the roads to get to his job: He worked as a forklift operator at a Home Depot in Belton, Missouri. Money was tight, and the gas gauge on his Chevrolet Impala was low, and Vasquez didn't make it, pulling over on the side of a highway entrance ramp to I-435 just past Stadium Drive. He called his cousin Felicia Miller, who rushed over in a Traverse, a can of gasoline in tow. She was joined by her five-year-old daughter, Ariel Young; her sister, Angela Saenz; and Saenz's young son. When the Impala wouldn't start with the added fuel, Miller returned to sit with her sister and their children in the Traverse, and Vasquez reached into his trunk through the back seat to grab jumper cables. The weak battery meant Vasquez's flashers weren't working as intended, but numerous cars safely passed them as they tried to get the Impala running.

Britt Reid, the son of Andy Reid, was leaving work at Arrowhead.

He had joined his father's staff in 2013, taking a coveted NFL position after years of legal issues in Pennsylvania, moving forward after the loss of his older brother, Garrett, to a drug overdose in 2012. Reid had been drinking enough to put his blood alcohol level above the legal limit. His past was marred by previous convictions for DUI, simple assault, and carrying a firearm without a license. Just a few months earlier, in the Kansas suburbs, he was investigated for an alleged road rage incident, although no charges were filed. After turning away from Stadium Drive, Reid accelerated in his truck to enter the highway, speeding up to 83 miles an hour, nearly 20 miles an hour above the speed limit. First, he banged into the left side of the Impala. He steered to the right and then back to his left, trying to regain control. Inside the Traverse, Miller saw beaming headlights in the rearview and braced for impact. Reid slammed his truck into her family at 67 miles an hour.

Miller and her sister were momentarily knocked unconscious. When they came to, their first thought was, "Where were our babies?" In the back seat, Ariel was not moving or responding. She did not wake up for eleven days.

ON February 7, the Chiefs played the Buccaneers in the Super Bowl. Britt Reid wasn't there. He was hospitalized with minor injuries the night of the crash. He was not arrested, but the Chiefs suspended him, and he did not travel to Tampa Bay. Team management did not address whether Reid had been drinking at the office—or whether anyone knew about it. They never would. A couple of hours before the game, on the CBS pregame show, sideline reporter Tracy Wolfson highlighted the well-being of Andy Reid; a source told her he had done everything to avoid a "distraction." During the broadcast, commentators Jim Nantz and Tony Romo didn't bring up anything about the crash, which everyone knew had severely injured a five-year-old girl, until late in the fourth quarter.

The game was long over by that point. Tom Brady, forty-three years old, was still Tom Brady, and the Buccaneers defense ravaged a Chiefs offensive line that had been decimated by injuries throughout the season, pressuring Mahomes on twenty-nine of his fifty-six drop-backs, the most in Super Bowl history. According to advanced track-ing, the Buccaneers forced Mahomes, playing on an injured toe, to cover 497 yards before attempting a pass or being sacked, the highest number recorded since the NFL began measuring. At one point in the fourth quarter, Mahomes scrambled around for eight seconds before unleashing a diving throw that hit his receiver in the hands at the goal line. It was dropped. For the first time in the Mahomes era, the Chiefs failed to score a touchdown. There would be no parade by the Liberty Memorial.

TWENTY-ONE months later, a few minutes before 1:30 P.M. on No-vember 1, 2022, golden elevator doors swung open on the fourth floor of a downtown courthouse. Britt Reid, dressed in a slate gray suit and a patterned tie, betrayed no emotion as he walked alongside his law-yer, J.R. Hobbs, hurrying past a row of TV cameras and reporters holding notepads. Felicia Miller's family was already in the court-room. They wore white T-shirts emblazoned in blue with the phrase "Justice for Ariel." Ariel Young was there, too, holding her mother's hand. Her shirt read "Ariel Strong."

Everyone rose when Judge Charles McKenzie entered the court-room. Reid, after tendering a guilty plea for felony DWI, faced a prison sentence of up to four years. His lawyer sought probation, de-scribing Reid as somebody who was trying to stay clean, who had completed an alcohol-treatment program in 2020 and enrolled in an-other after the crash. (The Chiefs reached a financial settlement agree-ment with the family in 2021.) The prosecuting attorneys ran through the basics of that February night: the drinking ("presumably around a work setting"), the choice to drive, the speeding. They read Miller's victim impact statement for the court, laying out Ariel's story. When she awoke from the coma, she didn't recognize her mother, she couldn't walk, and she had to relearn how to speak and eat. She still needed a feeding tube after leaving the hospital. When she went to therapy the first several times, Miller carried her into the building. But she made strides. Ariel started walking again, and she rejoined her classmates at school. "She's Ariel strong," Miller's statement read. "[Reid is] not strong like her."

Reid had apologized for the first time a few weeks earlier when he pleaded guilty, and he took to the lectern to apologize once again. He looked back at Miller and her family for a moment but mostly faced McKenzie. "Whatever the sentence is, I understand," Reid said, "and I accept the responsibility for what I did that night."

McKenzie took about an hour to reach his decision and shared it with the courtroom without much preamble: three years in prison. Reid, McKenzie announced, would start the sentence immediately. His lawyer could bring along any possessions. A couple minutes later, two deputies led Reid down a dank staircase to the street, his wife following closely. The county jail was a couple of blocks away.

Miller and her family didn't wait around to watch Reid's exit, leaving as soon as McKenzie ended the hearing. They wanted a longer sentence. Ariel's condition had certainly improved, but her right foot dragged when she walked, she often experienced motion sickness during car rides, and she had fallen behind her peers at school. Before the crash, Ariel had wanted to pursue gymnastics. That no longer seemed to be a possibility. "She'll never play sports," Miller's victim statement read.

The family did not accept Reid's apology—not on the day of the sentencing and not when Reid had announced plans to plead guilty a few weeks earlier. That first apology came from his lawyer, and it was part of an expression of contrition directed not only toward Ariel but to "the Hunt family, the Chiefs organization, and Chiefs Kingdom."

The sports references gave Miller a feeling of disbelief: an apology to football fans for injuring a child? "This," she wrote in her statement, "is not a game."

THIRTEEN SECONDS

I t was just past 3:35 P.M. outside Arrowhead Stadium when a football fan climbed onto the bed of a white pickup truck in the middle of Lot G. A crowd of eager onlookers had already gathered to watch. The man, looking no older than a college student, wore a gray hooded sweatshirt under a Buffalo Bills throwback jersey. He raised one finger in the air, took a step forward, glanced at an empty folding table below, and jumped.

It was January 23, 2022, a Sunday in Kansas City, and in exactly two hours and fifty-five minutes the Chiefs would face the Bills in the Divisional Round of the AFC playoffs. The parking lot was already a bacchanalian carnival. Under wispy clouds and a low afternoon sky, thousands of fans crammed into the Truman Sports Complex, setting up temporary tents and extravagant setups—complete with kegs, speakers, and ice sculpture "shot luges." The air was crisp and smelled of charcoal. Nineties rap music blared. A few spaces down, a group of old friends from a local Catholic high school was hosting a large tailgate with a ceremonial toast involving the rock band Ween. They had wedged between cars an "outhouse" tent containing two 5-gallon industrial buckets full of urine. Everyone was thinking about the looming quarterback duel between Patrick Mahomes and the Bills' Josh Allen, his emerging rival. But first, somebody had to go through a table.

If there's an NFL fan base as steadfast and committed as Chiefs Kingdom, it's probably Buffalo's—code name "Bills Mafia"—a seemingly unhinged cohort from Western New York. Bills fans shared the heartbreak gene. They also had a similar affinity for Zubaz, the baggy, zebra-patterned pants that had captured NFL fans in the '90s. More than anything, members of the Bills Mafia loved leaping off the backs of trucks and crashing through folding tables, like professional wrestlers. The man in Lot G was sacrificing himself for the cause.

The miracle of the moment—prime-time playoff game, Arrowhead Stadium, out-of-town fans going through tables—was that for much of the 2022 season, Kansas City hadn't been sure if it would arrive. In the months after the blowout loss to the Bucs in Super Bowl LV, the Chiefs had regrouped and rebuilt their offensive line, hoping to better protect Mahomes. Fans talked openly of a Patrick Mahomes Revenge Tour—a scorched-earth campaign unleashed on the rest of the league. But it didn't happen that way. The Chiefs opened the season 3-4, including a humbling blowout loss to the rising Bills and a humiliating 27–3 demolition at the hands of the Tennessee Titans. For the first time in his career, Mahomes was . . . kind of struggling.

It all seemed weird. He had thrown nine interceptions and fumbled twice in the Chiefs' first seven games. (In what felt like a misprint, he was tied with Jets rookie Zach Wilson for most interceptions in the NFL.) Some of the giveaways came on tipped balls and fluky deflections, and the underlying offensive numbers—the fundamentals of the Chiefs' economy, you might say—were still strong. But when Mahomes posted a shoddy 74.8 passer rating in a 20–17 victory over the New York Giants the next week, Nate Silver's analytical website FiveThirtyEight ran a study that confirmed the hypothesis: "It's undeniable," the writer Neil Paine wrote, "that quarterback Patrick Mahomes is in a slump."

The conventional theory was NFL teams wised up and realized there was a smarter way to contain Mahomes: Stop blitzing. Throughout football history, defenses had operated under a simple principle: Blitzing—the act of sending linebackers and defensive backs to help the defensive line pressure the quarterback—was one of the surest ways to sabotage elite passers who stood in the pocket and dissected defenses with downfield throws. Mahomes, however, had broken the sport. To blitz him only removed defenders from the secondary and invited the sort of chaos that usually resulted in him slipping away from the rush and uncorking a pass that defied physics. So defenses made a counterintuitive gamble: In October, the Bills blitzed zero times in their 38–20 win at Arrowhead Stadium. "I don't know if I've ever been in a game where we didn't pressure at least once," Bills defensive coordinator Leslie Frazier said.

Opposing teams often combined the lack of blitzing with a defensive scheme called "two high or two-high shell": two deep safeties, guarding against the deep ball, while the rest of the secondary played man coverage. If that wasn't enough, they regularly disguised their looks. "When I first got in the league, blitzes were relatively simple," Andy Reid said. "But these defensive coordinators are so creative; they're bringing people from everywhere except the popcorn vendor." But that was the thing: Teams weren't really blitzing at all. Instead they were selling out to blanket Mahomes's two top targets, Tyreek Hill and Travis Kelce. Mahomes had pushed the league to try something nearly unprecedented, and for a while, it seemed to work. "Safeties would start 20 or 25 yards deep, which was ridiculous," said Chad Henne, the Chiefs' backup quarterback. At times, Mahomes appeared impatient. He had always excelled on the so-called off-script plays, but he was leaving the pocket even when he didn't have to. In Week 9, the Chiefs improved to 5-4 by beating the Green Bay Packers (who were without quarterback Aaron Rodgers). But Mahomes passed for just 166 yards. "I feel like we're close," he told reporters.

Then, as the season beat on and Reid adjusted to the league's adjustment, the sport's gravity tilted back toward Kansas City. The Chiefs rolled off eight straight victories. The defense shined. Reid unleashed Hill as a souped-up "possession" receiver, deploying him in the open spaces underneath the deep safeties. In the quarterback room, coaches preached a simple mantra: "All that underneath stuff was there," Henne said.

Kansas City finished the regular season 12-5, winning the AFC West for the sixth straight year. In the worst year of his career, Mahomes finished with 4,839 yards passing and thirty-seven touchdowns. He had faced two-high defenses nearly 67 percent of the time—nearly one hundred more plays than any other quarterback in football, and at some point, his photographic memory cataloged the different looks and his mind solved the puzzle. He started taking the occasional short throw. The easy ones. Sometimes, he was just too good, no matter the defense. "You figure out answers," he said.

The Chiefs earned the No. 2 seed in the AFC playoffs and slaughtered the Pittsburgh Steelers 42–21 in the wild-card round. Which brought a rematch with the Buffalo Bills in Kansas City, two of the best teams in the NFL meeting in the divisional round. The table was set.

Now somebody just had to go through it.

FROM the moment Mahomes arrived in 2018, one question had hovered just below the surface: He was the best young quarterback in football. But would anyone challenge the throne? Tom Brady was in his forties. Drew Brees was retired. Aaron Rodgers couldn't play forever. For a while it seemed like it might be Deshaun Watson . . . or Lamar Jackson . . . or whatever latest quarterback was lighting up the league. Yet by the end of the 2021 season, another challenger emerged: Josh Allen, the twenty-five-year-old signal caller of the Buffalo Bills.

Allen grew up on a cotton farm in rural California, attended the University of Wyoming, and was drafted by the Bills with the seventh pick in 2018—one year after the Chiefs traded with the Bills to pick Mahomes. Like Mahomes, Allen possessed a military-grade bazooka for a right arm. He was also built like a Ford F-150—six feet five, 250 pounds—and while he didn't have the wizardry of Mahomes, he existed as a brute-force brawler, running over defenders, keeping plays alive, changing the game with the flick of his right wrist. He had nearly won the MVP in 2020, and he'd beaten Mahomes at Arrowhead

Stadium in October, but the Bills had slumped in November and December, allowing the surprising Titans to earn the No. 1 seed in the AFC. As Allen stood on the field before kickoff, he looked at his teammates huddled around him: "It's our [expletive] night," he yelled.

A quarterback duel unfolded across four quarters, Allen pounding forward with his trademark runs, Mahomes answering with a "Superman" dive for the end zone. "You guys just keep covering," Bills defensive backs coach John Butler yelled at his secondary. "He can't scramble all game!" The Chiefs built a 23–14 lead in the third quarter, scoring on a 25-yard jet sweep run from receiver Mecole Hardman. Momentum lasted all of ten seconds. On the first play of the next drive, Allen hit receiver Gabe Davis on a 75-yard bomb over the top. The Chiefs responded with a field goal to push the lead to 26–21 with just under nine minutes left. But Allen landed another broadside on fourth-and-13 from the Chiefs' 27 with two minutes left, firing a strike to an open Davis in the end zone. When Allen found Stefon Diggs for a two-point conversion, the Bills led 29–26. Which set up two of the wildest minutes in NFL history.

There is an adage—more like a football cliché—that you do not want to score too quickly in the final minutes, lest the other team have time to go back down the field. With one minute and fifty-four seconds left, the Bills surely left too much time for Mahomes and the Chiefs offense. What no one inside Arrowhead Stadium understood, however, was that Mahomes would then leave too much time for Allen to *again* leave too much time for Mahomes. If you tried to work out the math on how that was possible in 1:54, it would have made little sense. But then Mahomes hit a streaking Tyreek Hill in the middle of the field for a 64-yard touchdown, giving the Chiefs a 33–29 lead with one minute and two seconds left, and Allen responded again, engineering a six-play drive in forty-nine seconds that culminated in another touchdown pass to Davis, his fourth of the night. The Chiefs trailed 36–33. There were thirteen seconds left.

Mahomes stood along the sideline, near Eric Bieniemy, the Chiefs' offensive coordinator. "We've got three timeouts left," Bieniemy said. There is not much a football team can do in thirteen seconds. A typical play lasts about four seconds, and that's on a relatively short gain. Hill, one of the fastest players ever, would need at least ten seconds just to run the length of the field. The Chiefs, though, didn't need to go that far. "Just get in field goal range," Mahomes said out loud. That made the timeouts key. The Chiefs caught another break when the Bills sent the kickoff through the end zone, wasting no time. They just needed to cover roughly 40 yards in under thirteen seconds, leaving time for a long field goal. It wasn't impossible, but it would require perfection.

"When it's grim," Reid would say, "be the grim reaper."

On the first play, from the 25-yard line, Reid called a quick screen pass to Hill, who caught the ball and darted upfield for 19 yards. Mahomes signaled for timeout. The officials spotted the ball at the Chiefs' own 44. Eight seconds on the clock. As Mahomes walked toward the sideline, he passed Travis Kelce, who had an urgent idea. "Hey, hey," Kelce said, getting Mahomes to stop. He spoke in a quiet voice. "If they play it like that, that seam is open."

When Reid arrived in Kansas City nearly a decade earlier, he established a program that empowered his players. He asked them to be creative, to color outside the lines. If a player had an idea for a new play, Reid carved out practice time to look at it. He liked to say he retained 51 percent of the vote—veto power—but no idea was too weird. "We absolutely borrow things," Reid said. The culture manifested itself in strange ways; assistant coaches noted that a whiteboard in the Chiefs' facility often looked like the work of mathematician John Nash in the movie *A Beautiful Mind*. In the early years, the Chiefs ran a play called "Hungry Pig Right," where a 350-pound nose tackle named Dontari Poe lined up as a slot receiver in a diamond formation and hauled in a lateral pass for a touchdown. "Cut the beef loose," Reid said. When Mahomes arrived in 2017, the culture manifested in new techniques for shovel passes and other exotic shifts. If Mahomes wanted to try something new, he just had to prove it would work.

As Kelce stood next to Mahomes, he decided to take the ethos to the extreme. On first down, he had noticed that the defensive back was covering him on the outside, leaving acres of open space in the middle of the field. Kelce wanted to let Mahomes know: If the defense lined up the same way, he wasn't going to run the correct route. He was going to cut straight up the field, to the open space. *The seam was open.* As the Chiefs lined up, Mahomes was in the shotgun. He peered to his left and saw the defense. They were lined up the same.

"Do it, Kels!" Mahomes yelled out. "Do it, do it, Kels!"

Mahomes took the snap, pumped once, then fired a pass to an open Kelce, who was bolting up the seam. From the snap to the catch, it took less than three seconds. Kelce cradled the football with two hands and kept galloping, gaining another 10 yards as he slid down at the Bills' 31-yard line. As he finished the play, Kelce would say that he felt like Michael Jordan before a game-winning shot, counting down the seconds in his head. Timeout. Three seconds on the clock. Harrison Butker split the uprights on a 49-yard field goal, sending the game to overtime.

Three years earlier, the Chiefs had watched Tom Brady lead a game-winning touchdown drive on the first possession of overtime in the AFC Championship Game. This time, Mahomes had the ball. He completed all six of his passes on an eight-play drive, the final coming on an 8-yard back-shoulder throw to Kelce in the right corner of the end zone. As Kelce hauled in the pass against Bills linebacker Matt Milano and fell to the turf, Mahomes ripped off his helmet and sprinted toward a mob in the end zone. He wrapped his right arm around Kelce's neck. "Great [expletive] ball!" Kelce said.

"I love you, man," Mahomes said.

Before Arrowhead Stadium could empty out, before the euphoria wore off and the party had migrated to the parking lot, Mahomes changed into a beige coat and walked to a press conference inside the bowels of the stadium. He had thrown for 378 yards and rushed for another 69 yards, and when the Chiefs faced the Bengals the next Sunday, he would be the first quarterback in NFL history to start in four conference championship games before the age of twenty-seven. Kansas City would be the first city ever to host four straight conference championships. In the moment, he could really say only one thing:

He would remember this night for the rest of his life.

ONE week later, on a Sunday afternoon in Kansas City, the Chiefs built a 21–3 lead against the Bengals in the AFC Championship. Everything seemed fine. The Bengals trimmed the lead to 21–10 with a minute left before halftime, but Mahomes was cooking, leading touchdown drives on the Chiefs' first three possessions, and the offense again raced down the field in five plays—a pass interference penalty putting the ball at the 1-yard line with nine seconds left in the half. Mahomes threw incomplete on first down, which gave the Chiefs five seconds for one more shot at a touchdown or a field goal, and with no timeouts left, Reid trusted Mahomes to run one more play before bringing on the field-goal unit. But Mahomes threw a quick screen pass to Tyreek Hill, who—instead of sprinting toward the pylon—tried to awkwardly spin past Bengals cornerback Eli Apple. Hill went down short of the end zone. The clock ran out. The Chiefs gave away 3 points. As Johnny Mahomes watched the play, he was stunned. "I've never seen Patrick do that," Mahomes's grandfather said.

Neither had anyone inside Arrowhead Stadium. To Johnny Mahomes, it was like his grandson "had a brain fart."

"To me that turned around the game," he said. "They were never the same after that."

The Chiefs had six possessions in the second half. They punted four times. Mahomes threw an interception. The game began to unravel. The Bengals did what the league had done all year: They stopped worrying about blitzing and instead dropped as many as eight defenders into the secondary. In the second half alone, the Cincinnati defense dropped at least eight men into coverage on 45 percent of their plays. Mahomes finished the day seven for thirteen for 59 yards with an interception against those looks. The Chiefs needed a 44-yard field goal in the final seconds to tie the game at 24–24 and send it to overtime. And when they won the toss in overtime, Mahomes did the unthinkable, throwing an interception on the third play. Eight plays later, the Bengals kicked a game-winning field goal. "When you're up 21–3," Mahomes said, "you can't lose it."

The collapse matched the largest in AFC Championship Game history, while Mahomes had been 37-0 in his career when leading by at least 15 points, and if there was a reason for the pain, it seemed to come from somewhere deep down: The idea of another Super Bowl parade had been put on hold, this time for a second straight year, and a crushing loss had stirred up old feelings. The next day, Kansas City went into its ritualistic mourning phase, enduring the usual recriminations, consternations, and sports talk-radio calls. The worst part was the truth. Maybe it was the scheme. Maybe it was the randomness of sports. Maybe he just played badly.

For once, Mahomes had not come through.

"I put that on myself," he said.

THE BULL'S HORNS

On August 17, 2022, about three weeks before the start of the NFL season, a woman walked to a dais on the twenty-sixth floor of city hall, slid a mask to the side of her face, and addressed Mayor Quinton Lucas and a few members of the city council. Behind her, some seventy-five people were clad in yellow T-shirts with "KC Tenants" scrawled on the front. The name was printed above a bull logo, a design inspired by an old Charlie Parker poster and meant to evoke Kansas City's cow town, stockyard roots—with a twist. KC Tenants believed their work had transformed an iconic Kansas City symbol into something powerful, unapologetic, and bold. Although they were seated in an ornate chamber room—designed long ago to fulfill the grandiose vision of Tom Pendergast—and had endured two hours of a marathon session of the Neighborhood Planning and Development Committee, the group was as animated as spectators at a football game. They jeered when a staffer for the mayor described the price range for apartments under a new proposal. They clapped when a local nonprofit leader compared housing developers to children who wanted dessert before finishing their vegetables.

The woman at the podium, however, was about to elicit the loudest applause of the afternoon.

"My name," she began, "is Diane Charity."

Charity wore the same yellow shirt, pairing it with yellow earrings. A black KC Tenants hat was perched atop her gray hair. She was seventy-two, yet still as skeptical of municipal government as when her grandmother's entire block had been destroyed for a highway, still as pugnacious as when she had protested for equal accommodations for Black Kansas Citians at her mother's side in the early 1960s. Over the years, Charity had become a fixture among the city's civically engaged: a leader at Parade Park, a mostly Black public housing co-op that stood out for decades as a rare success story from the urban-renewal era; a onetime candidate to recall an unpopular East Side council member; a neighborhood organizer who helped prevent crime and catalyze the citywide replacement of streetlights; and a member of an East Side Catholic parish that drew statewide political candidates who wanted to win over the Black community. Over the last sixty years, she had developed an absolute love of Kansas City, although sometimes she wanted "to take it and wring it up."

This was one of those times.

The Neighborhood Planning and Development Committee, a subgroup within the larger city council, was discussing a bill proposed by Lucas—Ordinance 220700—that would redefine what constituted affordable housing in Kansas City. Beginning in early 2021, any developer who negotiated for incentives with the city had to set aside a portion of the new housing as affordable. According to that previous legislation, half the affordable portion had to be *deeply affordable*, which came to around $600 a month for a one-bedroom home, while the other half had to be *moderately affordable*, about $1,200 a month. No developers built anything under those terms, however, and Lucas believed the city had to change course after roughly eighteen months. In his proposal, he nixed the deeply affordable requirement, so developers would set aside only a portion of moderately affordable housing. The result was a version of "affordable" that translated to roughly $1,200 for a one-bedroom home for a person making less than $41,034 a year.

It sounded good for San Francisco or Austin or Prairie Village, but this was Kansas City. A $1,200 one-bedroom apartment would stretch the city's median renter household, which made around $38,000 a year.

To Lucas, the proposed ordinance offered Kansas City an opportunity to stimulate housing growth for the middle class, and he believed the city could use other strategies to build housing for the working class. Charity and the KC Tenants saw something else: an unrealistic definition of "affordable" that betrayed tens of thousands.

Charity had cofounded the group in 2019 with three women. As George Floyd's murder faded out of the news cycle and many social justice movements weakened, KC Tenants got stronger, growing to 4,500 members. Its mission was basically twofold: unionize renters, who made up nearly half the city's population, and advocate for better affordable housing, with a north star goal of bringing thousands of units of social housing to the city—homes permanently supported by a sustainable public revenue source with rents based on the quality of the units and what people could afford—similar to models in European metros like Vienna but also comparable to Parade Park. That complex, built near Eighteenth and Vine as a nationally unprecedented partnership between Reynolds Metals Company, the city, and the federal government in the early 1960s, functioned as a public housing co-op. Parade Park residents—who ranged from laborers to then councilman Bruce R. Watkins and young baseball star Reggie Jackson— made a small down payment for collective ownership of the property (as low as $100 to $150 in the early 1960s), paid monthly carrying fees, and accumulated equity. "We owned it. We knew that it was ours," Charity said. "And we took care of it as though it was ours."

The mission of KC Tenants regularly brought its members to apartment complexes run by slumlords to demand satisfactory conditions, as well as to the council chambers at city hall, where they tracked eye-glazing legislation that could drastically change the city. At the Neighborhood Planning and Development Committee meeting, several members spoke against the plan. Maya Neal feared she would no longer be able to raise her son in the city. Denise Brown said $1,200 was "a smack in the face." Aaron Ratigan didn't want to be on the wrong side of a policy that the group believed would lead to displacement.

Then it was time for Diane Charity, who alluded to a question that Kansas City, and every up-and-coming city in America, had not sufficiently answered during their modern revivals: Where were the people who never abandoned urban living, who never left Kansas City during its lean years, supposed to go? The ordinance, Charity said, sounded like a plan to move her "and all the poor and working-class Kansas Citians out of the beloved city we call home."

FOUR years earlier, Charity had been celebrating her birthday one of the best ways she knew: attending a municipal government meeting. This one, hosted by Kansas City's health department, was about evictions, and the house was packed. As Charity searched for an empty chair, she muttered about not being able to find anywhere to sit on her birthday. Immediately, she heard the voice of Tara Raghuveer, who was giving a presentation. "Sit over there, birthday girl," she said, pointing to an empty chair.

On the surface, Raghuveer was Charity's opposite: a millennial Indian American Harvard graduate who was born in Australia and grew up in Mission Woods, Kansas, a small Nichols-planned city that hugged State Line Road. Developed in 1937, Mission Woods was hailed by Nichols as bringing "the man of moderate income opportunities . . . the refinements of living hitherto enjoyed only by the wealthy." The opportunity, per the Nichols Company's modus operandi, was offered exclusively to white families via his racial covenants. When Raghuveer's parents moved to the city in 2001, 165 people lived in the woodsy enclave, and 160 were white. Mission Woods residents gained entry to some of the best public schools in Kansas, which is why Raghuveer's parents sought to purchase and rehabilitate the cheapest house they could find. At Harvard, when Raghuveer took sociology courses on racism, she started to reflect on how cities had been shaped. "I kept reading about Kansas City, and about J.C. Nichols, and being like, 'Oh, damn,'" she recalled. "I did not understand my little pocket of a neighborhood in a Kansas suburb to be as connected to this national story as it ultimately turned out to be."

Raghuveer studied segregation patterns and redlining, and developed a thesis on evictions and affordable housing. The research provided a foundation for a data set on Kansas City evictions, meticulously compiled by Raghuveer, researchers, lawyers, and community leaders. The data showed evictions for late rent in 2015 and 2016 were on par with those in the early years of the Great Recession even though the economy had recovered. It indicated residents living East of Troost faced the greatest concentration of evictions, and race, even when researchers were controlling for income, most predicted someone's likelihood of being evicted, with Black women affected more than any other group.

Her data hit the city at an inflection point. Everything was going up. The Power and Light District, the downtown entertainment venue across from the Sprint Center, rocked with excitement during sporting events. A glassy apartment tower called One Light, the city's first new high-rise residence building in decades, opened in 2015, followed by Two Light and Three Light. The Troost Wall began to blur in certain neighborhoods as young people, Black and white, populated new apartments, and entrepreneurs opened businesses on Troost Avenue. A new streetcar, which prompted the city to pass a revolutionary zero-fare transit initiative, chugged through downtown. In 2020, the city earned federal funding to expand the system north to the Missouri River, where the Kansas City Current was building the country's first sports facility for a professional women's soccer team.

The new Kansas City seemed to be getting everything: a smattering of craft breweries in the Crossroads, a $1.5 billion makeover to bring the airport into the twenty-first century, an inordinate number of Kansas City T-shirts worn by people as they wandered through their own city. The Heart of America was pumping again.

To many locals, the progress—downtown's population had increased almost fivefold since the late 1990s—was a point of pride; it certainly beat a crumbling downtown. But Kansas City's past still lingered. Decades ago, Nichols, developers, and the FHA had steered a racialized shift of population, economic opportunity, and wealth into the neighborhoods of the Country Club District and the suburbs. While redlined neighborhoods struggled under the burdens of urban renewal, highway building, and the refusal of many banks to offer loans, Nichols's innovations allowed his neighborhoods to stay frozen in amber. In and around the Country Club District, zoning laws and Nichols's self-perpetuating covenants on land use—which, unlike the racial restrictions, were in many cases still valid—prevented most new construction, leading to existing homes becoming more valuable. Now that the population was coming back, many people who might have settled in Nichols's Armour Hills or Brookside, if not for the scarcity of housing, looked to once neglected neighborhoods. The new demand increased prices before the city had done enough to stimulate investments that aided the longtime residents, who now faced a paradox: Their homes were more valuable, but their neighborhoods were changing—sometimes with new features and buildings they didn't like—and it was hard to stick around and reap the benefits.

In the gentrifying Westside, a mostly working-class Mexican American and Latino neighborhood scarred by urban renewal in the 1950s, home values doubled in a two-year period, leading more than 25 percent of the neighborhood's residents to become delinquent on property taxes. (Eventually, the Westside convinced the city council to pass a property tax reduction program for lower-income residents.) In Beacon Hill, a predominantly middle-class Black neighborhood on the East Side, newcomers built $600,000 luxury homes. Jeanene Dunn's family had owned a house in the neighborhood since the late 1940s, when they were the first African Americans on a block of Twenty-Eighth Street. Shortly before her mother died, in 2013, she told Dunn she could do anything she wanted with the house, with a caveat: "If you do leave this area," Dunn recalled her mother saying, "you won't be able to afford to get back here."

Many of the new homes in Beacon Hill received tax breaks. Kansas City handed out such incentives regularly. To jump-start downtown, the city forked over $295 million to the developers of the Power and Light entertainment district. It gave the same developers—who were accused of racial discrimination—millions more for parking garages at One Light, Two Light, and Three Light. In Kansas City, the gifts were granted for essentially nothing in return. Developers who received incentives did not have to guarantee a designated amount of affordable housing until 2021 or donate to a fund the city could use to finance more homes. (Kansas City didn't start a housing trust fund until 2018, years after other cities.) For anyone priced out by escalating rent or property taxes, there was nothing new coming along they could afford. A studio at Three Light started at $1,461 a month.

The East Side was hit hard. The new businesses and developments were mostly in downtown or other neighborhoods west of Troost, so there were no major reinvestments to create improved economic opportunities for longtime residents. "You add features to the city; that's good for everyone. But the trickle-down for our community just is not there," said Gwen Grant, a civil rights activist and CEO of the Urban League of Greater Kansas City. Instead the East Side saw an influx of out-of-town LLCs, based anywhere from Leawood, Kansas, to Abu Dhabi, buying up rental properties after the financial crisis and hiking the rent. It all meant that many longtime East Side residents, the majority of whom were Black and who rented their homes, now dealt with the decades-old problems of concentrated poverty—underserved schools, a lack of nearby jobs—and paid a higher premium. During a recent one-year period, average rent in the eastern part of Kansas City went up at double the rate for the city as a whole, outpacing growth in wages.

In other words, the new Kansas City could still hold up a mirror and see a glaring flaw in its reflection: Just as during the era of Nichols, the FHA, and urban renewal, thousands of working-class and middle-class people were being displaced and steered into certain areas, in many cases out of the city. As the population of Kansas City swelled after 2000, its first real growth in a generation, the Black population leveled off, representing a declining share of the city.

To understand the complex situation at hand, you could have prepared a thesis. Or you could have just lived on the East Side. To Charity, Raghuveer "affirmed everything I had been saying for twenty years. She just had the data to prove it."

The women exchanged phone numbers and got lunch. In 2019, along with Tiana Caldwell and Brandy Granados, they formed KC Tenants to represent the city's renters. KC Tenants grew quickly, and its thousands of members, most of whom had experienced the housing problems they sought to fix, represented a diverse mix of age, income, and race. The group had no exclusive leader, and newcomers regularly gravitated into significant roles, whether they researched legislation, showed up for meetings about development projects, or organized tenants to band together in neighborhood-based unions. Kansas City had never seen anything like them. "They're the people most affected," said Dianne Cleaver, a longtime nonprofit leader. "When you can go in and say, 'I can't afford a place to live,' that has a different impact."

At one KC Tenants meeting on the East Side, a newcomer summarized what he learned from the group by paraphrasing a passage from the Book of Numbers: "Don't be a victim, be a victor." The KC Tenants' victories were leading to incremental gains. Its members wrote legislation that guaranteed free legal counsel for Kansas Citians facing evictions and pushed for the passage of the 2021 law requiring developers to produce a portion of affordable housing anytime they received financial incentives. They helped renters at a large East Side apartment complex organize after the air-conditioning cut out for weeks, and they convinced the city council to scrap an incentive for a big-time developer and give $10 million to the housing trust fund instead.

At the group's offices, inside Trinity United Methodist Church in Midtown, one of the most rapidly developing areas of Kansas City, a display listed their goals and outlook, their allies and critics, many of whom saw KC Tenants as too aggressive, too socialist, too anti-development. Hardly anyone would deny they had changed Kansas City. Anytime the city considered incentive packages for a high-rise, they showed up decked out in yellow shirts with bull logos, reminding the people who held the most power—the developers, the politicians, the residents of the Country Club District—that it was past time to give some back.

THE night before the Neighborhood Planning and Development Committee meeting, several members of KC Tenants attended an outdoor theatrical production of *Sister Act*. It was a standard performance, except for one detail: Lucas made a cameo appearance as the pope. When he appeared onstage, the group's members, hoisting a yellow banner calling out the mayor by name, heckled him with a chant: "The rent, the rent, the rent is too damn high."

KC Tenants had often worked with Lucas. As a councilman, he had led the passage of legislation that originally defined affordable housing at a level considered deeply affordable, capped incentives for developers, and helped create the city's housing trust fund. He spent one of his first nights as mayor at the home of a KC Tenants organizer to see her struggles firsthand and worked with the group in 2019 to author a renters' bill of rights. But ahead of the Neighborhood Planning and Development Committee meeting, his decision to propose a new definition for affordable housing made him a traitor in their eyes. Members of KC Tenants weren't the only ones questioning the proposal. A policy strategist for the Kansas City school district testified that a $1,200 one-bedroom apartment would be unaffordable for teachers on starting salaries. Another nonprofit had crunched numbers showing that Kansas City most needed the deeply affordable housing, and the city's own data revealed the same thing. At the committee meeting, no members of the public had spoken in favor of the proposal, a sign to KC Tenants and others of the influence of developers, who had contributed to the campaigns of Lucas, past mayors, and city council members.

Lucas insisted the reality was more complicated. He didn't want Kansas City to resemble Denver or San Francisco, he explained, "where there are only two types of housing being built: very expensive housing for those who can afford it and only low-income housing centered in certain areas." It was true that, especially after the pandemic, more people felt squeezed. In Kansas City, as in many cities, newly built starter homes and modern apartments priced for people with average incomes were becoming rare, a result of skyrocketing building expenses and developers growing accustomed to handouts. Most builders constructed luxury housing—unless incentives were offered.

Summing up his proposal, Lucas said he wanted to promote more opportunities for the middle class, to bring more apartments "for people at all income levels" in downtown and other highly coveted neighborhoods. There would be other avenues for deeply affordable housing, he said. KC Tenants was not swayed. When the committee voted to approve the proposal, the activists erupted into a chant, halting the meeting.

Later, outside the north entrance to city hall, Charity, Raghuveer, and others met for a debriefing. Raghuveer called for a "code red," saying KC Tenants needed to "muck up the process that's messing up our lives." The proposal might have been approved, but they could still exert pressure to carry over to future housing policy battles. She asked the group for suggestions. How could they make sure the city realized they weren't backing down?

"No idea," Raghuveer told them, "is a bad idea."

THE ANKLE

O n a Friday afternoon in the fall of 2022, Pat Mahomes Sr. put on a gray fleece jacket and a ball cap and headed to an empty baseball diamond in Tyler, Texas. He rode through the busy intersections of Broadway Avenue—past a mini mall, a Holiday Inn, and a conveyor belt of American chain restaurants—until a row of pine trees signaled he had come upon Faulkner Park, where he guided a visitor to a parking spot at an athletic complex surrounded by a skate park and a nature trail. The baseball diamond was still and quiet, and as Pat Sr. stepped out into the sun, he walked to a spot just beyond the outfield fence. "There was actually a car parked right there," he said, pointing at the concrete.

It was October 21, nine months after the Chiefs' loss to the Bengals in the AFC Championship Game, and two days before Patrick Mahomes would lead a comeback win on the road against the San Francisco 49ers. The victory pushed the Chiefs to 5-2, first place in the AFC West. But the season was just getting underway, and back in Texas, Pat Sr. was trying to explain how his son had become the NFL's ultimate escape artist, a Harry Houdini in shoulder pads. He began with a story about Faulkner Park.

When Mahomes was in middle school, he played baseball for Rose Capital East, the same team that would qualify for the Junior League World Series. In one game that summer, Rose Capital East faced a travel ball team from the Houston area. The score was tied 0–0 in the late innings, and Mahomes, as usual, was pitching a shutout. By then, everyone understood that Mahomes was unique. He had hit home runs off the tee in T-ball. He had showcased his arm from shortstop as a six-year old. When he was around eight, he had attended a basketball camp at Whitehouse High School and drained a 60-foot heave to send a game to overtime. Junior League baseball, however, was a different level, a little more serious, the dimensions of the diamond at Faulkner Park better suited for high school players. Before that day, according to Pat Sr., Mahomes had never hit a home run on the field.

When Mahomes was a kid, his father had noticed his son acted differently in clutch situations. He would get "quiet," as Pat Sr. put it, the moment going by in "slow motion," as if his son could manipulate time with his mind. As Mahomes stepped to the plate at Faulkner Park, Pat Sr. said, "that's the way he was." The opposing pitcher delivered a pitch, and Mahomes connected in a way he never had before. The ball pinged off his aluminum bat and soared into the air. It cleared the left-field fence and landed in the parking lot, exactly where a Honda Accord was parked. For a middle school kid, it was a moon shot, the distance measured at 382 feet. Rose Capital East won the game.

Memory, of course, can be a fickle thing. Pat Sr. remembers the moment in vivid detail: a family member missing the homer because they were at the concession stand, the baseball coming perilously close to the foul pole, the make and model of the car. But no journalists were covering middle school baseball, no written accounts exist, so the only thing we know for sure is how it made Pat Sr. feel.

One thing we can say: Patrick Mahomes probably did smash a car window. Chad Parker, the coach of the team, remembered a similar story, and his son Jake recalled the wildest detail: The ball didn't stop when it hit the car in the parking lot. It crashed through the rear window and landed in the back seat.

THIRTY days after Pat Sr. wandered around Faulkner Park, Henry Winkler was standing along the sidelines at SoFi Stadium in Inglewood,

California, the palatial home of the Los Angeles Chargers and Rams. Winkler, a seventy-seven-year-old actor best known for his role as Arthur "Fonzie" Fonzarelli on *Happy Days*, had come to watch Patrick Mahomes play football, which itself was a strange story. A few years earlier, his son Max, a Hollywood director, had started coming over to watch football on Sundays. Winkler, a New York City native who had lived in Southern California for most of his life, found himself transfixed by the young quarterback for Kansas City, gobsmacked by the same quality Pat Sr. had noticed all those years ago at Faulkner Park: "the absolute magical second when he must slow time down in his brain," Winkler said.

Winkler wore a red sweater and gazed around the football field. His secret reverence for Mahomes had become public five months earlier, during an appearance on a national radio show. He asked Mahomes over for dinner—promising chicken stuffed with ricotta—and Mahomes reciprocated by inviting him to a game, which is how Winkler had ended up here, standing among some members of the Mahomes family, explaining how a quarterback in a sport he followed only casually had made him reconsider the art of improvisation. The way Winkler saw it, some actors could create a moment between two others, revealing something beautiful and resonant—a moment "that you never would have considered existed." Mahomes was always making those moments.

Of all the traits that had come to define him, perhaps the most astonishing was Mahomes's ability to create a moment when the odds were bleak, when the Chiefs needed to forge a comeback, in the magical seconds when time seemed to stop. As Winkler waited for the Chiefs to play the Chargers on *Sunday Night Football*, Mahomes had started eighty-three games in his career. In twenty-two of those games, the Chiefs had fallen behind by at least 10 points, a significant margin in a football game. Mahomes had a 13-9 record in those games, or put another way, he won nearly 60 percent of the time when his team trailed by 10. Tom Brady, widely considered the most clutch quarterback in history, was second; he won those games 38 percent of the time. "There's concentration," Winkler was saying. "There is grace." And minutes later, there was Mahomes, jogging across the field during warm-ups, toting an autographed Chiefs jersey with "Winkler" on the back. "I'm gonna take you up on that dinner," he said.

It was November 20, and the mood in Kansas City was hopeful. The Chiefs were 7-2, in command of the AFC West race. Mahomes was the frontrunner for MVP. One of the defining plays of the season had come in Week 4, when the Chiefs faced Brady and the Bucs in Tampa, and Mahomes had scrambled to his right near the goal line, spun away from a linebacker near the sideline, stopped at the line of scrimmage as if he'd reached the edge of a cliff, then flipped a one-handed, pop-a-shot touchdown pass. "Patty Mahomes," tweeted LeBron James, who happened to be watching. "So damn good!!" (Mahomes didn't quite concur until he pulled up the clip on his flight back to Kansas City. "When I saw the spin and jump-shot throw I made, I even was like, 'Man, this is pretty cool.'")

The only setbacks came in a bizarre road loss to the Indianapolis Colts and a 24–20 loss to Josh Allen and the Bills at Arrowhead Stadium in October. A lot of people around the NFL had expected much worse. Back in March, in the days after Mahomes married Brittany Matthews, his high school sweetheart, on a beach in Maui, he had received word from Brett Veach. The team was about to trade receiver Tyreek Hill. Mahomes had one reaction: *Why?*

The Chiefs did not want to trade Hill. A few weeks prior, in early March, Veach had met with Hill's agent, Drew Rosenhaus, at the NFL Scouting Combine, hoping to make headway on a contract extension. But then things went haywire. The Jacksonville Jaguars signed Christian Kirk—a decent-enough receiver—to a flabbergasting four-year, $72 million contract, and the Las Vegas Raiders traded for Packers star Davante Adams, handing him a record contract worth $141.25 million. "The market went to another world," Veach said. The NFL salary cap—the league-wide limit on team payroll—is a black box of loopholes and fine print. It demands a MacGyver level of creativity, a yearly game of sacrifices, trade-offs and bombs defused by hand. The Chiefs could pay Hill the market rate, around $30 million a year. That wasn't a problem. But they would lose the ability to invest in their defense or sign key players the next year. Veach did not want to teeter on the edge of salary-cap purgatory. So they traded Hill to the Miami Dolphins for a bundle of draft picks and opted to spread the money around. It was shrewd business; the news still hit the NFL like a bomb. Some Chiefs fans were bewildered. Division rivals smelled blood. Mahomes had lost his most electric weapon—his cheetah and his wasp.

Veach viewed the maneuver in chess terms; they just needed to rearrange the pieces. The front office planned to load up on rookie defensive players and rebuild their receiving corps with cheaper options. It was, Veach told reporters, the best way to ensure a sustainable Super Bowl contender. But after the Broncos traded for Seahawks quarterback Russell Wilson, the Raiders acquired Adams, and the Chiefs lost Hill, a narrative congealed around the AFC West: The division would be one of the toughest in NFL history. The Chiefs' run of six straight AFC West titles was in jeopardy. "This is the time when the Chiefs are in rebuild mode," ESPN analyst Domonique Foxworth said on the morning show *First Take*.

Mahomes wasn't so sure. In April, he invited the Chiefs receivers and running backs to a summit in Fort Worth, Texas, near his off-season training base. The group included Travis Kelce and newcomers JuJu Smith-Schuster, Marquez Valdes-Scantling, and Justin Watson. A lot of NFL quarterbacks host their receivers in the springtime, but Mahomes wanted something different, something more formal, a camp to serve as the first phase of the Chiefs' off-season activity. He wanted a chance to teach. The agenda included play installations, throwing sessions, and barbecue. Mahomes went to work coaching up his new targets. "He didn't treat anybody any differently," Watson said. Mahomes had always been a talker, vocal in the locker room, his raspy voice projecting in the huddle, but in the months after the Bengals loss, he realized he needed to be more. "I had to become a better leader," he said. He texted out the invites himself. He and Kelce did most of the instruction, outlining the freedom inherent in the Chiefs offense—the spacing, the routes, the little details that he wanted to see. When he arrived at training camp, he kept on talking, running through extra film sessions with his new wideouts. He had watched NFL defenses adjust, taking away the deep throws and filling the secondary with defenders, so he spent the off-season throwing more than ever before.

Seven months later, Mahomes was standing in the huddle at SoFi Stadium. The Chiefs trailed the Chargers 27–23 with a minute and forty-six seconds left. They needed to go 75 yards to escape with a victory. It seemed like half the receivers from the off-season summit were on the sideline. Smith-Schuster had a concussion. Mecole Hardman was out with an abdomen injury. Kadarius Toney, a midseason pickup from the New York Giants, left the game early with a hamstring injury. Mahomes looked around the huddle. It all felt routine. "Everybody was just like, 'Let's just do it,'" Mahomes would say.

So they did.

Mahomes hit Valdes-Scantling for 18 yards, found rookie Skyy Moore for a big gain, and then took off up the middle for a 16-yard run that put the ball on the 17-yard line. On the next play—the sixth of the drive—Mahomes found Kelce on a crossing pattern for a touchdown with 31 seconds left. The AFC West race was over before Thanksgiving. Back in the Chiefs' locker room, Mahomes put on a black long-sleeve shirt and a pair of flower-patterned basketball shorts and walked to a press conference inside a spacious back room that looked like a high school multipurpose area. "There was no doubt that we were gonna go down there and score," he said.

The Chiefs would suffer just one more loss, a third straight defeat to Cincinnati on December 4, a road setback that confirmed Joe

Burrow and the Bengals as Kansas City's new foil and injected a measure of doubt into the bloodstream.

But by then, everyone in Kansas City was already thinking about the playoffs.

WHEN Mahomes was a senior at Whitehouse High School, he hurt his foot. The specifics of the injury were a minor mystery, even to his coaches. Most believed it was a lingering ailment from summer baseball, and Mahomes occasionally sat out football practices during the fall, managing the pain while winning the Texas state player of the year honors. It wasn't until basketball season, however, that Brent Kelley, the Whitehouse varsity basketball coach, really began to worry. Mahomes already had a football scholarship to Texas Tech and interest from MLB teams, and when district basketball play started in January, he hurt his foot again. The school's trainer told Kelley that Mahomes should sit for a week and see how the foot felt. Kelley wondered if Mahomes should have been playing at all. Mahomes told Kelley something different:

"No, I'm playing."

Mahomes nursed his foot for the rest of the year, wearing a boot around school, rationing his work at practice. But he never missed a game. Sometimes the pain was so severe that Kelley would call timeout and let Mahomes sit down and rest for a minute while he grimaced and grabbed at the injured foot. But he always got up. "It was really him just gutting it out," Kelley said. To Mahomes, it was the only option. His best friends were counting on him. The pain was only mental, another hurdle for an athlete to overcome.

For those who knew Mahomes, the high school story lingered for years, from his time at Texas Tech, when he played through a sprained shoulder and broken wrist, to his second full season as the Chiefs starter, when he returned from a dislocated kneecap in Denver. But it all came flooding back again on the evening of January 21, 2023, when the Chiefs opened the playoffs against the Jacksonville Jaguars in the AFC divisional round, and Mahomes stepped up in the pocket. As he looked downfield and tried to evade the rush, he became sandwiched between two pass rushers and felt Jaguars linebacker Arden Key awkwardly fall onto his right leg, buckling his ankle inward. All around Arrowhead Stadium, everyone had the same thought:

No.

The Chiefs had earned the No. 1 seed in the AFC with a 14-3 record. If they beat the Jaguars, they would face the Bills or Bengals in the AFC Championship Game. But as Mahomes hobbled to the sideline and Andy Reid called timeout, Cris Collinsworth, the NBC color analyst, watched the replay on a monitor, which showed Mahomes's lower leg trapped like a toothpick between the ground and the force of Key's left knee. "Things just changed," Collinsworth said.

The Arrowhead crowd grew quiet, and Mahomes limped back onto the field, where he had to hop on his left foot to hand the ball off to Jerick McKinnon, and for a moment, the sport of football—the entire project of fandom and hope—felt especially cruel. Mahomes was in visible distress. His superpower—his ability to scramble and make plays—was gone. The drive stalled, and the Chiefs settled for a 50-yard field goal to take a 10–7 lead in the second quarter.

Even if the Chiefs could handle the Jaguars with Mahomes on one leg, there would still be an AFC Championship Game against one of the best teams in the NFL the next week, a team that had beaten a healthy Mahomes earlier that season. Inside Arrowhead Stadium, and all around Kansas City, everyone tussled with the same reality: Had the Super Bowl dream just died? On the sideline, meanwhile, Mahomes was dealing with his own problem: Reid had just told him that he was not going back in the game until he got an X-ray on his right leg.

"No! No!" Mahomes said, his voice cracking. "Not a chance. Let me finish one more drive at least."

Reid wasn't going to relent. So Mahomes hobbled back down a tunnel to the locker room as Chad Henne, a thirty-seven-year-old backup, entered the game. Henne, who once starred at the University of Michigan before embarking on a life as an NFL journeyman, had arrived in Kansas City in 2018, taking on an older-brother role in the Chiefs' quarterback room. Mahomes and Henne were a decade apart in age, but they bonded over a shared interest. "We're beer drinkers," Henne said.

Henne was experienced in the art of beer pong—former team-mates touted his amazing accuracy—easy to get along with, an intelligent football mind in meetings, and fairly clutch, which was all the more impressive because he almost never played. Two years earlier, he had come on in relief of Mahomes during the divisional round and completed a fourth-down pass to secure the win. "Henne thing is possible, baby," Kelce had said. So as Mahomes returned to the locker room, Henne calmly went to work, leading the Chiefs on a 98-yard touchdown drive—a methodical twelve-play sequence of timing passes, long runs, and a touchdown pass to Kelce, which gave the Chiefs a 17–7 lead.

Mahomes's X-ray results, meanwhile, came back negative. He had an ankle sprain. But his leg was intact, so he watched as a staffer re-taped his ankle, and then headed back onto the field for the second half. His ankle *was* wobbly; he seemed to possess the mobility of a shopping cart, and he couldn't always plant to throw. But he was used to passing from odd angles with his feet out of position, so he tried to gut it out.

In the opening minutes of the fourth quarter, as the Chiefs held on to a 20–17 lead, Mahomes seemed to find a rhythm. He hit Kelce twice, pushing the ball across midfield. He found Smith-Schuster against single coverage. On the tenth play of the drive, as he limped to the line of scrimmage, he took the snap, skipped forward in the pocket, hopped in the air on his left leg, and hit Valdes-Scantling in the back of the end zone. The Chiefs survived with a 27–20 victory. The Bengals demolished the Bills 27–10 the next day. In a week, the Chiefs would host Cincinnati in an AFC Championship Game rematch.

Only one question seemed to matter: Would Mahomes be healthy enough to play?

TWO days later, Mahomes brought his one-year-old daughter, Sterling, to a Monday workout session with Bobby Stroupe. The official diagnosis was a high-ankle sprain—or damage to the ligaments that connect the tibia bone to the fibula. It fell somewhere on the spectrum between a low grade 2, in which ligaments are partially torn, and grade 3, which includes a full rupture. To Brett Veach, few people understood just how badly Mahomes was hurt. It was an injury that could keep a quarterback out for a month—or longer. Mahomes had seven days. As he sat with Stroupe inside a local athletic facility, attempting his usual weekly routine, he wore a pair of Adidas tennis shoes. No walking boot. No crutches. He was adamant. *No, I'm playing.* "Of all the players in the world to deal with anything," Stroupe would say, "Patrick is the most adaptable athlete of all time."

Just hours after the victory, the Chiefs sports medicine staff started working around the clock. Julie Frymyer, an assistant athletic trainer and physical therapist, designed a rehab program. Mahomes started treatment that night. The program, a secretive, proprietary amalgamation of ice and heat and resistance bands and any number of futuristic-looking therapy gizmos, forced Mahomes to report to the team facility at 6 A.M. and stay past 6 P.M. The treatments continued after press conferences and practice, which Mahomes never missed, and bled into team meetings. If he needed a push, a source of quiet inspiration during the ceaseless rehab, he told a reporter from *Sports Illustrated*, he would pull out his phone and watch clips of Michael Jordan in game 5 of the 1997 NBA Finals, known as the "Flu Game," when Jordan scored 38 points while battling severe illness, later revealed to be food poisoning.

Not that Mahomes needed extra motivation. He might have been the presumptive MVP—his second in five seasons—but he was 0-3 against Bengals quarterback Joe Burrow, with all three losses coming by 3 points. What would it mean to lose again? What could he say then? He certainly wouldn't have a comeback for "Burrowhead," the Bengals' new nickname for Arrowhead Stadium. And what could he say about the mayor of Cincinnati, Aftab Pureval, who had issued a proclamation two days before the game: "Whereas, Joseph Lee Burrow, who's 3–0 against Mahomes, has been asked by officials to take a paternity test confirming whether or not he's his father."

Mahomes still held on to the loss from the previous year, the weight of the disappointment, the emptiness, the way he felt like he had let his teammates down. He thought back to his first two seasons as a starter, when he had claimed the MVP and won the Super Bowl, and maybe he had taken it for granted. "I thought that's just kind of how it went," he would say. "You were gonna play, I listened to what Coach Reid said, and that stuff happens."

When the AFC Championship Game finally kicked off on Sunday evening, every emotion was swirling in the frigid Kansas City air: Burrowhead. The Mayor. The Ankle. The Super Bowl appearance at stake. When Mahomes combed Twitter and scanned what the media were saying, he deemed that only "5 percent" were picking the Chiefs to win. It wasn't *literally* true—the Chiefs were the Vegas favorite and picked by a *slightly* higher number than that—but that Mahomes thought it was true might have been just as telling. He still cared what people said.

The Chiefs built a 13–6 lead in the first half, as Mahomes winged passes from the pocket and defensive tackle Chris Jones kept smashing through the Cincinnati line. Mahomes had figured that he wouldn't be able to run but kept pushing the ankle to the max. He rolled out to his right and hit Kelce for a touchdown on fourth down. He tiptoed around the pocket, moving like he was holding a drink. And with 4:15 to go in the third quarter, he scooted forward on third down and fired a 19-yard touchdown strike to Valdes-Scantling, giving the Chiefs a 20–13 lead.

The only real sign that Mahomes was playing with a debilitating ankle injury would come minutes later, after the defense forced a punt and Mahomes took a snap near midfield. The Bengals sent pressure. Mahomes tried to fire a short pass to Valdes-Scantling. The ball just slipped out of his hands—one of those plays that didn't make sense. The weather was dry. The temperature was in the teens. But the ball just slipped, and when Mahomes went to recover it, he felt his ankle tweak. The worst pain of the night.

The Chiefs defense would force another punt, but the momentum was gone. The Bengals tied the game at 20–20 with 13:30 left. Smith-Schuster, Hardman, and Toney were injured. It was easy to wonder if that was it: The Bengals would come back. Burrow would do it again. It was inevitable. But then something different happened: The Chiefs defense wouldn't let Mahomes lose. Jones crashed through the line. The young secondary made plays. And when rookie Skyy Moore returned a punt 29 yards to the Chiefs' 47 with thirty seconds left, Mahomes had the ball. As Matt Nagy, now the Chiefs quarterbacks coach, would say: "We knew we were gonna win."

All week, Mahomes had pushed his ankle: Round-the-clock treatment. Practice. Business as usual. At one point, Stroupe figured that Mahomes would need to make a play with his feet. He would need to adapt again. The moment finally came on third-and-4 from just beyond midfield with seventeen seconds left, when Mahomes dropped back, scanned the field, slipped away from pressure, then decided it was time to run.

He sprinted toward the first-down marker, racing to the sideline. In moments, he would reach a peak speed of 18 miles an hour. When he stepped out of bounds at the Bengals' 42-yard line, he felt a shove on his back. It was the right hand of Joseph Ossai, a 263-pound defensive end. Mahomes went crashing into the Cincinnati bench, attempting a barrel roll to protect his ankle. A second later, he saw the flag. Late hit; 15 yards. Harrison Butker trotted onto the field and kicked a 45-yard field goal through the wind to send the Chiefs to the Super Bowl.

What followed was an epic release: Kelce would call the Cincinnati mayor a "jabroni," Pat Mahomes Sr. would light up a victory cigar ("a Joe Burrow"), and Clark Hunt would think about his father as he cradled the Lamar Hunt Trophy for a third time in four years. Mahomes, meanwhile, just walked in from the cold, carrying his daughter in his arms as he moved through a foyer outside the locker room, where Paul Rudd was standing and smiling. The celebration was on, the Super Bowl in Glendale, Arizona, was up next, and as the rest of the players and coaches paraded by, on their way back to the locker room, Quinton Lucas, the Kansas City mayor, came walking through, bumping into Brittany Mahomes. She had a message for Aftab Pureval, the Cincinnati mayor.

"Tell him that's not the way to run a city."

THE KANSAS CITY SPIRIT II

There were two rallies held in Kansas City in 2022.

The first was about soccer and the influence of the Hunt family. It was in the middle of June at the Power and Light District, where hundreds of people braved a heat index of 106 degrees to watch a selection show that revealed whether Kansas City would be chosen as one of sixteen North American host cities for the 2026 World Cup. Some attendees dressed in USA regalia, but many more wore T-shirts celebrating the Chiefs, the Royals, and the city's two professional soccer teams.

Nate Bukaty, a radio host, waved an American flag and kicked off the festivities. "I want to welcome you," he said, "to one of the most significant days in the history of this amazing city." There was a slight pause before he added, "When it comes to sports."

The future was on the line, but the past lingered in the air, too—echoes of that summer in 1899 when Kansas City boosters gathered at the Convention Hall and raised funds to prove it could host the Democratic National Convention; echoes of the hotel ballroom where politicians and businessmen gave speeches all night trying to draw enough support for the Liberty Memorial. City leaders were just as eager for the World Cup. For the past year, a ninety-by-ninety-foot banner with a blunt message hung on Main Street: "WE WANT THE WORLD CUP." At stake, beyond hosting soccer games, was the city's growing optimism, its Patrick Mahomes–fueled view of itself.

The selection show began with many of North America's most prominent western cities named as hosts: Los Angeles, San Francisco, Vancouver, Seattle, and Guadalajara. Then it came time to announce the Central Region's hosts, and an image of Kansas City's skyline popped up on the telecast. Before the words "Kansas City" fully appeared, a roar pulsated through Power and Light, and golden sparks shot into the air. One person cried and another uncorked champagne, and the venue became a sweaty mess of high fives, hugs, and spilled beers. Moments later, Mahomes appeared in a prerecorded message to explain that the world's loudest stadium, Arrowhead, would now be the site of the World Cup. But you couldn't hear him above the pandemonium.

Of the US cities selected, the Kansas City metro area was the smallest by 1.7 million people and the farthest from a beach. Washington, DC, would not be hosting World Cup matches, but Kansas City would be hosting several, along with tens of thousands of international visitors. In the end, FIFA officials claimed, Kansas City earned the bid because the city wanted it more than anywhere else.

After the crowd quieted down, Clark Hunt gave a speech, telling the story of how his father, Lamar Hunt, had attended the 1966 World Cup final in London and dreamed of bringing the event to America, to Kansas City specifically. By one estimate, the World Cup would lead to $620 million in economic development. Economists could quibble with the numbers, but one thing was clear: The city was set to host the NFL Draft in spring 2023, just weeks after opening a new $1.5 billion airport. Add that to the presence of Mahomes, and civic leaders could convince themselves of the city's new position in the national firmament.

As Hartzell Gray saw it, "Kansas City has a very unique window, and it is still open." It was easy to wonder just what that meant.

Gray was onstage that afternoon, leading the crowd in "USA, USA" chants. People knew him as the in-stadium voice for the Sporting KC Major League Soccer team, the cohost of a popular local podcast, and one of the city's most fervent supporters. ("If I was a wrestler," Gray said later, "I'd be Mr. Kansas City, and my finishing move would be the Plaza Lights.") His family had been in the area for generations: His great-grandmother owned a house in Beacon Hill, near where the freeway buzzed through, and his grandparents worked for J.C. Nichols, helping raise the family's heirs. "They were the help," Gray said. "They saw all the secrets in real time." Members of the Nichols family spoke at his grandfather's funeral.

To Gray, this window wasn't simply about hosting mega-events and basking in a rebuilt downtown. Instead he saw an opportunity for the city to be more intentional about its trajectory. The World Cup would bring economic development. But where, and for whom? Like others, Gray wanted the city's new boom era to emphasize improvements for a wider range of people and neighborhoods. "Because," Gray explained, "the only reason why Kansas City is on the precipice of truly something spectacular is because of the folks who made it."

Four months later, Gray was at the second rally, again leading the crowd as a hype man. This one was about housing and the influence KC Tenants hoped to attain through a new sibling organization, KC Tenants Power, a political arm meant to turn the group's housing activism into a force inside city hall. The rally was downtown at Ilus Davis Park on a Saturday in early October. About two hundred people waved signs and listened to the rhythm of the Center High School drumline and the Swahili church songs of the Salvation Choir. Here, too, the future was on the line while the past lingered in the air — echoes of policies and barriers erected long ago. Gray kicked off the festivities by saying that everybody there was making a statement. "From undesirable," he said, "to undeniable."

Gray introduced Diane Charity, who launched into the story of Kansas City. She saw it as one of "redlining, displacement, evictions, and closed schools." Just as much, however, she saw it as "Chiefs games on Sundays . . . immigrant communities and listening to jazz at the Phoenix."

"I love this city," Charity said. "I *love* this city. But I'm trying to get this city to love me, too."

At stake, beyond the formation of KC Tenants Power, was the direction Kansas City would take as it evolved. KC Tenants Power wanted to reshape the way the city made key decisions—with the working class and marginalized groups part of every conversation. As the rally wound down, Gray told the crowd he hoped people would remember the moment as the beginning of something special. This day, he shouted, was "a historic day in Kansas City."

A few weeks later, the new offshoot of KC Tenants faced an immediate challenge, akin to, in the football world, skipping past the preseason and regular season and directly into the playoffs. On November 8, Kansas City residents would vote on Question Two, a proposal to inject $50 million into the city's housing trust fund, money that would be made available to nonprofits, developers, and neighborhood organizations to subsidize the construction and renovation of affordable housing. Mayor Quinton Lucas and the city council had finalized the ballot question in late August, in the aftermath of the contentious decision to alter the definition of affordable housing for developers who received incentives. The proposed $50 million was slated for deeply affordable housing, the type where a one bedroom would go for around $600, meaning it would be used for the housing the city lacked most. KC Tenants was behind the "deeply affordable" stipulation, having cowritten the requirement into a bill, which was sponsored by Lucas and six members of city council. After the stipulation passed, KC Tenants posed for a picture with Lucas and other city council members at city hall and wrote thank-you notes—appreciation, Tara Raghuveer believed, was as important as accountability.

But it would all be for naught unless Kansas Citians approved a bond proposal for the city to dedicate more money to affordable housing than it ever had. The city's residents could be fickle when it came to tax money. In recent years, voters agreed to pay for a general infrastructure fund, but these types of questions often dealt with higher-profile projects. In 2004, they approved the downtown arena, and they voted in 2006 to renovate Arrowhead Stadium. In those elections, Kansas Citians made choices they believed were necessary to maintain status as a so-called major-league city. Whether enough people would understand the need for—and benefit of—an infusion of affordable homes was a thornier prospect.

So KC Tenants Power started knocking on doors, speaking to thousands of people in October and November, explaining how the homes would be priced at levels for the working class and how voting yes for the affordable housing wouldn't raise taxes. Two days before the election, a few dozen members geared up for a final canvassing. Raghuveer headed to the Old Northeast, others went to Midtown and South Kansas City, and Charity went to the East Side, near the same neighborhoods where she'd helped get out the vote as a teenager in the '60s. At one of the first homes on her list, a man sat outside on a porch. "Have you voted yet?" she asked. He had, and he'd said yes to Question Two. When people weren't home, Charity affixed brochures to their door handles. She parked her car on Mersington Avenue and got out next to a one-story home with vinyl siding. A twentysomething woman named Elisabeth Bedwell answered. She ran a cleaning business. She had taken on debt to attend college but hadn't graduated. She was worried about rising prices and was shocked about new apartments near Troost, where she said studios went for $950. Was she going to vote? "Absolutely," Bedwell said.

Two days later, Charity was in the basement of the KC Tenants' headquarters at Trinity United Methodist Church, where, a couple of hours after the polls closed, she helped lead a chant that spread around the room: *"Fifty milli for the people. Fifty milli for the people."* With every precinct reporting, around 71 percent of Kansas Citians supported the measure to fund affordable housing. That was far more than the 58 percent who had approved the Sprint Center to revitalize downtown in 2004, far more than the 54 percent who had wanted to renovate Arrowhead Stadium in 2006.

The Kansas City Spirit had a way of surfacing when it mattered most.

The city had never invested near that amount in affordable housing. Just a few years earlier it didn't even have a fund to subsidize housing. It didn't have a renters' bill of rights, either, and it didn't have a mayor and a city council that made housing a priority, pushed into action by several grassroots organizations that kept them in check, none more prominently than KC Tenants. "It's the right time, right group, right moment," said Geoff Jolley, the leader of the Greater Kansas City Local Initiatives Support Corporation. "I think when we look back five to ten years from now, that we won't be wherever we'll be but for KC Tenants."

There was also a sobering reality: The $50 million was "not actually that much," Raghuveer believed. The sum would cover the development of perhaps two thousand affordable homes. One ballot question—even one that, for Kansas City, was the equivalent of a Super Bowl—could not unwind the enduring policies that made housing unequal. It could not provide support for all the people fighting to stay in their city.

Kansas City needed these victories over and over.

WHEN the Chiefs defeated the Bengals in the AFC Championship, an unlikely fan attended the game: Raghuveer, the Harvard-educated housing activist. She'd never seen professional football in person, and she'd watched maybe three games ever, but a friend from Cincinnati bought her a ticket, so they bundled up for the bitter weather and trudged up a steep staircase in the upper deck, to the second-to-last row from the top.

Raghuveer was charmed by the crowd, which seemed impervious to the cold. Save for the occasional Bengals fan, everybody wore red clothing. They chanted in unison after touchdowns and field goals, and she could hear several fans cheering and calling out plays as though they believed their dedication could change the outcome of the game. Everyone in that stadium, Raghuveer realized, was "so hungry for connection." They didn't go to the game, she believed, because they hated the Bengals; they went because "people love the Chiefs."

As she reflected on the experience the next couple of weeks, Raghuveer considered her trip to Arrowhead one of the most important organizing lessons of her life. It reinforced for her the idea that she and the others fighting for change through KC Tenants showed up at meetings in church basements and rallied outside city hall—in matching yellow clothing—for the same reason Chiefs fans watched football in frigid weather. Any dislike they harbored for developers or the political process was outweighed by love for their neighbors, love for their city, and the belief they could make something good happen.

The group often reminded themselves of that optimism by reciting a cheer that was as prevalent in the sports world as in the organizing world: *I believe that we will win.*

"The first thing you have to believe is that you will win," Raghuveer said. "If we don't start with that belief, we're not going to get anywhere."

MASTERPIECE

Patrick Mahomes sat in the back corner of a ritzy hotel ballroom at the Hyatt Regency Scottsdale Resort and Spa, a desert ranch transformed into a Super Bowl compound. Outside, on the other side of the hotel foyer, bomb-sniffing dogs inspected visitors, and uniformed security manned the perimeter. Inside, reporters from all over the world milled about, covering the last official media session before the game on Sunday.

Mahomes was almost finished when a reporter from Europe walked up. He wanted to ask a "political" question. Mahomes nodded.

It was February 9, 2023, and in three days, the Chiefs would play the Philadelphia Eagles in Super Bowl LVII. There was no shortage of story lines. Andy Reid was set to coach a Super Bowl against his old team, where he'd first met an intern named Brett Veach. Travis Kelce was playing against his older brother, Jason, the Eagles' All-Pro center. And then there was Mahomes's right ankle, which he had feverishly rehabbed in the ten days since the win over the Bengals. There was also something else: Mahomes was facing off against Eagles quarterback Jalen Hurts, which meant that for the first time in fifty-seven years, two Black quarterbacks were starting in the Super Bowl.

"Could you put that into political perspective?" the reporter asked. "What it means for society in the US."

Mahomes had been answering the question for more than a week, and it made him think about history, the way it ebbs and flows, the way each generation builds on the next. It had been only fifty-four years since Marlin Briscoe had become the first Black quarterback to start a game. It had been only forty-four years since Warren Moon was undrafted and forced to go to Canada. Mahomes had considered quarterbacking pioneers like James "Shack" Harris and Doug Williams. He had thought about Jackie Robinson and the men who broke the color barrier in baseball. It wasn't that they didn't have the talent. It was that a system of prejudice had undermined their chances for success, and it wasn't ancient history, either. It was only a few decades ago. "The Black quarterback went through such a hard time to even be consistent starting quarterbacks in the NFL," Mahomes said. "And it seemed like when they were, they were always looking to be replaced."

As Mahomes kept speaking, it was easy to think of the moment as inevitable. He was at the vanguard of a generation of Black quarterbacks. He was the best player in the NFL and the biggest reason why people thought the Chiefs could win. The Eagles, favored by 1.5 points, had the deeper roster and the better defense and the best pass rush in football—at least that was the presumption. But the Chiefs had Patrick Mahomes.

The number of star Black quarterbacks had increased for years. ("We're moving forward," Mahomes said.) Four of the last eight NFL MVP awards had gone to Black quarterbacks. Hurts, like Mahomes, was a native Texan who played the position in his own style, borrowing the designed quarterback runs of the college game and pairing them with a strong and accurate arm. The moment, however, was not inevitable. It was the result of decades of work, of sweat and sacrifice and pushing against the system in place.

And as Mahomes considered his place in the story, he knew something else:

He was ready to put on a show.

BACK in Kansas City, on the morning of the Super Bowl, the doors to the Power and Light District opened just after 10 A.M. The first person walked in carrying a set of goggles, prepared, it seemed, to spray champagne. Over the next seven hours, the beers flowed and the crowd multiplied, and soon thousands of fans packed into the open-air party venue in the heart of downtown, while hundreds more spilled out onto Grand Boulevard to watch on a colossal TV screen. A generation ago, nothing like it would have seemed remotely possible. That was before Andy Reid and Brett Veach and the 2017 draft, before people started moving back downtown, before Patrick Mahomes asked to run Jet Chip Wasp.

Even by Kansas City standards, the city was buzzing. You could see the excitement in the windows of churches and local businesses, where the boldest signs quoted Travis Kelce's takedown of the Cincinnati mayor. You could hear it on the streetcar, where people yelled "Go, Chiefs" when they exited at their stop. You could taste it at Cafe Cà Phê, a Vietnamese coffee shop where baristas infused drinks with red-velvet condensed milk. For one week in February, Kansas City had transformed into a heartland, sports-centric parallel of Munich during Oktoberfest or Rio de Janeiro during Carnival, reaching a state of temporary urban nirvana.

The first Super Bowl championship had brought joy to a city that never seemed to be good enough, but somehow the stakes this time seemed higher. Mahomes could collect his second championship ring and start chasing the GOATs. The city could validate a decades-long revival. At least, that's what everyone hoped. The thing about sports, of course, is that the wins are not inevitable, either, and the pending result of Super Bowl LVII felt like a coin flip, as if it would come down to a single play. But as kickoff loomed just forty-five minutes away, and Kansas City tried to calm its nerves, a local radio host stood up on a stage in front of ten thousand people in the Power and Light District.

"Could you imagine," he asked over a loudspeaker, "not having Patrick Mahomes as your quarterback?"

HAD you stood on the Chiefs sideline at just past 6:04 P.M. on the night of February 12, you would have been forgiven for thinking that the Super Bowl was over. It was then, on a small patch of sideline in the middle of State Farm Stadium, that you would have heard the anguished cries of Patrick Mahomes. He limped off the field with 1:33 left in the second quarter. He hobbled over to the bench. He sat down next to Rick Burkholder, the Chiefs' top athletic trainer. He appeared to be in agony. "He rolled it," Mahomes said, wincing, pulling off his helmet and collapsing into a slouch. His face betrayed the acute pain coursing through his right ankle. He took one deep breath, and then gasped for another. "[Expletive]!" When yelling did not help, he leaned over and rested his forehead on Burkholder's shoulder.

The first half of Super Bowl LVII was turning into a nightmare. The Eagles owned a 21–14 lead and were threatening to score again. Mahomes was on the sideline in what seemed like excruciating pain, his sprained ankle twisted on a shoestring tackle by Philadelphia linebacker T.J. Edwards. The Eagles offense had scored touchdowns on three of their first five drives, shredding the Chiefs on third down and overpowering them with quarterback sneaks. The only thing keeping Kansas City in the game was a strange fumble from Hurts, who had sensed pressure, tried to protect the football, and dropped it onto the turf, watching as linebacker Nick Bolton scooped it up and returned it 36 yards for a touchdown. When the Eagles kicked a field goal to go up 24–14 on the final play of the half, Mahomes tried to jog back to the locker room. He still had a noticeable limp.

As Mahomes stepped back into the Chiefs' locker room, the pop star Rihanna was taking her place on an aerial platform stage for the halftime show. The Chiefs had around twenty-five minutes to regroup, which gave Mahomes time to work on his ankle. He received a fresh tape job. He tried to loosen it up. (He later said he did not take "a pain-killing shot.") More than a healthy ankle, what Mahomes wanted most was the chance to speak. He had always played football with a sense of wonder and experimentation, a joie de vivre that existed in every off-platform throw and unscripted play. Football was a kid's game, he liked to say, and it was important to treat it as such. He told his teammates to embrace the moment. One play at a time. He wanted to see joy. "He just needed that energy," Chad Henne said.

On the opening drive of the second half, the Chiefs received the kickoff and marched 75 yards in five and a half minutes. Running backs Isiah Pacheco and Jerick McKinnon gashed the Eagles' front line. Mahomes hit Kelce for 11 yards. On second down from the Eagles' 17, Mahomes moved right and scrambled for 14 yards. On the sideline, Eagles coach Nick Sirianni spoke into his headset: "Looked like he was moving fine there." Pacheco bowled in from the 1.

Eagles 24, Chiefs 21.

The Eagles responded with a marathon seventeen-play drive of their own, pushing the ball to the Chiefs' 15. But when it resulted in only a short field goal, Mahomes kept his foot on the gas, completing five straight passes as the offense raced down the field and back into the red zone. It was around then that Andy Reid started thinking about a play called "Corn Dog."

In the weeks before the Super Bowl, the Chiefs' coaching staff had discovered a tell: When the Eagles lined up in man coverage, they tended to overcompensate if an offense sent a receiver in a motion that looked like a jet sweep. In a typical jet sweep play, a receiver lined up outside, motioned back toward to the middle of the field before the snap, then took a handoff (or forward pitch) from the quarterback while running at top speed. The play, or at least one variation, had trickled upward from the college game, and Reid became a believer, borrowing the concept and using his fastest receivers to put a strain on defenses. But this time, Reid and his staff had unearthed something akin to a cheat code. They noticed that if a receiver went in motion in the red zone, the Eagles liked to switch the defender responsible for the receiver in motion—a defensive maneuver called "rocking and rolling." The tactic protected against the jet sweep, but it left the defense vulnerable against a fake. In a film session before the Super Bowl, offensive coordinator Eric Bieniemy had put a play up on the screen. It came from the Eagles' game against the Jaguars earlier in the season, and it featured Jacksonville receiver Jamal Agnew faking a jet sweep motion before stopping, reversing course, and breaking open for a touchdown pass in the flat. The message, as Henne would share later, was clear: "If they do this, this guy is wide open."

The Chiefs had their own version of the Agnew play. It was named "Duo Left 35Y Corn Dog." (One receiver would run a "corner" route, and the other would run a "drag." Hence, the name.) They had, according to Reid, run it just one time all season, in the season opener against the Arizona Cardinals in this stadium, on the twenty-third snap of the season. But on third-and-goal from the 3, with twelve minutes left in the Super Bowl, they ran it again. Kadarius Toney lined up wide to the right. Kelce lined up to his left, worried about the slick field conditions that had flummoxed both teams all game. Before the snap, Kelce turned to Toney and delivered a reminder: "Under control." Then Toney motioned left toward Mahomes, stopped in his tracks, and sprinted to the corner of the end zone.

Mahomes whipped a quick pass out to the flat. Toney was wide open.

"Great call!" Mahomes yelled, running back to the bench. "Great call!"

Chiefs 28, Eagles 27.

The momentum had changed. You could feel it inside State Farm Stadium, where Kelce stalked the sideline and shouted, "More, more, more!" You could feel it back in the Power and Light, where fans erupted when the Chiefs defense forced another three-and-out. On the ensuing punt, Eagles punter Arryn Siposs hit an ugly liner. Toney returned it 65 yards to the Eagles' 5-yard line, the longest punt return in Super Bowl history. Two plays later, on another third-and-goal, this time with 9:26 left, the Chiefs returned to the jet sweep motion. The play wasn't Corn Dog. At least, that's what Reid would say. The receivers lined up wrong, too. The result was the same: Skyy Moore lined up to the left, faked a jet sweep motion back to the middle, and hauled in a short touchdown pass without a defensive player in the frame. As quarterback coach Matt Nagy would tell Mahomes on the sideline just moments later: "That jet motion's killing them."

Chiefs 35, Eagles 27.

The game, however, was not over. Aside from his fumble, Hurts played brilliantly, and once again, the Eagles moved the ball. On first-and-10 with 5:45 left, Hurts chucked a 45-yard pass to receiver DeVonta Smith. On the next play, he plunged in from the 2-yard line. The Eagles needed only a two-point conversion to tie the score, and when Hurts rushed in again from the 2, the Chiefs had the ball with 5:15 left and the score tied at 35–35.

It had been a classic Super Bowl. Hurts had thrown for 305 yards and rushed for another 70. Mahomes had been effectively perfect in the second half. Fans expected a storybook finish. In reality, Mahomes was about to go off-script. On the sixth play of the drive, a first down from the Eagles' 43-yard line, Mahomes dropped back into the pocket and scanned the field, a mass of bodies crashing around him. As his eyes drifted downfield, he sensed the pocket starting to collapse.

To his left, guard Joe Thuney was winning a one-on-one battle with Eagles defensive tackle Javon Hargrave. To his right, defensive tackle Ndamukong Suh was forcing his way past guard Trey Smith. On his left flank, Pacheco was helping left tackle Orlando Brown Jr. with a defensive end. On his far right, Eagles edge rusher Haason Reddick was pushing his way into the picture. Two seconds had passed when Mahomes realized his receivers were covered. He needed to run.

It was at this moment that you could understand the essence of Patrick Mahomes. It would be easy to say that he did not have time to consider his compromised ankle, that he did not have time to worry about the pain, that he just trusted his instincts, the innate athletic skills that had been honed across three different sports for his entire life. But that would not be entirely correct. The most amazing thing about Patrick Mahomes is not his instincts or his awareness or his ability to make something up on the fly. It's that he always has enough time.

"Someone was just right on my back," he would say.

That someone was Reddick, one of the fastest pass rushers in the NFL. As Mahomes approached the line of scrimmage, he turned his head and peered behind him. He had a step, he thought, so he kept running into the open field, into a space that Thuney saw out of the corner of his eye, "a huge expanse of green field."

When it came into focus, Mahomes was sprinting down the middle of the field, pulling away from the defense on one good ankle, tucking the football as he ran, chased down at the Eagles' 17-yard line and rolling across the turf. It was a 26-yard run. The Chiefs were in position to win the Super Bowl.

"Nothing like the biggest moments in sports, right?" Henne would say."

Added Matt Nagy: "He's just made different. We always joke about it. He was made in a lab."

The final two minutes and seven seconds of Super Bowl LVII were not without controversy. The Chiefs were in field goal position. But when Eagles cornerback James Bradberry grabbed the jersey of receiver JuJu Smith-Schuster on third down with 1:54 left, it provided a first down and the chance to salt away the rest of the clock. The Chiefs went into what they called "church mode." When the Eagles tried to let them score on a running play, McKinnon slid down at the 2-yard line, wasting more time. Two plays later, Harrison Butker kicked a 27-yard field goal with eight seconds left. When the Eagles' Hail Mary attempt fell harmlessly to the turf, the Kansas City Chiefs were Super Bowl champs—again.

Chiefs 38, Eagles 35.

IN the hour after the Super Bowl, Patrick Mahomes left the field in his pads and was escorted through a tunnel to a podium in a temporary press conference room, where he fielded questions from reporters for eleven minutes. He had already hoisted the Vince Lombardi Trophy, hugged his father and listened to his wife: "You played your ass off!" Brittany told him. He had become the sixth player ever to be named Super Bowl MVP twice. When the final question was answered, he walked down the hall to the Chiefs locker room, where he pressed through a doorway, wedged his body through a crowd of bodies and wrapped his right arm around Chad Henne, who was talking to two reporters near the front of the room.

"I love you," Mahomes said.

"Good shit," Henne said.

Mahomes left Henne to his interview and started to take a lap around the room, stopping to embrace each teammate. He thanked his offensive linemen, who had not allowed a sack, and he praised his wide receivers, who joked about smoking another "Joe Burrow" as cigar smoke wafted in the air. He kept walking, weaving through reporters and hugging staffers and joking about the Coors Lights he wanted to drink, before he headed to the other side of the room, where half of the defense was sitting in a row, and after handing out another hug—"What a story!" he said—he cut a diagonal across the room and found defensive tackle Chris Jones, who had been sitting all alone.

"Two of them," Jones said, wrapping Mahomes in a hug.

"I know," Mahomes said. "Two of them."

Somewhere, in another corner of the stadium, Andy Reid was off doing another interview, telling reporters that his quarterback wanted to be the "best player of all time," and somewhere else, Brett Veach was taking it all in, an intern who had become a scout and then a GM who had built a two-time Super Bowl champion. But back in the locker room, Mahomes was ready to sit down. Minutes earlier, he had talked about his first Super Bowl, when the Chiefs had come back against the 49ers and he had felt "like a little kid winning a prize at the fair." This time, it was different. He had climbed the mountaintop once, and then he came to understand how it felt to lose.

He did not want to use the word "dynasty." That would come later. He just wanted to enjoy the moment.

THE FUTURE

Three days later, Kansas City held another parade. The party, as always, started on Grand Boulevard. Fans showed up at 6 A.M., six hours before any Chiefs players would pass by. The fans planted lawn chairs on the sidewalk, covered up in stocking caps and blankets, grilled eggs and bacon at mini tailgates. Children, granted the day off by the region's school districts, threw footballs near the Power and Light District, where bleary-eyed twentysomethings formed a line outside the bars. It was February 15, but it felt like Groundhog Day.

Patrick Mahomes wore a sparkly WWE belt emblazoned with a Chiefs logo. He posed with his MVP trophy as though he might toss it into the crowd. He ventured into a porta-potty set up along the parade route and emerged to a rapturous ovation.

As confetti fell from the sky, Mahomes and his teammates crowded onto a stage at Union Station in the shadow of the Liberty Memorial.

"Kansas City!" Mahomes shouted. "How we feelin' today, baby?"

Here it was, the second championship parade in four seasons—the third in eight years if you included the Royals' 2015 World Series—and Kansas Citians wondered how many more they would win. Three? Four? Five? There were no limits to the imagination. Once upon a time, a generation ago, Kansas City was a hollowed-out city in the heartland, and its football team knew only heartbreak, and on this Wednesday morning in February, it was celebrating one of its happiest days since the Hannibal Bridge opened in 1869. Locals could debate whether it was *this* Super Bowl parade, or the last one, or the World Series celebration before that. That made it all the more surreal.

"I'll make sure to hit y'all back next year," Mahomes said, "and I hope the crowd's the same."

It is admittedly strange to be from a place where the presence of a quarterback can change the mood of an entire city, where the level of pride and optimism and overall happiness can rest on the result of a football game, but Kansas City is admittedly that kind of place, a town where football can be both unifier and balm, and in the days before the Super Bowl, as the city hoped for the best, Clark Hunt considered the power of Patrick Mahomes.

"He's really raised everybody's level of joy, right?" Hunt said. "He is the single most important person in Kansas City right now, and you can argue that maybe it shouldn't be a sports figure. But it is."

The only question was what might happen next.

IT may not surprise you to hear that on the day of the parade, the legacy of a controversial developer was in the news. As hundreds of thousands of Chiefs fans swarmed the streets of Kansas City, the Kansas Legislature met at 9 A.M. in room 281-N of the state capitol, sixty miles away in Topeka, to discuss racial housing covenants. It had been roughly seventy-five years since the US Supreme Court ruled against the covenants and seventy-three years since the FHA discouraged their use. The covenants had been, for decades, unenforceable. But because of the complicated self-perpetuating restrictions championed by J.C. Nichols, the clauses appeared on many official records. The bill sought to fix that, offering local governments and homeowners in the Kansas City suburbs an easy method for dissolving the racial covenants.

Later, before a vote on the house floor, Rui Xu, a Kansas City–area lawmaker who lives in a Nichols suburb, described the covenants as "a painful vestige of an unacceptable past." "You can still see the effects of this on my district today," he said. Some of the cities Xu represented—wealthy communities like Prairie Village and Mission Hills—remain around 90 percent white and 1 percent Black. Racism, Xu believed, was "pervasive and enduring," far harder to eradicate than a paragraph on a deed.

In fall 2020, when the authors began the research for this book, the premise was simple: Kansas City was changing, growing in population, rehabilitating its self-image, pushing toward a bigger future, and asking questions it rarely had before. The work of J.C. Nichols and others—combined with white people's hostility toward desegregation—had left scars that divided the city, a Troost Wall that separated Black and white, freeways that displaced thousands, a history that seeped into the city's bloodstream. (The city was reminded of its divisions when, two months after the parade, Andrew Lester, an 84-year-old white man, shot Ralph Yarl, a 16-year-old Black boy who knocked on his door in a predominantly white Kansas City neighborhood.)

When the writer Shaemas O'Sheel visited Kansas City in 1928, he believed it to represent the center of the "national psychology." But almost nobody outside Kansas City—and only a few people in it—understood just how accurate he was. The scars left by Nichols and those who shaped the city were America's scars, too. "Every force and current and influence that has made, and is making, America flows and eddies here," O'Sheel wrote. You could argue it still does.

For parts of three years, we talked to people in Kansas City: politicians and activists, historians and writers, businesspeople and athletes.

There was Diane Charity, who'd grown up on the East Side, not far from Municipal Stadium, where the Chiefs arrived in 1963 and near where the freeway took her grandmother's house. A few days after the Super Bowl, Charity appeared on a local PBS program about civil rights leaders, explaining how her mother inspired her to fight for equality all these years. In the 1960s, as they held signs and protested against segregation at downtown stores, Charity realized her mother was showing her something: "This is what we *got to* do. This is what we *got to* do."

There was Mike Garrett, the Chiefs star who moved to town in

1966 and was denied an apartment on the Country Club Plaza, who left the city once and then came back, who worked as the athletic director at his alma mater, USC, for nearly two decades and now owns a home in the Country Club District. He recently helped start a nonprofit that plans to provide paths to homeownership for lower-income Kansas Citians. One thing Garrett loves about Kansas City, he said, is that it feels like things can change. "If you're doing an experiment," he said, the city is "just the right size."

There was J.C. Nichols III, the grandson of J.C. Nichols, who lives in Westwood Hills, Kansas, a tiny Nichols-planned city just on the other side of State Line Road. The Nichols Company operated until the 1990s, when an investor group from New York initiated a hostile takeover. The family continued to maintain a philanthropic organization and in the summer of 2020 released a statement supporting the renaming of the J.C. Nichols Fountain. But Nichols III, who turned eighty-three in 2022, wondered if the reexamination of his grandfather, and the segregation he wrought, was "modern sensibilities projected on the past."

"Look," he said, "what would Kansas City have been without him?"

THE East Side of Kansas City can still feel a world away from the Country Club District. In fall 2022, Quinton Lucas led us to a rental home where he'd grown up, next to US Highway 71. The city had received a federal grant to study how to make the freeway more palatable to residents, perhaps by improving the pedestrian bridges, rethinking intersections where cars idle and emit thick clouds of exhaust, and creating more business opportunities for the nearby Prospect Corridor. "Even if you got rid of it, the world changes so much," Lucas said. "Would a bunch of people just build new houses in the middle?"

Kansas City cannot start over. It can't change the past or bring old houses back. But perhaps it can find a lesson from an article published just after the Chiefs won the Super Bowl. Their *first* Super Bowl.

In February 1970, just weeks after the Chiefs beat the Vikings in

Super Bowl IV, and as the Black United Students organization and educators at Kent State University ushered in the first celebration of Black History Month, Alvin Brooks, then the leader of Kansas City's human relations department, wrote a column for *The Call*. Brooks was frustrated by the lack of progress in Kansas City, and he wondered whether the new designation would lead Americans to truly reflect on Black history. Two years earlier, in 1968, the city had examined race relations in the wake of riots following the assassination of Martin Luther King Jr., and released a report from the Mayor's Commission on Civil Disorder. The report stated that racism was systemic, existing "in Kansas City and the institutions which comprise the city," leading to social and economic inequality for the Black community. It offered forty-three recommendations, stating in the first few paragraphs that an enormous issue was Missouri's control of the Kansas City Police Department. "With the complex problems existing today in urban areas," the report read, "there would seem to be little reason why Kansas Citians could not better understand their local needs than can state legislators and officials." For housing, the report explained the need to improve substandard housing in the core of the city and to destroy the myth that property values plummet in neighborhoods with Black residents. A starting point for any solutions, Brooks wrote in his column, was for people—especially white people—to consider the way racism had been embedded in America throughout its history. If not, he believed, Kansas City, and the country, would be talking about the same things fifty years later.

Brooks, who celebrated his ninetieth birthday in May 2022, dug up the old column while working on his memoir. It was easy to see what had changed—numerous people had pushed the city forward—and what had not. The state of Missouri still controlled the Kansas City Police Department. The status quo enacted by racial covenants had never been totally unwound. Although people could choose where to live, studies over the years, including one by Brooks, have indicated that Kansas City's Black and Latino residents are more likely to be denied home loans than white residents making comparable incomes. And the core of Kansas City is still bereft of quality affordable housing.

During a phone call in summer 2022, Brooks was energetic about his pride for Kansas City, blunt about its failings, and dismayed at what he's seen as a growing movement around the country to conceal the past. Brooks was certain we'd be having these same conversations fifty years from now if America didn't accept what had already been done.

"You can't reconcile something unless you deal with the truth," he said.

AFTER the last strips of confetti fell and the sea of red began to dissipate around the Liberty Memorial, Patrick Mahomes left the stage and slipped into the grand hall of Union Station. He had been everywhere since Sunday. Two days earlier, he'd visited Disneyland. The same night, he returned to *Jimmy Kimmel Live!* He was still seven months shy of his twenty-eighth birthday, just entering the phase of his career when his photographic memory and mental football catalog would catch up to his immense physical gifts. Mahomes's personal trainer had suggested that he would continue getting faster until he was thirty-three, that he was only getting better, that this really was just the beginning, and if that's true, it's easy to fear for the rest of the NFL.

Mahomes, still wearing a pair of sports goggles on the side of his head, strolled across the hall's marble floors—past a "world champions" light sculpture and a Chiefs Kingdom banner—surrounded by an entourage that included wife, Brittany, a high school friend, and somebody carrying his MVP trophy. The hall bustled with VIP parade attendees, who warmed up from the February cold. They grabbed another drink from a cash bar and made plans to keep the party going. They didn't notice the city's quarterback. Mahomes took an escalator to the basement level, turned a corner to a doorway manned by two security guards, and stepped outside. He was on to the next thing.

ACKNOWLEDGMENTS

In September 2020, a few months after the Chiefs won their first Super Bowl in fifty years, Rustin and I started talking about Kansas City and Patrick Mahomes. The Royals had won the World Series in 2015, but this felt different. Kansas City was looking forward to a future with a transcendent superstar and looking critically at the past. What would this mean for the city? We followed the reporting where it took us, and three years later here we are.

Daniel Greenberg, our agent, was intrigued by our pitch and got back to us right away. Thank you for seeing the potential in our story and offering your support. Jill Schwartzman, our editor, recognized the important connection between football teams and mid-size American cities immediately and was as enthused as we were. Thank you for your guidance and for making this book better. Thank you to everyone else at Dutton who provided an assist, including Charlotte Peters, Nancy Inglis, Frank Walgren, Madeline Hopkins, Nicole Jarvis, Jamie Knapp, Janice Barral, Tiffany Estreicher, and Steve Meditz.

To report this book, we talked to around one hundred people, and I'm thankful for everyone who shared their time and insights. In addition to those interviews, our book was the product of research. Thank you to the librarians at the Kansas City Public Library and the State Historical Society of Missouri for use of the archives and special collections. Thank you to historians like Kevin Fox Gotham, Sherry Schirmer, and Charles E. Coulter for writing highly detailed histories of Kansas City. Thank you to local journalists, past and present, from

The Kansas City Star to *The Kansas City Call*, to KCUR and more, whose indispensable work has brought Kansas City's rich stories to life.

Thank you to so many people who've helped in my career. I wouldn't have lasted a year in journalism without guidance from friends at the KU student newspaper and professors like Malcolm Gibson and Susanne Shaw. In Philadelphia, coworkers like Chris Krewson, Anna Orso, and Cassie Owens helped me better understand what makes a good story. My current editors, Brad Wolverton and Zack Crockett, still teach me new ways to fine-tune and structure narratives, and were totally cool with me working on this book. Journalists Jason Fagone and Mary Pilon showed me how to write book pitches and proposals, and Ryan Jones let me drop his name when we reached out to Daniel Greenberg. To friends like Wes, Pat, Mike, Scott, and so many others I know from Kansas City, Philly, State College, Fort Worth, and beyond, thanks for all the support.

Rustin has been one of my closest friends and collaborators since college. Thank you for showing me how to be a great journalist for years, and always knowing how to organize the chapters in this book. We covered the 2008 NCAA championship together, but this was even better.

Finally, thanks to my siblings, Rachel and Mike, and parents, Paul and Debbie. Mom and Dad, you were always reading the *Star* for hours and telling me to read it, and you gave Rachel, Mike, and I plenty of unstructured time to play basketball, watch TV shows we probably shouldn't have, and listen to Mix 93.3 and record mixtapes on a boombox in the basement. I'm pretty sure that's how we learned to be creative. Thanks the most to Lo for being a part of my life from that Friday in October 2005 to now, for listening to all of my ideas, and for making me happy every day. I love you.

And one more thing: The Kansas City Spirit is real in so many good ways. Thank you to Kansas City and everyone who makes it a special place.

—MARK

Every morning when I was a kid, I woke up early before school at Nall Hills Elementary, walked downstairs to the kitchen, and read the pages of *The Kansas City Star*. Had my parents, Frank and Mary, not subscribed to the local newspaper, I'm quite certain this book would not exist. My mother read me *The Berenstain Bears* before bedtime. My father was my first basketball coach. Thank you for showing me how to be empathetic, thankful, curious, and conscientious. Around the breakfast table were my three older siblings: Regan, Ryan, and Reilly. My three role models and best friends. Thank you for filling my head with so many words before I understood what any of them meant.

In late 2020, just eighteen months after I had moved to New York, Mark called me with an idea: He thought we should write a book about Kansas City. Some time later, after months of research, interviews, one published story, a pandemic, and dozens of phone calls back and forth, we realized we really needed to write a book about J.C. Nichols. Without Mark, this book wouldn't exist either, in part because I never would have learned how to write a proper newspaper story had Mark not been my classmate in journalism school at the University of Kansas.

Thank you to our agent, Daniel Greenberg, and our editor at Dutton, Jill Schwartzman, for believing in (and truly understanding) our idea to write a book about Patrick Mahomes, J.C. Nichols, redlining, and the resonant history of a city in the middle of the country. The aforementioned team at Dutton was beyond helpful in stewarding this project.

Thank you to a long list of colleagues and dear friends whose knowledge, expertise, and writing is all over this book: Pedro Moura, Andy McCullough, Jayson Jenks, Marc Carig, Steph Apstein, Nick Piecoro, Ken Rosenthal, Michael Rosenberg, Sam McDowell, Lindsey Adler, Evan Drellich, Jeff Passan, Sam Mellinger, Kent Babb, Nate Taylor, Lindsay Jones, and Mike Sando.

Thank you to my editors at *The Athletic*—Paul Fichtenbaum, Emma Span, Kaci Borowski, Chris Strauss, Sarah Goldstein, Dan

Uthman, and Brendan Roberts—for being supportive of this project.

Thank you to so many old friends—from Kansas City to New York and everywhere else—for your encouragement and advice: Todd Brown, Corban Goble, Claire Noland, Paige Cornwell, Aaron Randle, Bailey Grover, Rachel Bain, Rachel Ullrich, Edwin Vohland, Matt Trofholz, Matt Potchad, Reeves Weideman, Azmat Khan, and Sarah Tankard Bradshaw.

I watched Patrick Mahomes injure his ankle against the Jacksonville Jaguars at the Horseshoe Bar (7B) in the East Village with Jack Spangler, David Wilcox, Sampson Yimer, and dozens of other Kansas Citians; I exchanged thousands of text messages about the Chiefs with Daniel Fredrick, Greg Slovick, and the 75 Connection group text: Scott, Salamat, Tosh, Joe, Tommy, and Jeff. I streamed hours and hours of Nate Bukaty, Steven St. John, Todd Leabo, Soren Petro, and Kurtis Seaboldt on Kansas City radio. I listened to podcasts with Josh Brisco and Seth Keysor. Thank you all for helping me stay connected to back home.

Finally, a couple of special mentions: the New York Public Library, which always made me think of my friend Vahe Gregorian and his father—and where I spent hours writing and revising this book; the generations of reporters from *The Kansas City Call* newspaper, who were covering the consequences of restrictive covenants before anyone else; and the late Terez Paylor and his partner, Ebony Reed—we all know Terez was destined to write an amazing book about Patrick Mahomes. I thought of him often while writing.

—RUSTIN

NOTES

PROLOGUE

1 **at precisely 11 a.m.:** "Change the Parade Route," *Kansas City Star*, October 24, 1919, 1, Newspapers.com.

1 **seven thousand marchers:** "Cheer Approval!," *Kansas City Star*, October 25, 1919, 1, Newspapers.com.

1 **in the thousands:** "Cheer Approval!," *Kansas City Star*.

1 **played patriotic tunes:** "A Hero Carried the Colors," *Kansas City Star*, October 25, 1919, 2, Newspapers.com.

1 **441 local men:** David Von Drehle, *Time*, April 6, 2017, https://time.com /4728314/kansas-city-still-remembers/.

2 **"bigger, broader and grander":** "Demand a Real Memorial," *Kansas City Star*, October 24, 1919, 1, Newspapers.com.

2 **"a wholly unnecessary inferiority complex":** Shaemas O'Sheel, "Kansas City: Crossroads of a Continent," *New Republic*, May 16, 1928.

2 **"imperishable stone":** "A Vision for Kansas City," *Kansas City Star*, October 23, 1919, 1, Newspapers.com.

3 **"White City":** "A Vision for Kansas City," *Kansas City Star*.

3 **"hundred thousand dollar town":** "To Make It Worthy," *Kansas City Star*, October 24, 1919, 1, Newspapers.com.

3 **164th Field Artillery Brigade:** "At the Turn of the Road," *Kansas City Star*, October 24, 1919, 1, Newspapers.com.

3 **chasing stories around Kansas City:** "H.R. Palmer to St. Louis," *Kansas City Star*, July 31, 1922, Newspapers.com.

3 **career in advertising:** "Palmer to Potts-Turnbull," *Kansas City Star*, October 26, 1919, Newspapers.com.

3 **On the day before:** "At the Turn of the Road," *Kansas City Star*.

3 **"a great, ugly town":** "At the Turn of the Road," *Kansas City Star*.

4 **looked like a movie:** Interview with Quinton Lucas, December 16, 2020.

4 **started to chug:** Chris Weems, "Mahomes Catch and Chug," February 21, 2020, YouTube video, https://www.youtube.com/watch?v=Ehn4N9Orx8c.

5 **"I love this city"**: "Went Over the Top," *Kansas City Times*, November 6, 1919, 2, Newspapers.com.

5 **simple headline:** "Come On!," *Kansas City Star*, November 3, 1919, 1, Newspapers.com.

5 **"If we can't make"**: "Not Giving Enough," *Kansas City Star*, October 28, 1919, 1, Newspapers.com.

6 **"taken before Judge Kennedy"**: "In 2 Hours, $146,000," *Kansas City Star*, November 3, 1919, 2, Newspapers.com.

6 **two and a half minutes:** "Went Over the Top," *Kansas City Times*.

6 **"It is a wonderful thing"**: "Went Over the Top," *Kansas City Times*.

7 **"I love that style"**: Press conference interview with Steph Curry, July 7, 2022.

8 **was hired:** "Genius into Stone Next," *Kansas City Star*, June 29, 1921, 46, Newspapers.com.

8 **the city's spirit:** "Throng of 150,000," *Kansas City Star*, November 11, 1926, 1, Newspapers.com.

9 **"Looked more like a silo"**: "A Witty Rogers on WDAF," *Kansas City Times*, November 16, 1926, Newspapers.com.

9 **wasn't a fan:** "Expect 200,000 at Rededication of Kansas City Memorial This Weekend," *Tri-County News*, November 10, 1961, Newspapers.com.

9 **like a saltshaker:** "National Affairs: And a Speech," *Time*, November 22, 1926, https://content.time.com/time/subscriber/article/0,33009,722735,00 .html.

9 **deterioration extended:** Steve Penn, "Officials Closing Liberty Memorial," *Kansas City Star*, November 9, 1994, 72, Newspapers.com.

9 **structure's sub-deck:** Steve Penn, "Memorial Awaits Help," *Kansas City Star*, December 11, 1994, 1, Newspapers.com.

10 **"just plain central"**: "Our City's Skyline with Buildings Well Spaced Appeals to an Eastern Visitor," *Kansas City Star*, November 11, 1945, Newspapers .com.

10 **"Paris reminded me of Kansas City"**: Richard Pearson, "Composer, Music Critic Virgil Thomson Dies," *Washington Post*, October 1, 1989.

10 **"America flows and eddies here"**: O'Sheel, "Kansas City."

11 **came in third:** Peggy Krebs, "Homeownership at Higher Point in U.S. History," *Tennessean*, February 26, 1999.

11 **more miles of freeway:** "Highway Statistics 2018," Federal Highway Administration, https://www.fhwa.dot.gov/policyinformation/statistics/2018/hm72 .cfm; and "Highway Statistics 1999," Federal Highway Administration via the Texas Transportation Institute, http://www.publicpurpose.com/hwy-tti99ratio .htm.

11 **"When I was in high school"**: Interview with Jason Kander, November 23, 2021.

NO BOUNDARIES

15 **At least, that's how it started:** Paul Kirkman, *The Battle of Westport: Missouri's Great Confederate Raid* (Cheltenham, UK: History Press, 2011); and Diane Euston, "The Land Dispute That Led to the Town of Kansas," *Martin City Telegraph*, June 30, 2018, https://martincitytelegraph.com/2018/06/30/the-land-dispute-that-led-to-the-town-of-kansas/.

15 **Hopewell settlements:** Natalie Wallington, "Venture to Indian Mound in Northeast KC," *Kansas City Star*, January 14, 2023, https://www.kansascity.com/kc-city-guides/article271173312.html.

15 **in the region:** "The Osage Nation and Jackson County," Jackson County Historical Society, https://www.jchs.org/osage-tribe; "Kaws (or Kanzas, Kansas)," Kansas State Historical Society, https://www.kshs.org/kansapedia/kaws-or-kanzas-kansas/17371; and interviews with the historians Jason Roe and Brooks Blevins.

15 **The Osage:** Jackson County Historical Society, "The Osage Nation in Jackson County," https://www.jchs.org/osage-tribe and Osage Nation Foundation, "Osage Nation History," https://www.osagefoundation.org/about.

16 **forcibly removed:** "Treaty with the Osage, 1825," Tribal Treaties Database, Oklahoma State University Library, https://treaties.okstate.edu/treaties/treaty-with-the-osage-1825-0217; and "Treaty with the Kansa," University of Tulsa Library, http://resources.utulsa.edu/law/classes/rice/Treaties/07_Stat_244_KANSA.htm.

16 **from the federal government in 1831:** "Gabriel Prudhomme," Missouri Valley Special Collections, https://kchistory.org/islandora/object/kchistory%3A115441/datastream/OBJ/download/Biography_of_Gabriel_Prudhomme___1791-1831____Early_Settler.pdf.

16 **pooled their resources together:** Mildred Cecile Cox, "Town of Kansas: Medley of Beginnings at Kawsmouth," The History of Kansas City Project, 1957.

16 **"nobody could think of anything better":** Shirl Kasper, "Birth of a City," *Kansas City Star*, January 29, 1998, Newspapers.com.

17 **twenty miles east:** James Shortridge, *Kansas City and How It Grew, 1822–2011* (Lawrence: University Press of Kansas, 2012), 7.

17 **Congress said no again:** Shortridge, *Kansas City*, 7.

17 **Scoping out the vast plains:** Henry C. Haskell Jr. and Richard B. Fowler, *City of the Future: The Story of Kansas City, 1850–1950* (Kansas City, MO: Frank Glenn Publishing, 1950), 23.

17 **"Great American Desert":** Haskell and Fowler, *City of the Future*, 23.

18 **Midwest for years:** Simone Amardeil Johnson, "The French Presence in Kansas: 1673–1854," 4–7, https://kuscholarworks.ku.edu/bitstream/handle/1808/21248/Dinneen_FrenchInKS_wSupplement.pdf?sequence=5.

18 **as the Nebraska Territory:** Michael Wells, "Why Are Two Cities Named Kansas City?," Kansas City Public Library, https://kchistory.org/blog/why-are -two-cities-named-kansas-city.

18 **had done the copying:** Wells, "Why Are Two Cities Named Kansas City?"

18 **He could not have chosen:** "Bleeding Kansas," PBS, https://www.pbs.org /wgbh/aia/part4/4p2952.html.

19 **moved with her to Europe:** George Martin, "The Boundary Lines of Kansas" (*Kansas State Historical Society*, 1909), 25, https://archive.org/details/boundar ylinesofk00mart/page/n1/mode/2up?view=theater.

19 **torrent of violence:** "Bleeding Kansas," PBS.

20 **mayor lobbied:** Robert W. Patrick, "When Kansas City, Mo., Came Close to Being a City in Kansas," Kansas State Historical Society, 1978, https://www .kshs.org/publicat/history/1978winter_patrick.pdf.

20 **"Half the people of the East":** "Annexation," *Kansas City Times*, January 1, 1879, Newspapers.com.

20 **"promising city in the land":** Martin, "The Boundary Lines," 7.

22 **"throughout the average day":** Chris Riebschlager, "Speed Levitch in City of Fountains," *The 816*, https://blog.the816.com/post/36788321915/speed-levitch -in-city-of-fountains-i-was.

ARM TALENT

23 **third-string defense:** Brett Veach, interview with Ross Tucker, *Ross Tucker Football Podcast*, podcast audio, February 17, 2020, https://www.podchaser .com/podcasts/ross-tucker-football-podcast-n-5240/episodes/chiefs-gm -brett-veach-53630082.

24 **what they might've missed:** Interview with Matt Nagy, February 6, 2023.

24 **"It was like a phenomenon":** Lindsay Jones and Nate Taylor, "From No-Look Snaps to Behind-the-Back Passes, Chiefs Share Moments When Patrick Mahomes Left Them Amazed," *The Athletic*, January 30, 2020, https://theathletic .com/1572644/2020/01/30/chiefs-share-moments-when-patrick-mahomes -left-them-amazed/.

24 **"a long way to go before that":** Press conference interview with Andy Reid, April 27, 2017.

25 **"part of the development":** Interview with Emmett Jones, August 27, 2023.

25 **"practicing this shit":** Jayson Jenks, Rustin Dodd, and Nate Taylor, "Ping Pong, Rollerblades and Trick Passes: The Essence of Patrick Mahomes in 15 Stories," *The Athletic*, October 7, 2021, https://theathletic.com/2861980/2021 /10/07/ping-pong-rollerblades-and-trick-passes-the-essence-of-patrick -mahomes-in-15-stories/.

25 **"a no-look pass":** Jenks, Dodd, and Taylor, "Ping Pong, Rollerblades and Trick Passes."

26 **"He really just did that":** Jenks, Dodd, and Taylor, "Ping-Pong, Rollerblades and Trick Passes."

26 **"You knew you had something":** Jones and Taylor, "From No-look Snaps."

27 **"Quite a play":** Press conference interview with Andy Reid, August 31, 2017.

"KANSAS CITY FROM NOW ON WILL BOOM"

28 **On April 13, 1856:** Laura Coates Reed, *In Memoriam: Sarah Walter Chandler Coates* (Kansas City, MO: Hudson and Kimberling, 1898), 41.

28 **It wasn't that Sarah:** Coates Reed, *In Memoriam*, 15–30.

29 **under Thaddeus Stevens:** "Col. Coates Dead," *Kansas City Star*, April 25, 1887, Newspapers.com.

29 **"Gullytown":** "Bridge to the Future," KC History, Kansas City Public Library, https://kchistory.org/week-kansas-city-history/bridge-future.

29 **Buildings were erected:** James Shortridge, *Kansas City and How It Grew, 1822–2011* (Lawrence: University Press of Kansas, 2012), 19–21.

29 **In 1860:** US Census Bureau, Census 1860, https://www2.census.gov/library /publications/decennial/1860/population/1860a-23.pdf.

29 **Sarah's sacrifice:** Coates Reed, *In Memoriam*, 39–40.

29 **They kept a Sharps rifle:** Coates Reed, *In Memoriam*, 42.

29 **"'Be Brave' said the spirit within me":** Coates Reed, *In Memoriam*, 41–42.

30 **buy $6,000 of land:** "Col. Coates," *Kansas City Star*.

30 **"the purchase of a crazy man":** "Col. Coates," *Kansas City Star*.

30 **red brick:** Henry C. Haskell Jr. and Richard B. Fowler, *City of the Future: The Story of Kansas City, 1850–1950* (Kansas City, MO: Frank Glenn Publishing, 1950), 24.

30 **In 1857:** "The Worst Fire in Kansas City History," KC History, Kansas City Public Library, https://kchistory.org/week-kansas-city-history/worst-fire-kansas -city-history.

30 **Kersey took Sarah for walks:** Coates Reed, *In Memoriam*, 46–48.

30 **more than four thousand:** William S. Worley, *J.C. Nichols and the Shaping of Kansas City: Innovation in Planned Residential Communities* (Columbia: University of Missouri Press, 1993), 42.

30 **a social scene:** A. Theodore Brown, *K.C.: A History of Kansas City, Missouri* (Boulder, CO: Pruett Publishing, 1978), 23–27.

30 **"unbounded, unquestioning faith":** "The Kansas City the Steamboats Knew," *Kansas City Star*, March 8, 1925, Newspapers.com.

30 **the Battle of Westport:** "Gettysburg of the West," KC History, Kansas City Public Library, https://kchistory.org/week-kansas-city-history/gettysburg-west.

30 **declined by a third:** Shortridge, *Kansas City*, 30.

31 **population that boomed to twenty thousand:** M.H. Hoeflich, "A Rare Edition of the Leavenworth City Charter and Ordinances: A Vignette of Life in 1870 Kansas," *Kansas Law Review* 69 (2020–21): 636, https://kuscholarworks.

ku.edu/bitstream/handle/1808/32774/3.%20Hoeflich_FINAL%20to%
20Publisher.pdf?sequence=1&isAllowed=y.

31 **Inside a Boston office:** Haskell and Fowler, *City of the Future*, 46–47.

31 **On July 3, 1869:** "Bridge to the Future," KC History.

31 **in a headline:** Cited in "The Bridge That Made Kansas City," *Kansas City Star*, July 27, 1924, Newspapers.com.

31 **his train pulled:** James Dallas Bowser "Reminiscences" in *Kansas City Sun* in Charles E. Coulter, *"Take Up the Black Man's Burden": Kansas City's African American Communities, 1865–1939* (Columbia: University of Missouri Press, 2016), 21–23.

32 **the first school:** Penn School, African American Heritage Trail of Kansas City, MO, https://aahtkc.org/pennschool.

32 **two hundred students:** Alice Hartman, "Lincoln: Rebirth or Death?" *Kansas City Times*, April 27, 1978, Newspapers.com. https://www.newspapers.com /image/677438463/.

32 **he nearly convinced:** "James D. Bowser, journalist born," African American Registry, https://aaregistry.org/story/james-d-bowser-born/.

32 **"leading Black intellectual":** Coulter, *"Take Up,"* 22.

32 **"a fortune to be made":** Bowser in *Kansas City Sun* in Coulter, *"Take Up,"* 21.

33 **more buildings were constructed:** Richard P. Coleman, *The Kansas City Establishment: Leadership Through Two Centuries in a Midwestern Metropolis* (KS Publishing, 2006), 30.

33 **thirty-four rail lines:** John Herron, "Making Meat: Race, Labor, and the Kansas City Stockyards," The Pendergast Years, Kansas City Public Library, https://pendergastkc.org/article/making-meat-race-labor-and-kansas -city-stockyards.

33 **eighteen thousand cattle a day:** "In Kansas City: Impressions of a Busy West-ern Metropolis," *Baltimore Sun*, December 5, 1899, Newspapers.com.

33 **the "Great Exodus":** "Exodusters," Homestead National Historical Park, April 10, 2015, https://www.nps.gov/home/learn/historyculture/exodusters .htm#:~:text=Many%20individuals%20and%20families%20were,it% 20were%20called%20%22exodusters.%22.

33 **alongside immigrants:** Herron, "Making Meat." Joseph Hernandez, "Trails, rails, revolution: How 4 Kansas City neighborhoods became hubs of Hispanic culture," *Kansas City Star*, November 6, 2022, https://www.kansascity.com /news/your-kcq/article268242572.html.

33 **neighborhood in 1880:** Shortridge, *Kansas City*, 86; and Coulter, *"Take Up,"* 25.

33 **stayed in the same:** Coulter, *"Take Up,"* 24.

33 **far from equal:** Coulter, *"Take Up,"* 24; and Herron, "Making Meat."

34 **a famous rebuttal:** "Educators' Gifts to Fledgling City," *Kansas City Star*, Feb-ruary 17, 2004, Newspapers.com.

34 **backed up his abolitionist beliefs:** Worley, *J.C. Nichols,* 44.

34 **At his funeral:** "Laid to Rest," *Kansas City Times*, April 28, 1887, Newspapers .com.

34 **Coates House Hotel:** "Coates House Hotel," KC History, Kansas City Public Library, https://kchistory.org/image/coates-house-hotel-20.

34 **Susan B. Anthony stayed:** Brian Burnes, "Kansas City's Long Road to Women's Suffrage," *Flatland KC*, October 8, 2020, https://flatlandkc.org/news-issues /kansas-citys-long-road-to-womens-suffrage/.

34 **"It is something":** Reed Coates, *In Memoriam*, 33.

35 **On a muggy July night:** "A Good Start," *Kansas City Star*, July 9, 1899, News papers.com.

35 **Leaders were already discussing:** "Can It Be Done in Time?" *Kansas City Star*, April 5, 1900, Newspapers.com.

35 **testified that Kansas City:** "For the New Hall," Kansas City Star, April 4, 1900, Newspapers.com.

35 **"I live in Kansas City":** "As Kansas City Looks Upon It," *St. Louis Post-Dispatch*, June 28, 1900, Newspapers.com.

THE PINE CURTAIN SUPERSTAR

36 **"Good Country Livin'":** Patrick Reusse, "Pressure Suits Mahomes Fine," *Minneapolis Star Tribune*, April 9, 1992, Newspapers.com.

36 **once described:** Asher Price, *Earl Campbell: Yards After Contact* (Austin: University of Texas Press, 2019), 14.

36 **Sometime after the Civil War:** Texas Department of Health Bureau of Vital Statistics, death certificates for Wilber Mahomes and Mary Price; and US Census Bureau, 1880 Census, Precinct 7, Smith, Texas. (Census records give the name of Cuma Homes for Que Mahomes, but his name appears as Q. Mahomes and Que Mahomes on death certificates for two of his children. Johnny Mahomes was unaware of the identity of his ancestor.)

36 **a 25-to-1 margin:** Price, *Earl Campbell*, 18.

37 **at least five:** William Lange, "Texas African American History," East Texas History, https://easttexashistory.org/items/show/344.

37 **"ran in my family":** Interview with Johnny Mahomes, August 30, 2022.

37 **three children:** Interview with Johnny Mahomes, August 30, 2022.

37 **picking blackberries:** Interview with Johnny Mahomes, August 30, 2022.

37 **"for the most part":** Reusse, "Pressure Suits Mahomes Fine."

37 **finished a psychology degree:** Dennis Brackin, "Mother Knows Best," *Minneapolis Star Tribune*, May 17, 1992, https://www.newspapers.com/image /193008255/?terms=%22Augusta%20Mahomes%22&match=1.

37 **By his senior year:** Olin Buchanan, "Top East Texas Athletes," *Tyler Morning Telegraph*, December 27, 1987, Newspapers.com.

38 **National Honor Society:** Brackin, "Mother Knows Best."

38 **her friend:** Interview with Pat Mahomes Sr., August 4, 2022.

38 **"tries to be himself":** Buchanan, "Top East Texas Athletes."

38 **"A lot of it stemmed":** Interview with Pat Mahomes Sr., August 4, 2022.

38 **as a quarterback:** Buchanan, "Top East Texas Athletes."

38 **high jump:** "ET Track Elite," *Tyler Morning Telegraph*, May 12, 1988, Newspapers.com.

38 **in baseball:** Reusse, "Pressure Suits Mahomes Fine."

38 **named Brett Favre:** Interview with Pat Mahomes Sr., August 4, 2022.

39 **Johnny's mind was made up:** Interviews with Johnny Mahomes and Pat Mahomes.

39 **affiliate in Tennessee:** "Tyler's Jimmie Pullins Chooses Braves," *Tyler Courier Times*, June 7, 1988, Newspapers.com.

39 **ball back to his parents:** Reusse, "Pressure Suits Mahomes Fine."

39 **junior best man:** "Mahomes-Martin Wedding at Colonial Hills Baptist," November 22, 1988, Newspapers.com.

40 **Mahomes later recalled:** Press conference with Patrick Mahomes, February 2023.

40 **How did she get him not to do it?:** Cindy McDermott, "Randi Mahomes: 'The Work of Parenting Is Never Done,'" *Her Life*, https://www.herlifemagazine .com/kansascity/inspirations/randi-mahomes-the-work-of-parenting -is-never-done/.

40 **eager to swim in Moore's pool:** Interview with Reno Moore, November 8, 2021.

41 **smashed the first baseman's glasses:** Interview with Pat Mahomes Sr., August 4, 2022.

41 **favorite movie was a throwback:** Junior League World Series 2010, ESPN.

41 **he wore a backward baseball cap:** Interview with Adam Cook, November 5, 2021.

42 **He was also laid-back enough:** Interview with Chad Parker, November 12, 2021.

42 **One of the few activities:** Interview with Pat Mahomes Sr., August 4, 2022.

42 **The lessons lasted several weeks:** Interviews with Reno Moore, November 8, 2021, and Adam Cook, November 5, 2021.

44 **In fall 2009:** Interview with Reno Moore, November 8, 2021.

45 **If you search:** DFW Inside High School Sports, "Playoffs Week 3: Mesquite Poteet Pirates at Whitehouse Wildcats," YouTube video, https://www.youtube .com/watch?v=8E-FaGW9sfY.

45 **as the No. 55 player in Texas:** "2014 American Statesman Fabulous 55," *Austin American-Statesman*, February 17, 2013, Newspapers.com.

45 **"For the life of me":** Interview with Sonny Cumbie, March 28, 2022.

45 **In September 2012:** Interview with Sonny Cumbie, March 28, 2022.

46 **All Kingsbury had seen:** Josh Weinfuss, "'We Went After Him Hard': How Kliff Kingsbury Got the Jump on Recruiting High Schooler Patrick Mahomes," ESPN, September 10, 2022, https://www.espn.com/blog/arizona-cardinals/post/_/id/35837/we-went-after-him-hard-how-kliff-kingsbury-got-the-jump-on-recruiting-high-schooler-patrick-mahomes.

46 **One youth coach said:** Interview with Chad Parker, November 12, 2021.

46 **One time during basketball season:** Interview with Brent Kelley, former Whitehouse basketball coach, November 11, 2021.

46 **"There's no major airport":** Interview with David Bailiff, July 26, 2022.

46 **"didn't always spin the football perfectly:** Wescott Eberts, "Patrick Mahomes Commits to the Texas Tech Red Raiders," *SB Nation*, April 22, 2013, https://www.sbnation.com/college-football-recruiting/2013/4/22/4254006/patrick-mahomes-commits-texas-tech-red-raiders-spring-game.

47 **When he wasn't splitting time at QB:** Interview with Adam Cook, November 5, 2021.

47 **the University of Texas invited Mahomes to a camp:** Interview with Pat Mahomes Sr., August 4, 2022.

47 **Mahomes decided to keep playing for one reason:** Interview with Pat Mahomes Sr., August 4, 2022.

48 **"He liked being the guy":** Interview with Randy McFarlin, November 5, 2021.

48 **it was too late for the biggest college football programs:** Interview with Pat Mahomes Sr., October 21, 2022.

48 **coached some of his early teams:** Interviews with Johnny Mahomes, August 30, 2022, and Pat Mahomes Sr., August 4, 2022.

48–49 **a fairly normal life:** This info came from public social media accounts, the 2014 Whitehouse Yearbook, and interviews with Chad Parker.

49 **Her name was Brittany Matthews:** Johnni Macke, "Patrick Mahomes and Brittany Matthews' Relationship Timeline," *US Weekly*, October 19, 2022, https://www.usmagazine.com/celebrity-news/pictures/patrick-mahomes-brittany-matthews-relationship-timeline/may-2013-9/.

49 **Sometime on that first day:** Interview with Pat Mahomes Sr., August 4, 2022.

49 **According to a Diamondbacks official:** Interview with Diamondbacks official, November 16, 2022.

THE BOSS AND THE DEVELOPER

51 **Toward the end of 1894:** Lawrence H. Larsen and Nancy J. Hulston, *Pendergast!* (Columbia: University of Missouri Press, 1997), 22.

51 **On Union Avenue:** William M. Reddig, *Tom's Town: Kansas City and the Pendergast Legend* (Columbia: University of Missouri Press, 1986), 26.

51 **"Wettest Block in the World":** Reddig, *Tom's Town*, 27.

Notes

51 **A.J. Kelly Foundry:** Maurice M. Milligan, *Missouri Waltz: The Inside Story of the Pendergast Machine by the Man Who Smashed It* (New York: Charles Scribner's Sons, 1948), 40.

51 **The legend goes:** Larsen and Hulston, *Pendergast!*, 16–17.

52 **Jim had another bar:** Larsen and Hulston, *Pendergast!*, 16, 22.

52 **a coterie of WASPs:** Larsen and Hulston, *Pendergast!*, 26–27.

52 **Nelson recruited:** A. Theodore Brown, *The Politics of Reform: Kansas City's Municipal Government, 1925–1950* (Kansas City, MO: Community Studies, 1958), 16.

52 **de facto zoning system:** William S. Worley, *J.C. Nichols and the Shaping of Kansas City: Innovation in Planned Residential Communities* (Columbia: University of Missouri Press, 1993), 56.

52 **The plan demolished:** James Shortridge, *Kansas City and How It Grew, 1822–2011* (Lawrence: University Press of Kansas, 2012), 63–64.

52 **The Commercial Club cared little:** Larsen and Hulston, *Pendergast!*, 26.

52 **Jim Pendergast saw:** Reddig, *Tom's Town*, 47, 71.

53 **"All there is to it":** Reddig, *Tom's Town*, 28.

53 **"a glass of lemonade":** Milligan, *Missouri Waltz*, 48.

53 **their chosen mark:** J. Michael Cronan, *James A. Reed: Legendary Lawyer; Marplot in the Senate* (Bloomington, IN: iUniverse, 2018), 12; and Larsen and Hulston, *Pendergast!*, 30.

53 **More than 70 percent:** Larsen and Hulston, *Pendergast!*, 35.

53 **508 Main Street:** Larsen and Hulston, *Pendergast!*, 31.

53 **learning that most people:** Larsen and Hulston, *Pendergast!*, 35.

53 **Far from the West Bottoms:** "The Class of '97," *Olathe News*, May 20, 1897, Newspapers.com.

54 **The Hayes Opera House:** "Opera House," *Olathe News*, November 1, 1894, Newspapers.com.

54 **Nichols worked there:** Robert Pearson and Brad Pearson, *The J.C. Nichols Chronicle: The Authorized Story, His Company, and His Legacy, 1880–1994* (Kansas City, MO: Country Club Plaza Press, 1994), 13.

55 **"They did not run":** J.C. Nichols, "Jesse Clyde Nichols (1880–1950) Memoir," *Planning for Permanence: The Speeches of J.C. Nichols*, Western Historical Manuscript Collection–Kansas City, 2007, 7.

55 **Nichols lectured in the dark:** Nichols, "Jesse Clyde Nichols," 7.

55 **After graduation:** Nichols, "Jesse Clyde Nichols," 7–8; and Pearson and Pearson, *The J.C. Nichols Chronicle*, 17–18.

55 **"I came to know":** Nichols, "Jesse Clyde Nichols," 7.

56 **entered the black financially:** Pearson and Pearson, *The J.C. Nichols Chronicle*, 18.

56 **Nichols was lauded:** "Nichols Earned It," *Topeka State Journal*, June 21, 1902, Newspapers.com.

56 **Before his senior year:** Nichols, "Jesse Clyde Nichols," 10.

56 **A course titled Economics 6:** "How J.C. Nichols Reached His Turning Point," *Kansas City Star*, December 8, 1929, Newspapers.com.

57 **hit up his Olathe contacts:** Pearson and Pearson, *The J.C. Nichols Chronicle*, 23.

57 **Fort Worth hotel room:** Nichols, "Jesse Clyde Nichols," 11.

57 **Back in Olathe:** "Miller-Nichols," *Olathe News*, June 29, 1905, Newspapers .com.

57 **he reached out to his father:** Pearson and Pearson, *The J.C. Nichols Chronicle*, 34–36.

57 **There was only one complication:** Pearson and Pearson, *The J.C. Nichols Chronicle*, 36.

THE COACH AND THE INTERN

58 **"a bomb":** Jerry Kellar, "Warning Signs Were Clear Before Brown Bomb Hit," *Times Leader,* November 24, 1986, Newspapers.com.

58 **what football could mean:** Brett Veach, interview with Ross Tucker, *Ross Tucker Football Podcast,* podcast audio, February 17, 2020, https://www .podchaser.com/podcasts/ross-tucker-football-podcast-n-5240/episodes /chiefs-gm-brett-veach-53630082.

58 **in the late 1960s:** Jack Roland, "Rolan' Along," *Republican-Herald*, October 2, 1968, Newspapers.com.

58 **dated back to 1893:** Mike Kelly, "Little Mount Carmel Is Big on Football," *Pittsburgh Post-Gazette*, December 13, 1998.

59 **swaths of the country:** Hugh A. Jones, "Mount Carmel Historical District Self-Guided Walking Tour," Susquehanna River Valley Visitors Bureau, 2004, visitcentralpa.org.

59 **in the history of Mount Carmel:** Interview with Dave "Whitey" Williams. January 17, 2021.

59 **repeating the eighth grade:** Vahe Gregorian, "Why Brett Veach's Football-Steeped Coal Country Heritage Is Perfect Fit for KC Chiefs," *Kansas City Star*, December 27, 2021.

59 **"on the dance floor":** Interview with Dave "Whitey" Williams, January 17, 2021.

59 **leading rusher in school history:** Charlie Lentz, "Veach Goes Out like Champion," *Daily Item*, December 8, 1996, Newspapers.com.

59 **"that's where I go":** Lentz, "Veach Goes Out like Champion."

59 **"75 Go":** Interview with Dave "Whitey" Williams, January 17, 2021.

59–60 **a 65-yard touchdown:** Chris Courogen, "Red Tornadoes Advance to State Final," *Pottsville Republican and Evening Herald*, November 30, 1996, Newspapers.com.

60 **in the Coal Region:** Chris Courogen, "Mt. Carmel Wins One for Coal Region," *Pottsville Republican and Evening Herald*, November 30, 1996, Newspapers.com.

60 **Veach was too small:** Interview with Dave "Whitey" Williams, January 17, 2021.

60 **switched to receiver:** Kevin Tresolini, "A Well-Received Change," *News Journal*, November 1, 2000, Newspapers.com.

60 **football staffer and mentor:** Interview with Jerry Oravitz, January 17, 2021.

60 **for receiver Terrell Owens:** Brett Veach, interview with Albert Breer, *MMQB NFL Podcast*, podcast audio, July 15, 2020, https://podcasts.apple.com/us/podcast/one-on-one-with-brett-veach-Wednesday-mailbag/id916244917?i=1000485009899.

61 **the unknown of the NFL:** Interview with Jerry Oravitz, January 17, 2021.

61 **window to the NFL had closed:** Brett Veach, interview with Albert Breer, *MMQB NFL Podcast*, July 15, 2020.

61 **notice the call:** Jayson Jenks, Nate Taylor, Mike Sando, and Dan Pompei, "What It Took for Chiefs to Land Patrick Mahomes," *The Athletic*, January 21, 2021, https://theathletic.com/2330642/2021/01/21/chiefs-draft-trade-patrick-mahomes/.

61 **"you saw Brett Veach":** Jenks et al., "What It Took for Chiefs to Land Patrick Mahomes."

62 **best young minds in football:** Interview with Joe Banner, January 2021.

62 **Banner knew he had the right guy:** Interview with Joe Banner, January 2021.

62 **Drawing up plays:** NFL Films, "Tracking Andy Reid's Historically Impressive Coaching Tree," YouTube video, December 18, 2017, https://www.youtube.com/watch?v=YRe51o9tvQg.

62 *What do you see?:* Brett Veach, interview with Albert Breer, *MMQB NFL Podcast*, July 15, 2020.

62 **Playoff rival at Mount Carmel:** Brett Veach, interview with Albert Breer, *MMQB NFL Podcast*, July 15, 2020.

62 **Dorothy Chandler Pavilion:** Sam Farmer, "Andy Reid Draws from California Roots, and Now Brings His Masterpiece of a Chiefs Offense to Face the Rams in L.A.," *Los Angeles Times*, November 13, 2018.

63 **Was a radiologist:** "The Andy Reid Story," Chiefs.com, January 28, 2020, https://www.chiefs.com/news/the-andy-reid-story.

63 **"can of whup-ass":** Sam Farmer, "Before He Was 'Big Red,' Andy Reid Lived the Big Life with His Friends in L.A.," *Los Angeles Times*, February 21, 2021.

63 **Model A Ford to practice:** David Fleming, "Mahomes, Favre, Other NFL Stars Reveal Larger-Than-Life Tales Behind Andy Reid," ESPN, October 9, 2019, https://www.espn.com/nfl/story/_/id/27736041/the-larger-life-tales-andy-reid-told-mahomes-favre-other-nfl-stars.

63 **Reid's teammate Randy Tidwell:** Interview with Mike Sheppard, 2022.

63 **"grandfatherly":** Fleming, "Mahomes, Favre, Other NFL Stars Reveal."

63 **crafting his own prose:** BJ Kissel, "The Andy Reid Story," Chiefs.com, January 28, 2020, https://www.chiefs.com/news/the-andy-reid-story.

64 **considered coaching:** Kissel, "The Andy Reid Story."

64 **Curious mind:** Interview with Joe Banner, January 2021.

64 **artistic side coming out:** Farmer, "Andy Reid Draws from California Roots."

64 **"Don't judge":** Andy Reid, conference-call interview with reporters, December 5, 2018, transcript courtesy of the Baltimore Ravens.

64 **"I want to teach":** Andy Reid, conference-call interview with reporters, December 5, 2018, transcript courtesy of the Baltimore Ravens.

65 *Find the Winning Edge*: Fleming, "Mahomes, Favre, Other NFL Stars Reveal."

65 **talent at the margins:** Brett Veach, interview with Albert Breer, *MMQB NFL Podcast*, July 15, 2020.

65 **"learn everything he could":** Interview with Joe Banner, January 2021.

65 **sketched out the design and presented it:** Interview with Jerry Oravitz, January 17, 2021.

65 **"He was a maniac":** Interview with Matt Nagy, February 6, 2023.

65 *needed* a salesman: Jenks et al., "What It Took for Chiefs to Land Patrick Mahomes"; and Interview with Matt Nagy, February 6, 2023.

66 **different path: scouting:** Brett Veach, interview with Albert Breer, *MMQB NFL Podcast*, July 15, 2020.

66 *I'm gonna be a GM*: Interview with Dave "Whitey" Williams, January 17, 2021.

CONCRETE AND THE COUNT

69 **wasn't sure how he got to the hospital:** Count Basie, *Good Morning Blues: The Autobiography of Count Basie* (Minneapolis: University of Minnesota Press, 2016), 12.

69 **glimmering diamond:** Bud Klement, *Count Basie: Bandleader and Musician* (Los Angeles: Melrose Square, 1994), 57.

69 **A visiting critic from Chicago:** Basie, *Good Morning Blues*, 101.

70 **carved out spaces and institutions:** Charles E. Coulter, *"Take Up the Black Man's Burden": Kansas City's African American Communities, 1865–1939* (Columbia: University of Missouri Press, 2016), 6.

70 **Black-owned:** "Historical Resources of the 18th and Vine Area of Kansas City, Missouri," National Register of Historic Places application, United States Department of the Interior, 10–11, https://www.kcmo.gov/Home/ShowDocument?id=799.

70 **played pool:** Coulter, *"Take Up,"* 121.

Notes

70 **Perry smoked beef:** Daniel Coleman, "Henry Perry," The Pendergast Years, Kansas City Public Library, https://pendergastkc.org/article/biography /henry-perry.

70 **were a first:** Samuel U. Rogers, "Kansas City General Hospital No. 2, A Historical Summary," *Journal of the National Medical Association* 54, no. 5 (September 1962): 527.

70 **Around one-third to one-half:** Jason Roe, "'As Good As Money Could Buy': Kansas City's Black Public Hospital," Kansas City Public Library, https:// pendergastkc.org/article/kansas-city%E2%80%99s-black-public-hospital; "New Hospital Is Ready," *Kansas City Star*, February 26, 1930, Newspapers .com. https://www.newspapers.com/image/655430830/?terms=%22general %20hospital%202%22&match=1.

71 **While Basie recuperated:** Basie, *Good Morning Blues*, 14.

71 **at the Eblon Theater:** Basie, *Good Morning Blues*, 15.

71 **handed out business cards:** Basie, *Good Morning Blues*, 18–19.

71 **two hundred jazz clubs:** Zeb Larson, "There Goes the Neighborhood: What Really Caused the Decline of 18th and Vine," *Scalawag*, December 8, 2020,https://scalawagmagazine.org/2020/12/kansas-city-mo-black-music -history/.

71 **fifty of them:** Harper Barnes, "Kansas City Modern: Growing Pains and Pleasures," *The Atlantic*, February 1974, https://www.theatlantic.com/magazine /archive/1974/02/kansas-city-modern-growing-pains-and-pleasures/662 660/.

71 **State Line Tavern:** "Old-Timey Jazz Joints," Squeezebox City, http://www .squeezeboxcity.com/old-timey-jazz-joints/; and "Kansas City Jazz," map of jazz clubs, The Pendergast Years, Kansas City Public Library, https://pendergastkc .org/topics/jazz/map.

71 **Sometimes Basie even heard:** Basie, *Good Morning Blues*, 109.

71 **At one point, Basie thought:** Nathan Pearson, *Goin' to Kansas City* (Champaign: University of Illinois Press, 1994), 108.

71 **Found a young Thelonious Monk:** Walter Ray Watson, "The Women Who Made Thelonious Monk," NPR, December 30, 2009, https://www.npr.org /sections/ablogsupreme/2009/12/the_women_who_made_thelonious_monk .html.

71 **changed his playing forever:** Jeff Mores, "Jazz Grew Up in . . . Kansas City?," *Medium*, January 29, 2021, https://medium.com/@MoresJeff/jazz-grew-up -in-kansas-city-e972640dab9d.

72 **During their songs:** Clint Ashlock, "Kansas City Jazz History Part 3: The Kansas City Style," the Kansas City Jazz Orchestra, YouTube video, 2020, https://www.youtube.com/watch?v=8eGu9snRdoU; and "Count Basie," The Pendergast Years, Kansas City Public Library, https://pendergastkc.org/article /biography/william-count-basie.

72 **"wheels on all four bars":** John S. Wilson, "Count Basie, 79, Band Leader and Master of Swing, Dead," *New York Times*, April 27, 1984, https://www.nytimes .com/1984/04/27/arts/count-basie-79-band-leader-and-master-of-swing-dead .html.

72 **Ronald Reagan commented:** Martin Chilton, "Count Basie: A Jazz Pioneer Who Still Inspires," *The Telegraph*, August 21, 2014, https://www.telegraph .co.uk/culture/music/worldfolkandjazz/11045834/Count-Basie-a-jazz-pioneer -who-still-inspires.html.

72 **Seamy hole-in-the-wall:** Pearson, *Goin' to KC*, 106, 138.

72 **In fifth grade:** American Jazz Museum, "His Childhood, Saxophone Supreme: The Life & Music of Charlie Parker," https://artsandculture.google.com/story /his-childhood-saxophone-supreme-the-life-music-of-charlie-parker-american -jazz-museum/-AVBZmysO1LsKQ?hl=en.

72 **Parker grabbed his instrument:** Stanley Crouch, *Kansas City Lightning: The Rise and Times of Charlie Parker* (New York: Harper, 2013), 155.

72 **Jesse Stone once said:** Katie Baker, "Those Kansas City Blues," *Daily Beast*, October 24, 2014, https://www.thedailybeast.com/those-kansas-city-blues-a -family-history-1.

73 **Big Joe Turner later explained:** "Boss of the Blues," *Ebony*, March 1954, 105.

73 **Pendergast held court:** Pearson, *Goin' to KC*, 88.

73 **Political insiders referred:** Rudolph H. Hartmann, *The Kansas City Investigation: Pendergast's Downfall, 1938–1939* (Columbia: University of Missouri Press, 1999), 8–9.

73 **Paying musicians double:** Pearson, *Goin' to KC*, 94.

73 **Said to be higher:** Orlando K. Armstrong, "Feed 'Em and Vote 'Em," *Baltimore Sun*, October 14, 1934, Newspapers.com.

74 **$32 million a year:** Lawrence H. Larsen and Nancy J. Hulston, *Pendergast!* (Columbia: University of Missouri Press, 1997), 101.

74 **Made $100 million:** Larsen and Hulston, *Pendergast!*, 100.

74 **Compared Kansas City to:** Larsen and Hulston, *Pendergast!*, 100.

74 **Naked waitresses:** Pearson, *Goin' to KC*, 100.

75 **Ten-Year Plan:** "Ten-Year Plan Approved," The Pendergast Years, Kansas City Public Library, https://pendergastkc.org/timeline/ten-year-plan-approved; and "To City of Future," *Kansas City Star*, September 19, 1935, Newspapers.com.

75 **"In Kansas City":** "Greatest Inland City," *Kansas City Times*, May 22, 1930, Newspapers.com.

75 **"couldn't afford three dollars":** Pearson, *Goin' to KC*, 108.

75 **When a British parliamentarian:** "British Woman Talks with American Boss," *Times-Tribune*, October 12, 1933, Newspapers.com.

75 **quarters in his pockets:** Louis LaCoss, "Missouri Machine Rivals Tammany's, *New York Times*, February 21, 1932, https://timesmachine.nytimes.com /timesmachine/1932/02/21/105784176.html?pageNumber=60.

Notes

75 **police brutality had declined:** Sherry Schirmer, *A City Divided: The Racial Landscape of Kansas City, 1900–1960* (Columbia: University of Missouri Press, 2016), 161.

75 **to Black communities:** Schirmer, *A City Divided*, 164; and interview with Charles E. Coulter, April 20, 2022.

75 **masked the need:** John McKerley, "The Long Struggle over Black Voting Rights and the Origins of the Pendergast Machine," The Pendergast Years, Kansas City Public Library, https://pendergastkc.org/article/long-struggle-over -black-voting-rights-and-origins-pendergast-machine.

76 **city of one million:** Henry C. Haskell Jr. and Richard B. Fowler, *City of the Future: The Story of Kansas City, 1850–1950* (Kansas City, MO: Frank Glenn Publishing, 1950), 158.

76 **"a cracker town":** David McCullough, *Truman* (New York: Simon and Schuster, 1993), 237.

THE SIGN

77 **traveled four hundred feet:** Interview with Hunter Rittimann, September 2021.

77 **When Mahomes was a freshman:** Jayson Jenks, Rustin Dodd, and Nate Taylor, "Ping Pong, Rollerblades and Trick Passes: The Essence of Patrick Mahomes in 15 Stories," *The Athletic*, October 7, 2021, https://theathletic.com /2861980/2021/10/07/ping-pong-rollerblades-and-trick-passes-the-essence -of-patrick-mahomes-in-15-stories/.

77 **"I have a picture of it":** Interview with Coleman Patterson, September 2021.

77 **"really deep with receivers":** *Lubbock Avalanche Journal*, October 22, 2016, Newsbank.

78 **Mahomes tweeted:** Patrick Mahomes (@PatrickMahomes), "I really want the royals to win . . ." Twitter post, September 30, 2014, https://twitter.com /PatrickMahomes/status/517164826443796481?s=20 (ellipses in original).

THE COUNTRY CLUB AND THE COVENANTS

79 **J.C. Nichols took an oath:** Diane Euston, "Dissecting the Troost Divide," *New Santa Fe Trailer*, https://newsantafetrailer.blogspot.com/2020/06/dissecting -troost-divide-and-racial.html.

79 **his next cigarette:** Interview with J.C. Nichols III, October 27, 2022.

79 **In 1908, he began advertising:** Advertisement, *Kansas City Star*, July 12, 1908.

79 **He had learned:** J.C. Nichols, "When You Buy a Home Site," *Good Housekeeping*, February 1923.

80 **"character of residential neighborhoods":** J.C. Nichols, "Developer's View of Deed Restrictions," speech, *Planning for Permanence: The Speeches of J.C. Nichols*, Western Historical Manuscript Collection–Kansas City.

326

80 **The first parts:** Nichols, "When You Buy a Home Site"; and Euston, "Dissecting the Troost Divide."

81 **"No part of the property":** Euston, "Dissecting the Troost Divide."

81 **They had been around:** Interview with Robert M. Fogelson, author and urban historian, April 6, 2022.

81 **by the early 1900s:** Robert M. Fogelson, *Bourgeois Nightmares: Suburbia, 1870–1930* (New Haven, CT: Yale University Press, 2005), 95.

81 **among the first:** Kevin Fox Gotham, *Race, Real Estate, and Uneven Development: The Kansas City Experience, 1900–2010* (Albany: State University of New York Press, 2014), 41; and Sara Stevens, "J.C. Nichols and Neighborhood Infrastructure" in *Wide-Open Town: Kansas City in the Pendergast Era*, eds. Diane Mutti Burke, Jason Roe, John Herron (Lawrence: University of Kansas Press, 2018), 68–69.

81 **albeit lower-paying jobs:** Charles E. Coulter, *"Take Up the Black Man's Burden": Kansas City's African American Communities, 1865–1939* (Columbia: University of Missouri Press, 2016), 58.

81 **Black and white people lived:** James Shortridge, *Kansas City and How It Grew, 1822–2011* (Lawrence: University Press of Kansas, 2012), 86; and Gotham, *Uneven Development*, 28–31.

81 **out of their homes:** Sherry Schirmer, *A City Divided: The Racial Landscape of Kansas City, 1900–1960* (Columbia: University of Missouri Press, 2016), 16–17.

81 **more acutely aware:** Shortridge, *Kansas* City, 62–65.

82 **As progress continued:** Urban Land Institute Advisory Services Program, Parks and Boulevard System: Kansas City, Missouri: Providing a More Equitable Approach to Investing in Parks and Recreation, December 2019, 8, https://knowledge.uli.org/-/media/files/advisory-service-panels/uli-asp _report_kansascitymo_2019_final.pdf?rev=9ee95631b53a4626b17c3ba 5fc0e1cd1&hash=FAF6D8C90041CD78A01C81486FDC48CA.

82 **Walls went up elsewhere, too:** Schirmer, *A City Divided*, 42.

82 **was the streetcar:** Schirmer, *A City Divided*, 95.

82 **In March 1908:** John W. McKerley, "The Other Tom's Town," in *Wide-Open Town: Kansas City in the Pendergast Era*, eds. Diane Mutti Burke, Jason Roe, and John Herron (Lawrence: University Press of Kansas), 20.

82 **one of his first ads:** Advertisement, *Kansas City Star*, August 30, 1908, Newspapers.com.

82 **Another boasted:** Advertisement, *Kansas City Star*, August 8, 1909, News papers.com.

82 **"Complete uniformity is here assured":** Advertisement, *Kansas City Star*, February 21, 1909, Newspapers.com.

82 **Courts had been iffy:** Fogelson, *Bourgeois Nightmares*, 107.

82 **devised a work-around:** Nichols, "When You Buy a Home Site"; J.C. Nichols, "From Beauty in Planning," *Good Housekeeping*, April 1937; and Fogelson, *Bourgeois Nightmares*, 108–9.

83 **establish homeowner associations:** William S. Worley, *J.C. Nichols and the Shaping of Kansas City: Innovation in Planned Residential Communities* (Columbia: University of Missouri Press, 1993), 7; and Fogelson, *Bourgeois Nightmares*, 106.

83 **At such a wide scale:** Worley, *J.C. Nichols*, 6.

83 **Saw roses cascading over walls:** "Kansas City: The Crossroads of the Continent," *New Republic*, May 16, 1928.

83 **He bought his first house:** "Pendergast Residence," Kansas City Public Library, https://kchistory.org/islandora/object/kchistory%3A92085.

83 **According to family lore:** Interview with J.C. Nichols III, October 27, 2022.

83 **plunked down $5,000:** Lawrence H. Larsen and Nancy J. Hulston, *Pendergast!* (Columbia: University of Missouri Press, 1997), 79.

84 **cost him $5 million:** Robert Pearson and Brad Pearson, *The J.C. Nichols Chronicle: The Authorized Story, His Company, and His Legacy, 1880–1994* (Kansas City, MO: Country Club Plaza Press, 1994), 97.

84 **Around half the land:** Pearson and Pearson, *The J.C. Nichols Chronicle*, 93.

84 **first planned shopping center:** Kenneth T. Jackson, *Crabgrass Frontier: The Suburbanization of the United States* (Oxford: Oxford University Press, 1987).

84 **"Nichols's folly":** Gaile Dugas, "He Built with Bricks and Beauty," *St. Louis Post-Dispatch*, December 28, 1947, Newspapers.com.

84 **visiting Henry Ford in Detroit:** Interview with J.C. Nichols III, October 27, 2022.

84 **In 1908:** Pearson and Pearson, *The J.C. Nichols Chronicle*, 49.

84 **In 1925:** Pearson and Pearson, *The J.C. Nichols Chronicle*, 105.

84 **Nichols showed off:** Dugas, "He Built with Bricks and Beauty."

84 **little black book:** Interview with J.C. Nichols III, October 27, 2022.

85 **Nichols believed an abundance:** Pearson and Pearson, *The J.C. Nichols Chronicle*, 62–63.

85 **"stood head and shoulders above":** Fogelson, *Bourgeois Nightmares*, 66.

85 **"If Webster was asked":** Edward Meisburger, "Nichols Worked with Pick and Shovel in Becoming Builder of 'City Beautiful,'" *Brooklyn Daily Eagle*, July 12, 1925, Newspapers.com.

85 **eighteen-room mansion:** Pearson and Pearson, *The J.C. Nichols Chronicle*, 54–55.

85 **drinks on a silver tray:** Interview with J.C. Nichols III, October 27, 2022.

85 **"Hoover china":** Interview with J.C. Nichols III, October 27, 2022.

85 **"Not another spot":** Pearson and Pearson, *The J.C. Nichols Chronicle*, xv.

86 **"I cannot sell"**: J.C. Nichols, "Real Estate Subdivisions: The Best Manner of Handling Them," 1912 speech, National Association of Real Estate Boards.

86 **"Cities are handmade"**: Meisburger, "Nichols Worked."

BIG RED'S ARRIVAL

88 **"Roman Coliseum"**: Joel Thorman, "Fans Cheering Matt Cassel's Injury Are 'Sickening,'" *Arrowhead Pride*, October 7, 2012.

89 **"I'm not exactly sure either"**: Dave Skretta, "Losses Piling Up During Chiefs' Lost Season," Associated Press, October 29, 2012.

89 **against the Cincinnati Bengals:** Interview with Marty McDonald, longtime Chiefs fan, June 2022.

89 **Goldman Sachs analyst:** Bill Reiter, "A Rising Son," *Kansas City Star*, December 17, 2006, Newspapers.com.

89 **Chiefs chairman:** Randy Covitz, "The Son Also Rises," *Kansas City Star*, November 25, 2005, Newspapers.com.

89 **came across Jovan Belcher:** Jason M. Vaughn, "Police Release Full Report on Belcher Murder-Suicide Case," Fox 4 Kansas City WDAF-TV, December 18, 2012.

89 **Bentley Continental GT:** Kevin Armstrong, "Dead on Arrival," *New York Daily News*, December 3, 2012, Newspapers.com.

89 **unlikely NFL prospect:** Bruce Buratti, "Sports Writer's Old College Roommate Tries to Make Sense of Kansas City Chiefs Tragedy," *Express-Times*, December 4, 2012.

90 **"I'm sorry, Scott":** Report, Kansas City Police Department, released December 2012.

90 **"in good spirits":** Christine Vendel, "Facts of Belcher's Death Spiral Emerge," *Kansas City Star*, December 18, 2012, Newspapers.com.

90 **did not immediately intervene:** Report, Kansas City Police Department, released December 2012.

90 **influence of alcohol:** Report of the medical examiner, Office of the Jackson County Medical Examiner, December 13, 2012.

90 **dementia and depression:** Steve Delsohn, "Belcher's Brain Had CTE Signs," ESPN, September 29, 2014.

90 **shot Perkins nine times:** Rachel George, "Jovan Belcher's Blood Alcohol Content Was Twice Legal Limit," *USA Today*, January 14, 2013.

91 **shot himself in the head:** Kansas City Police Department report, released December 2012.

91 **victims of domestic violence:** Matt Williams, "Kansas City Chiefs Observe Moment of Silence for Domestic Violence Victims," *The Guardian*, December 2, 2012, https://www.theguardian.com/world/2012/dec/02/kansas-city-chiefs-moment-silence.

91 **Andy Reid answered:** Interview with Clark Hunt. February 6, 2023. Sam Mellinger, "The Meeting That Brought Andy Reid to Kansas City and Changed the Chiefs' Fortunes," *Kansas City Star*, January 11, 2019, www.kansascity .com/sports/nfl/kansas-city-chiefs/article224241440.html.

91 **"Sometimes change is good":** Jeff McLane, "Tearful Reid Says Goodbye," *Philadelphia Inquirer*, January 1, 2013, Newspapers.com.

91 **at Eagles training camp:** Jeff McLane, "Reid's Son Is Found Dead," *Philadelphia Inquirer*, August 6, 2012, Newspapers.com.

92 **"long-standing battle with addiction":** Michael Rubinkam, "Coroner: Reid Died from Accidental Heroin Overdose," Associated Press, October 18, 2012, https://apnews.com/article/philadelphia-eagles-nfl-sports-andy-reid -easton-43b8a3baa0a74216947c12b0e2620085.

92 **"This is what I do":** Andy Reid, press conference interview with reporters, transcript courtesy of the Chiefs, January 7, 2013.

92 **the Arizona Cardinals:** Adam Schefter (@AdamSchefter), "One league source . . . ," Twitter post, January 1, 2013, https://twitter.com/adamschefter /status/286222710571425792.

92 **Nobody touched it:** Mellinger, "The Meeting That Brought Andy Reid to Kansas City."

92 **could seem so . . . warm:** Clark Hunt, press conference interview with reporters, transcript courtesy of the Chiefs, January 7, 2013.

92 **"I was supposed to get on that":** Clark Hunt, interview with Peter Schrager, *The Season with Peter Schrager*, podcast audio, February 8, 2023.

92 **followed him around town:** Sam Mellinger, "Now the Hard Part Begins for New Coach," *Kansas City Star*, January 8, 2013, Newspapers.com.

93 **"right thing to do":** Andy Reid, press conference interview with reporters, transcript courtesy of the Chiefs, January 7, 2013.

93 **the next Len Dawson:** Andy Reid, press conference interview with reporters, transcript courtesy of the Chiefs, January 7, 2013.

THE BATTLE FOR LINWOOD

94 **When NAACP leader:** Roy Wilkins, *Standing Fast: The Autobiography of Roy Wilkins* (New York: Viking, 1982), 53–54.

94 **One day, Wilkins told:** Wilkins, *Standing Fast*, 60.

94 **At the Orpheum Theater:** Wilkins, *Standing Fast*, 63.

95 **"nearly ate my heart out":** Wilkins, *Standing Fast*, 60.

95 **outside these boundaries:** Interview with Carmaletta Williams, executive director of the Black Archives of Mid-America, February 27, 2023.

95 **neighborhoods like Beacon Hill:** "A Short History of Beacon Hill," Beacon Hill Homeowners Association, https://www.beaconhillkcmo.com/contact -your-hoa.

95 **fireplace and spacious library:** "Troy Hall," *Kansas City Sun*, December 27, 1919. Newspapers.com.

95 **at NAACP conferences:** Charles A. Starks, "The National Conference," *Kansas City Sun*, May 23, 1914. Newspapers.com.

95 **"social and cultural center":** "Professor J. Dallas Bowser," *Kansas City Sun*, October 16, 1920, Newspapers.com.

95 **It wasn't unusual:** "'Only Wanted a Home' Says Woman from Bombed House," *Kansas City Call*, June 20, 1924.

95 **"There is little area":** Thomas A. Webster, "Community Planning to Improve the Housing Conditions of the Negro Population of Kansas City, 1940–1947" (master's thesis, University of Kansas, 1949), 166–67; and Kevin Fox Gotham, *Race, Real Estate, and Uneven Development: The Kansas City Experience, 1900–2010* (Albany: State University of New York Press, 2014), 67.

95 **The Urban League estimated:** Gotham, *Uneven Development*, 70.

95 **The Call reported:** Jerry A. Slingsby, "Racial Covenants in Kansas City: An Historical View of their Effect on Housing Choice" (master's thesis, University of Kansas, 1980), 41; and *The Call*, May 17, 1940.

95 **"It seems impossible":** "'Only Wanted a Home,'" *Kansas City Call*.

96 **The development featured:** "The Country Clubber," *Time*, December 1, 1947, https://content.time.com/time/subscriber/article/0,33009,779494-1,00.html; and Mary Francis Ivey, "Jesse Clyde Nichols," The Pendergast Years, Kansas City Public Library, https://pendergastkc.org/article/biography/jesse-clyde-nichols.

96 **Around 76 percent:** Slingsby, "Racial Covenants," 112.

96 **The segregation compounded:** Gotham, *Uneven Development*, 48, 50; and Sherry Schirmer, *A City Divided: The Racial Landscape of Kansas City, 1900–1960* (Columbia: University of Missouri Press, 2016), 108–9.

96 **Sherry Schirmer later reflected:** Schirmer, *A City Divided*, 123.

96 **The cycle made Nichols's neighborhoods:** Schirmer, *A City Divided*, 108; Gotham, *Uneven Development*, 50; Kevin Fox Gotham, *Constructing the Segregated City: Housing, Neighborhoods, and Racial Division in Kansas City, 1880–Present* (Lawrence: University Press of Kansas, 1997), 113–15; and interview with Kevin Fox Gotham, September 1, 2022.

97 **"professional duty":** Interview with Kevin Fox Gotham, September 1, 2022.

97 **One East Side notary:** Schirmer, *A City Divided*, 110.

97 **In 1910 and 1911:** Schirmer, *A City Divided*, 42.

97 **Many of that area's residents:** Charles E. Coulter, *"Take Up the Black Man's Burden": Kansas City's African American Communities, 1865–1939* (Columbia: University of Missouri Press, 2016), 250–52.

97 **bombed Priscilla Quarles's house:** "Hear Us, Police Commissioners," *Kansas City Sun*, September 28, 1918, Chronicling America, Library of Congress.

97 **noticed a pattern:** "Hear Us, Police Commissioners," *Kansas City Sun*.

98 **seven bombings a year:** Schirmer, *A City Divided*, 101, 110, 111.

98 **for the third time:** "Third Bomb Hits Home of Teacher," *Kansas City Call*, February 23, 1923.

98 **"There didn't seem to be":** Wilkins, *Standing Fast*, 63.

98 **The struggle reached a crescendo:** Schirmer, *A City Divided*, 112–14; and Wilkins, *Standing Fast*, 63–64.

98 **for ten years:** "'Negroes Must Not Come Up Here—Edict," *Kansas City Call*, June 4, 1926.

98 **Wilkins fought:** Wilkins, *Standing Fast*, 64.

99 **Rev. D.A. Holmes:** Schirmer, *A City Divided*, 113.

99 **To separate jazz:** Marc Rice, "'The Event of the Season': Charity, Politics, Dancing, and Jazz Near 18th and Vine in the 1920s," The Pendergast Years, Kansas City Public Library, https://pendergastkc.org/article/event-season-charity -politics-dancing-and-jazz-near-18th-and-vine-1920s.

99 **Despite being overcrowded:** Wilkins, *Standing Fast*, 68.

99 **received a threatening letter:** Schirmer, *A City Divided*, 115.

99 **"Anyone who could feel":** Wilkins, *Standing Fast*, 63.

THE DRAFT

100 **a blank canvas:** Brett Veach, interview with Albert Breer, *MMQB NFL Podcast*, podcast audio, July 15, 2020, https://podcasts.apple.com/us/podcast/one -on-one-with-brett-veach-Wednesday-mailbag/id916244917?i=10004 85009899.

100 **training camp for scouts:** Brett Veach, interview with Albert Breer, *MMQB NFL Podcast*, July 15, 2020.

101 **in his mind and his gut:** Brett Veach, interview with Albert Breer, *MMQB NFL Podcast*, July 15, 2020.

102 **blue waters of Newport Bay:** Interview with Leigh Steinberg, May 2, 2022.

102 **killing one bystander:** "Berkeley Riot Victim Succumbs in Hospital," *United Press International*, 1969, Newspapers.com.

102 **told a local newspaper a year later:** Dexter Waugh, "UC's Young Man with a Message," *San Francisco Examiner*, July 12, 1970, Newspapers.com.

102 **he told a reporter:** Waugh, "UC's Young Man with a Message."

103 **believed it was Patrick Mahomes:** Interview with Leigh Steinberg, May 2, 2022.

103 **next year's draft class:** Sam Mellinger, "The Inside Story of a Legendary Agent's Successful Recruitment of Patrick Mahomes," *Kansas City Star*, August 25, 2019, Newspapers.com.

103 **"was miraculous":** Interview with Leigh Steinberg, May 2, 2022.

103 **she called back:** Interview with Leigh Steinberg, May 2, 2022.

104 **"the standpoint of a technician":** Interview with Leigh Steinberg, May 2, 2022.

104 ***Wait until the season is over:*** Brett Veach, interview with Ross Tucker, *Ross Tucker Football Podcast*, podcast audio, February 17, 2020, https://www.podchaser.com/podcasts/ross-tucker-football-podcast-n-5240/episodes/chiefs-gm-brett-veach-53630082.

105 **wasn't even listed:** Brett Veach, interview with Ross Tucker, *Ross Tucker Football Podcast*, February 17, 2020.

105 **"mechanics are all over the place":** Todd McShay, "How the Chiefs QB Changed the Way Todd McShay Scouts the Position," ESPN, January 22, 2022, https://www.espn.com/nfl/draft2022/story/_/id/33145124/patrick-mahomes-evolving-nfl-draft-quarterback-evaluation-how-chiefs-qb-changed-way-todd-mcshay-scouts-position.

105 **in the draft:** Mike Mayock, "Mike Mayock's 2017 Draft Position Rankings," NFL Media, February 14, 2017, https://www.nfl.com/news/mike-mayock-s-2017-nfl-draft-position-rankings-0ap3000000785722.

105 **a second-round pick:** Interview with Leigh Steinberg, May 2, 2022.

105 **"The Draft's Rorschach Test":** Emily Kaplan, "The Draft's Rorschach Test: What Will Each Team See in Patrick Mahomes?," *Sports Illustrated*, March 1, 2017, https://www.si.com/nfl/2017/03/01/nfl-draft-patrick-mahomes-ii-texas-tech-quarterback-first-round-prospect.

105 **recalled Kingsbury saying:** Patrick Mahomes, interview with WHOOP, *WHOOP Podcast*, podcast audio, May 19, 2021, https://www.youtube.com/watch?v=azP_kImHHR8.

106 **"There's some dumb throws":** ESPN Throwback, "Patrick Mahomes Goes Through Gruden's QB Camp (2017)," ESPN, YouTube video, September 19, 2019, https://www.youtube.com/watch?v=_PW3Gsilfrg.

106 **"He was a likable dude":** Interview with Mike Sheppard, August 14, 2022.

107 **"smarter than maybe anybody knew":** Interview with Mike Sheppard, August 14, 2022.

107 **"Somehow":** Interview with Leigh Steinberg, May 2, 2022.

107 **"Holy cow":** Sam Farmer, "Chiefs' Patrick Mahomes has thrown NFL for a loop . . . ," *Los Angeles Times*, September 20, 2018, https://www.latimes.com/sports/nfl/la-sp-chiefs-mahomes-farmer-20180920-story.html.

107 **owner Terry Pegula:** Tyler Dunne, "The Pressure Is on Josh Allen," *Go Long* newsletter, November 25, 2020, https://www.golongtd.com/p/part-i-the-pressure-is-on-josh-allen.

107 **"best quarterback I've ever evaluated":** Sean Payton, interview with *Good Morning Football*, NFL Network, February 3, 2021.

108 **He loved Mahomes:** Terez A. Paylor, "How the Chiefs Finally Found Their Franchise Quarterback in Patrick Mahomes," Yahoo! Sports, September 21,

2018, https://www.yahoo.com/news/chiefs-finally-found-franchise-quarterback -patrick-mahomes-165452074.html.

108 **It fit Patrick Mahomes:** Interview with Leigh Steinberg, May 2, 2022.

108 **"a city that's just all in for you":** KCTV5 News, "Raw: Chiefs Introduce Newly Drafted QB Patrick Mahomes," YouTube video, April 28, 2017, https:// www.youtube.com/watch?v=ZGI3dEqmSVs.

108 **"But that was a special situation":** Interview with Clark Hunt, February 6, 2023.

108 **on a conference call:** Interview with Brett Veach, February 9, 2023.

109 **with speed and skill:** Brett Veach, interview with Albert Breer, *MMQB NFL Podcast*, July 15, 2020.

109 **laid out the various scenarios for Hunt:** Interview with Brett Veach, February 9, 2023.

109 **"I think he's Brett Favre":** Interview with Mike Sheppard, August 14, 2022.

109 **"Go, Chiefs":** Interview with Brett Veach, February 9, 2023.

110 **"Don't get scared now":** Jayson Jenks, Dan Pompei, Mike Sando, and Nate Taylor, "Conviction, Loyalty, Subterfuge: What It Took for Chiefs to Land Patrick Mahomes," *The Athletic*, January 21, 2021, https://theathletic.com/2330 642/2021/01/21/chiefs-draft-trade-patrick-mahomes/.

110 **with other executives:** Bob McGinn, "The Talk About Pat Mahomes Before the 2017 Draft," *The Athletic*, January 30, 2020, https://theathletic.com /1572145/2020/01/30/the-mcginn-files-he-pulls-plays-out-of-his-ass-likIouldnt -believe-the-talk-about-pat-mahomes-before-the-2017-draft.

110 **they wanted Mahomes:** McGinn, "The Talk About Pat Mahomes Before the 2017 Draft."

110 **aging Philip Rivers:** McGinn, "The Talk About Pat Mahomes Before the 2017 Draft."

110 **catch the entire league by surprise:** Interview with Brett Veach, February 9, 2023.

111 **"I wanted to be here":** Patrick Mahomes, interview with Jason and Travis Kelce, *New Heights with Jason and Travis Kelce*, podcast, podcast audio, December 1, 2022.

111 **Texas Tech logo:** Interview with Brett Veach, February 9, 2023.

111 **the Saints' Drew Brees:** Chicago Bears, "Ryan Pace Full Draft Day 1 Press Conference," YouTube video, April 27, 2022, https://www.youtube.com/watch ?v=kd8e3anjXuM.

111 **"Watch them Chiefs":** Interview with Adam Cook. November 5, 2022.

111 **"Let's get it done":** Jenks et al., "Conviction, Loyalty, Subterfuge."

112 **another Texas Tech logo:** Adam Kilgore, "The Inside Story of How Patrick Mahomes Landed with the Chiefs," *Washington Post*, January 9, 2019.

112 **a text from Brett Veach:** Interview with Brett Veach, February 9, 2023.

NICHOLS AND THE NATION

113 **soaked in garlic:** Frank Barhydt, "Real to Reel: Excerpts from Frank Byhardt's research transcripts highlights this area's rich oral history," *Kansas City Star*, August 18, 1996, Newspapers.com.

113 **he cried:** "Shots Fatal to Lazia," *Kansas City Star*, July 10, 1934; and Robert Pearman, "Shots Ended the Reign of John Lazia," *Kansas City Star*, April 21, 1966, Newspapers.com.

114 **In the spring of 1934:** Paul J. Haskins, "Kansas City 1934," *Kansas City Times*, December 6, 1974, Newspapers.com.

115 **"Terror Reign":** Associated Press, "Terror Reign Marks Kansas City Voting," *New York Daily News*, March 28, 1934, Newspapers.com.

115 **curious vote ratio:** "FBI Involvement in Early Election Fraud Case in Kansas City," Federal Bureau of Investigation, https://www.fbi.gov/news/stories/fbi -involvement-in-early-election-fraud-case-in-kansas-city.

115 **the Pendergast way:** Background on this is from sources including Lawrence H. Larsen and Nancy J. Hulston, *Pendergast!* (Columbia: University of Missouri Press, 1997); and Maurice M. Milligan, *Missouri Waltz: The Inside Story of the Pendergast Machine by the Man Who Smashed It* (New York: Charles Scribner's Sons, 1948).

115 **He lost some $600,000:** Associated Press, "Tom Pendergast Draws Year and Three Months in Prison," *St. Joseph News-Press*, May 22, 1939, Newspapers.com.

115 **Al Capone treatment:** Associated Press, "Pendergast Draws."

115 **state insurance settlement:** Associated Press, "'Gift' of $750,000 Promised to Boss in Insurance Deal," *St. Joseph News-Press*, May 22, 1939, Newspapers.com.

115 **While Roosevelt didn't:** Larsen and Hulston, *Pendergast!*, 136.

115 **he told the assembled crowd:** "T.J. Pendergast Is Indicted," *Kansas City Star*, April 7, 1939, Newspapers.com.

115 **fifteen-month prison sentence:** Associated Press, "Pendergast Draws."

115 **His wife left him:** Larsen and Hulston, *Pendergast!*, 185.

115 **Harry Truman stayed loyal:** Justin L. Faherty, "Roosevelt Objectives Continue with Office," *St. Louis Globe-Democrat*, Newspapers.com.

116 **handful of signatories:** Larsen and Hulston, *Pendergast!*, 174.

116 **unable to climb stairs:** Larsen and Hulston, *Pendergast!*, 174.

116 **wrought-iron door:** Milligan, *Missouri Waltz*, 87.

116 **couldn't cross the state line:** Milligan, *Missouri Waltz*, 212–13.

116 **commuting every other month:** J.C. Nichols, "Jesse Clyde Nichols (1880–1950) Memoir," *Planning for Permanence: The Speeches of J.C. Nichols*, Western Historical Manuscript Collection–Kansas City, 2007, 27.

116 **National Capital Park:** Nichols, "Jesse Clyde Nichols," 27.

116 **Nichols counted:** Nichols, "Jesse Clyde Nichols," 27.

116 **had defaulted on their mortgages:** Lew Sichelman, "The Housing Crisis in 1933 and Today," MarketWatch, October 10, 2015, https://www.marketwatch .com/story/the-housing-crisis-in-1933-and-today-2010-10-15.

116 **loan associations failed:** Kevin Fox Gotham, *Race, Real Estate, and Uneven Development: The Kansas City Experience, 1900–2010* (Albany: State University of New York Press, 2014), 53–54; and United States Department of Labor, "Nonfarm Housing Starts, 1889–1958," Bulletin No. 1260, https://fraser .stlouisfed.org/files/docs/publications/bls/bls_1260_1959.pdf.

116 **circulating a memorandum:** "Federal Loans Are Urged for Home Building," *Nashville Banner*, October 8, 1933, Newspapers.com.

116 **House Resolution 9620:** National Housing Act, 1934, Public No. 479–73D Congress, H.R. 9620, 72rd Cong., https://fraser.stlouisfed.org/files/docs /historical/martin/54_01_19340627.pdf.

117 **with friendlier rates:** Kevin Fox Gotham, "Racialization and the State: The Housing Act of 1934 and the Creation of the Federal Housing Administration," *Sociological Perspectives* 43, no. 2 (Summer 2002): 292, https://www .jstor.org/stable/1389798?seq=1.

117 **by following the cardinal tenets:** Federal Housing Administration, "Underwriting Manual," 1938, https://www.huduser.gov/portal/sites/default/files/pdf /Federal-Housing-Administration-Underwriting-Manual.pdf.

117 **false belief:** John Kimble, "Insuring Inequality: The Role of the Federal Housing Administration in the Urban Ghettoization of African Americans," *Law and Social Inquiry* 32, no. 2 (Spring 2007): 404, https://www.jstor.org/stable /20108708?read-now=1&refreqid=excelsior%3A62069c6b1a92881a 207e0df108cc4940&seq=6; and Katie Nodjimbadem, "The Racial Segregation of American Cities Was Anything but Accidental," *Smithsonian*, May 30, 2017, https:// www.smithsonianmag.com/ history/ how-federal-government -intentionally-racially-segregated-american-cities-180963494/.

117 **"social and racial classes":** Federal Housing Administration, "Underwriting Manual," 1938, Section 937.

117 **The FHA deemed:** Price V. Fishback, Jonathan Rose, Kenneth A. Snowden, and Thomas Storrs, "New Evidence on Redlining by Federal Housing Programs in the 1930s," Working Paper, National Bureau of Economic Research, 2021, https://www.nber.org/papers/w29244; Price V. Fishback, Jessica LaVoice, Allison Shertzer, and Randall Walsh, "The HOLC Maps: How Race and Poverty Influenced Real Estate Professionals' Evaluation of Lending Risk in the 1930s," Working Paper, National Bureau of Economic Research, 2020, https://www. nber.org/system/files/working_papers/w28146/w28146.pdf; Richard Rothstein, *The Color of Law: A Forgotten History of How Our Government Segregated America* (New York: W.W. Norton, 2017); and interview with historian Allison Shertzer, July 1, 2022.

117 **organization's manual called for:** Federal Housing Administration, "Underwriting Manual," 1938, Section 980.

117 **three of every five homes:** Gotham, "Racialization and the State," 292.

118 **"almost verbatim":** Gotham, *Uneven Development*, 59.

118 **desperately annexed in Missouri:** Annexation map, Kansas City, https://data.kcmo.org/api/file_data/kWzvO0c87TcRoH6skCMePtjBTYVPU6fjqvdnhjb9lIE?filename=Annex_2013.pdf.

118 **as suburban as possible:** James Shortridge, *Kansas City and How It Grew, 1822–2011* (Lawrence: University Press of Kansas, 2012), 102.

118 **purposefully destroyed:** Fishback et al., "New Evidence on Redlining."

118 **for Black families:** Urban Land Institute Advisory Services Program, *Parks and Boulevard System: Kansas City, Missouri: Providing a More Equitable Approach to Investing in Parks and Recreation*, December 2019, 10, https://knowledge.uli.org/-/media/files/advisory-service-panels/uli-asp_report_kansascitymo_2019_final.pdf?rev=9ee95631b53a4626b17c3ba5fc0e1cd1&hash=FAF6D8C90041CD78A01C81486FDC48CA.

118 **The agency, he believed:** Joy Milligan, "Remembering the Constitution and Federally Funded Apartheid," *University of Chicago Law Review* 89, no. 1: 84, https://chicagounbound.uchicago.edu/cgi/viewcontent.cgi?article=6278&context=uclrev.

118 **gave a snapshot:** Interview with Allison Shertzer, July 1, 2022; and Fishback et al., "New Evidence on Redlining," 21–22.

118 **as described by the HOLC:** "Mapping Inequality: Redlining in New Deal America," University of Richmond, https://dsl.richmond.edu/panorama/redlining/#loc=12/39.063/-94.66&city=greater-kansas-city-mo&area=D25.

119 **Kansas City was redder:** "Mapping Inequality," University of Richmond.

119 **modern features:** "Twenty New Homes Sold in Prairie Village," *Kansas City Star*, September 14, 1941, Newspapers.com.

119 **twenty-five Cape Cod–style homes:** "Twenty New Homes Sold," *Kansas City Star*.

120 **ad announcing the new subdivision:** Advertisement, *Kansas City Star*, August 17, 1941, Newspapers.com.

120 **"a pioneer":** "Name of a Name of a Name!," *Newsday*, February 25, 1948, Newspapers.com.

120 **company claimed:** Advertisement, *Kansas City Star*, August 17, 1941.

120 **such as Howard McEachen:** Howard McEachen, Johnson County Museum Oral Histories, oral history interview, June 7, 1973.

120 **The first batch of houses:** Advertisement, *Kansas City Star*, August 17, 1941.

120 **In 1942:** Besse Kibbey Palmer, "This Little Home Went to Market," *Better Homes and Gardens*, January 1942, https://www.bhg.com/account/signin

?regSource=9797&returnURL=https://archive.bhg.com/issue/1942/1/; and advertisement, *Kansas City Star*, March 8, 1942.

120 **best planned community:** "History," City of Prairie Village, https://www .pvkansas.com/about/history.

120 **prime minister of Pakistan:** "Reflections: A History of Prairie Village," Prairie Village Bicentennial Commission, 1976, https://www.pvkansas.com/home /showdocument?id=3592, 50; and "Home Furor over Visit," *Kansas City Star*, May 9, 1950, Newspapers.com.

121 **first city council meetings:** "Reflections: A History of Prairie Village," Prairie Village Bicentennial Commission, 13.

121 **"helped preserve your identity":** Marisa Agha, "First Mayor of PV Recalls Birth of City," *Kansas City Star*, August 9, 1995, Newspapers.com.

121 **"When you rear children":** "The Country Clubber," *Time*, December 1, 1947, https://content.time.com/time/subscriber/article/0,33009,779494-1,00.html.

121 **"all-out fight":** "Meeting Sunday at Centennial," *Kansas City Call*, December 14, 1945.

121 **brought in 1947:** "Upholds Restrictive Covenant," *Kansas City Call*, September 19, 1947.

121 **facing years of pressure:** Louis Lee Woods III, "Almost 'No Negro Veteran . . . Could Get a Loan': African Americans, the GI Bill, and the NAACP Campaign Against Residential Segregation, 1917–1960," *Journal of African American History* 98, no. 3 (Summer 2013): 402, https://www.jstor.org/stable /10.5323/jafriamerhist.98.3.0392?seq=11#metadata_info_tab_contents.

122 **The new conditions:** Associated Press, "FHA Explains Rules on Restrictive Covenants," *Hammond Times*, December 18, 1949, Newspapers.com; and National Association of Real Estate Boards, *Headline's: Real Estate's Newsletter for Today and Tomorrow* 16, no. 52 (December 26, 1949).

122 **except for "the Aryan race":** Geneva Hunter Simmons to Frank Grant, J.C. Nichols Company Records, 1896–2007, State Historical Society of Missouri at the University of Missouri Kansas City, K0106, box 249, folder 31.

122 **"As a matter of fact":** Frank Grant to Geneva Hunter Simmons, J.C. Nichols Company Records, K0106, box 249, folder 31.

122 **"Negro clause":** Miller Nichols to Mr. Kennard, June 21, 1948, J.C. Nichols Company Records 1896–2007, The State Historical Society of Missouri at the University of Missouri Kansas City, K0106, box 249, folder 31.

122 **an informal deterrent:** Nancy H. Welsh, "Racially Restrictive Covenants in the United States: A Call to Action," *Agora Journal of Planning and Design*, 2018, 136, https://deepblue.lib.umich.edu/bitstream/handle/2027.42/143831 /A_12%20Racially%20Restrictive%20Covenants%20in%20the%20US.pdf.

122 **company imposed restrictions:** Various plats from Nichols neighborhoods from February 1950, J.C. Nichols Company Records, K0106, box 249, folders 31 and 22.

122 **"The answer is no":** Urban League of Greater Kansas City, *Matter of Fact* 5, no. 1, newsletter (Autumn 1948).

123 **"distinguished public servant":** "Word Here from Truman," *Kansas City Star*, February 20, 1950, Newspapers.com.

123 **praised James Kem:** "Senate Tribute Paid to J.C. Nichols by Kem," *Kansas City Star,* February 20, 1950, Newspapers.com.

123 **At a church:** "Tribute to a Builder," *Kansas City Star*, February 19, 1950, Newspapers.com.

MAHOMES THE APPRENTICE

127 **"This doesn't happen anywhere else":** KSHB 41, "Flip the Switch on the 2017 KCP&L Plaza Lights," YouTube video, November 23, 2017, https://www.youtube.com/watch?v=xhLhU5i3peI.

128 **"I get it, right":** Terez A. Paylor, "Chiefs Still Committed to Smith as Starting QB," *Kansas City Star*, May 18, 2017, Newspapers.com.

128 **research study he'd heard about:** Sam Mellinger, "Chiefs QB Smith Blocks Social Media, but Not Wife's Words," *Kansas City Star*, August 27, 2017, Newspapers.com.

128 **"everything to do with tolerance":** Adam Teicher, "Chiefs' Alex Smith Says Safety Pin Wasn't a Political Statement," ESPN, November 16, 2016, https://www.espn.com/blog/kansas-city-chiefs/post/_/id/19151/alex-smith-said-safety-pin-wasnt-a-political-statement.

128 **"Alex goes by the book":** Interview with Derrick Johnson, September 16, 2022.

128 **University of Utah:** Pete Thamel, "Little Degree of Difficulty at Utah," *New York Times*, September 22, 2004, https://www.nytimes.com/2004/09/22/sports/ncaafootball/little-degree-of-difficulty-at-utah.html.

128 **think Ivy League:** Pete Thamel, "Alex Smith's Lost Legacy," Yahoo! Sports, April 20, 2021, https://sports.yahoo.com/alex-smiths-lost-legacy-leading-the-team-that-changed-college-football-193310288.html.

128 **competitive speech class:** University of Utah, "Alex Smith Delivers the 2014 Commencement Address," YouTube video, May 2, 2014, https://www.youtube.com/watch?v=4E-2AtyI_I8.

129 **to the receiver:** Urban Meyer, interview with Rob Stone, *Big Noon Kickoff* Fox Sports, August 31, 2019.

129 **"he won't throw it":** Paul Domowitch, "Smith Believes 49ers Made a Smart Choice," *Philadelphia Daily News*, April 25, 2005, Newspapers.com.

129 **"thought we couldn't do it":** Nate Taylor, "Fresh Start for Chiefs' Leaders on Team with Lingering Pain," *New York Times*, August 10, 2013, https://www.nytimes.com/2013/08/11/sports/football/leaders-of-the-chiefs-seek-fresh-start-on-team-that-needs-one.html.

130 **best season of his career:** The Herd with Colin Cowherd, "Andy Reid Discusses Tyreek Hill Trade, Chiefs Game Plan, Patrick Mahomes–Alex Smith," YouTube video, May 6, 2022, https://www.youtube.com/watch?v=8wabo9kCYiA.

130 **"natural friends":** Alex Smith, interview with Matt McMullen, Chiefs.com, September 25, 2021.

130 **"a gift from God":** Terez A. Paylor, "Scout QB to MVP: How Patrick Mahomes' 'Redshirt' Year and Alex Smith Led to a Historic Season," Yahoo! Sports, January 17, 2019, https://sports.yahoo.com/scout-qb-mvp-patrick -mahomes-redshirt-year-alex-smith-led-historic-season-083412040.html.

131 **Smith teamed with Tyler Bray:** Interview with Joel Stave, November 2021.

131 **"'I don't know if I make that one'":** Interview with Joel Stave, November 2021.

131 **"After a play, he'd just look to his left and kind of smile":** Interview with Matt Nagy, February 6, 2023.

131 **"We used to get in trouble":** Interview with Derrick Johnson, September 16, 2022.

132 **"'we can't stop this quarterback'":** Interview with Derrick Johnson, September 16, 2022.

132 **"Keep shooting, buddy":** Interview with Brad Childress, September 2021.

132 **"Who said we can't do something?":** The Herd with Colin Cowherd, "Andy Reid Discusses Tyreek Hill Trade."

132 **"wanted to see him take chances":** Interview with Brad Childress, September 2021.

133 **"'I'd throw the post'":** Interview with Brad Childress, September 2021.

134 **in a suite:** Interview with Pat Mahomes Sr., August 4, 2022.

134 **"*this kid is special*":** Interview with Dustin Colquitt, September 2021.

135 **"quarterback of the future":** Associated Press, "Mahomes Leads Chiefs Past Broncos 27–24 in 1st Start," December 31, 2017, ESPN.com.

135 **let the kid do his thing:** Brett Veach, interview with Ross Tucker, *Ross Tucker Football Podcast*, podcast audio, February 17, 2020, https://www.podchaser .com/podcasts/ross-tucker-football-podcast-n-5240/episodes/chiefs-gm -brett-veach-53630082.

136 **adjacent to the Kansas Speedway:** Pete Grathoff and Sam McDowell, "Chiefs Patrick Mahomes Turned Heads with His Fashion Choice at Kansas Speedway," *Kansas City Star*, May 14, 2018, https://www.kansascity.com/sports /spt-columns-blogs/for-petes-sake/article211082229.html.

THE GAMBLER'S SON

137 **waited for his ride:** Michael MacCambridge, *Lamar Hunt: A Life in Sports* (Kansas City: Andrews McMeel Publishing, 2012); and James J. Fisher, "Bartle

Behind Chiefs Move," *Kansas City Times*, January 13, 1970, https://www
.newspapers.com/image/675522629.

138 **shoes properly repaired:** Jack Olsen, "Biggest Cheapskate in Big D," *Sports
Illustrated*, June 19, 1972.

138 **Lockwood told reporters:** Joe McGuff, "A.F.L. May Come Here," *Kansas City
Times*, June 23, 1962, Newspapers.com.

138 **New Orleans and Atlanta:** Associated Press, "A.F.L. to Judge Bids by Three,"
Kansas City Times, June 26, 1962, Newspapers.com.

139 **"Bubbles Champagne":** "April Flowers Starred," *Kansas City Star*, October 27,
1973, Newspapers.com.

139 **The Missouri River swelled:** Katie Hill, "Rivers Rise: KCQ Examines the
1951 Flood," Kansas City Public Library, https://kchistory.org/blog/rivers-rise
-kcq-examines-1951-flood; and Frank Reeves, "Black Friday Very Real to K.C.
Stockyards People," *Fort Worth Star-Telegram*, July 30, 1951, Newspapers.com.

139 **noted an influential Realtor:** Fred Fitzsimmons, "Kansas City's Downtown:
Where Does It Stand?," *Kansas City Star*, January 12, 1964, Newspapers.com.

139 **woman named Daisy Bradford:** Stanley Brown, "Let's Make a Deal," *Texas
Monthly*, August 1976, https://www.texasmonthly.com/news-politics/lets-make
-a-deal/.

140 **Texas Tech University:** MacCambridge, *Lamar Hunt*.

140 **"I make up games":** Jack Olsen, "Biggest Cheapskate in Big D."

140 **all-caps headline:** "We Go Big League Tuesday!," *Kansas City Star*, April 10,
1955, Newspapers.com.

141 **took up the cause:** "Stadium and the Big Chance," *Kansas City Times*, August
14, 1953, Newspapers.com.

141 **the city's spirit:** Kim Clark, "Tribute to That Kansas City Spirit," *Kansas
City Star*, April 10, 1955, https://www.newspapers.com/image/657573078
/?terms=%22Tribute%20to%20That%20Kansas%20City%20Spirit%22&
match=1.

141 **Boy Scouts in 1928:** Steve Murphy, "Roe Bartle Has Worked Hard in
Many Fields to Win Success," *Kansas City Star*, January 30, 1955, Newspapers.
com.

141 **chieftain of the same name:** "History of the Mic-O-Say," Boy Scouts of America, Heart of America Council, https://www.hoac-bsa.org/mic-o-say-history.

141 **Boy Scout Oath:** John Keasler, "'Mr. Big' of Kansas City," *St. Louis Post-
Dispatch*, April 17, 1955, Newspapers.com, https://www.newspapers.com
/image/139753532/?terms=%22Roe%20Bartle%22%20%22Major%
20League%22&match=1.

142 **Nichols's Armour Hills:** Murphy, "Roe Bartle Has Worked Hard."

142 **act of concentration:** Keasler, "'Mr. Big' of Kansas City."

142 **rules of secrecy:** Dan Jenkins, "Too Many Chiefs Made Too Many Touchdowns," *Sports Illustrated*, September 16, 1963.

Notes

142 **"have I not":** Jenkins, "Too Many Chiefs Made Too Many Touchdowns."

142 **"reason to change our minds":** Associated Press, "Kansas City Bids for Dallas Club," *Austin American*, February 9, 1963, Newspapers.com.

143 **fifty season tickets:** Jenkins, "Too Many Chiefs Made Too Many Touchdowns."

143 **old neighborhoods:** Interview with Graham Stark, Ray Evans's grandson, May 21, 2022.

143 **a cow town:** MacCambridge, *Lamar Hunt*.

143 **tribute to Roe Bartle:** Vahe Gregorian, "It's Time for the Chiefs to Defuse the Cultural Offenses They Enable and Reflect," *Kansas City Star*, July 13, 2020, https://www.kansascity.com/sports/spt-columns-blogs/vahe-gregorian/article244153762.html.

143 **"appear in headlines":** Jack Sareault, "Texans Migrate to KC as Chiefs," *The Olympian*, May 30, 1963; and United Press International, "Transplanted Texans Renamed KC Chiefs," *Shreveport Times*, May 26, 1963, Newspapers.com.

THE FREEWAY

144 **Where Diane Charity lived:** Interview with Diane Charity, July 21, 2022.

145 **two distinct cities:** Kevin Fox Gotham, *Constructing the Segregated City: Housing, Neighborhoods, and Racial Division in Kansas City, 1880–Present* (Lawrence: University of Kansas Press, 1997), 113–15.

145 **slave owner Benoist Troost:** Channa Steinmetz, "Truth Not Troost: A New Effort Seeks to Rename Kansas City Corridor over Slavery Ties," *Startland New*s, July 3, 2022, https://www.kcur.org/housing-development-section/2022-07-03/truth-not-troost-a-new-effort-seeks-to-rename-kansas-city-corridor-over-slavery-ties.

145 **"West of Troost":** Advertisements, *Kansas City Star*, August 3, 1968; August 7, 1961; and May 12, 1970, Newspapers.com.

145 **nearly one hundred thousand white people:** Gotham, *Constructing the Segregated City*, 182.

145 **He expressed concern:** J.C. Nichols, "Planning for Permanence," speech, New York City, November 18, 1948, in *Planning for Permanence: The Speeches of J.C. Nichols*, Western Historical Manuscript Collection–Kansas City, https://files.shsmo.org/manuscripts/kansas-city/nichols/JCN083.pdf.

146 **in the early 1940s:** Robert Pearson and Brad Pearson, *The J.C. Nichols Chronicle: The Authorized Story, His Company, and His Legacy, 1880–1994* (Kansas City, MO: Country Club Plaza Press, 1994), 163.

146 **blamed the cities themselves:** Kevin Fox Gotham, "A City Without Slums: Urban Renewal, Public Housing, and Downtown Revitalization in Kansas City, Missouri," *American Journal of Economics and Sociology* 60, no. 1 (2001): 131, 137–38.

146 **Greenwich Village as blighted:** Anthony Paletta, "Story of Cities 32: Jane Jacobs v Robert Moses, Battle of New York's Urban Titans," *The Guardian*, April 28, 2016, https://www.theguardian.com/cities/2016/apr/28/story-cities-32 -new-york-jane-jacobs-robert-moses.

146 **came to mean:** Gotham, "A City Without Slums," 131, 137–38.

146 **In late spring 1942:** "Urban Land Institute Proposes Large-Scale Rebuilding Plans to Avoid Postwar Slump," *Hartford Courant*, June 21, 1942, Newspapers .com.

146 **Related policies:** Interview with Kevin Fox Gotham, September 1, 2022; and Diana Ionescu, "What Is Urban Renewal?," Planetizen, https://www.planetizen .com/definition/urban-renewal.

146 **Federal Highway Act of 1956:** Michael Wells, "Kansas City's Downtown Loop," Kansas City Public Library, November 7, 2019, https://kclibrary.org /blog/kc-q-kansas-citys-downtown-loop.

147 **envisioned as temporary housing:** Interview with Kevin Fox Gotham, September 1, 2022.

147 **They also segregated:** Kevin Fox Gotham, *Race, Real Estate, and Uneven Development: The Kansas City Experience, 1900–2010* (Albany: State University of New York Press, 2014), 81–83.

147 **every four units demolished:** Emily Badger, "Why Trump's Use of the Words 'Urban Renewal' Is Scary for Cities," *New York Times*, December 7, 2016, https://www.nytimes.com/2016/12/07/upshot/why-trumps-use-of-the-words -urban-renewal-is-scary-for-cities.html; and Herbert J. Gans, "The Failure of Urban Renewal," *Commentary*, April 1965, https://www.commentary.org /articles/herbert-gans/the-failure-of-urban-renewal/.

147 **"It means Negro removal":** Vince Graham, "Urban Renewal Means Negro Removal—James Baldwin 1963," Baldwin interview with Kenneth Clark, YouTube video, https://www.youtube.com/watch?v=T8Abhj17kYU.

147 **"dean" of big-city managers:** Carolyn Olson, "Manager Stepped Out to Head Off Council," *Kansas City Star*, March 31, 1974, Newspapers.com.

147 **all-state lineman:** James W. Scott, "The Cookingham Way—Skill Plus Vision," *Kansas City Times*, March 26, 1959; and Henry Van Brunt, "Profile of a City Manager," *Kansas City* Star, November 3, 1940, Newspapers .com.

147 **He immediately cut:** Martha Perego, "Cookingham's Legacy," International City/County Management Association, September 21, 2016, https://icma.org /articles/article/cookinghams-legacy.

147 **made up 12 percent:** Gotham, "A City Without Slums," 138.

147 **highway plan in 1947:** James Shortridge, *Kansas City and How It Grew, 1822– 2011* (Lawrence: University Press of Kansas, 2012), 106.

148 **"The stranger visiting Kansas City":** "The Kansas City Blitz," *Kansas City Star*, August 26, 1954, Newspapers.com.

Notes

148 **When the highway was finished:** "Faith in Course," *Kansas City Times*, October 8, 1957; "Tour New Sites," *Kansas City Times*, October 8, 1957; and "Hail Vital City Stride," *Kansas City Star*, October 7, 1957, Newspapers.com.

148 **"a great urban renaissance":** "Faith in Course," *Kansas City Times*.

148 **citation of honor:** Gotham, *Uneven Development*, 84.

148 **Black residents protested:** Gotham, *Uneven Development*, 86–87.

148 **60 percent occupied:** Jillian Mincer, "Kansas City, Mo: Failed Project Is Demolished," *New York Times*, March 8, 1987, https://www.nytimes.com/1987/03/08/realestate/national-notebook-kansas-city-mo-failed-project-is-demolished.html.

148 **Two elevators got stuck:** "Wayne Miner Public Housing," KC History, Kansas City Public Library, https://kchistory.org/islandora/object/kchistory%3A66744.

148 **never been to Kansas City:** Paul Zollo, "Behind the Song 'Kansas City' by Leiber and Stoller," https://americansongwriter.com/behind-the-song-kansas-city.

149 **crumbled under urban renewal:** "Historical Resources of the 18th and Vine Area of Kansas City, Missouri," National Register of Historic Places application, United States Department of the Interior, 22, https://www.kcmo.gov/Home/ShowDocument?id=799.

149 **replaced by heavy industry:** "Historical Resources of the 18th and Vine Area of Kansas City, Missouri," National Register of Historic Places application, United States Department of the Interior, 22, https://www.kcmo.gov/Home/ShowDocument?id=799.

149 **"no place left to jump":** Charles Thomas Stites, "Jazz Hoes Hard Row," *Kansas City Star*, November 7, 1965, Newspapers.com.

149 **Thousands of Kansas City families:** Gotham, *Uneven Development*, 88.

149 **"no longer a viable":** Dennis Nodin Valdés, *Barrio Norteños: St. Paul and Midwestern Mexican Communities in the Twentieth Century* (Austin: University of Texas Press, 2000), 183.

149 **West Terrace Park:** "West Terrace Park, Palisades," KC History, Kansas City Public Library, https://kchistory.org/islandora/object/kchistory%3A108771.

149 **Black families were just starting:** "Freedom Inc. Asks for Active Public Interest in South Midtown Freeway," *The Call*, February 13–19, 1976.

150 **It would run:** "Briefs Council on Road Study," *Kansas City Times*, October 1, 1963, Newspapers.com.

150 **Officials were split:** "Into Freeway Routes South," *Kansas City Star*, February 5, 1965.

150 **still have their homes:** "Briefs Council," *Kansas City Times*.

150 **expressed support:** LaDene Morton, *The Brookside Story: Shops of Every Necessary Character* (Cheltenham, UK: History Press, 2010), 73; and "Votes to Retain Freeway," *Wednesday Magazine*, October 25, 1961.

150 **Company president Miller Nichols:** "Form Freeway Organization," *Wednesday Magazine*, November 8, 1961.

151 **some fifty attorneys:** "Country Club Freeway Condemnation Case Begins," *Wednesday Magazine*, June 14, 1961.

151 **legal objections:** "Important Notice—Arguments for Repeal: The Country Club Freeway Ordinance," October 1964, vertical file "Freeways: Country Club (Proposed)," Kansas City Public Library.

151 **pondered why the city:** "The Country Club Freeway," *Wednesday Magazine*, October 4, 1961.

151 **approved both routes:** "Choice to City," *Kansas City Star*, November 4, 1964, Newspapers.com.

151 **"demoralizing effects on property values:** "Views on Freeway by Six Candidates," *Kansas City Times*, February 20, 1963, Newspapers.com.

151 **regional planner warned:** "Told to Be Quiet on Freeway Route," *Kansas City Times*, November 18, 1967, Newspapers.com.

151 **to pick the South Midtown:** "The City Makes a Choice on a South Freeway," *Kansas City Star*, November 8, 1965, Newspapers.com.

151 **petition at city hall:** Matt Campbell, "Bruce R. Watkins Drive Nears End of Long, Bumpy Road to Completion," *Kansas City Star*, October 21, 2001, Newspapers.com.

151 **by about $15 million:** "Choice to City," *Kansas City Star*.

151 **a legal ruling:** "Halt a Condemnation," *Kansas City Times*, September 13, 1966, Newspapers.com.

152 **The cost:** "South Midtown Freeway Starts with Human Problems," *Kansas City Times*, August 29, 1970, Newspapers.com.

152 **could have purchased:** "To Stay on Tramway," *Kansas City Star*, June 30, 1964, Newspapers.com.

152 **regained control:** Brian Burnes, "An Old Way of Moving Is Timely Once More," *Kansas City Star*, June 23, 2007, Newspapers.com.

152 **"The affluent people":** "Asks Alert in Freeway Plan," *Kansas City Star*, November 9, 1967, Newspapers.com.

152 **seventeen churches:** Doris Handy, "Other Side of the Tracks Now Other Side of the Freeway," *The Call*, February 20–26, 1976.

152 **three schools:** "Told to Be Quiet," *Kansas City Times*.

152 **razed out of the earth:** Campbell, "Bruce R. Watkins Drive Nears End."

152 **"We had a beautiful neighborhood":** Interview with Carmaletta Williams, February 27, 2023.

152 **as long as she could:** Handy, "Other Side of the Tracks."

152 **"an area under siege":** Campbell, "Bruce R. Watkins Drive Nears End."

152 **some ten thousand people:** "Suit Filed by Freeway Opponents," *Kansas City Star*, June 21, 1973, Newspapers.com; and Campbell, "Bruce R. Watkins Drive Nears End."

Notes

153 **their appraised value:** Campbell, "Bruce R. Watkins Drive Nears End."

153 **"have been stolen":** Handy, "Other Side of the Tracks."

153 **The highway route missed:** Interviews with Diane Charity, July 21, 2022, and August 11, 2022.

EVOLUTION

154 **to the next group:** Tyler Dunne, "The Legend of Patrick Mahomes," *Bleacher Report*, December 5, 2019, https://bleacherreport.com/articles/2865233-the -legend-of-patrick-mahomes.

154 **his forty-first birthday:** Patrick Mahomes (@PatrickMahomes), "Man he is still faster than me," Twitter post, May 2, 2021, https://twitter.com /PatrickMahomes/status/1388956604175994881?s=20.

154 **never quite seem to change:** Patrick Mahomes, interview with Dan Katz and Eric Sollenberger, *Pardon My Take*, podcast audio, May 20, 2019.

156 **gone to hell:** NBC Sports, "Patrick Mahomes Recreates No-Look Pass, Goes In-Depth on Football with Peter King," YouTube video, January 10, 2019, https://www.youtube.com/watch?v=rpxGjrSDxDE.

157 **"'how did he do that?'":** Lindsay Jones and Nate Taylor, "From No-Look Snaps to Behind-the-Back Passes, Chiefs Share Moments When Patrick Mahomes Left Them Amazed," *The Athletic*, January 30, 2020, https://theathletic .com/1572644/2020/01/30/chiefs-share-moments-when-patrick-mahomes -left-them-amazed/.

157 **"Two fucking plays, man":** Sam Mellinger, "What It Felt Like to Be on the Other Side of Patrick Mahomes' Magic," *Kansas City Star*, October 3, 2018.

157 **"single play is insane":** Mitchell Schwartz (@MitchSchwartz71), "His ability to manipulate speed and tempo . . . ," Twitter post, September 12, 2021.

157 **"Football Year's Death Harvest":** "Football Year's Death Harvest," *Chicago Tribune*, November 5, 1905, Newspapers.com.

158 **"or forsake it":** Michael Beschloss, "T.R.'s Son Inspired Him to Help Rescue Football," *New York Times*, August 1, 2014, https://www.nytimes.com/2014 /08/02/upshot/trs-son-inspired-him-to-help-rescue-football.html; and James Warren, "The Government Has Tried to Fix Football Before," *The Atlantic*, March 27, 2012, https://www.theatlantic.com/entertainment/archive/2012 /03/the-government-has-tried-to-fix-football-before/255059/.

158 **"the last extremity":** "New Football a Chaos, Experts Declare," *New York Times*, September 30, 1906.

159 **throw a baseball:** J.E. Wray, "Wray's Column," *St. Louis Post-Dispatch*, November 12, 1940, Newspapers.com.

159 **"overhead projectile spiral pass":** Michael Weinreb, "The First Forward Passes: In a Decade of Change, Eddie Cochems and Saint Louis Saw the Fu-

ture of Football," *The Athletic*, March 11, 2019, https://theathletic.com/858132
/2019/03/11/1906-saint-louis-eddie-cochems-college-football-forward
-pass-legalized/.

159 **40 yards in the air:** J.E. Wray, "Wray's Column," *St. Louis Post-Dispatch*,
January 11, 1943, Newspapers.com.

159 **"Mid West and Western football":** Knute Rockne, "The First Army Notre
Dame Game and the Forward Pass," in *Oh, How They Played the Game*, ed.
Allison Danzig (New York: Macmillan, 1971), 189.

160 **the league's best-paid quarterback:** Leonard Shapiro,"Simpson was paid
$806,668 in 1979," *Washington Post*, February 1, 1980.

160 **"franchise quarterback":** Interview with Leigh Steinberg, May 2, 2022.

160 **"set quarterback play back":** Interview with Bobby Stroupe, October 6,
2022.

161 **Pass on your left:** Missouri Department of Transportation (@MoDot), "Take
a note from @PatrickMahomes5 and the @Chiefs," Twitter post and photo,
October 3, 2018, https://twitter.com/MoDOT/status/1047481232232251394.

162 **delivered the ball:** Connor Orr, "In the Throws of Change," *Sports Illustrated*,
November 16, 2021, https://www.si.com/nfl/2021/11/16/cover-story-how-the
-qb-evolution-sparked-a-coaching-revolution.

162 **"you are my idol":** Patrick Mahomes (@PatrickMahomes), "Rodgers this is
why you are my idol," Twitter post, January 16, 2016, https://twitter.com
/PatrickMahomes/status/688578245055221762?s=20&t=SCqR2IELaad
Khtlm2Rqxlg.

162 **speeding up the play:** Orr, "In the Throws of Change."

162 **turning into a strength:** Interview with Bobby Stroupe, October 6, 2022.

163 **running straight:** Interview with Bobby Stroupe, October 6, 2022.

163 **"to its full measure":** Interview with Steve Young, July 9, 2022.

163 **"It's a dream," he said:** Interview with Steve Young, July 9, 2022.

THE BALLAD OF LLOYD WELLS

164 **once told a reporter:** "Lenny Dawson, Icy Stare, Warm Humor," *St. Louis
Post-Dispatch*, February 2, 1987, Newspapers.com.

164 **felt like an eternity:** Michael MacCambridge, *69 Chiefs: A Team, a Season,
and the Birth of Modern Kansas City* (Kansas City, MO: Andrews McMeel
Publishing, 2019), 133–34.

164 **"force of his presence":** "Lenny Dawson, Icy Stare," *St. Louis Post-Dispatch*.

165 **he overheard:** Joe Posnanski, "It's Been a Wonderful Life for Chiefs' Best
Quarterback," *Kansas City Star*, December 25, 2001, Newspapers.com.

165 **different meanings of his stares:** Ernest Mehl, "Sporting Comment," *Kansas
City Star*, November 12, 1964, Newspapers.com.

166 **"The best thing":** Interview with Bobby Bell, January 2021.

166 **a Hollywood agent:** Interview with Mike Garrett, August 15, 2022.

166 **"The Man":** David Bell, "Chiefs: Revisiting a Sad Day in Houston—Lloyd Wells Passes," *Arrowhead One,* July 26, 2019, https://arrowheadone.com /chiefs-revisiting-a-sad-day-in-houston-lloyd-wells-passes/.

166 **Wells targeted Otis Taylor:** Rustin Dodd, "The Legacy Bowl: How a Bold Scout, HBCU Talent Elevated Chiefs—and Football," *The Athletic,* February 4, 2021, https://theathletic.com/2356066/2021/02/04/the-legacy-bowl-how-a -bold-scout-hbcu-talent-elevated-chiefs-and-football/.

167 **"as pure as it could be":** Interview with Willie Lanier, January 2021.

167 **5:45 flight:** Gary D. Warner, "Garrett Stays a Halfback—Stram," *Kansas City Star,* March 21, 1966, Newspapers.com.

167 **too short:** Joe McGuff, "Sporting Comment," *Kansas City Star,* January 18, 1966, Newspapers.com.

168 **to recruit him:** McGuff, "Sporting Comment."

168 **horses and buggies:** Interview with Mike Garrett, August 15, 2022.

168 **around the Plaza:** Interview with Mike Garrett, August 15, 2022.

168 **enough food on the table:** Warner, "Garrett Stays a Halfback."

168 **starred at Roosevelt High School:** Mark Sachs, "Return to Glory," *Los Angeles Times,* January 29, 1995, https://www.latimes.com/archives/la-xpm-1995-01-29 -ci-25590-story.html.

168 **"capture the moment":** Sachs, "Return to Glory."

168 **Wilshire Boulevard:** Interview with Mike Garrett, August 15, 2022.

169 **Nothing was available:** Interview with Mike Garrett, August 15, 2022.

169 **"I was hoping":** Interview with Mike Garrett, August 15, 2022.

169 **One day in 1950:** Brady McCollough, "Playing Through," *Kansas City Star,* July 17, 2005, Newspapers.com.

169 **public swimming pool:** Aarón Torres, "Kansas City Closed This Public Pool for Two Years Instead of Letting Black People In," October 1, 2021, Kansas City Public Library, https://kclibrary.org/blog/kansas-city-closed-public-pool -two-years-instead-letting-black-people.

169 **as high as ten inches:** "Brave Winter Weather to Walk Picket Line," *The Call,* January 16–23, 1959.

169 **Their boycott was covered extensively:** Brian Burnes, "Journalist Lucile Bluford Dies," *Kansas City Star,* June 14, 2003, Newspapers.com.

169 **amusement park:** Charles E. Coulter, "Civic Affairs," *Kansas City Star,* September 18, 2005, Newspapers.com.

169 **Kansas City Council passed:** Edgar Chasteen, "Public Accommodations: Social Movements in Conflict," *Phylon* 30, no. 3 (1969), https://www.jstor.org /stable/273473?seq=4#metadata_info_tab_contents.

170 **referendum on the ordinance:** Chasteen, "Public Accommodations."

170 **wanted a house:** Interview with Bobby Bell, January 2021.

170 **had no impact:** Interview with Bobby Bell, January 2021.

170 **"thinking of the people":** Bobby Bell, "Not So Welcome Wagon," *Kansas City Star*, August 29, 2004, Newspapers.com.

170 **seven dollars a week:** Kent Pulliam, "McClinton's Strength Is Game of Life," *Kansas City Star,* February 26, 1995, Newspapers.com; and Geri Gosa, "Ex-Chief Still a Winner," *Kansas City Star*, August 3, 1972, Newspapers.com.

170 **"represented the Black element":** "Local Accent in Fair Housing," *Kansas City Star*, January 24, 1966, Newspapers.com.

170 **He wondered:** Tom Marshall, "McClinton Is the Driving Type," November 3, 1965, *Kansas City Star*, Newspapers.com.

171 **"what the housing situation was":** Marshall, "Driving Type."

171 **loved classical music:** Gosa, "Ex-Chief Still a Winner."

171 **looked up to Paul Robeson:** Pulliam, "Game of Life."

171 **Cleveland Summit:** Robert Anthony Bennett III, "You Can't Have Black Power Without Green Power: Black Economic Union" (dissertation, Ohio State University, 2013), 118, https://etd.ohiolink.edu/apexprod/rws_etd/send_file/send?accession=osu1365514328&disposition=inline.

171 **the first time:** William C. Rhoden, "Ex-Brown Walter Beach Recalls Black Athletes' Support of Ali," *New York Times*, September 28, 2014, https://www.nytimes.com/2014/09/29/sports/football/ex-brown-walter-beach-recalls-black-athletes-support-of-ali.html.

171 **to develop McClinton Courts:** Marshall, "Driving Type."

171 **He joined Watkins:** Gosa, "Ex-Chief Still a Winner."

172 **Alvin Brooks remembered:** Pulliam, "Game of Life."

172 **with Bell, Buchanan, and Taylor:** Interview with Alvin Brooks, July 20, 2022.

172 **catalyze a housing movement:** Pulliam, "Game of Life."

172 **spoken at rallies:** "Fair Housing," *Kansas City Star*.

172 **"No one likes":** "Urged to Assume Role in Fair Housing Drive," *Kansas City Star*, February 7, 1966, Newspapers.com.

172 **hostile opposition:** "Meet on Fair Housing," *Kansas City Times*, August 10, 1967, Newspapers.com.

172 **passed a fair-housing law:** "O.K. Fair Housing Act," *Kansas City Times*, July 22, 1967, Newspapers.com.

172 **Garrett realized:** Interview with Mike Garrett, August 15, 2022.

173 **"We've never questioned":** "City Prepares Fair Housing Ordinance," *Kansas City Times*, May 17, 1968, Newspapers.com.

173 **Bell finally did get:** Bell, "Not So Welcome Wagon."

173 **willing mortgage underwriter:** Interview with Bobby Bell, January 2021.

173 **ostracized by the community:** Interview with Bobby Bell, January 2021.

173 **They were organizing:** Bell, "Not So Welcome Wagon."

174 **Sixty-Five Toss Power Trap:** *Sports Illustrated*, "Len Dawson Recalls 65 Toss Power Trap in Super Bowl IV," YouTube Video, September 18, 2015, https://www.youtube.com/watch?v=4UtyyDkRFJY.

Notes

174 **The play worked great:** Interview with Mike Garrett, August 15, 2022.

174 **"I got it":** Interview with Mike Garrett, August 15, 2022.

174 **Taylor bawled:** Gary D. Warner, "Chiefs Happy for Selves—and Len Dawson," *Kansas City Times*, January 12, 1970, Newspapers.com.

174 **Dawson stood:** Joe McGuff, "Len Dawson Triumphs Despite Adversity," *Kansas City Times*, January 12, 1970, Newspapers.com.

174 **The next afternoon:** Michael J. Satchell, "Jubilant on Top of Football World," *Kansas City Times*, January 13, 1970, Newspapers.com.

175 **"You still had the redlining":** Interview with Mike Garrett, August 15, 2022.

PRIME TIME

176 **"in their division":** Joseph Kaye, "New Yorkers Briefed: Promoters Sing Praises of Kansas City," *Kansas City Star*, March 28, 1972, Newspapers.com.

176 **Hall told the audience:** Kaye, "New Yorkers Briefed."

177 **to the country:** Robert Sanford, "Kansas City Whoops Up Its Image," *St. Louis Post-Dispatch*, May 23, 1976, Newspapers.com.

177 **in newspaper ads:** "Vendo Is Proud to Be Part of 'One of the Few Liveable Cities Left,'" advertisement, *Kansas City Star*, January 20, 1974.

177 **actor Barry Sullivan:** Joe Roberts, "Kansas City TV Commercial Cited," *Kansas City Star*, February 27, 1974, Newspapers.com.

177 **top 100 in 1974:** Roberts, "Kansas City TV Commercial Cited"; and "Civic Groups Take New Directions," *Kansas City Star*, July 2, 1975, Newspapers.com.

177 **the exec said:** Jeff Bremser, "Kansas City—One Terrific Place to Live," letter to the editor, *Kansas City Star*, June 29, 1980, Newspapers.com.

178 **deep-rooted segregation:** Richard Rhodes, "Convention Fever in Kansas City," *Harper's*, May 1976.

178 **supersonic air travel:** "Superjet Center Planned by T.W.A.," *New York Times*, August 20, 1967, https://timesmachine.nytimes.com/timesmachine/1967/08/20/107196635.html?pageNumber=90.

179 **parking for seven thousand cars:** Associated Press, "Kansas City Getting a New Look," *Journal News*, August 2, 1972, Newspapers.com.

179 **"inside its lobby:** "For 300 Million Years, It Was Just a Hill," Crown Center advertisement, *Kansas City Star*, May 6, 1973, Newspapers.com.

179 **"downtown suburb":** "Hotel Only a Step in Big Center Plan," *Kansas City Star*, May 6, 1973.

179 **four-story lobby atrium:** United Press International, "Hyatt 'Greeted with Great Anticipation,'" *Kansas City Star*, July 19, 1981, Newspapers.com.

180 **TWA sales manager:** Tom Wolf, "Airline Marketers Aim at Businessmen," *Kansas City Star*, July 5, 1981, Newspapers.com.

180 **to Southern California:** Paul Rudd, interview with Marc Maron, *WTF with Marc Maron*, podcast audio, July 1, 2018.

180 **famed American Royal:** Michael Rudd, "Still Some Whys," letter to the editor, *Kansas City Star*, June 27, 1985; and "Respect for Animals," letter to the editor, *Kansas City Star*, November 8, 1988.

180 **rival district Blue Valley:** Shawnee Mission West Yearbook, 1987.

180 **"because of this class":** James Fussell, "It's a Mad, Mad, Mad, Mad World in High School Forensics Class," *Kansas City Star*, January 1, 1987, Newspapers .com.

180 **part-time job:** Jon Niccum, "Hometown Hero," *Kansas City Star*, July 12, 2015, Newspapers.com.

181 **1982 documentary:** Tom Shales, "The Mall," *Washington Post*, August 4, 1982, https://www.washingtonpost.com/archive/lifestyle/1982/08/04/the-mall -38/5523c99a-cc7c-4706-9134-a2696bf6e51f/.

181 **"where you have to look":** Charles Kuralt, "After the Dream Comes True," *CBS Reports*, 1982.

181 **sprung up in 1975:** Joe Roberts, "Mall's Official Debut Is Tomorrow," *Kansas City Star*, August 27, 1975, Newspapers.com.

181 **by the Nichols Co.:** "J.C. Nichols Company Presents," Oak Park Manor advertisement, *Kansas City Star*, October 24, 1979.

181 **job at Imagery:** Niccum, "Hometown Hero."

181 **other novelty inflatables:** "Back to School Equals Back to Oak Park Mall," *Kansas City Star*, August 7, 1985, Newspapers.com.

181 **surprising bits of art and culture:** Paul Rudd, interview with Marc Maron, *WTF with Marc Maron*, July 1, 2018.

182 **"good for your head":** Chris Heath, "You Know You're Paul Rudd When . . . ," *GQ*, March 31, 2009.

182 **playing on FM radio:** Paul Rudd, interview with Marc Maron, *WTF with Marc Maron*, July 1, 2018.

182 **capital improvement sales tax:** John A. Dvorak, "Neighborhood Group Hears Sales Tax Views," *Kansas City Star*, July 17, 1981.

183 **Country Club District:** Interview with Brent Wright, Karen Jeter's son, November 11, 2022.

183 **big band traditions:** Interview with Micheal Mahoney, November 11, 2022.

183 **survey the wreckage:** Robert Campbell, "Arena Falls While Designer at Architects Meeting Nearby," *Boston Globe*, June 6, 1979, Newspapers.com.

183 **throughout the city:** Kimberly Mills, "Officials Arrive to Begin Study of Deaths from Heat Wave," *Kansas City Star*, July 29, 1980, Newspapers.com.

184 **"dingy, sometimes ugly":** Editorial Board, "Fresh Hope for Downtown," *Kansas City Star*, July 11, 1981, Newspapers.com.

184 **local company Hallmark:** Paul Goldberger, "Hyatt Tragedy Raises Questions of Responsibility," *New York Times*, July 28, 1981, https://www.nytimes.com /1981/07/28/us/hyatt-tragedy-raises-questions-of-responsibility.html.

184 **from KMBC-TV (channel 9):** Haley Harrison, "KMBC 9 Chronicle: The Skywalk Tapes," KMBC 9 News, updated July 14, 2021.

184 **unremarkable Friday night:** Interview with Micheal Mahoney, November 11, 2022.

184 **when he heard it:** Interview with Micheal Mahoney, November 11, 2022.

185 **Wright continued to work:** Interview with Brett Wright, November 11, 2022.

185 **waiting for help:** Associated Press, "Mother, Son Tell Hyatt Hotel Horror," *Kansas City Star,* July 23, 1981, Newspapers.com.

185 **man did not survive:** Harrison, "KMBC 9 Chronicle: The Skywalk Tapes."

185 **visit his brother:** "In Memoriam," *Kansas City Times*, July 25, 1981, Newspapers.com.

185 **none of the engineers had detected:** Harrison, "KMBC 9 Chronicle: The Skywalk Tapes."

186 **twelve shorter rods:** Kevin Murphy, Rick Alm, and Carol Powers, *The Last Dance* (Kansas City: Kansas City Star Books, 2011).

186 **Winstead's for steakburgers:** Interview with Brent Wright, November 11, 2022.

THE VILLAIN'S NAME WAS TOM

188 **"It's supposed to hurt":** Patrick Mahomes press conference.

188 **"odd feeling in your heart":** Interview with Chris Jones, February 2, 2020.

188 **through a back door:** Dan Wetzel, "Tom Brady's Message for Patrick Mahomes After Their AFC Title Duel," Yahoo! Sports, January 21, 2019, https://sports.yahoo.com/tom-bradys-message-patrick-mahomes-afc-title-duel-0648 38899.html.

188 **doing it the right way:** Rick Stroud, "The Most Important Meeting Between Tom Brady and Patrick Mahomes Took Place off the Field," *Tampa Bay Times*, November 25, 2020, https://www.tampabay.com/sports/bucs/2020/11/25/the -most-important-meeting-between-tom-brady-and-patrick-mahomes-took -place-off-the-field/.

THE MARTYBALL '90S

189 **He once sketched out:** Interview with Quincy Bennett, October 20, 2022.

190 **That first summer:** Interview with Quinton Lucas, October 7, 2022.

190 **experienced a very different life:** Interviews with Quincy Bennett, October 20, 2022, and Quinton Lucas, October 7, 2022.

191 **Lucas saw that:** Interview with Quinton Lucas, October 7, 2022.

191 **Lucas usually watched:** Interview with Quinton Lucas, October 7, 2022.

192 **He first glimpsed Arrowhead Stadium:** Interview with Carl Peterson, December 14, 2020.

192 **to stimulate interest:** Interview with Carl Peterson, December 14, 2020.

192 **Jerry Rice described him:** Rick Gosselin, "State Your Case: Why Forgotten CB Albert Lewis Deserves a HOF Look," *Sports Illustrated*, September 25, 2018, https://www.si.com/nfl/talkoffame/nfl/state-your-case-why-forgotten -cb-albert-lewis-deserves-a-hof-look.

194 **Lucas wrote after a game:** Quinton Lucas, "The Quinton Lucas Sports Journal."

194 **"worst restaurant in San Francisco":** Michael Silver, "Fussy Steve Bono Has Put Starch in 9-1 Chiefs," *Sports Illustrated*, November 20, 1995, https://vault .si.com/vault/1995/11/20/the-all-pro-bono-fussy-steve-bono-has-put -starch-in-the-9-1-chiefs.

194 **a hilarious miscommunication:** Jayson Jenks, "How Was Elvis Gbrac Named *People*'s Sexiest Athlete Alive?," *The Athletic*, January 23, 2020, https:// theathletic.com/1554275/2020/01/23/how-was-elvis-grbac-named-peoples -sexiest-athlete-alive/.

195 **"that we'll make it someday":** Interview with Quinton Lucas, December 16, 2020.

THE VOICE

196 **Travis Kelce started laughing:** Patrick Mahomes, interview with Dan Katz and Eric Sollenberger, *Pardon My Take*, podcast audio, May 20, 2019.

196 **Kermit the Frog:** Tyreek Hill interview, Super Bowl media day, 2020.

196 **"What's going on?":** Patrick Mahomes, interview with Dan Katz and Eric Sollenberger, *Pardon My Take*, May 20, 2019.

196 **"Kermit" moniker:** Interview with Adam Cook., November 5, 2022.

196 **"since I was in, like, seventh grade":** Patrick Mahomes, press conference interview, 2018.

197 **damage from the festivities:** *Jimmy Kimmel Live!*, "Patrick Mahomes on Kansas City, Bachelor Party and Crazy Fans," YouTube video, July 9, 2019, https:// www.youtube.com/watch?v=8BunxlLH78M.

197 **another with Essentia water:** Terez A. Paylor, "Patrick Mahomes' Plan to Be Even Better," Yahoo! Sports, July 2, 2019, https://www.yahoo.com/video /patrick-mahomes-plan-to-be-even-better-165235040.html.

197 **"Do you want to come?":** Interview with Dustin Colquitt, September 2021.

197 **"in, like, forty-two minutes":** Interview with Dustin Colquitt, September 2021.

198 **munching on chicken fingers:** NBC Sports Hockey (@NBCSportsHockey), "@PatrickMahomes and @tkelce showing some support . . . ," Twitter post and video, June 1, 2019, https://twitter.com/tkelce/status/11349976403227 19751.

199 **for smoking marijuana:** Les Bowen, "A Big Brother's Guiding Hand," *Philadelphia Inquirer*, September 14, 2017, Newspapers.com.

Notes

199 **"I was just getting yelled at every single day":** Travis Kelce press conference, February 6, 2023.

200 **"something I haven't seen yet":** *Dan Patrick Show,* "Chiefs TE Travis Kelce on *The Dan Patrick Show,*" January 31, 2018, YouTube video, https://www .youtube.com/watch?v=EN86dJ5f9GI.

200 **Kelce had been late, too:** Patrick Mahomes, interview with Jason and Travis Kelce, *New Heights with Jason and Travis Kelce,* podcast audio, December 1, 2022.

201 **from his college days:** Paylor, "Patrick Mahomes' Plan to Be Even Better."

201 **sixteen hours to complete:** Interview with David Leach, December 20, 2022.

REVENGE OF THE COW

202 **knew it colloquially as "BOB":** "The Hereford Bull," Kansas City Parks and Recreation, https://kcparks.org/places/the-hereford-bull/.

202 **some people swore:** Mike Hendricks, "Bovine Intervention Revives Bull," *Kansas City Star,* October 23, 2002, Newspapers.com.

202 **President Dwight Eisenhower flew in:** "Ike in by Plane Today," *Kansas City Times,* October 15, 1953, Newspapers.com.

202 **he addressed a crowd:** "In Good Spirits," *Kansas City Times,* October 17, 1953, Newspapers.com.

203 **by Paul Decker:** "To Hoist a Lofty Symbol of Beef," *Kansas City Star,* October 10, 1954.

203 **stuffed the statue's scrotum:** Calvin Trillin, "The Bull Vanishes," *New Yorker,* June 11, 2001.

203 **so the bull could glow:** "To Hoist," *Kansas City Times;* and Trillin, "The Bull Vanishes."

203 **"the lights be turned on":** "A Hereford Fete," *Kansas City Times,* October 19, 1954, Newspapers.com.

203 **"The people of Kansas City":** "A Bull to Make Us Proud," *Kansas City Star,* April 5, 1954, Newspapers.com.

203 **"Not a good smell":** Interview with Calvin Trillin, December 2020.

204 **"I love that bull":** Trillin, "The Bull Vanishes."

205 **The stretch of highway:** Elaine Adams, "Ground Broken for Bruce Watkins Drive," *Kansas City Star,* October 11, 1987.

205 **"the beginning of the end":** Chelsey Parkman, "Missouri v. Jenkins: The Beginning of the End for Desegregation," *Loyola University Chicago Law Journal* 27, no. 3 (Spring 1996), https://lawcommons.luc.edu/cgi/viewcontent .cgi?article=2530&context=luclj.

205 **Around six thousand people:** Jeffrey Spivak and Kevin Collison, "City's Ailing Center in Search of Revival," *Kansas City Star,* September 22, 2002, Newspapers.com, https://www.newspapers.com/image/legacy/687174121/.

205 **In a four-block zone:** Spivak and Collison, "City's Ailing Center."

205 **"Downtown was an eyesore":** Interview with Sly James, September 20, 2022.

205 **James bet another attorney:** Interview with Sly James, September 20, 2022.

206 **proposed an elaborate entertainment zone:** Bill Graham, "Downtown District Holds Area Benefits," *Kansas City Star*, January 8, 1998, Newspapers.com.

206 **"last, best hope":** Mark P. Couch, "City Council Votes to End Power & Light District," *Kansas City Star*, October 13, 2000, Newspapers.com.

206 **applied some spin:** Couch, "City Council Votes."

206 **Barnes noticed funky water levels:** Interview with Kay Barnes, December 3, 2020.

207 **she tried channeling JFK:** Lynn Horsley and Gromer Jeffers Jr., "Mayor Barnes Urges Residents to Help Shape City's Future," *Kansas City Star*, April 11, 1999, Newspapers.com.

207 **more to her idea:** Dan Margolies, Julius A. Karash, and Lynn Horsley, "Mayor Maps $1.8 Billion Blueprint for KC's Future," *Kansas City Star*, December 1, 2001, Newspapers.com; and Jeffrey Spivak and Lynn Horsley, "KC Touts Major Step Forward, *Kansas City Star*, May 13, 2004, Newspapers.com.

207 **naming-rights contract:** Spivak and Horsley, "Major Step Forward."

207 **"in a bad sitcom":** Michael Hurd, "Flaws Blur Mayor's KC Vision," *Olathe News*, December 4, 2001, Newspapers.com.

207 **"A mistake":** Barbara Shelly, "Build It, but Don't Manage It," *Kansas City Star*, December 13, 2001, Newspapers.com.

207 **"I've learned not to say never":** Randy Covitz, "Arena Plan Gets Attention in Big Leagues," *Kansas City Star*, July 28, 2004, Newspapers.com.

208 **"economic engine":** Yael T. Abouhalkah, "All Hail Johnson County," *Kansas City Star*, May 6, 2004, Newspapers.com.

208 **A collection of odd bedfellows:** Lynn Horsley, "Opponents of Arena Fee Unite," *Kansas City Star*, July 15, 2004, Newspapers.com; and "Coalition Broadcast Campaign Takes Aim at KC Arena Project," *Sports Business Journal*, July 20, 2004, https://www.sportsbusinessjournal.com/Daily/Issues/2004/07/20/Facilities-Venues/Coalition-Broadcast-Campaign-Takes-Aim-At-KC-Arena-Project.aspx.

208 **spelled economic disaster:** Joe Posnanski, "Rental Car Company Has Bad Case of Footnote-in-Mouth Disease," *Kansas City Star*, July 30, 2004, Newspapers.com.

208 **a bizarre mural:** Joe Posnanski, "Arena Foes Are Taxing on the Ears," *Kansas City Star*, July 20, 2004, Newspapers.com.

208 **Sometimes they said:** Posnanski, "Rental Car Company."

208 **"I'm not going to let":** Kevin Collison, "Sprint Says It Will Pay for Name on Arena," *Kansas City Star*, July 23, 2004, Newspapers.com.

208 **A varied group:** Lynn Horsley, "Does KC Want a Downtown Arena?," *Kansas City Star*, July 28, 2004.

Notes

209 **Lamar Hunt voiced his support:** Randy Covitz, "Hunt Steamed by Those Who Say Downtown Facility Will Hurt Chiefs," *Kansas City Star*, July 30, 2004, Newspapers.com.

209 **a simple message:** Kay Barnes, "Should Voters OK Arena Plan?," *Kansas City Star*, August 1, 2004, Newspapers.com.

209 **The company bused in:** Interview with Kay Barnes, December 3, 2020.

209 **wearing Chiefs gear:** Interview with Kay Barnes, December 3, 2020.

209 **for a tailgate:** "New Downtown Arena on the Way," *Kansas City Star*, August 4, 2004, Newspapers.com.

209 **A supergroup:** David W. Landis, "Curtain Up," *Structure Magazine*, January 2006, https://www.structuremag.org/wp-content/uploads/2014/09/Sprint -Center-Feature1.pdf.

209 **two thousand glass panels:** Steve Rock, "It's a Downtown Jewel," *Kansas City Star*, October 11, 2007, Newspapers.com.

210 **three thousand people to see Wilco:** Rick Montgomery and Joyce Smith, "The Music Begins," *Kansas City Star*, October 14, 2007, Newspapers.com.

210 **Third Fridays:** Tony Cardarella, "First Fridays Aren't the Only Happening Nights Around," *Kansas City Star*, April 20, 2005, Newspapers.com.

210 **His first track:** Montgomery and Smith, "Music Begins."

THE ELECTION

211 **limit incentives for developers:** Bill Turque, "KC Councilman Lucas Enters 2019 Mayoral Race," *Kansas City Star*, June 24, 2018, Newspapers.com.

211 **helped pursue revival plans:** Turque, "KC Councilman Lucas."

211 **gave a citywide definition:** Bill Turque, "KC Council Defines Affordable Housing Rents," *Kansas City Star*, May 25, 2018, Newspapers.com.

212 **better-funded candidate:** Joel Williams, "May Fundraising Reports: Justus Raises Twice as Much as Lucas in KC Mayoral Election," *Ballotpedia News*, https://news.ballotpedia.org/2019/05/13/may-fundraising-reports-justus -raises-twice-as-much-as-lucas-in-kc-mayoral-election/.

213 **change the song:** Interview with Emma Shankland, Lucas campaign official.

213 **They were not included:** Sam McDowell, "Debate About the Chiefs' Name, and Its Ties to Native Americans Rages On. Here's Why," *Kansas City Star*, October 9, 2020, https://www.kansascity.com/sports/nfl/kansas-city-chiefs /article246195195.html.

214 **"they choose to perform nonsense chants":** Rhonda LeValdo, "The Kansas City Chiefs' 'Arrowhead Chop' isn't a tribute to people like me. It's racist." *Vox*, February 6, 2021, https://www.vox.com/first-person/2020/2/1/21115858 /super-bowl-chiefs-kansas-city.

214 **"If no offense is intended":** Kent Pulliam, "Indian Chief Vows a Fight with KC over Chop," *Kansas City Star*, October 12, 1992, Newspapers.com.

214 **He did not partake:** John Eligon, "Celebrating the Kansas City Chiefs, the Chop Divides," *New York Times,* January 29, 2020, https://www.nytimes.com/2020/01/29/sports/football/chiefs-tomahawk-chop.html.

215 **about the city's blemishes:** Rachel Schultz, "The Power of a City," *The Ampersand*, Washington State University in St. Louis alumni magazine, September 2, 2021, https://artsci.wustl.edu/ampersand/power-city.

JET CHIP WASP

216 **after big Chiefs wins:** Interview with Jason Kander, November 23, 2021.

216 **weekly pep rally:** "Red Friday: A Kansas City Tradition," Chiefs.com, September 17, 2015; and interview with Carl Peterson, former Chiefs president, December 14, 2020.

217 **trailing only the Patriots:** "2019 Preseason Odds," Pro Football Reference, SportsOddsHistory.com.

217 **"It's out":** Adam Teicher, "Kelce on Mahomes: 'His Knee Didn't Even Look like a Knee,'" ESPN, October 19, 2019, https://www.espn.com/blog/kansas-city-chiefs/post/_/id/26909/kelce-on-mahomes-his-knee-didnt-even-look-like-a-knee.

217 **a voice told him:** Teicher, "Kelce on Mahomes."

218 **Kelce would say:** NFL Films, "Mahomes Reveals Veach's Super Bowl LIV Prophecy," YouTube video, September 9, 2020, https://www.youtube.com/watch?v=JZayjGdRW1A.

218 **crouched down:** Ian Rapoport, "Chiefs' Doc Knew Mahomes Would Return Quickly from Knee Injury," NFL.com, February 1, 2020, https://www.nfl.com/news/chiefs-doc-knew-mahomes-would-return-quickly-from-knee-injury-0ap3000001100488.

218 **Refused a cart:** Teicher, "Kelce on Mahomes."

218 **he told his wife:** Interview with Pat Mahomes Sr., August 4, 2022.

218 **after they won the Super Bowl:** NFL Films, "Mahomes Reveals Veach's Super Bowl LIV Prophecy"; and Sam McDowell, "One Year Later: How Patrick Mahomes Turned a Serious Injury into a Blip on the Radar," *Kansas City Star,* October 16, 2020, https://www.kansascity.com/sports/nfl/kansas-city-chiefs/article246472470.html.

219 **"it's not broke":** Interview with Bobby Stroupe, October 6, 2022.

219 **treadmill two days later:** Interview with Bobby Stroupe, October 6, 2022; and McDowell, "One Year Later."

219 **a genetic gift he received from his mother:** Interview with Pat Mahomes Sr., October 21, 2022.

219 **"Houdini of our era":** Kevin Patra, "Chiefs TE Travis Kelce on QB Patrick Mahomes," NFL.com, October 3, 2022, https://www.nfl.com/news/chiefs-te-travis-kelce-on-qb-patrick-mahomes-he-s-the-houdini-of-our-era.

220 **"playing man coverage":** NFL Films (@NFLFilms), "Down by 24, @PatrickMahomes led the @Chiefs in a playoff comeback for the ages. All starting with this TD," Twitter post and video, *Inside the NFL*, Showtime, January 13, 2020.

220 **stood up and left:** Charles Penn (@cpenn4thewin), Twitter post with a peace emoji and video, January 12, 2020, https://twitter.com/cpenn4thewin/status /1216461092412690433.

220 **Frank Clark said:** Sam McDowell, "'Let's Go Do Something Special.' A Patrick Mahomes Speech Sparked Chiefs' Big Comeback," *Kansas City Star*, January 13, 2020, https://www.kansascity.com/sports/nfl/kansas-city-chiefs /article239179418.html#storylink=cpy.

221 **"You like Wasp?":** NFL Films, "How Mahomes Made 3rd & 15 Magic in Super Bowl LIV," *NFL Turning Point*, YouTube video, February 7, 2020, https://www.youtube.com/watch?v=t-t6tbS5waE.

222 **"Yeah," Shanahan said:** NFL Films, "How Mahomes Made 3rd & 15 Magic in Super Bowl LIV"; and NFL Films, "Super Bowl LIV Mic'd Up, 'I'm a BEAST down Here . . . HIT ME!,'" *Game Day All-Access*, YouTube video, February 5, 2020, https://www.youtube.com/watch?v=tyoRfDTLaR8.

223 **"you just keep firing":** NFL Films, "Super Bowl LIV Mic'd Up, 'I'm a BEAST down Here.'"

224 **"I'm believing":** NFL Films, "Super Bowl LIV Mic'd Up, 'I'm a BEAST down Here.'"

224 **"Make 'em tighten up":** NFL Films, "Super Bowl LIV Mic'd Up, 'I'm a BEAST down Here.'"

224 **inspired by insects:** Vahe Gregorian, "'Jet Chip Wasp' Was a Moment That Will Last Forever, But Also Speaks to Chiefs' Future," *Kansas City Star*, September 6, 2020, https://www.kansascity.com/sports/spt-columns-blogs/vahe -gregorian/article245243430.html.

225 **against the Atlanta Falcons:** NFL, "Chiefs vs. Falcons Highlights: NFL 2018 Preseason Week 2," YouTube video, August 17, 2018, https://www.youtube .com/watch?v=-JzAvloSXKY; and Shannon Sharpe and Skip Bayless, "Patrick Mahomes Speaks on His Super Bowl Victory and $500M Mega Deal with Chiefs," *Skip and Shannon: Undisputed*, YouTube video, August 12, 2020, https://www.youtube.com/watch?v=5xeYFZwYScU.

225 **"Any down and distance":** NFL Films, "How Mahomes Made 3rd & 15 Magic in Super Bowl LIV."

225 **in-game strategy:** Interview with Chad Parker, November 12, 2021.

225 **"and I love you":** Interview with Pat Mahomes Sr., August 4, 2022.

225 **"You be working!":** NFL Films, "How Mahomes Made 3rd & 15 Magic in Super Bowl LIV"; and NFL Films, "Super Bowl LIV Mic'd Up, 'I'm a BEAST down Here.'"

226 **"Let's go get it":** NFL Films, "How Mahomes Made 3rd & 15 Magic in Super Bowl LIV; and NFL Films, "Super Bowl LIV Mic'd Up, 'I'm a BEAST down Here.'"

227 **"We did it, baby":** NFL Films, "Super Bowl LIV Mic'd Up, 'I'm a BEAST down Here'"; and interview with Pat Mahomes Sr., August 4, 2022.

227 **In the suburbs:** Interview with Bobby Bell, January 2021.

227 **he told a reporter:** Fox Sports: NFL (@NFLonFox), "The happiest people in the stadium?," Twitter post and video, interview with Peter Schrager, February 3, 2020, https://twitter.com/NFLonFOX/status/1224199691014791168.

227 **"the Golden State Warriors, baby":** Interview with Chris Jones, February 2, 2020.

A FOUNTAIN AND A RECKONING

231 **Patrick Mahomes jersey:** Kelcie McKenney and Travis Young, "Today's Rally Was Aptly Titled 'Black Lives Matter. Enough Is Enough,'" *The Pitch*, May 31, 2020, https://www.thepitchkc.com/kc-rally-black-lives-matter-enough-is-enough/pic/614513/.

231 **"It looked like an ocean":** Interview with Justice Horn, September 19, 2022.

231 **atmosphere grew tense at night:** Cortlynn Stark and Luke Nozicka, "Police Car Engulfed in Flames, More Tear Gas Deployed at KC Plaza Saturday Night," *Kansas City Star*, May 31, 2020, https://www.kansascity.com/news/article243129326.html; and Luke Nozicka, Katie Moore, and Anna Spoerre, "Kansas City Curfew Ordered Sunday as Protests Mount," *Kansas City Star*, June 1, 2020, Newspapers.com.

232 **"Power to the people":** Nozicka, Moore, and Spoerre, "Kansas City Curfew Ordered."

232 **Several speakers:** Interviews with Justice Horn, September, 19, 2022, and Lindsey Aquino, protest organizer, September 30, 2022.

232 **"Resurrection City":** Robert W. Butler, "Resurrection City Attracts Rich, Poor and the Curious," *Kansas City Times*, July 25, 1972, Newspapers.com.

232 **showing Kansas City's most powerful:** "Tent City for Urban Poor," *Kansas City Star*, June 28, 1972, Newspapers.com.

232 **"Protest is righteous":** *Kansas City Star*, "US Rep. Emanuel Cleaver II Called the Midday Protest 'Righteous' in Kansas City," May 31, 2020, YouTube video, https://www.youtube.com/watch?v=oiHs0q4M-fE.

232 **"This is about as beautiful":** *Kansas City Star*, "US Rep. Emanuel Cleaver II."

232 **They claimed protesters:** Lisa Rodriguez, Frank Morris, Laura Spencer, Kyle Palmer, and Laura Ziegler, "Third Day of Kansas City Protests Draws Biggest Crowds Yet," KCUR, May 31, 2020, https://www.kcur.org/2020-05-31/following-night-of-demonstration-and-destruction-a-third-day-of-protest

-planned-in-kansas-city; and Katie Moore and Kaitlyn Schwers, "KC Police Chief Defends Response to Plaza Protests," *Kansas City Star*, June 2, 2020, Newspapers.com.

232 **Horn noticed what felt:** Interview with Justice Horn, September 19, 2022.

233 **"We were there standing":** Interview with Justice Horn, September 19, 2022.

233 **fifteen years lower:** Dave D'Marko, "Living in Certain Parts of Kansas City Could Take 15 Years Off Your Life," *Fox 4*, October 17, 2018, https://fox4kc .com/news/living-in-certain-parts-of-kansas-city-could-take-15-years -off-your-life/.

233 **Black Kansas Citians were more likely:** Urban League of Greater Kansas City, *2021 State of Black Kansas City: Is Equity Enough?*, 20–28, https://static1. squarespace.com/static/59c3f63f49fc2b9eb12a6663/t/61846fee0c2ad b21ffbe9835/1636069365443/2021+SOBKC+Charting+the+Path+Forward +flipbook_PDF.pdf.

233 **list of demands:** Micheal Mahoney, "Mayor Quinton Lucas Signs List of Changes Black Lives Matter Leaders Want to See in Kansas City," KMBC, June 5, 2020, https://www.kmbc.com/article/mayor-quinton-lucas-signs-list -of-changes-black-lives-matter-leaders-want-to-see-made-in-kansas-city -missouri/32783237.

234 **"look around":** "Tribute to a Builder," *Kansas City Star*, February 19, 1950, Newspapers.com.

234 **one-fifth as much:** Michelle Tyrene Johnson, "Past Housing Discrimination Contributed to Wealth Gap," KCUR, August 10, 2018, https://www.kcur.org /community/2018-08-10/past-housing-discrimination-contributed-to-wealth -gap-between-blacks-and-whites-in-kansas-city.

234 **median net worth:** Urban League of Greater Kansas City, "Urban Education: Still Separate and Unequal," *2019 State of Black Kansas City*, 9, https://static1 .squarespace.com/static/59c3f63f49fc2b9eb12a6663/t/5d8d739af8f69c 0524180f42/1569551275926/ULSOBKC2019.pdf.

235 **"and it went national":** Interview with Pastor Ron Lindsay, October 11, 2022.

235 **"I definitely knew":** Interview with Gabe Coppage, Kansas City activist and artist.

235 **"You did not discuss":** Interview with Whitney Terrell, May 9, 2022.

235 **Terrell had an inside glimpse:** Interview with Whitney Terrell, May 9, 2022.

236 **show them the deed:** Interview with Sara Stevens, historian, March 8, 2022.

236 **"national embarrassment":** Judy L. Thomas, "Curse of Covenant Persists," *Kansas City Star*, July 27, 2016, https://www.kansascity.com/news/local/article 92156112.html.

236 **"'Holy shit'":** Interview with Whitney Terrell, May 9, 2022.

236 **called to do something:** Interview with Chris Goode, March 3, 2023.

236 **daycare on Troost Avenue:** Interview with Chris Goode, March 3, 2023.

237 **"It was just home":** Interview with Chris Goode, March 3, 2023.

237 **long communal table:** Tommy Felts, "Wonder No More: Ruby Jean's Taking Juice to Troost," *Startland News*, September 13, 2017, https://www.startlandnews.com/2017/09/ruby-jeans-taking-juice-troost/.

237 **near-even mix:** David Frese, "Troost Renaissance: Revitalization or Gentrification? Or Can It Be Both?," *In Kansas City*, December 1, 2018, https://www.inkansascity.com/innovators-influencers/local-news/troost-renaissance-revitalization-or-gentrification-or-can-it-be-both/.

237 **A community mural:** Felts, "Wonder No More."

237 **Goode saw Kansas City:** Chris Goode, "Unity Memo," from Chris Goode to KCMO Parks Commissioners and Staff, June 4, 2020, https://kcparks.org/wp-content/uploads/2020/06/unitymemo.pdf.

237 **On June 4:** Goode, "Unity Memo."

237 **Goode prayed:** *Kansas City Star*, "Chris Goode," YouTube video, https://www.youtube.com/watch?v=cRAFexiwc-s.

238 **voted to restore:** John Eligon, "Kansas City Voters Remove Martin Luther King's Name from Boulevard," *New York Times*, November 5, 2019, https://www.nytimes.com/2019/11/05/us/mlk-paseo-election-kansas-city.html.

238 **partnered with Roosevelt Lyons:** Interview with Roosevelt Lyons, September 23, 2022.

238 **spoke with Whitney Terrell:** Interview with Whitney Terrell, May 9, 2022.

238 **contacted Justice Horn:** Interview with Justice Horn, September 19, 2022.

238 **removed a plaque:** "J.C. Nichols Plaques Removed from Fountain Sidewalk in the Plaza," Fox 4, July 1, 2020, https://fox4kc.com/news/jc-nichols-plaques-removed-from-fountain-sidewalk-in-the-plaza/.

238 **"Few men":** "The Jesse Clyde Nichols Memorial Fountain," Historical Marker Database, https://www.hmdb.org/m.asp?m=88238.

238 **a disruption of the status quo:** Interview with Chris Goode, March 3, 2023.

A QUARTERBACK'S HOME

239 **It was an old ranch house:** "Ranch Dressing," *Spaces Kansas City*, August–September 2006, https://static1.squarespace.com/static/58a335bce58c6260ac2faeb4/t/5fb55fe23e7ad6489f10f018/1605722084909/KCSpaces+-+Ranch+Dressing.pdf.

239 **"a big step in our life":** *Bleacher Report*, "Patrick Mahomes' Dream House Has Closet with 180 Pairs of His Shoes," YouTube video, https://www.youtube.com/watch?v=v8akMdYecv4.

239 **The previous owners:** Plat of Sunset Hill (SBD 08-3077), Missouri Recorder of Deeds, February 1919.

240 **Nichols knew he had struck gold:** Advertisements, *Kansas City Star*, October 8, 1916, Newspapers.com.

240 **The restrictions took up sixteen pages:** Plat of Sunset Hill (SBD 08-3077), Missouri Recorder of Deeds, February 1919.

240 **The comptroller's endorsement:** Advertisement, *Kansas City Star*, March 13, 1921, Newspapers.com.

240 **"copied by developers":** Advertisement, *Kansas City Star*, March 13, 1921, Newspapers.com.

241 **Post Malone got a tattoo:** Clay Skipper, "How Patrick Mahomes Became the Superstar the NFL Needs Right Now," *GQ*, July 14, 2020, https://www.gq.com/story/patrick-mahomes-cover-profile-august-2020.

241 **he couldn't bring himself to finish it:** Arrowhead Pride, "Patrick Mahomes Realizes How Critical His Participation in the Black Lives Matter Video Was for the NFL," press conference, YouTube video, June 10, 2020, https://www.youtube.com/watch?v=2jB5YhlxqxU.

242 **He had been largely sheltered:** Interviews with Pat Mahomes Sr., August 4, 2022, and Johnny Mahomes, August 30, 2022; and Arrowhead Pride, "Patrick Mahomes Realizes."

242 **considered himself blessed:** Arrowhead Pride, "Patrick Mahomes Realizes."

243 **So in the spring of 1968:** Charles Maher, "Why No Negro Quarterback," *Washington Post–Los Angeles Times* News Service, March 27, 1968.

244 **"They said you couldn't even play":** Interview with Bobby Bell, January 2021.

244 **"greatest arm I have ever seen":** Ben Swanson, "Briscoe's Pioneering Path in Pro Football," DenverBroncos.com, February 23, 2022, https://www.denverbroncos.com/news/the-making-of-the-magician-marlin-briscoe-s-pioneering-path-in-pro-football.

245 **"If it has to do with race":** Interview with Warren Moon, August 25, 2022.

245 **"something about him":** Jason Reid, *The Rise of the Black Quarterback: What It Means for America* (Bristol, CT: Andscape, 2022), 277.

245 **to create barriers between:** Urban Land Institute Advisory Services Program, *Parks and Boulevard System: Kansas City, Missouri: Providing a More Equitable Approach to Investing in Parks and Recreation*, December 2019, 8, https://knowledge.uli.org/-/media/files/advisory-service-panels/uli-asp_report_kansascitymo_2019_final.pdf?rev=9ee95631b53a4626b17c3ba5fc0e1cd1&hash=FAF6D8C90041CD78A01C81486FDC48CA.

246 **The city received:** Interview with Roosevelt Lyons, September 23, 2022.

247 **"there were people who booed":** Interview with Quinton Lucas, October 7, 2022.

247 **As he hung up the phone:** Interview with Quinton Lucas, October 7, 2022.

247 **"So often here in Kansas City":** Emma James, "Kansas City Leaders, Fans React to Booing at Chiefs-Texans Moment of Unity," KSHB, September 11, 2020, https://www.kshb.com/news/local-news/kansas-city-leaders-fans-react-to-booing-at-chiefs-texans-moment-of-unity.

THE CRASH

249 **what one official termed:** Michael J. Satchell, "Gear Up for Arena Drive," *Kansas City Star*, September 4, 1971, Newspapers.com.

249 **were used by everyone:** Jean Peters Baker, prosecutor sentencing statement, November 1, 2022.

249 **That night:** Charging document, Kansas City Police Department, Case No. 2116-CR, https://www.jacksoncountyprosecutor.com/DocumentCenter /View/1715/BReid_Redacted.

250 **above the legal limit:** Charging document, Kansas City Police Department, Case No. 2116-CR.

250 **previous convictions:** Meredith Deliso, "Ex-NFL coach sentenced to 3 years over DWI crash that severely injured child," ABC News, November 1, 2022, https://abcnews.go.com/US/nfl-coach-britt-reid-sentenced-dwi-crash-left/story ?id=92475995#:~:text=%2C%20incl . . . -,Former%20Kansas%20City%20 Chiefs%20assistant%20coach%20Britt%20Reid%20was%20sentenced,an%20 attorney%20for%20the%20victims.

250 **Just a few months earlier:** Defendant sentencing memorandum, Jackson County Circuit Court, Case No. 2116-CR01457-01.

250 **When they came to:** Felicia Miller and family, victim impact statement read by district attorney's office, November 1, 2022.

250 **Tracy Wolfson highlighted:** Ben Strauss, "CBS Discussed Multiple-Vehicle Crash Involving Britt Reid," *Washington Post*, February 7, 2021, https://www .washingtonpost.com/sports/2021/02/07/super-bowl-chiefs-buccaneers -score-live-updates/#link-4TYWL7GL4BCUXBSHLFKMNXK4LY.

252 **That first apology:** David Medina, "Former Chiefs Assistant Britt Reid to Plead Guilty Sept. 12 in DWI Case That Injured Girl," KSHB, September 6, 2022, https://www.kshb.com/news/crime/former-chiefs-assistant-britt-reid -to-plead-guilty-sept-12-in-dui-case-that-injured-girl.

THIRTEEN SECONDS

254 **"in a slump":** Neil Paine, "Yes, Patrick Mahomes Is Struggling. But No QB Avoided His First Career Slump Longer," FiveThirtyEight, November 4, 2021, https://fivethirtyeight.com/features/yes-patrick-mahomes-is-struggling -but-no-qb-avoided-his-first-career-slump-longer/.

255 **"I don't know":** Mark Gaughan, "Analysis: Leslie Frazier Relies on Bills' Front Floor and No Blitzes to Corral Chiefs," *Buffalo News*, October 12, 2021.

255 **"When I first got in the league":** Andy Reid press conference, 2021.

255 **"which was ridiculous":** Interview with Chad Henne, February 8, 2023.

255 **"I feel like we're close":** Associated Press, "Chiefs Edge Rodgers-less Packers 13–7 in Defensive Slugfest," November 7, 2021.

256 **another quarterback in football:** Next Gen Stats, "Chiefs Offensive Adjustments Not Slowing Down Mahomes," video, NFL, 2022, https://www.nfl

.com/videos/chiefs-offensive-adjustments-not-slowing-down-mahomes-next-gen-edge.

256 **"You figure out answers"**: Ron Kopp Jr., "Patrick Mahomes Continues to 'Figure Out Answers' for Combating Cover 2," Arrowhead Pride, December 30, 2021, https://www.arrowheadpride.com/2021/12/30/22859758/kansas-city-chiefs-qb-patrick-mahomes-figuring-out-playing-against-cover-2-defenses.

257 **"It's our [expletive] night"**: NFL Films, "NFL Mic'd Up Divisional Round 'I Almost Popped a Blood Vessel,'" *Game Day All-Access*, YouTube video, January 26, 2022, https://www.youtube.com/watch?v=5AjkZ5RL4BA.

257 **"He can't scramble all game"**: NFL Films, "NFL Mic'd Up Divisional Round 'I Almost Popped a Blood Vessel.'"

258 **"We've got three timeouts left"**: NFL Films, "NFL Mic'd Up Divisional Round 'I Almost Popped a Blood Vessel.'"

258 **"be the grim reaper"**: Andy Reid press conference, January 23, 2022.

258 **"that seam is open"**: NFL Films, "NFL Mic'd Up Divisional Round 'I Almost Popped a Blood Vessel.'"

258 **"We absolutely borrow things"**: Mark Craig, "Chiefs Coach Andy Reid's 'Beautiful Mind' Always Searching for the Next Imaginative Play," *Minneapolis Star-Tribune*, January 30, 2020.

259 **middle of the field:** Travis Kelce press conference, January 23, 2022.

259 **in his head:** Travis Kelce press conference, January 23, 2022.

259 **"Great [expletive] ball"**: NFL Films, "NFL Mic'd Up Divisional Round 'I Almost Popped a Blood Vessel.'"

259 **"I love you, man"**: Patrick Mahomes postgame press conference, January 23, 2023.

260 **the rest of his life:** Patrick Mahomes postgame press conference, January 23, 2023.

260 **"I've never seen Patrick do that"**: Interview with Johnny Mahomes August 30, 2022.

261 **45 percent of their plays:** Next Gen Stats (@NextGenStats), "The #Bengals almost doubled their usage of dropping 8+ defenders in coverage in the second half and overtime," Twitter post, January 30, 2022, https://twitter.com/NextGenStats/status/1487934892054761473?s=20&t=r-MwnugCcSVSv2x_9sle-g.

261 **against those looks:** Next Gen Stats (@NextGenStats), "Patrick Mahomes struggled against 8+ defenders in coverage," Twitter post, January 30, 2022, https://twitter.com/NextGenStats/status/1487934888665776130?s=20&t=BYxnbWMP9qweMcwK7vPzfQ.

261 **"I put that on myself"**: Nate Taylor, "Known for Their Comebacks in Recent Years, Chiefs Suffer Demoralizing Collapse vs. Bengals in AFC Title Game," *The Athletic*, January 30, 2022, https://theathletic.com/3102033/2022/01/30/

known-for-their-comebacks-in-recent-years-chiefs-suffer-demoralizing
-collapse-vs-bengals-in-afc-title-game/.

THE BULL'S HORNS

263 **"wring it up":** Interview with Diane Charity, July 21, 2022.

263 **a version of "affordable":** "KCMO Set Aside Price Sheet 2022, 30 to 100 Percent," KCMO.Gov, https://docs.google.com/spreadsheets/d/1HZVoNUg _ujYp5MFlFUFYx15alzZb8wZp/edit#gid=943630900, https://docs.google .com/spreadsheets/d/1JfnlnmrmvEfWpCx0M6PtH-dkHPZpfxQM/edit#gid =286574157.

263 **around $38,000 a year:** US Census Bureau, American Community Survey 2020 Five-Year Estimates, generated by Point2Homes.com, https://www.poin t2homes.com/US/Average-Rent/MO/Kansas-City.html; and KC Tenants, "The Rent Is Too Damn High: KC Tenants Call to Action," August 2022, https://docs.google.com/document/d/1Xuy7OyeR6dVuE7VhuQ7V5Gyfu-7VoJzewUMdg2VRyjsk/edit.

264 **nationally unprecedented partnership:** "Residents Take Title to Apartments," *Kansas City Star*, August 15, 1963, Newspapers.com, https://www .newspapers.com/image/648385562/?terms=%22reynolds%22%20and%20 %22parade%20Park%22&match=1.

264 **baseball star Reggie Jackson:** Anna Spoerre, "Black Wealth, Pride and Decent Housing: Why Parade Park Matters to Kansas City," *Kansas City Star*, May 11, 2022, https://www.kansascity.com/news/article261118937.html.

264 **"We owned it":** Interview with Diane Charity, August 11, 2022.

265 **Mission Woods was hailed:** Advertisement, "Mission Woods," *Kansas City Star*, September 26, 1937, Newspapers.com, https://www.newspapers.com /image/657031461/?terms=%22mission%20woods%22%20and%20%22nich ols%22&match=1.

265 **160 were white:** US Census Bureau, Census 2000, summary file, generated by the University of Kansas, https://ipsr.ku.edu/ksdata/census/2000/sf1/city/sf1pr 2047425.pdf.

266 **"I kept reading about":** Interview with Tara Raghuveer, April 13, 2022.

266 **were on par with:** Tara Raghuveer, "Eviction in Kansas City," August 26, 2017, https://static1.squarespace.com/static/5075895f84ae84c1f4ec0443/t /59a6e665893fc02cee005290/1504110191834/Eviction+in+Kansas+City+-+ August+2017.pdf.

266 **It indicated residents:** KC Tenants, "KC Tenants Power People's Platform," 2, https://kctenantspower.org/platform.

266 **most predicted:** Tommy Felts, "With 42 KC Evictions per Day, Civic Hackers Pinpoint Action with Data," *Flatland KC*, September 5, 2017, https://www .startlandnews.com/2017/09/kc-evictions-civic-hackers-data/.

Notes

266 **more than any other group:** KC Tenants, "KC Tenants Power People's Platform," 2.

267 **increased almost fivefold:** Jeffrey Spivak and Kevin Collison, "City's Ailing Center in Search of Revival," *Kansas City Star*, September 22, 2002, Newspapers.com, https://www.newspapers.com/image/legacy/687174121/; and Kevin Collison, "Greater Downtown Population Jumps 29% in New Census," *Flatland KC*, August 17, 2021, https://flatlandkc.org/news-issues/greater-downtown-population-jumps-29-in-new-census-results/.

267 **Kansas City's past still lingered:** Interviews with University of Missouri–Kansas City professor Brent Never, Dianne Cleaver, Diane Charity, Tara Raghuveer, Michael Savwoir, Black Archives of Mid-America executive director Carmaletta Williams, and Quinton Lucas.

267 **home values doubled:** Celisa Calacal, "As Taxes Explode on Kansas City's Westside, Homeowners Get Breaks Normally Reserved for Developers," KCUR, January 5, 2023, https://www.kcur.org/housing-development-section/2023-01-05/as-taxes-explode-on-kansas-citys-westside-homeowners-get-breaks-normally-saved-for-developers.

267 **$600,000 luxury homes:** Aaron Randle and Eric Adler, "The New 'East of Troost': Chef's Kitchens, Lap Pools, $600k Homes—and Class Tensions," *Kansas City Star*, May 2, 2019, https://www.kansascity.com/news/business/development/article177276366.html.

268 **"If you do leave":** Interview with Jeanene Dunn, April 21, 2022.

268 **received tax breaks:** Randle and Adler, "The New 'East of Troost,'"; and Beacon Hill Developers LLC, Beacon Hill 353 Tax Abatement, https://www.beaconhillkansascity.com/documents/353ProcessAndRequirements.pdf.

268 **forked over $295 million:** Lynn Horsley, "Despite Large Power & Light District Crowds, Taxpayers Are Still on the Hook," *Kansas City Star*, February 7, 2015, https://www.kansascity.com/news/politics-government/article9530081.html.

268 **accused of racial discrimination:** Dan Margolies and Laura Ziegler, "Appeals Court Reinstates Racial Discrimination Claim Against Kansas City Power & Light Operator," KCUR, July 5, 2017, https://www.kcur.org/community/2017-07-05/appeals-court-reinstates-racial-discrimination-claim-against-kansas-city-power-light-operator.

268 **millions more for parking garages:** Lisa Rodriguez, "Kansas City Council Approves Tax Break for Luxury Apartment Tower Downtown," KCUR, June 21, 2018, https://www.kcur.org/economy/2018-06-21/kansas-city-council-approves-tax-break-for-luxury-apartment-tower-downtown.

268 **years after other cities:** Bill Turque, "KC Gearing Up to Adopt First Affordable Housing Plan," *Kansas City Star*, September 12, 2018, Newspapers.com, https://www.newspapers.com/image/657164175/?terms=%22housing%20trust%20fund%22&match=1.

268 **$1,461 a month:** Three Light, "Our Floor Plans," Three Light Apartment Portal, https://threelight.prospectportal.com/kansas-city/three-light-luxury-apartments/. Accessed March 8, 2023.

268 **"just is not there":** Interview with Gwen Grant, October 26, 2022.

268 **out-of-town LLCs:** Interviews with Tara Raghuveer, April 13, 2022, and Brent *Never*, December 15, 2022; and Raghuveer, "Eviction in Kansas City."

268 **outpacing growth in wages:** Gina Kaufmann, "Rent Is Going Up So Fast, It's Not Just Pricing Out Residents—It's Hurting Kansas City," KCUR, October 17, 2021, https://www.kcur.org/housing-development-section/2021-10-17/kansas-city-rent-priced-out-apartments.

269 **declining share of the city:** US Census Bureau, Census 2010, generated by Mark Dent using data.census.gov, https://data.census.gov/table?q=Kansas+City+city,+Missouri&tid=DECENNIALPL2010.P1; and US Census Bureau, American Community Survey 2021 Five-Year Estimates, generated by Mark Dent using data.census.gov, https://data.census.gov/table?q=Kansas+City+city,+Missouri&tid=ACSDP5Y2021.DP05.

269 **"They're the people most affected":** Interview with Dianne Cleaver, December 13, 2022.

270 **"the rent is too damn high":** Taylor Johnson @NewsladyTay, "Last night the group showed up to Kansas City Starlight in protest . . . ," August 17, 2022, https://twitter.com/NewsladyTay/status/1559969755636940804.

270 **As a councilman:** Bill Turque, "KC Councilman Lucas Enters 2019 Mayoral Race," *Kansas City Star*, June 24, 2018, Newspapers.com, https://www.newspapers.com/image/657129506/?terms=%22quinton%20lucas%22%20and%20%22mayor%22&match=1.

270 **He spent one:** Allison Kite, "Lucas Begins Term at Tenants' Home Talking Affordable Housing," *Kansas City Star*, August 3, 2019, Newspapers.com, https://www.newspapers.com/image/657352623/?terms=%22quinton%20lucas%22&match=1.

270 **renters' bill of rights:** Laura Ziegler and Lisa Rodriguez, "Mayor and Housing Advocates Claim Victory as Kansas City Council Passes Renters' 'Bill of Rights,'" KCUR, December 12, 2019, https://www.kcur.org/community/2019-12-12/mayor-and-housing-advocates-claim-victory-as-kansas-city-council-passes-renters-bill-of-rights.

271 **Kansas City most needed:** Urban Neighborhood Initiative, "Recommendations and Analysis for Kansas City's Housing Trust Fund," April 30, 2021, https://uni-kc.org/wp-content/uploads/2021/09/PEN-Housing-Trust-Fund-Recommendations_Final_04302021-1.pdf.

271 **"centered in certain areas":** Facebook Live session with Quinton Lucas, "Questions with Q," August 14, 2022, https://www.facebook.com/watch/live/?ref=watch_permalink&v=375476524745364.

Notes

THE ANKLE

272 **pointing at the concrete:** Interview with Pat Mahomes Sr., October 21, 2022.

273 **at Whitehouse High School:** Alex Guerrero, "Patrick Mahomes Home Video Shooting a Full Court Game Winner at 8 Years Old," YouTube video, October 21, 2018, https://www.youtube.com/watch?v=5Ool9YoOd0M.

273 **"that's the way he was":** Interview with Pat Mahomes Sr., October 21, 2022.

273 **remembered a similar story:** Interview with Chad Parker, February 3, 2023.

274 **"in his brain":** Pete Grathoff, "Legendary Actor Henry Winkler Explains Why He Calls Chiefs' Patrick Mahomes a Hero," *Kansas City Star*, December 22, 2022, https://www.kansascity.com/sports/spt-columns-blogs/for-petes-sake /article268832802.html#storylink=cpy; and interview with Henry Winkler, November 20, 2022.

275 **"There is grace":** Interview with Henry Winkler, November 20, 2022.

275 **"'Man, this is pretty cool'":** Timothy Rapp, "Chiefs' Patrick Mahomes Says Wild TD Pass vs Buccaneers Was 'Cooler Than I Thought,'" *Bleacher Report*, October 3, 2022, https://bleacherreport.com/articles/10051136-chiefs -patrick-mahomes-says-wild-td-pass-vs-buccaneers-was-cooler-than -i-thought.

275 **had one reaction:** Patrick Mahomes press conference interview, February 12, 2023.

275 **"went to another world":** Brett Veach interview with Pat McAfee, "Chiefs GM Talks Building a Dynasty Team and Treating Mahomes like a Business Partner," *The Pat McAfee Show*, YouTube video, February 14, 2023, https:// www.youtube.com/watch?v=v2ZtWL9O5w8.

276 **"anybody any differently":** Interview with Justin Watson, February 7, 2023.

277 **"become a better leader":** Patrick Mahomes press conference, February 12, 2023.

277 **texted out the invites himself:** Interview with Justin Watson, February 7, 2023.

277 **more than ever before:** Bobby Stroupe, interview with Will Ahmed, *Whoop Podcast*, podcast audio, February 8, 2023.

277 **"'Let's just do it'":** Patrick Mahomes press conference interview, November 20, 2022, Inglewood, California.

277 **"go down there and score":** Patrick Mahomes press conference, November 20, 2022, Inglewood, California.

278 **"No, I'm playing":** Interview with Brent Kelley, January 25, 2023.

278 **a boot around school:** Interview with Brent Kelley, January 25, 2023.

278 **"just gutting it out":** Interview with Brent Kelley, January 25, 2023.

279 **"Let me finish one more drive at least":** NFL Films (@NFLFilms), "True competitor . . . ," Twitter post and video, January 26, 2023, https://twitter .com/NFLFilms/status/1618662144383270923.

280 **"We're beer drinkers":** Interview with Chad Henne, February 8, 2023.

281 **bone to the fibula:** Ian Rapoport, "Chiefs Athletic Trainer Julie Frymyer: Patrick Mahomes' Third-Down Scramble the Only Highlight I Wanted," NFL.com, February 12, 2023.

281 **how badly Mahomes was hurt:** Brett Veach press conference, January 29, 2023.

281 **"most adaptable athlete of all time":** Bobby Stroupe (@stroupebob), "1. Thoughts on @patrickmahomes hitting 18.14 mph . . . ," Instagram post.

281 **designed a rehab program:** Rick Burkholder (@proatc), "Thanks for the support and if you loved the way Patrick played then love this person, Julie Frymeyer [sic]," Twitter post, January 29, 2023, https://twitter.com/proatc/status/1619907969805844480.

281 **stay past 6 p.m.:** Rapoport, "Chiefs Athletic Trainer Julie Frymyer."

281 **told a reporter from _Sports Illustrated_:** Greg Bishop and Conor Orr, "A Different Kind of Team. A Different Kind of Adversity. Another Chiefs Super Bowl," _Sports Illustrated_, February 13, 2023, https://www.si.com/nfl/2023/02/13/mahomes-reid-veach-on-stories-of-their-super-bowl-lvii-season-daily-cover.

282 **"confirming whether or not he's the father":** Aftab Pureval (@aftabpureval), "A WHO DEY proclamation from Mayor," Twitter post and video, January 27, 2023, https://twitter.com/AftabPureval/status/1619020031941279744.

282 **"that stuff happens":** Patrick Mahomes press conference, January 29, 2023.

282 **"5 percent":** Patrick Mahomes press conference, January 29, 2023.

283 **fire a short pass to Valdes-Scantling:** Patrick Mahomes press conference, January 29, 2023.

283 **worst pain of the night:** Patrick Mahomes press conference, January 29, 2023.

283 **"We knew we were gonna win":** Interview with Matt Nagy, February 6, 2023.

284 **third time in four years:** Interview with Clark Hunt, February 6, 2023.

THE KANSAS CITY SPIRIT II

286 **FIFA officials claimed:** Dave D'Marko, "Kansas City Should See Millions in Economic Impact from 2026 World Cup," Fox 4, June 18, 2022, https://fox4kc.com/sports/2026-world-cup/kansas-city-should-see-millions-in-economic-impact-from-2026-world-cup/.

286 **$620 million in economic development:** D'Marko, "Kansas City Should See Millions," Fox 4.

286 **"Kansas City has":** Interview with Hartzell Gray, November 12, 2022.

288 **which was sponsored:** Kansas City Council, Resolution 220902, October 6, 2022, https://kansascity.legistar.com/LegislationDetail.aspx?ID=586608

2&GUID=832F715F-335B-4205-A387-F23403EFB187&G=D2E89A09
-8736-4EFB-B4AE-572E0903BD5A&Options=&Search=.

288 **as important as accountability:** Steve Kraske, Claire Powell, and Danie Alexander, "KC Tenants Flexes Its Political Muscle," KCUR, October 13, 2022, https://www.kcur.org/podcast/up-to-date/2022-10-13/kc-tenants-flexes-its-political-muscle.

290 **"It's the right time":** Interview with Geoff Jolley, October 28, 2022.

290 **"not actually that much":** Interview with Tara Raghuveer, February 16, 2023.

290 **an unlikely fan attended:** Interview with Tara Raghuveer, February 16, 2023.

THE MASTERPIECE

293 **"looking to be replaced":** Interview with Patrick Mahomes, February 9, 2023.

293 **"We're moving forward":** Interview with Patrick Mahomes, February 9, 2023.

295 **"He rolled it":** NFL Films, "NFL Super Bowl LVII Mic'd Up, 'We Have to Put Up 7,'" *Game Day All-Access*, YouTube video, February 16, 2023, https://www.youtube.com/watch?v=r0sl7jsbWUc.

295 **"a pain-killing shot":** Patrick Mahomes press conference, February 12, 2023.

296 **"He just needed that energy":** Interview with Chad Henne, February 12, 2023.

296 **"Looked like he was moving fine there":** NFL Films, "NFL Super Bowl LVII Mic'd Up, 'We Have to Put Up 7.'"

297 **"Duo Left 35Y Corn Dog":** Peter King, "FMIA: Jonathan Gannon on Philly's Defensive Breakdown, and More from My Super Bowl Notebook," NBC Sports, February 20, 2023; and NFL Films, "NFL Super Bowl LVII Mic'd Up, 'We Have to Put Up 7.'"

297 **"Great call!":** NFL Films, "NFL Super Bowl LVII Mic'd Up, 'We Have to Put Up 7.'"

298 **"That jet motion's killing them":** NFL Films, "NFL Super Bowl LVII Mic'd Up, 'We Have to Put Up 7.'"

299 **"Someone was just right on my back":** Patrick Mahomes press conference, February 12, 2023.

299 **"huge expanse of green field":** Interview with Joe Thuney, February 12, 2023.

299 **"Nothing like the biggest moments in sports, right?":** Interview with Chad Henne, February 12, 2023.

299 **"made in a lab":** Interview with Matt Nagy, February 6, 2023.

299–300 **"You played your ass off!":** NFL Films, "NFL Super Bowl LVII Mic'd Up, 'We Have to Put Up 7.'"

300 **"best player of all time":** Andy Reid press conference interview, February 12, 2023.

THE FUTURE

302 **The bill:** House Bill 2376, Kansas House, 2023, https://legiscan.com/KS/bill /HB2376/2023.

302 **"a painful vestige":** Rui Xu, Kansas House Chamber Proceedings, House Bill 2376, February 23, 2023, YouTube video, https://www.youtube.com/watch?v= wAUBKkpIKNE&list=PLGnUWv2THZAi2p9iHJ2REOOb2zfm HSxQe&index=33.

303 **a local PBS program:** "Passing the Baton," *Flatland in Focus*, season 2, episode 8, Kansas City PBS, February 16, 2023, https://flatlandkc.org/in-focus /conversations-passing-the-baton/.

304 **"just the right size":** Interview with Mike Garrett, August 15, 2022.

304 **"without him":** Interview with J.C. Nichols III, October 27, 2022.

305 **the first celebration:** "Tracing the Origins of Black History Month," Kent State University, February 1, 2023, https://www.kent.edu/today/news/tracing -origins-black-history-month.

305 **Brooks was frustrated:** Interview with Alvin Brooks, July 20, 2022.

305 **The report stated:** Full text of report, *Kansas City Star*, August 18, 1968, Newspapers.com, https://www.newspapers.com/image/675343840/.

305 **If not, he believed:** Interview with Alvin Brooks, July 20, 2022.

305 **studies over the years:** Shawn Donnan, Ann Choi, Hannah Levitt, and Christopher Cannon, "Wells Fargo Rejected Half Its Black Applicants in Mortgage Boom," *Bloomberg*, March 10, 2022, https://www.bloomberg.com/graphics /2022-wells-fargo-black-home-loan-refinancing/?sref=3Ac2yX40; and Mark Davis, "Black Borrowers Face More Denial," *Kansas City Star*, October 26, 1991, Newspapers.com, https://www.newspapers.com/image/682056507/.

INDEX

Index

Index

Index

Index

Index

Index

Index

ABOUT THE AUTHORS

Mark Dent is a journalist whose work has appeared in *The New York Times*, *Texas Monthly*, *Vox*, *Wired*, *The Kansas City Star*, and elsewhere. He is also a senior writer at *The Hustle*. His work has been cited as a notable mention in *The Best American Sports Writing*, and he has also been named Texas Sportswriter of the Year. Dent grew up in the Kansas City area and lives in Dallas.

Rustin Dodd is a senior writer at *The Athletic*. He previously worked as a sportswriter at *The Kansas City Star* from 2010 to 2017. His work has been honored by the Associated Press Sports Editors. Dodd grew up in the Kansas City area and lives in Brooklyn. He is a graduate of the University of Kansas.